The Early Jews an.
of England and Wales

ALSO BY ELIZABETH CALDWELL HIRSCHMAN
and DONALD N. YATES

*When Scotland Was Jewish: DNA Evidence, Archeology,
Analysis of Migrations, and Public and Family Records Show
Twelfth Century Semitic Roots* (McFarland 2007; paperback 2013)

*Jews and Muslims in British Colonial America:
A Genealogical History* (McFarland 2012)

ALSO BY DONALD N. YATES

*Old World Roots of the Cherokee: How DNA, Ancient Alphabets
and Religion Explain the Origins of America's
Largest Indian Nation* (McFarland 2012)

The Early Jews and Muslims of England and Wales

A Genetic and Genealogical History

ELIZABETH CALDWELL HIRSCHMAN
and DONALD N. YATES

McFarland & Company, Inc., Publishers
Jefferson, North Carolina

LIBRARY OF CONGRESS CATALOGUING-IN-PUBLICATION DATA

Hirschman, Elizabeth Caldwell, 1949– author.
The early Jews and Muslims of England and Wales :
a genetic and genealogical history /
Elizabeth Caldwell Hirschman and Donald N. Yates.
p.   cm.
Includes bibliographical references and index.

ISBN 978-0-7864-7684-8 (softcover : acid free paper) ∞
ISBN 978-1-4766-1343-7 (ebook)

1. Jews—England—History.   2. Jews—England—Genealogy.
3. English—History.   4. Ethnology—England—History.
5. Ethnohistory—England.   6. Human population genetics—England.
7. Muslims—England—History.
I. Yates, Donald N., 1950– author.   II. Title.

DS135.E5H567 2014   942.0049'24—dc23   2014003334

BRITISH LIBRARY CATALOGUING DATA ARE AVAILABLE

On the cover: Tree of Jesse window with a Star of David, York Minster in
York, England. It was regarded as their national genealogy by the English
for hundreds of years and includes the oldest surviving fragments of
stained glass windows in the world (photograph by Jim Poyner)

Printed in the United States of America

*McFarland & Company, Inc., Publishers
Box 611, Jefferson, North Carolina 28640
www.mcfarlandpub.com*

Table of Contents

Introduction

"Every age is the same to God." With these words, the founder of modern source-based historical writing, Leopold von Ranke, asserted in 1854 that the value of any given period rests not on what it produces in terms of events and results, in how it might advance the plot of a national storyline or fulfill some sense of destiny, but "in its existence itself, in its own selfhood." From that position, he wrote, the study of history takes on a special, unique fascination. Every historical era must be regarded as something intrinsically important in and of itself, richly repaying the effort to understand it. Every topic is worth investigating for its own sake.

In approaching the history of Jews in England and Wales we have been guided by von Ranke's attitude. Out of convenience, we have divided the story of Britain's Jews and Muslims into twelve chapters, beginning with the Romans and concluding with the Age of Enlightenment, a period that witnessed the spread of British culture (the word "civilization" had not yet been coined) and its mercantile values around the world. But all these episodes are of a piece. The thread of Judaism runs throughout them. At no time in British history has the influence of the Mediterranean world and ancient Middle East been absent or lacking. In each successive era, Hebrew and Arabic names stamp the changing landscape and color the canvas of history. Jewish and Islamic concepts permeate English laws, religion, literature, science, social forms, business, industry and commerce.

We have endeavored to respect the intrinsic "selfhood" of all these fields of study, realizing that certain areas will always guard their secrets. Scotland, Phoenicia, Ireland and most of pre–Roman Britain, for different reasons, were left out of our purview. Geographically, our interest here focuses on England and Wales—the two countries' annals, records, literature and historiography. What was their history like "as it actually happened?" We start *in medias res* with Pythias the Greek geographer, who left in scattered echoes the first account of the island of Great Britain. Prehistory is ignored except in peripheral genetic, archeological and linguistic notes. The same may be said for the whole domain of British myth and legend. We analyze Roman descriptions of the province of Britannia and learn that the first recorded name of a suspected Jew with British ties was a member of the imperial Julio-Claudian family. Pomponia Graecina was the wife of the first governor of the colony, Aulus Plautius. It is not known for certain whether she accompanied her husband to Britain, but in 57 CE Pomponia was in Rome, where she was charged with practicing a "foreign superstition." Israeli historian Shlomo Sand believes this could only have been Judaism. Pomponia's high position and convert status are certainly appropriate. She well embodies the British aristocracy's belief in a royal bloodline that went back to Julius Caesar, Brutus and Aeneas and grafted onto itself the ancestry and religion of King David and the Rod of Jesse.

Even though both the scholarly and popular literature on the subject of Jews in Britain is uncommitted about what forms of Judaism were most typical and distinctive, "most English"

1

if you will, the leitmotif of Sepharad and Sephardic Jews sounds its note in our first pages and recurs prominently in chapter 2, "Black Swan." Following the better part of the evidence, we think that Gildas the Wise, author of the sixth-century work known as *The Conquest and Ruin of Britain*, bears a North African name for a reason. He was very probably a Jewish semi-convert. In this chapter, we document the presence and influence of Visigothic, Vandal, Ostrogothic, Berber and pre–Islamic Arabic incursions into Britain as Roman rule slowly disintegrated.

Chapter 3 is titled "Saxons, Vikings and Muslims." It tells the tale of two invaders who descended serially on Britain and left their marks in varying degree. At the end of it all, we are still able to identify Jews, and now Muslims, in England. One of these People of the Book signed his name to a manuscript produced at Canterbury Cathedral around 1020. Eadwig Basan, the inventor of a chancery script that inspired today's sturdy Times Roman, was not alone. This chapter documents two vigorous English Jewish bloodlines that survive from Anglo-Saxon times to the present day, Basan and Jobe.

The next chapter seeks to "contextualize" the Normans, whose entry into British history in 1066 was neither as sudden nor sweeping nor irrational as one might think. William the Conqueror's mother was Jewish, as we show, and many of his retainers and well-wishers in England were of Jewish ancestry as well.

Chapters 5 and 6 present a meticulous tour through that microcosm of English property records named Domesday Book. From Devon to Dover, from the Midlands to Lancashire and Cheshire, we examine the names, holdings and family connections of England's property owners "on the day King Edward was alive and dead," the fifth of January 1066, and the year 1086, exactly twenty years after the Normans had consolidated their power. The snapshot of English society that emerges captures some surprising portraits of Jews and crypto–Jews, Muslims and crypto–Muslims. Many of England's enduring crypto–Jewish family names are found in Domesday: Stuart, Bruce, Raleigh, Greville, Drake, Clare, Taisson, Giffard, De Vere, Devereux, Warren, Montgomery, Montfort, Bagot, Bigot, Bowhay, Blund, Hamo, Delacy, Ascham, Durand, Hervey, Mortain, Emory, Malet, Pagnel, Wateman, Latimer, Morel, Rabel, Levin, Boia, Cheever, Cooper, Braos, Beauchamp, Chaworth, Mowbray, Grey, Laval, Lovett, Gold, Mortimer, Totnes, Lovel, Payne, Gamel, Lee, Picot, Pole, Rayner and Tosny. The majority of the surnames are interwoven in the titled lineages that lasted until Elizabethan times. They have intrinsic interest because of their Jewish connections.

Chapter 7, "The Jews in England 1066–1290," covers well-trampled territory. Hardly a stone has been left unturned by Cecil Roth, Joseph Jacobs, Salo Baron and others. Into this forbidding academic wasteland, however, we venture with the honest quest to determine what exactly happened to the thousands of avowed Jews when Edward I gave them the choice of leaving the country or converting. A hint to the answer comes from the absence of contemporary records mentioning *one* case of emigration. Despite the abundance of "beautiful deaths" portrayed in rabbinical literature during this crisis no English Jew seems to have chosen martyrdom over conversion or at least the semblance of it. Instead, Britain's Jews blended and adapted. It is especially important not to lose sight of them during this formative period, as it is widely believed that it was the Angevin rulers behind the "expulsion" who gave the kingdom its lasting tone and shape. Moreover, the times of the first Parliament and Magna Carta are of crucial interest to generations of historians pursuing that grail of the national character, English constitutionalism.

Chapter 8 takes us on "A Necessary Excursion to Wales." We experience some of the differences that make the Welsh ... well, Welsh. Properly speaking, we should refer to them as

"British," upholders of the autochthonous race and culture of the island called Britain. We learn that many of the Welsh heroes, as well as the bards who sang their deeds, had Berber and Arabic names. Our favorite candidate for puncturing Celtic pretensions is Cadwaladr, a name that means "first-born son" in Arabic. Arthur and his family also have Arabic names.

"The Irony of It All: English Jews and Muslims 1300–1450" (Chapter 9) draws together various strains of late medieval English Jewries, particularly from the records of several great commercial firms and in the persons involved in London's Domus Conversorum (House of Converts). Foremost among the latter is the ancestor of Thomas Cromwell, a German Jew. We also chronicle the rise of the Welsh-Polish De la Poles, one of whom nearly was elected pope in 1549. Other Jewish bloodlines appearing in this context are the Zouches, Bardi and Peruzzi families, Brisco, Green, Hagg, Sallay, Sandys, Vavasour, Crosse, Ferriby, Ellis, Eyre, Horne, Barnard, Bassett, Chaworth, Burghley, Seymour and Sackville. From Appendix C, "Medieval Merchants," we might add Alexander, Aubrey, Bacon, Bledlow, Boleyn, Box, Cavendish, Chichele, Fish, Gardner, Franke, Grantham, Hyde, Hill, Jordan, Kingsmill, Olney, Osborn, Paris, Shelley, Wade and Wood.

Chapter 10 introduces the Welsh Tudors, who, we show, probably came from Greek-speaking Jewish origins. Their name Twdwr is the same as that of the Babylonian exilarch Todros, King of the Jews in Narbonne.

Philo-Semitism, that very British pursuit, is the subject of Chapter 11. Puritan millenarianism was mentioned by John Pocock (*The Ancient Constitution and the Feudal Law*) as one of the three main "historical texts" or themes driving England's emergence into the modern period. It is not surprising that Jewish and crypto–Jewish voices ranging from John Selden, the chief proponent of Noahic or natural law, to Sir Robert Bruce Cotton of Huntingdon, founder of the celebrated Cotton Library, were among the intellectual architects of state and empire-to-be. As in other pivotal eras of transformation, the national debate over future directions owed not a little to ancestral memories of Jewishness peculiarly British.

Finally, we come to "Daniel Defoe and Robinson Crusoe," the last chapter in our history. It has as its model "Jews in the National Consciousness of Scotland: Scott's *Ivanhoe*," which served as the concluding essay in our previous work *When Scotland Was Jewish*. Our intent this time is to open readers' eyes to a Jewish reading and appreciation of another great classic of British fiction, the world's first realistic action novel with psychological depth and a universal dimension. Robinson Crusoe is a man alone on a remote island in a similar way to Jews on the extraordinary island of Great Britain. He is transparently a foil for Defoe himself, whom we demonstrate to be a Sephardic Jew by ancestry—a De Foa descendant. Like the sovereign lord of the fictional island, the Jews of Britain had amazing adventures. Resembling the tirelessly industrious and optimistic Crusoe, they learned repeatedly how to be grateful to Providence.

So for God and glory, as the bard Taliesin exclaims, "Let there be an adventuring to Adonai!"

From Jerusalem, by William Blake (1804)

Here Los fix'd down the Fifty-two Counties of England & Wales,
The Thirty-six of Scotland, & the Thirty-four of Ireland,
With mighty power, when they fled out at Jerusalem's Gates,
Away from the Conflict of Luvah & Urizen, fixing the Gates
In the Twelve Counties of Wales, & thence Gates looking every way,
To the Four Points, conduct to England & Scotland & Ireland,
And thence to all the Kingdoms & Nations & Families of the Earth.

The Gate of Reuben in Carmarthenshire: the Gate of Simeon in
Cardiganshire: & the Gate of Levi in Montgomeryshire:
The Gate of Judah, Merionethshire: the Gate of Dan, Flintshire:
The Gate of Napthali, Radnorshire: the Gate of Gad, Pembrokeshire:
The Gate of Asher, Carnarvonshire: the Gate of Issachar, Brecknokshire:
The Gate of Zebulun, in Anglesea & Sodor, so is Wales divided,
The Gate of Joseph, Denbighshire: the Gate of Benjamin, Glamorganshire:
For the protection of the Twelve Emanations of Albion's Sons.
And the Forty Counties of England are thus divided in the Gates:
Of Reuben, Norfolk, Suffolk, Essex. Simeon, Lincoln, York, Lancashire.
Levi, Middlesex, Kent, Surrey. Judah, Somerset, Glouster, Wiltshire.
Dan, Cornwall, Devon, Dorset. Napthali, Warwick, Leicester, Worcester.
Gad, Oxford, Bucks, Harford. Asher, Sussex, Hampshire, Berkshire.
Issachar, Northampton, Rutland, Nottgham. Zebulun, Bedford, Huntgn, Camb.
Joseph, Stafford, Shrops, Heref. Benjamin, Derby, Cheshire, Monmouth.
And Cumberland, Northumberland, Westmoreland & Durham are
Divided in the (the) Gates of Reuben, Judah, Dan & Joseph.
And the Thirty-six Counties of Scotland, divided in the Gates:
Of Reuben, Kincard, Haddntn, Forfar. Simeon, Ayr, Argyll, Banff.
Levi, Edinburh, Roxbro, Ross. Judah, Abrdeen, Berwik, Dumfries.
Dan, Bute, Caitnes, Clakmanan. Napthali, Nairn, Invernes, Linlithgo.
Gad, Peebles, Perth, Renfru. Asher, Sutherlan, Stirling, Wigtoun.
Issachar, Selkirk, Dumbartn, Glasgo. Zebulun, Orkney, Shetland, Skye.
Joseph, Elgin, Lanerk, Kinros. Benjamin, Kromarty, Murra, Kirkubriht.

1

The First Jews in Britain

Benjamin Disraeli once remarked that "what a man believes as to his remote ancestral origins is often of more import than the dry, literal truth."[1] In the present volume we shall endeavor to overturn this logic and attempt to persuade readers that many inhabitants of Britain and its derivative colonies and ex-colonies, especially those with ancient pedigrees, are more likely to share ancestors with Benjamin Disraeli, a Jew, than they are with the Gentiles of Europe.

The central issue to be addressed is how early did Jews—people of Jewish ancestry or religion—settle in the British Isles. Leaving aside the generally discredited theory that some of the Lost Tribes ended up there (a supposition which the British genealogist L. G. Pine interestingly calls "possible, almost probable"[2]), our answer must depend on whether Phoenicians, the seafaring Canaanite neighbors of the ancient Judeans and northern tribes in Galilee, reached Britain. If they did, how significant was the footprint they left on the island's culture and demography? Most historians, with weighty exceptions, accept that the Phoenicians did smelt tin and copper ore in the British Isles and transported these metals to Gaul, North Africa, Iberia and indeed all over the Mediterranean.[3] The exact sites of Phoenician mining activities are no longer known with certainty, although mineralogical analyses attempting to match archeological copper with British ore continue to pursue proof.[4] At any rate, *someone* was mining copper at sites in central and northern Wales, such as at Parys Mountain, Amlwch and at Copa Hill, Cwmystwyth as long ago as 2000 BCE, and Welsh Bronze Age copper mines, particularly at Great Orme, Llandudno, provide leading evidence of early mining in Europe.

The Roman historian Strabo certainly linked Phoenician traders with tin in Cornwall, and an ancient tradition derives the name Britannia, rendered Prettanika or Bretanika by the Greeks, from the Phoenician word Bratanac, or Barat-anac (Country of Tin).[5] Although the word is widely and popularly believed today to come from a Celtic root similar to the Old Irish *brit,* meaning "painted, tattooed," the oldest occurrence of the name in an authentic document suggests otherwise. A Demotic Egyptian papyrus written in the early first century BCE uses the Semitic word *pretan* for "tin ... which was probably imported at the time from Cornwall to Egypt."[6] The Picts' true name, Cruithne, is simply the Scottish and Irish Q-Celtic equivalent of Priteni in P-Celtic Welsh or Breton. Myths project this common term for the islands' early inhabitants onto a hypothetical Cruithni, father of the Picts, in the same way that Brut or Brutus is "back dated" as the founder of the race of Britons in folk memory. Celtic regnal lists refer to Cruithne as the son of Cing and describe him as a type of judge from ancient Israel, giving his genealogy back to Noah.[7]

Diodorus Siculus, a writer in Rome and Alexandria during the same first century BCE, identifies Cornwall as one of Europe's main sources of tin. He refers both to the mining of surface deposits and manufacture and export to the Continent of "bone-like" ingots, oxhide or trapezoidal or reel-shaped forerunners to coins and tokens introduced by the Phoenicians. The Penwith peninsula of Land's End was an important station in the trade route where mer-

chants from the Rhone bought tin from the natives, as was the Isle of Wight.[8] From time immemorial two competing trade routes connected Britain to the Mediterranean. We will meet with the merchants and merchandise from the southern route that led by sea to Iberia as well as the northern land route that centered on the Rhone later in this chapter.

Middle East, Far West

Remarkably, certain place-names in England do invoke Middle Eastern influences. The main river in the Southwest is the Tamar, Hebrew and Arabic for date palm. Its Latin form is *phoenix*, enshrined in the name of the Phoenicians, who used the date palm as the emblem of state on their currency. There are ancient English towns named Marazion, Cairo and Menheniot. The latter name might come from the Hebrew *min ohiyot*, "from ships."[9] The name of the Hebrides (Hebrew Islands) is often cited as evidence that Jews lived in the British Isles from ancient times, while Hibernia, an early name for Ireland, also evokes Hebrews. The Roman

Benjamin Disraeli (1804–1881), the first Earl of Beaconsfield and twice prime minister of Great Britain. His parents were Jews from Italy (Print Collection, Miriam and Ira D. Wallach Division of Art, Prints and Photographs, The New York Public Library, Astor, Lenox and Tilden Foundations).

author Avienus derives the name of Ireland from the Greek adjective *hieros* and called it the Holy Island. Hence, the race of Hierni who inhabited it are "holy men." His work titled *Ora Maritima* was based on Greek sources going as far back as the sixth century BCE. It described the coastlines of the ancient world from the Black Sea to the British Isles. Rabbinical commentaries on the Talmud and Midrash speak of "the ships coming from Akharmania," which some scholars identify with *iyyē Britannia*, "isles of Britain."[10] Semitic studies professor Cyrus Gordon thought that southwestern England's Dumnoni or Danmoni (which he glossed as "Dan's Tin Mines") echoed the Irish founder myth of the Tuatha (tribe) de Danaan, identical with the Israelite tribe of Dan.[11]

In the eighteenth century, historians discovered evidence of a link between some Celtic languages and Phoenician, the Semitic language of ancient Carthage and its colonies. Among the plays of the Roman author Plautus (died 184 BCE) is a work called *Poenulus* ("The Puny Phoenician"). In it the dramatist places into the mouth of the character Hanno a specimen of what passed in early Rome for Phoenician (perhaps in reality a Celtiberian variant) and has the servant Milphio translate it into Latin.[12] The similarity between the Phoenician of Plautus' time and proto–Celtic was first proposed by Thomas Moore in his *History of Ireland*. This thesis was embraced by many antiquarians, including Charles Vallancy, Lord Rosse and Sir William Betham.[13] Celtic scholar John Rhys assembled strong evidence of Hebrew colonization of Britain in antiquity, when Ireland was known as Iberion and the common name of the Israelites was Ibri or Iberi, derived from the name Eber or Heber.[14] How much of this national passion for finding evidence of Jewish connections should be dismissed as archaic and misguided remains an open question.[15]

If we stick notwithstanding to the Celtic etymology of the word, and if it is an ethnonym, that is, a name the original inhabitants applied to themselves, it cannot be older than about 500 BCE, for this is the agreed-upon date when Celts from Gaul and Germany first set foot in the British Isles. The location and movements of the peoples we know as Celts are controversial subjects, but the consensus of archaeologists and historians is that it was this time period that marked the arrival of the La Tène civilization from the mainland with its amalgam of metallurgical designs drawn from Phoenician and Greek culture. An earlier Central European phase of Celtic culture called Hallstadt evidently skipped Britain, for no traces of it have been found there.[16] We daresay most people think of Britain as somehow quintessentially Celtic. But the Celticization of Britain in history does not predate 500 BCE, and the Celticization of fashionable attitudes about the past did not begin until the nineteenth century. Between the ancients' ethnographic observations about northern barbarians and the Scottish humanist George Buchanan's revival of the term Celt in the sixteenth century lies more than a millennium of silence about the people and culture often claimed to be typically British and native.

The pre–Celtic population of England before the Iron Age spoke an unidentified language. The original name for Great Britain was Alba or Albion ("the White Land") and its inhabitants were called the Albans.[17] The Anglo-Saxon Bede, writing in the early eighth century CE, described "five languages and four nations" in Britain.[18] Latin, of course, was the fifth language, brought by the Romans. The oldest known inhabitants were the Britons, speaking British, the idiom of the Welsh and Bretons. They were later joined by the Celts (Scotti), who spoke Irish, a so-called Goidelic or Q-Celtic language found in Celtiberian and in fragments of ancient Gallic and surviving in modern Irish and Scottish Gaelic. The Picts, "from Scythia," spoke a third, anomalous language. Pictish was, possibly, Brythonic or P-Celtic as in Galatian, Welsh, Cornish and Breton, but it was mixed unquestionably with other elements from a pre-existing linguistic stratum. Finally there were the Anglo-Saxon invaders from northern Germany who imposed their Germanic language on the populace beginning in the fifth century. After them, Bede called his people English and the country England. It is not clear why he favored the name Anglia, ignoring the Saxons and British, unless it was because in launching Augustine's mission to convert the island's population to Christianity Pope Gregory had made famous the fair-haired Angle boys he saw in a slave market as resembling "angels." That label apparently stuck because of its high endorsement and suitability to the Romanized east and south, with Canterbury the ecclesiastical capital. At any rate, in the eyes of Rome and all posterity Britain became England, a vaguely Teutonic land with ragged and unruly Celtic edges on the west and north.

Among Bede's four native languages, Pictish occupies a problematical place, since it was so different from Gaelic as to demand a translator according to medieval chroniclers. In the considered opinion of Nora Chadwick, "Pictish seems to have included a large element of Gaulish or Welsh, but of an early type no longer identical with the Welsh of today."[19] The emerging consensus of recent linguistic and genetic research is that the P and Q branches of the Celtic languages did not form until shortly before they arrived in Britain. Before that there was an older proto–Celtic or proto–Germanic as well as a non–Indo-European language perhaps similar to Basque spoken throughout the British Isles. There may also have been a Semitic tongue of some sort.

Pytheas the Greek

About the time of the conquest of Britain by Continental Celtic tribes, the explorer-geographer Pytheas journeyed forth from Marseilles, then a Greek colony, formerly a Phoenician one. He returned from his travels to compile a report of his navigations and inland journeys around northwestern Europe and its islands. He is believed to have visited Iceland and Jutland and circumnavigated Britain, or Albion as the main island of Great Britain was then called. Pytheas' work *The Ocean* was written in Greek in about 320 BCE. It is not preserved except in fragments and citations. These allow scholars to partially reconstruct Pytheas' geographical knowledge from later Greek and Roman writers like Strabo, Timaeus and Diodorus. Pytheas evidently observed firsthand the gold and tin mining and exporting operations of the local inhabitants of southern Britain, for Strabo quotes him as saying that "he traversed the whole of Brettanikē accessible by foot."[20] He noted that traders were carrying these metals from England to the European continent by horse and boat, and then transporting them down the Rhone River, a route that would give them access to the Mediterranean and North Africa. Were some of these traders Jews?

During the height of the Roman Empire Judaism attracted millions of converts. Eventually between one-tenth and one-quarter of the inhabitants within the boundaries of the Roman Empire professed Judaism.[21] Often it was a syncretistic form combined with disparate rites and beliefs. The story of a king converting to Judaism with many of his subjects and descendants following suit is a phenomenon documented from more than one time in history associated with mass conversions. The Hellenized Hasmonean dynasty established under Judas Maccabeus ruled the kingdom of Israel for over a hundred years, spreading Jewish religion to many others in the Middle East.[22] Bulan was a Khazar king who led the conversion of the Khazars to Judaism.[23] The Babylonian prince Makhiri or Machir, also known as Ha-Makhiri, Al-Makhiri, Natronai, Aymeri, Todros, Theodore, Theodoric, Dietrich, William and a host of other names, together with his followers carrying the titles Nasi ("patriarch"), Gaon (academy head) and Exilarch, converted most of the inhabitants of the kingdom of Narbonne or old province of Septimania in southern France.[24] Each of these expansions featured a distinctive rite with peculiar naming practices—Greek names like Phoebus and Alexander, favorites of the Khazars such as Obadiah and Menachem and Pesach, and the many Davidic derivatives of French converts.[25]

Plan of the Book

So much for the prehistoric backdrop to our study. Reliable history begins only with the arrival of Roman civilization in Britain. Our goal in the present effort is to revisit English records and historiography through the time of Cromwell with a particular eye toward Jewish and other Middle Eastern peoples. Specifically, we will present archaeological, documentary and DNA evidence that Jews, and later Muslims, were among the earliest *settlers* in England and Wales, not just curious visitors or traders passing through. Those of Jewish blood contributed substantially to British economic, political and religious development from Roman times to the 1600s. Recognizing that this claim will probably earn us a less than enthusiastic reception in some quarters, we ask only that readers weigh the material presented and make up their own minds as to whether our interpretation of the facts is justified.

Before reviewing some historical and archaeological witnesses for our case, let us introduce and touch on the compelling evidence of DNA. Britain has a history of invasions, reflected in its DNA. Its population structure has been shaped by successive waves of invaders as far back as we can see through the lenses of history, archaeology, linguistics, legend and myth. The resulting genetic story has only begun to be pieced together with the detective work of Oxford professor Stephen Oppenheimer.[26] Although once joined to the Continent through the now-submerged Doggerland, the British Isles were emptied of inhabitants with the Ice Age, leaving "a clean genetic sheet, a blank slate, until about 15,000 years ago."[27] In the Neolithic period, there were two general migrations into Britain, forming a pincher movement from the Mediterranean orbit. About 6,000 years ago came people "deriving ultimately from the very first farming communities in Turkey"—a tradition perhaps echoed in the founder myth that makes Brutus or Britus the grandson of Aeneas of Troy.

One genetic migration is essentially seaborne, with an arm crossing to Brittany and the river valleys of France and another encircling Spain. Both of these lead back to the Mediterranean and can be called the western route. Their impact was greater in Cornwall, Ireland and Wales than eastern or south central England and is demonstrated by a particular pottery type known as Cardial Impressed Ware.[28] The other migration path originates from the Black Sea region and travels up the Danube to cross over the North Sea to England from the Lowlands and northwest coast of Germany. The Brythonic and Goidelic branches of the Celts arrived in overlapping waves from both directions, both from the Iberian Peninsula and from central Europe.

Irish legend indeed speaks of six invasions, the first coming from "the Mediterranean region, in particular from or via Spain and even from Greece," Oppenheimer reminds us. These Mediterranean origins belie an oft-promoted Central European or "Thracian" thesis regarding the origins of the people we know today as Celts.[29] For instance, the Firbolgs are said to have fled Greece in ships. They were replaced in Irish king-lists by the incoming Tuatha de Danaan, who ruled until 1700 BCE.[30] The Milesians are described as originating in Spain, and also in Turkey or Asia Minor: This sounds like a definition of Phoenicia. All this is prologue, however. All these migrations would be over for a full millennium before the arrival of the last pre–Roman overlords, the Celtic tribes including mixed Gaulish and Germanic Belgae. The influence of the Celts was therefore late in coming, superficial and not long lasting or very penetrant. Only ten Celtic words ended up being adopted into the English language, most of them from Brythonic Welsh. The word "bard" is probably the best known (Welsh *bardd*). Paradoxically, as Oppenheimer recognizes, Celtic languages, art and DNA were "present in most parts of the British Isles at the time of the Roman invasion, although not as abundant in one place where there should be the most evidence—England."[31]

Jewish Gene Types

Oppenheimer goes on to identify the male and female gene types that correspond to these phases of British prehistory. Among them are the Middle Eastern haplotypes classified as T (formerly K), J and E1b1b (formerly E3b). He shows that according to present-day gene frequencies, there was a strong influx from Iberia into southwest England and northern Wales of the male lines E3b (now E1b1b1), IIb*, I1b2 (now I2) and J. A different suite of male hap-logroups made landfall on the east coast of Scotland and in eastern England, these coming pri-marily from Norway, northern Germany, Denmark and the Lowlands (I, R1a, R1b).[32] He proceeds to assign names to all these male founder types—Rory, Ian, Rob and the like—much as his colleague at Oxford and fellow geneticist Bryan Sykes had done in his *Saxons, Vikings, and Celts* with Oisin, Wodan and Eshu.[33]

The trouble with inferring the possible presence or contributions of ancient Jews in the DNA history of England is twofold. Not only is there no unequivocal "Jewish gene," but in the absence of ancient DNA we must form our generalizations on the basis of modern com-parisons. Inevitably, these comparisons are made on the basis of a divided, mixed and scattered population. Consequently, no founder type, no cluster, no branch, no lineage can be tied defi-nitely to a historical time or geographical place of origin. All our conclusions trying to make sense of the genetic record are based on projections. They assume gradual, random and con-tinuous models and have little room for the sudden leap of a diaspora, the non-random marriage pattern or discontinuous spread by long-distance travel. High frequencies for J, for instance, the "most Jewish" of Sykes' Daughters of Eve, in the Grampian Mountains of Scotland or Northumbria could relate simply to the survival of an archaic Neolithic population pushed into a remote region by the erratic tide of history. Or there could be other explanations equally plausible.[34]

A specific line claimed as Jewish may have sprung from deep history or it could have been planted in England in posterior times. Geneticists base their "times to coalescence" or point of genesis for a line on statistical formulae of population expansion that presume "star-like" growth following the contours of geography and known outlines of history. In genetics and evolution, as in geography and geology, a uniformitarian approach predominates in people's thinking, and this discounts chaotic or discontinuous causes. A small or anomalous episode of emigration or colonization from afar, such as those described in myths about the Firbolg kings of Ireland or tales about Joseph of Arimathea settling in Glastonbury, would be passed over and would be largely undetectable in the genetic record. Few would look for it; fewer still would see it.

However, the molecular clock of Y chromosome variation ticks faster than that of mito-chondrial. Study of male haplotypes provides greater capacity to pinpoint changes. Hence it becomes worthwhile to have a look at what patterns of male DNA may tell us about possible historical clusters of Jewish and other Middle Eastern lineages in the English population.[35] From this perspective, two male lineages, E1b1b and J, deserve our attention as conventional markers for Middle Eastern and probable Jewish ancestry. J is reported in 24 percent of Ashke-nazi Jews and 29 percent of Sephardim. Haplogroup E1b1b1, accounting for approximately 18 percent to 20 percent of Ashkenazi and 8.6 percent to 30 percent of Sephardic Y chromo-somes, appears to be one of the major founding lineages of the Jewish population.[36]

In Britain, these two lineages are absent or negligible in many towns and regions, but they are reported in elevated frequencies in the following: Wales (Llanidloes 7 percent, Llangefni 5 percent), the Midlands (Southwell, Nottinghamshire 12 percent, Uttoxeter 8 per-cent), Faversham in Kent (9 percent), Dorchester in the West Country with its historic harbors (7 percent), Midhurst in West Sussex commanding ancient seaports (5 percent) and the Chan-nel Islands, always an important crossroads of influences (5 percent).[37] Sykes' survey of paternal clans in England and Wales confirms significant traces of the E haplogroup (which he dubs Eshu) in southern England (4.9 percent) and Wales (3.1 percent).[38] E attains its highest fre-quency in Britain in Abergele, Wales (nearly 40 percent), a startling statistic that has been attributed to Roman soldiers of Balkan origin, but may have alternative and more complex explanations (see Appendix A, Jewish DNA Hot Spots).

Solving a DNA Mystery

Wales appears to be the epicenter for Jewish DNA. In 2011, Llangefni on Anglesey and Wrexham, the country's largest northern city, became the focus of a call for local men to provide samples of their unusual DNA. A team of scientists lead by Andy Grierson and Robert Johnston from the University of Sheffield hoped to link the migration of men from the Mediterranean to the copper mined at Parys Mountain on Anglesey and on the Great Orme promontory nearby. A preliminary analysis of 500 participants showed 30 percent of the men carried E1b1b, compared to 1 percent of men elsewhere in the United Kingdom.[39]

Significantly, Welsh tradition associates the Iron Age hilltop town on nearby Conwy Mountain known as Castell Caer Seion with a settlement of ancient Jews. This site overlooks Conwy Bay on the north coast of Wales and lies on the ancient road between Prestatyn in Denbighshire and Bangor in Gwynedd opposite Angelsey. In the *Black Book of Carmarthen*, the bard Taliesin remarks, in passing:

> When I return from Caer Seon,
> From contending with Jews,
> I will come to the city of Lleu and Gwidion.[40]

Lleu and Gwidion are the names of two legendary figures who are believed to be historical and are thought to have lived in the early centuries of the Common Era or anterior to it. We will return to these traces of Jews in Welsh history in chapter 8.

Another genetic signpost that deserves our attention is the rare haplogroup T, formerly called 12, 23, 25, 26, Eu15, Eu16, or K2. T is conjectured to be the worldwide signature of Phoenicians. It grabbed headlines when it was proved to be the patrilineal haplogroup of Thomas Jefferson, who traced his ancestry to Wales.[41] In Capelli's survey, T makes a solitary appearance in Llangefni, Wales (1 percent). Also linked to the Phoenicians in the genetics literature is mitochondrial haplogroup X.[42] Its worldwide center of diffusion was in Galilee and modern-day Lebanon. The highest incidence of X in Britain occurs in East Anglia (2.4 percent).[43]

Coming of the Romans

Although the Romans did not bring many actual people to Britain, their conquest and inclusion of Britain in the Roman Empire changed the island's population structure in various ways. The process of Romanization began in the first century BCE when Britain was visited twice by Roman general Julius Caesar and his legions. He mentions in *The Gallic War* that "the inland part of Britain is inhabited by tribes declared in their own tradition to be indigenous" and thus distinguishes between the Britons of the midland districts and the Celts of the southern, maritime part, chief among which were the Belgae. Caesar specifically mentions traders who were neither Gaulish nor British. "Nobody except traders," he complained, "journeys thither without good cause; and even traders know nothing except the sea-coast and the districts opposite Gaul" (IV.20).[44] Graves of this period contain rich imports

England and Wales in Roman times with precious metals and principal peoples and towns (Map by Donald N. Yates).

from the Mediterranean, so we can see that Britain's Mediterranean ties were strong even before the Romans.

These same traders owed no allegiance to Rome, for no sooner had Caesar summoned them for reconnaissance than they betrayed his plans to the Celtic chieftains across the Channel. A huge army was waiting for Caesar on the beaches of Dover when he landed on his first expedition. On his second attempt, Caesar chose a more secure landing site and proceeded north, crossing the Thames at Kew, where his soldiers had to wade across the river up to their necks in water. Learning of the enemy's stronghold through spies, Caesar lay siege to what is now Wheathampstead in the district of St. Albans in Hertfordshire and defeated the leader Cassivellaunus. Soon, however, he had to abandon the conquest because of the intrigues and guerrilla warfare of the Celtic tribes, as well as a devastating storm that sprang up. Despite his withdrawal, Roman influence and prestige only rose. The local chieftains began paying tribute and started sending their children to Rome to be educated.

First descent of Julius Caesar on the coast of Britain (eighteenth-century engraving) (Print Collection, Miriam and Ira D. Wallach Division of Art, Prints and Photographs, The New York Public Library, Astor, Lenox and Tilden Foundations).

Cassivellanus becomes, then, the first recorded name of a British person. There are many theories about who he was and what his origins, genealogy and ethnicity may have been. The name could in fact be a title, "leader of the Cassi." We will return to it in due course.

These preliminary expeditions were followed in 43 CE by a full-fledged army of invasion under the emperor Claudius. Four legions landed in southeast England and after a decisive victory at the Thames, the Romans occupied Colchester, the center of the important Catuvellauni tribe, which now included the mysterious Cassi. The troops quickly mopped up in the south and moved into Wales and the north before a revolt of the native tribes led by the fierce queen Boudicca in 60–61 CE destroyed Roman-occupied London, St. Albans and Colchester.

The Romans rebuilt in the south, but in Wales and in the north they decided to erect fortresses, eventually marking off the line approximated by Offa's Dyke on the Welsh border and firmly erecting Hadrian's Wall in the north as the boundaries of Roman rule. Britannia became one of the last provinces to be added to the Roman Empire. It was always regarded as a prized possession. Claudius' son was named Britannicus, and Britannicus would have followed Claudius as emperor had the boy not been put to death by Nero. Down through the ages in a kind of mutual admiration, Roman emperors carried the title Britannicus and British monarchs that of Augustus.

Tacitus' Anthropology

A picture of Roman life in the years of stabilization after Boudicca's revolt is provided by the historian Tacitus in the middle section of his *Agricola*. This work is a biography of his father-in-law, Gnaeus Julius Agricola, who governed Britain 77–84 CE. As with Tacitus' *Germania*, the *Agricola* presents an exacting and on the whole reliable ethnographic description of barbarian tribes on the northern frontier, even if it is colored by a Roman viewpoint. One of the questions Tacitus seeks to address, which we raised at the beginning of this chapter, is "whether the earliest inhabitants of Britain were an indigenous or an invading race." He writes that it is "an open question" and observes:

> Some evidence, however, may be drawn from the differences of physique that prevail. The red hair and large limbs of the Caledonian peoples testify to a German origin. The swarthy complexion of the Silures [in South Wales] and the frequency of curling hair among them, with the fact that Spain lies opposite their district, lead us to believe that the ancient Iberians [Basques] crossed the sea and settled in those parts.[45]

He delineates a third people among the "tribes that dwell nearest to the Gauls" who are physically and culturally similar to them because they are probably "originally descended from them." His threefold division seems to correspond to Bede's Britons, Scots and Picts, with the dark, curly-haired Silures in South Wales being the oldest inhabitants, Britain's genetic bedrock, as confirmed by the DNA studies cited above. Of them, Tacitus says that they "display more spirit, for they have never yet been long enough at peace to grow tame," although certain tribes who were "conquered some time ago ... have lost their valour ... a life of ease has bred in them an unwarlike temper."

In Roman Britain, the main military installations were located at Isca Silurum (Caerleon), Deva (Chester) and Eboracum (York). The largest urban centers besides London were Colchester, Gloucester, Wroxeter, Lincoln and York. The Latin suffix *castrum*, "camp," embedded in the names of Colchester, Gloucester and many other cities, remains as a memorial to England's

Roman past. Caerleon is Welsh for Camp of the Legions. There was a major pagan religious site at Aquae Calidae, or Aquae Solis (Bath), not far from Caerleon and the southern Welsh frontier. Certain places continued to fulfill the specialized functions of ports, mines, border defense and manufactures. Villas were spread across the countryside in the usual Roman pattern of great estates, essentially unaltered until the Industrial Revolution.

The huge archeological site that came to light at Southwell in Nottinghamshire when clergymen in the eighteenth century started digging up mosaics and frescos to decorate their libraries is centered on an ancient villa complex complete with baths and temple. As noted already, Southwell has Britain's highest concentration of Middle Eastern DNA. It grew into a religious community of uncertain character in the seventh century and eventually was crowned with a minister. Southwell provides a continual sequence of occupation from pre–Roman times through the Anglo-Saxon and Danish Dark Ages to the advent of the Normans.

An English Jerusalem

Syon House, home of the dukes of Northumberland for the past four hundred years, may top Southwell in historical importance. Barely ten miles from central London, and right across the river from royal Kew Gardens, it has recently yielded archeological finds stretching back to a gold Bronze Age bracelet and Roman farmhouses.[46] It was built by Edward Seymour in 1548 near the site where Julius Caesar crossed the Thames. Queen Elizabeth I granted it to Henry Percy, 9th earl of Northumberland, on his marriage to Dorothy Perrott, sister of her favorite, Robert Devereux, 2nd earl of Essex.[47]

Besides Syon House, another Roman site with interesting associations for our purposes is Verulamium, the capital and royal mint of the Catuvellauni tribe, later an important Roman municipality and, much later, the barony of Sir Francis Bacon.[48] It was the location of the martyrdom of the first English saint, Alban, a Roman patrician who may have been Jewish. The name conveys a distinctly Roman feel: Alba was the mother town of Rome, and classical poets used the adjective Alban in the sense of "Roman." Of course, the Edict of Caracalla or Constitutio Antoniniana of 212 declared that all free men in the empire were to be given full Roman citizenship and all free women in the empire were assigned the same rights as Roman women, a status previously enjoyed only in Italy, so Albanus may have been Roman in this wider sense. But the fact that he was remembered as a patrician argues against such an interpretation. According to tradition, Alban was from Rome and was "converted" by the Welsh priest Amphibalus to become, with his fellow saints Julius and Aaron, one of the three protomartyrs remembered from Roman Britain.

According to Gildas and Bede, these other two national saints, Aaron and Julius, were both from Caerleon in Wales. Aaron as a Jewish name requires no comment. But the Jewish liking for the name Julius deserves a brief note. Its popularity with Jews goes back to Julius Caesar, acclaimed as the savior of the Judean state in the first century BCE. This occurred after the Hasmonaean high priest and king of the Jews Hyrcanus helped the Roman general win Alexandria by sending 3,000 expeditionary forces from war-torn Judea. Upon his return to Rome Caesar repaid Hyrcanus by lifting the harsh degrees imposed under Pompey and allowed the Jews to rebuild Jerusalem. The Jewish people never forgot Caesar's magnanimity. He was particularly honored after he was assassinated in 44 BCE and Mark Antony betrayed them to the hated Herod. Ever afterwards the memory of Julius Caesar lived on, just like that of Alexander the Great. In turn-of-the-century Berlin, the given name Julius was invariably Jewish.[49] It was adopted for Joel and Judah in the double naming convention whereby a Jew carried a Hebrew, or private, name in his community and vernacular one (German, English, etc.) in public.[50]

Jewish or Christian?

If the names and other particulars of Albanus, Julius and Aaron are authentic and not invented, the timeframe for these first British converts to Christianity would likely have been between about 284 and 304 CE.[51] What was the religious life of Britons like in Roman Caerleon and Verulamium at that time? As in other provinces of the later empire, Roman Britain contained a confused welter of cults and spiritual practices with a great deal of syncretism and inter-influence between sects. Alongside the old religion of Republican Rome with its temples to the emperor and Victory there was the official Greco-Roman pantheon. By a convention observed everywhere in the empire, local gods and goddesses were "translated" into their Latin equivalent. For instance, the British Mother Goddess became Minerva at Bath.[52] Among the common religions practiced in Roman Britain were the cult of Sol Invictus (the faith of most emperors of the time and even Constantine, not baptized Christian until his death in 337), Mithraism (a Persian cult that arrived with barbarian legions mobilized in from the east), Manichees and other Dualists, the mysteries of Isis (Egyptian, often blended with Celtic paganism) and worship of Cybele or the Mater Magna from Asia Minor. Not to forget were the myriad pagan rites and rituals in British, Celtic and other iterations, notably at holy wells, rivers, streams, caves, crossroads and groves, including Druidism, and various schools of philosophy that substituted for religion such as Stoicism, Epicureanism and Neoplatonism. It was even possible to be an agnostic or skeptic, or to combine beliefs and practices. Only Judaism and Christianity were set apart as fundamentally different in popular opinion, and to an increasing extent, law. Both were monotheistic, oriented toward Jerusalem as a sacred and historical point of origin, and had laws, dogma, sacred writings, records and a system of communication between centers. It was sometimes hard to tell where Judaism left off and Christianity began.

Sand's Deconstruction of Jewish History

Around 300 CE, the Roman Empire was at its high point. An estimated seven to eight percent of the population within its boundaries was Jewish—Jewish not in the sense of Judeans, but within the meaning of the word that included the masses of proselytes and their descendants.[53] Jews were the empire's largest minority. Already in the fourth century Jerome remarked that "the Jews move from sea to sea and from the British to the Atlantic Ocean."[54] The destruction of the Temple in Jerusalem, however, did not empty Judea. University of Tel Aviv professor of European studies Shlomo Sand in his book *The Invention of the Jewish People* conducts a careful and thorough review of the historical sources. He makes a compelling, if shocking, case for rethinking many of our assumptions regarding ancient Jewish history. He shows that the Jews were *not* exiled from Judea following the destruction of the Second Temple by the Romans in 70 CE nor did they ever try to "return," but grew and spread by mass conversions, active proselytizing efforts and the natural increase of communities. He speaks authoritatively of a "wealth of evidence about the huge numbers of Jewish believers throughout the ancient world."[55]

"Ancient Judaism was not exclusive at all; it was, rather, as keen to propagate itself as Christianity and Islam would be in the future."[56] Already in 59 BCE the orator and consul

Roman ruins at Verulamium (Przemystaw Sakrajda, Wikimedia Commons).

Cicero complained about Jews in Rome, "You know how numerous that crowd is, how great is its unanimity, and of what weight it is in the popular assemblies."[57] Important convert populations were formed from Moabites, Ammonites, Babylonians, Armenians, Sumerians, Persians, Hasmoneans, Syrians, Phoenicians, Idumaeans, Itureans, Slavs, Germans, Gauls, Samaritans, Cyreneans, Carthaginians, Arabs and Iberians. There were as many Jews in Egypt as in the kingdom of Judea.[58]

In a relatively short span a rational Hellenistic version of Judaism gained believers "from the Arabian Peninsula to the lands of the Slavs, the Caucasus and the steppes between the Volga and the Don rivers, the areas around the destroyed and then rebuilt Carthage, the pre–Muslim Iberian Peninsula ... cultures ... all, of course, purely pagan."[59] The Roman Jewish historian Josephus quotes Strabo (died after 21 CE) as saying, "Now these Jews are already gotten into all cities; and it is hard to find a place in the habitable earth that hath not admitted this tribe of men, and is not possessed by them."[60]

Pomponia Graecina

If Roman Britain had cities, and we know it did, there were Jews in them. In fact, we have a tantalizing record of one British Jew, possibly. Pomponia Graecina was the aristocratic wife of the conqueror of Britain, the commander Aulus Plautius, who defeated the sons of Cunobelinus (Shakespeare's Cymbeline), seized the Celtic or Belgic capital of Camulodunum (Colchester) in Essex and secured the conquest of Britain for the emperor Claudius in 43 CE. Plautius became the first governor of the new colony. It is reasonable to think his wife lived with him during his governorship (43–47).

Ten years later, Pomponia Graecina was put on trial in Rome for a crime of character described as a "foreign superstition." She was a member of the imperial Julio-Claudian family. The same charge was brought about the same time against Poppaea, the future wife of Nero. Poppaea was rumored to be privately a Jewish convert and to favor Jews.[61] Although many commentators and fiction writers believe Pomponia Graecina's crime was the practice of Christianity, in the year 57 this would have been extremely unlikely. There were at that time very few Christians anywhere outside of Galilee. The apostles Peter and Paul were not yet dead. No Gospels had been set down in writing yet. In Rome Christians were a rarity far into the second century. They were so exotic even in the East that around 112 CE Pliny the Younger, then governor of Pontus and Bithynia, wrote the emperor Trajan for advice on how to identify and deal with them.[62]

The Christian epigrapher Giovanni Battista de Rossi in 1879 associated Pomponia with family members buried in the catacombs of St. Callistus in the third century. She was gradually transformed into the apocryphal St. Lucina, even figuring in the historical novel by Henryk Sienkiewicz titled, *Quo Vadis*. But a gap of over a hundred and fifty years seriously weakens de Rossi's theory. Sand identifies Pomponia Graecina as a Jewish convert, not a Christian.[63] She survived her husband by twenty years and died in about 83 CE.

Christianity struggled for several centuries to differentiate and distance itself from Judaism. Many of Britain's Jews around 300 were undoubtedly "semi-converts—people who formed broad peripheries around the Jewish community, took part in its ceremonies, attended the synagogues, but did not keep all the commandments."[64] After the legalization of Christianity by Constantine in 313, some Jews and "semi–Jews" presented themselves publicly as Christian, while thinking of themselves and their ancestors as still wholly Jewish. Sometimes families were divided in their allegiances. Timothy of the New Testament had a Jewish grandmother, Lois, and Jewish mother, Eunice, but a Greek father. When Timothy converted to Christianity in his native Anatolia, the apostle Paul performed a ceremony of circumcision on him (Acts 16:1–3). Most of Christianity's early converts came from Jews. Paul made a habit of preaching in synagogues.

As the Christianization of the Roman Empire accelerated during the fourth century, circumcision was forbidden to males who were not born Jews, the practice of converting one's slaves to Judaism or of owning Christian slaves was proscribed, Jewish women who were not born Jewish were barred from ritual baths and Jewish men of all persuasions were outlawed from marrying Christian women.[65] Endogamy—marrying cousins and other close relations—became ingrained among Jews attempting to hold themselves apart from Christians. All these developments tended to make secret Jews out of people who defiantly regarded themselves as Jewish and honored the commandments of Judaism to varying degrees, often without benefit of a rabbi, community, synagogue or Torah. It was not until the eleventh century that the Hebrew language was introduced to Europe, and its dissemination was spotty. Moreover, that Hebrew was no product of an autochthonous linguistic development, but the artificial creation of Jewish scholars.[66] In the rift, which covered most of the Middle Ages, the vast majority of European Jews were totally ignorant of Hebrew and were probably also not acquainted with rabbinical Judaism as it took shape in Judea and Western Asia.

Christianity's final triumph put an end to all proselytizing by Jews "and perhaps also prompted the desire to erase it from Jewish history."[67] In the centuries that followed, especially after the rise of Islam, rabbis and other keepers of the collective memory were pained by the apostasy of the Jewish people on such a continuingly large scale. They sought to deny what was obvious, considering anyone who gave up their Jewishness "dead." "Zionist historiography ... [turned] its back on any meaningful discussion of the issue," writes Sand. "Abandoning the Jewish religion was generally interpreted by modern sensibilities as betraying the 'nation,' and was best forgotten."[68]

The Romans held sway in Britain until 411 CE, although they had begun to withdraw and retrench as early as the third century. Yet as the modern historian Peter Hunter Blair observes of these centuries, "There is no single episode in the whole history of Roman Britain for which we have evidence deriving directly from two or three eye-witnesses, or two episodes for which we have even a single account that can be regarded as that of an eye-witness."[69] Blair's orientation, however, like most historians, has been toward political events. Shifting our inquiry to the cultural and economic realm, we can obtain a fairly complete and reliable picture at least of Britain's trade and commerce. Caesar's commentaries on Britain and Gaul, for instance, contain much valuable and relevant information, and this can be supplemented by the archeological record.

Commerce and Industry

Not only could Britons mine and refine iron, gold and tin, they also raised cattle and corn, spun wool, cured leather, manufactured bricks and tiles and wove cloth, all of which they exported across the channel to Gaul and by long-distance transport to the Mediterranean. The arrival of Roman technology, commerce and management practices transformed Britain. The Romans took over the export business for lead and tin, sending it throughout the empire. Latin became the standard written and spoken language, and a large proportion of the population gained literacy. A sizable number of Latinate words owe their entry into the English language to Britain having been a Roman province. Bronze and gold coins, together with wax accounting tablets, permitted a monetary financial system to emerge. The capitalist economy encouraged the accumulation of private wealth and acquisition of luxuries obtained from international trade. Blair reports that among the Roman-era items excavated in Britain were "glassware and pottery from Gaul, Baltic amber and bracelets and necklaces made of ivory."[70] The materials for these items would require trade routes stretching from western Europe to the Baltic and Africa.

It was most likely Roman Jewish merchants who transported these materials to Britain or acted as middlemen, for even before the addition of Britain to the empire they had established trade routes from Palestine to Egypt (e.g., Elephantine, Alexandria) and Tunisia (Djerba), onward through the Iberian Peninsula into Gaul, and from there to Britain. London had earlier on become the financial hub of Britain and the distinguished title of *Augusta* was awarded to the city. York, playing an even greater role in Roman economic development in Britain, was designated a *Colonia*. Lincoln also was an important municipal center. It was apparently these three cities, together with the tin and lead mining areas of Cornwall, that formed the foundation for the continuing presence of Jews in Britain from the Roman occupation onward.

One of the best-documented imports into Britain was wine. This was carried by mule train and river barges from Narbonne, the lower Rhone and the Garonne in southern France, loaded into ships that crossed the Channel in season, offloaded at the main ports in southern

England, Hengistbury Head, Poole Harbour, Portsmouth, Southampton, and distributed to the main cities on Roman roads. Finds of a standard shipping container known as Dressel IA amphorae document this route.[71]

Over the same well-traveled roads and sea lanes came Samian ware (the coveted equivalent of fine English bone china at the time, *de rigueur* for banquets), oil lamps, fish sauce, olive oil in a distinctive squat type of amphora, bronze tableware, blown glass, figs, olives, dates, nuts and luxury goods. Some of the latter items originated as far away as Egypt, Syria, Turkey and India.

Secrets of the Bath Drain

A collection of eighty-eight engraved gemstones was discovered during the 1979 excavation of the bath drain at the Roman fortress of Isca at Caerleon, all presumably lost by naked legionnaires during their ablutions. They are dated second or third century. The subjects range from good luck and love charms to occupational symbols and cult fetishes. One shows a long-tailed parrot (a Roman status symbol and luxury gift from India),[72] another an ibex beside a tree (Scythian). A large, strikingly abstract citrine cabochon, probably an ornament rather than a seal, exhibits a crescent and seven six-pointed stars, perhaps Jewish or Arab,[73] while a proper red jasper seal that was evidently carried around the neck of a merchant depicts a fighting rooster. It is the same as a distinctive motif often seen in Jewish art, where the cock (*tarnegol*) was called "the king's bird" and used as a diplomatic gift. "During the Roman period," according to food historian Gil Marks, "chicken emerged as a prominent feature of Jewish cooking, the Talmud considering it 'the choicest of birds.'"[74] We see Artemis, Apollo, Mars, Hercules, Athena, Roma, Victory, Cybele, Dionysus, Venus and other divinities, often assimilated to pagan Celtic and German belief systems according to the *interpretatio romana* or conventional scheme of

Roman seals from Caerleon: rooster, left, and crescent and stars, right (drawing by Donald Yates).

equivalencies. The merchant god Hermes with his money bag, traveler's staff and cap appears to have been a favorite, making us wonder if the legionnaires did not invite tradesmen to share the social pleasures of the bath with them.[75]

Strabo at the end of the first century wrote that Britain produced for export grain, cattle, gold, silver, iron, hides, slaves and hunting dogs. These staples filled the freight and cargo spaces occupied on the inbound journey predominately by luxury imports such as "ivory chains, necklaces, amber gems, glass vessels and other pretty wares of that sort."[76]

Gradually, the center of production moved from the Midi to northern France, the Loire and Rhineland. The North Sea trade increased, revitalizing ports of entry on the north Kent and Essex coast. London, of course, persisted as the most important commercial hub, being the farthest navigable town on the Thames. Tacitus described it as "teeming with traders and merchants." All in all, Britain "maintained social and economic systems that were deeply rooted in the past."[77]

End of the Beginning

In 410 CE, Alaric and the Goths sacked Rome, sending a shudder through the Roman world. Emperor Honorius, aware that the empire could no longer defend its westernmost possession, dispatched letters to the British cities informing them that they were essentially now on their own. A scant decade later, the monetary system of Britain was foundering. Rebecca Fraser in her survey provides a sobering description of the implosion of Britain's economic and cultural development after Roman abandonment: "Without a central taxation system, [characteristics of] Roman civilization, like roads, baths and government, simply fell away. The famous pottery factories ... vanished, as did the art of making glass.... Trade became local and was reduced to barter."[78]

Christians and Jews

Entire monographs have been written on the messiness of Jewish identity in the ancient world.[79] Whoever they were, and however many there were, British Jews belonged to the western branch of Sepharad. Most of them were converts. Whether they lived in Gaul, Iberia, North Africa or Britain, Sephardic Jews participated in the great transformations of Judaism during these centuries. But because they were increasingly part of a Diaspora, they evolved their own institutions and collective identities. We have seen that until the destruction of the Second Temple, Jews were a legally permitted and even admired foreign sect in the Roman Empire. There was at first no dichotomy between Judaism and Christianity. Not until the second century did Jewish religious authorities draw a clear line and rule that belief in Jesus was non–Jewish. The failure of the Bar Kokhba revolt (132–135 BCE) and subsequent birth of the movement we call rabbinical Judaism are often cited as the critical stage at which Jews and Christians parted ways, never to join again. But it should be noted that the initiatives striving to separate the two usually came from Jewish authorities. Rulings were binding only in an erratic and shifting fashion. For instance, "Under the rule of Raban Gamaliel II (c. 80–c. 115 CE), the Twelfth Benediction or *Birkat ha–Minim* ('Benediction concerning heretics') was recast to apply to Christians and this seems to have been the point at which the remaining Jewish followers of Christ were turned out of the synagogue."[80] Such decisions had little effect, especially far away from Palestine. Christians, for their part, fashioned their own unevenly articulated détente, retaining ambiguous types of self-identification, especially in the private sphere of the family.

With the establishment of the first synagogues and Talmudic academies, Jerusalem ceased to be the focal point of Jewish religious observance or for even self-identification purposes. Judaism changed from a traditional temple cult centered in Jerusalem to a household-focused religion oriented toward the Torah and sayings of rabbinic sages. Cassius Dio expressed the new definition of Judaism when he asserted in the third century "that the term 'Jew' no longer applied to people of Judean descent."[81] At the same time, there set in a growing strife between Christian churches and a fragmentation of the faith that many Jews were probably content to watch on the sidelines with indifference or secret satisfaction.[82]

As Professor Sand amply shows, the second and third centuries were a golden age for Jews. The myth of their mass removal

Drinking vessel from Roman catacombs depicting a family group, believed to be Greek-speaking converts of Jewish origin on the basis of their names, Sebere, Cosmas and Lea Zezes (Tzetzes) (© The Trustees of the British Museum).

by the Romans from the Land of Israel is unhistorical and false. Jews under Roman rule had little to hide or fear as long as they observed the forms of polite society, obeyed the law and paid their taxes. British Jews would have increasingly married within their faith and concentrated on creating a home environment in which biblical law could be observed and taught to their children. Many were undoubtedly illiterate and looked to well-to-do co-religionists and merchants as their link to the greater world of Judaism. Probably home weddings and funerals took the place of public ceremonies, for synagogues were only beginning to be established. Most of these were in the East.

The Romans at last thought it necessary to try to rein in Jewish proselytizing shortly after Christianity was legalized. In 336, a promulgation went out that "it shall be unlawful for the Jews to bother any man who has converted from Judaism to Christianity or to injure him in any way" (Codex Theodosianus 16.8.5). In 357, the emperor decreed that any "return" to Judaism was no longer an option: "If anyone converts from Christianity to Judaism and joins their sacrilegious assemblies ... we order his property forfeited to our treasury" (Codex Justinianus 1.7.1). This was followed by laws prohibiting Jews from marrying Christians (388) and holding secret marriage ceremonies (393).

One of the last regulations occurred in 408, when the governors of provinces were enjoined to prevent Jews from celebrating Purim in an anti–Christian manner or affixing crosses on their places of worship. At the same time, local authorities were forbidden to interfere with Jews observing their Sabbath, which fell on the day before Sunday, the Christian holiday.[83] It may be that away from centralized authority and imperial patronage in Constantinople, Rome and Alexandria, Jews continued to enjoy greater freedom and privileges. Perhaps, too, Christians in Britain evolved more lax and open practices. At any rate, the curtain was descending on the Roman world. Any British Jews faced the same dilemma as their fellow citizens— stay and fight the forces of chaos or leave for doubtful safety elsewhere.

2

Black Swan: Sepharad
in Post-Roman Britain

Into the economic and political vacuum left by the collapse of Roman rule in Britain poured barbarian invaders from Germania who brought the ruin of the entire country, according to standard accounts. Colchester, the initial capital of the province of Britain in what is now Essex, "became a backwater, a modest county town with no known history," and London "within fifty years of the departure of the last Roman soldier ... was completely deserted."[1] It is hard to imagine a more crushing clean sweep. Beginning in 447 CE and continuing until 460 CE, the mass movement of Teutonic peoples from the shores of the northern Netherlands, Jutland and the Baltic Sea southeast of Denmark resulted in the slaughter of the Romano-British, sacking of the main cities and conquest of much of the south and east of the country.[2] The Latin language died out; no Latin-derived vulgate like French or Spanish or Italian took its place. By 495 CE the newly established Angle, Saxon and Jute kingdoms extended north to York and west to Southampton. Historian Rebecca Fraser paints a dire picture of this five-decade process, writing that "under the onslaught of the Germanic tribes, the only hope for the Romano-British was to abandon their villas and cities.... In the first years of the Saxon invasion, the old population of England was very nearly destroyed."[3] Many fled to the British colony of Armorica in Gaul, which had been established in the late fourth century. So many Romano-British made their home in Brittany that to this day their descendants speak a version of the ancient British tongue similar to Welsh. The Breton Peninsula in France is named after them.

This period of English history is referred to as sub–Roman, a term derived from an archaeological label for its material culture. To archaeologists, the rough potsherds in sites of the fifth century and sixth century implied decadence from the higher standard set under the Roman Empire. Despite the calamities of this period, however, it was in some ways a rich and formative one. The discussion in Peter Hunter Blair's study, among others, paints a less drastic portrait of the Romano-British population in the aftermath of the Anglo-Saxon invasions.[4] For instance, Blair notes that rather than destroying what remained of Romano-British culture, the Anglo-Saxons and other Germanic incomers created settlements that "coincide with the Romano-British pattern ... such as Canterbury, Dover and Faversham [in Kent].... Eastern Kent shows evidence of a rapidly developing prosperity, characterized by advanced technical skills in the manufacture of [gold] jewelry ... and *by the import of luxury goods from the Continent*." Among these, he notes, are "gold coin-like jewels from Denmark, called bracteates, other kinds ... associated with the Rhine and northern France ... and quantities of glass imported from Rhenish glass factories.... [Indeed], it was in Kent that coins of Anglo-Saxon manufacture first came into circulation."[5]

To avoid the negative connotations of "sub–Roman," we will employ rather the expression post–Roman. As we shall see, the post–Roman is a period in which "history as it actually happened" emerges as something very peculiar and quite extraordinary. Little understood until recently, post–Roman Britain well deserves the title of a "black swan" phenomenon, that high-impact, hard-to-predict, rare event that inexplicably recurs in the history of a people and, in many ways, retrospectively defines them.

To appreciate the transition the post–Roman period marks from antiquity to medieval times, we must consider what the fallout in Britain was to a catastrophe on the other side of the world which scientists have pinpointed to the year 535 CE. As recorded in Chinese and other annals, the eruption of a super-volcano in Indonesia set off a calamitous chain of disasters. The following decades witnessed tsunamis and floods, darkness and cold, crop failures throughout Asia, famines, a pandemic of bubonic plague spreading from East Africa, dust storms and the collapse of societies in both the Eastern and Western Hemispheres. During these literal dark ages, the Roman Empire declined, the Maya and Tang civilizations fell and the new powers of Islam and Khazaria arose. In Britain, the same trade routes that transported Mediterranean luxury goods now brought rats and dying men. "Western Britain was wide open to plague infection—and was devastated ... Kent, so near to France, only started regular trade with the European mainland again in the 580s or 590s."[6] In the west, with its direct shipping ties to the Mediterranean, bubonic plague hit earliest, in 547. Everywhere, Germanic raiders and invaders swept in to take advantage of the circumstances. The South Midlands passed to the Saxons in 571. Soon Gloucester, Cirencester and Bath fell. "Wales was cut off from the other remaining Celtic British territories—the Cornwall/Devon peninsula and the northwest."[7] Effectively, Britain was partitioned. Large parts of it were laid waste either by pestilence or the scourge of the godless northerners.

Three important contemporary sources have come down to us for the early, seminal portion of this long era. We have two authentic letters by Patrick and we have the work known as *De Excidio et Conquestu Britanniae* (*On the Ruin and Conquest of Britain*) by Gildas. Both authors came from the Old North, the area centered on Glasgow in what is now Scotland. In today's language we would call both Patrick and Gildas Welshmen (Cymry). They regarded themselves as the upholders of an absent empire beating back the uncivilized pagan hordes. Patrick's *Confessio* and his *Letter to Coroticus* reveal aspects of life in post–Roman Britain showing that Christianity, although not of the variety promulgated later by the Catholic Church, was well ingrained in post–Roman Britain when he was captured at the age of 16 and taken as a slave to Ireland. He was born at Banna Venta Berniae, a location identified as Glannoventa or modern-day Ravenglass in Cumbria, the western region lying just within the northern bounds of Britannia.

Gildas probably lived from about 500 to 570 and spent his life divided between the Old North, Wales, Brittany, Rome and Gaul. A biography written at the Breton monastery of Rhuys several centuries later by an unnamed scribe says he was the son of Cauus (Caw, Caius, Kay) and was born in the district of Alt Clut (Rock of the Clyde, Dumbarton) in the Hen Ogledd (Old North), the Brythonic or Welsh-speaking region of northern Britain and southern Scotland. He was entrusted into the care of Saint Hildutus (Illtud) in the monastic college of Llan Illtud Fawr in the vale of Glamorgan in Wales along with Samson of Dol and Paul Aurelian. Like Patrick, then, Gildas came from a background of "Celtic" Christianity. More properly designated as British or Welsh, Celtic Christianity differed in several important respects from the Catholicism later brought by Palladius, Germanus and Augustine at the instigation of the Church in Rome.

The Old North

Norman Davies included Alt Clud (Alclud, Ald Cluid, Alcluith, Ail Cluaithe) or Dumbarton (Fortress of the Britons) or the Strathclyde principality as one of his "vanished kingdoms" in his book of that title. His history of the kingdom that became the symbol, along with Arthur, of Britain's last stand is a masterpiece of reconstruction. We cannot enter into all of the details, which pertain, at any rate, more to Scottish history than Welsh or British, but will attempt to convey some of his perspectives. First, as Davies says, in order to understand the true makeup and transformations of the Romano-Britons we must put the modern map of Great Britain out of our minds.

> In the era when Britannia was collapsing, there was no England, since the Anglo-Saxon ancestors of the English were still arriving; there was no Scotland, since the Scots had not even started to arrive; and there was no clearly defined Wales. The former Romano-Britons and their P-Celtic speech were spread over most if not all of *Prydain*, and as the ethno-linguistic jigsaw changed, "Wales" could be found in every pocket where Britons persisted.[8]

The Old North contained at least seven kingdoms, left a body of literature dwarfing Anglo-Saxon and kept alive for centuries a distinctive language, Cumbric, similar to Welsh. The kingdom of the Damnonii around the Firth of Clyde (their name means "the People of the Sea") was perhaps the grandest chapter in the history of a people whose king-lists stretch back to the second millennium BCE.

As we have gone into elsewhere in some depth, the Celtic Church was at variance not only in its date for the celebration of Easter but in many other ways.[9] The main currents for its development came from ascetic forms of monasticism spreading from Egypt and Syria, in other words the Middle East. Unlike Roman Catholicism, the Welsh religion, as we can well call it since Wales became its last stronghold, clung to Pelagianism, a doctrine named after one of its abbots. Morgan, whose Latin name was Pelagius, flourished 400 CE and his teachings were ambivalent about the divine nature of Jesus and operation of grace. Rather than parishes organized along urban and provincial lines and bishoprics subordinated to Rome, Alexandria or Jerusalem, British society emphasized land-based "academies" and independent abbot-ruled country estates combining the secular and sacred. Abbots could marry, have children and bear arms.

Britannia was one of the last provinces and first to go. Its relinquishment by Rome preceded the abdication of the last Roman emperor, Romulus Augustulus, by about seventy years.. The Latin language died out, and the rest of the world did not know what might take its place. In 582, after about a hundred and fifty years of Anglo-Saxon hegemony, when Pope Gregory sent Augustine and several other monks to missionize the English nation, "they were appalled at the idea of going to a barbarous, fierce, and pagan nation, of whose very language they were ignorant."[10] But Romano-British towns in the west and north had continued to thrive, more or less. Shifting fortunes left Wales, northwestern England and the Border Lands to negotiate their own cultural destinies.

For these lands, at least, it was not completely a dark age. In fact, Gildas does not inveigh so much against the Saxon barbarians as against his own decadent compatriots. "It is believed," says Welsh historian John Davies, "that the economy which had developed under the empire survived to a considerable extent for a century or more after its collapse ... [until] 650."[11] Moreover, "the years 400–600 are wholly central to the history of Wales and Britain ... when the nations of the Welsh, the English and the Scots crystallized." It is to Wales, Ireland and Scotland that one must look for strong continuity of civilization and its arts. "As the Romans, within regions where their authority was undisputed, had prohibited civilians from bearing arms, military traditions had withered among the men of southeastern Britain. The inhabitants of the less Romanized regions—those of Wales and the northern marches of Britannia—were less hesitant and within a few decades of the demise of the empire it would appear that authority had been seized by the men of the periphery."[12]

There is sparse but unmistakable evidence for Jewish communities in neighboring France during the years 300 to 600, and we might expect a similar situation in Britain. Norman Golb reports on the earliest written records of Jews residing in that country: "For those regions of Gaul spreading out from Lyon to the north, west and east, there are references in the fourth century (300 CE) only to the Jewish community of Cologne, in the fifth [century] to [French] Jewish inhabitants in general, and in the sixth [century] to Jews in Orleans, Bourges, Clemont-Ferrand and Paris. Decrees relating to the Jews are found ... during the fifth to the seventh centuries in Vannes, Epaone, Orleans, Macon, Paris and Reims."[13] We can assume that despite the raids and growing intrusions of the Saxons on the North Sea coast of England, the trade routes forged under the Romans continued to flow with imports, especially luxury goods. Timber and slaves and grain composed the main items exchanged. London and its hinterlands stretching toward Cirencester and the Cotswolds long held out against the barbarians' inroads. These centuries mark the appearance of the Radanite Jews, thought by some to be named for their concentration along the Rhone river (Radanus).

Why, if the British Isles were devoid of Jews between the Roman period and their reintroduction under the Normans, as standard histories claim, are there so many references to them in Anglo-Saxon and Welsh literature, legend and laws? Were there any Jews or ex–Jews in the "Celtic" Church? Could Gildas himself have come from a Jewish background?

Gildas as a Historian

Gildas' work is a unique testimony to a period for which he was a rare and eloquent eyewitness. Like the famous models of the historian from the ancient world—Cicero, Tacitus, Josephus—he wrote at the end of a public career and limned the character of his age in unforgettable fashion. The sixth century in Britain would otherwise be a blank page. Because of its singular status and literary value Gildas' history has been read and studied extensively. Arthurian enthusiasts have pored over the text, often wringing strange historical proofs from it, although Gildas does not mention Arthur by name. It has been thoroughly analyzed by the medievalist Robert Hanning, who places it solidly in the tradition of Orosius, Salvian, Augustine, Eusebius and other ecclesiastical writers.[14] Yet many readings of the Late Latin text we call *The Fall and Conquest of Britain* and opinions on its author, we submit, miss some very important and obvious points.

The closest thing to an original title is *Liber querulus* (A Plaintive Book). The title *The Fall (or Ruin) and Conquest of Britain* comes from later manuscripts, where the work became enmeshed with that of continuators, the so-called Nennian tradition. Gildas calls himself a monk and sources speak of him as Gildas Sapiens ("the Wise"). But the biggest mystery is Gildas' name. "Gildas" as a name is quite exceptional, neither Latin nor British.[15] As the critic Robert Vermaat writes in "Who Was Gildas"[16] and "Where Did Gildas Write,"[17] the "name 'Gildas' is very unusual." It is only elsewhere attested in the figure of a fifth-century North African rebel, "though there is no connection between these men ... neither man had a Latin name." A British origin for the name has been ruled out. Most modern-day scholars refuse to even attempt any etymology.

Could Gildas' name really have been Mauritanian or Berber or Carthaginian? It is possible. The name means "ruler" in the Lybico-Berber language and is connected to the modern Berber word for king, Agellid. As for Gildas' cultural milieu, it is evident from his fashionable rhetorical topoi and decorative allusions that he had a privileged education. African Latin writers contemporaneous with him include the mythographer Fulgentius, encyclopedist Martianus Capella, grammarian Priscian and Vandal Christian poets Luxorius and Dracontius, all of whose works are distinguished by an ornate, thickly allusive Latinity. "From his seemingly anachronistic prose style," comments one critic, "Gildas shows that he was a man with a classical education, which must have been very rare at that date. He was familiar with most of the books of the Bible, both the older Vetus Latina version as well as the newer Vulgate version from Jerome. He used works by Vergil (*Aeneid*), Rufinus, Orosius, Sulpicius Severus, John Cassian and Prudentius. These authors, together with his perfect grammar and syntax (no vulgarisms), show the high quality of his classical education."[18] Curiously, Gildas cites the Jewish Platonist and Pythagorean philosopher Philo of Alexandria (20 BCE–50 CE): "According to the maxim of Philo, 'We must have Divine assistance, when that of man fails'" (20). It is not the only learned reference that is recherché in Gildas. For all this, he is self-deprecatory about his style, calling it "cheap."[19]

Vera effigies Gildæ *qui ob insignem
Prudentiam, Morumq; Severitatem
Cognominatus est Sapiens
Floruit anno reparationis humanæ*
D·X·X·X·X·V·I·.   Will. Marshall sculp.

Gildas the Wise in an engraving by William Marshall, London, 1638 (© The Trustees of the British Museum).

Although all vouch for Gildas' historical value, even he admits that his sources were shaky and fragmentary. "I did as much as I could," he says, basing his account "not so much on the writings of my nation or memorials of its writers, if ever such existed, for they could not be found, having either been burnt up in the conflagrations of our foes or carried away in the ships of the exiles, but on the reports given to me overseas, themselves so beset by frequent interruptions as to be less than illuminating."[20] By "overseas," Gildas means Brittany. Before fleeing to that land from southwest Britain, he wrote the *Lorica Hymnus* preserved under his name, a chant to ward off plague (*mortalitas*). The *Lorica Hymnus* has been firmly dated to the year 547 in southwest Britain or Wales.[21] We will glance at its unusual forms of Latin a bit later.

We have seen in the first chapter that significant traces of North African DNA can be identified in the genetic population records of Wales, Cornwall and Devon, and to a lesser extent in other parts of Britain. Does history or archaeology support any North African influences persisting to the age of Gildas? The answer is a resounding yes. We know from the correspondence of Pope Gregory the Great that ships and even huge fleets linked Africa to Gaul, Italy, Spain and points north, where slaves known as *barbaresci* (Berbers) were traded.[22]

Basques, Berbers and Vandals

In the historical traditions collected under the name Nennius in the eighth century, later used by Geoffrey of Monmouth writing in the twelfth, we encounter Basques (Basclenses) from Spain. Significantly, in speaking of the Welsh kings of Caerleon before the Romans came, Geoffrey writes of one of them, Gurguit Barbtruc,[23] son of Belin:

> When Gurguit Barbtruc was returning home via the Orkney Islands ... he came upon thirty ships full of men and women. Gurguit asked what they were doing there. Their leader, whose name was Partholoim, went up to Gurguit, did obeisance to him and asked for his pardon and peace. Partholoim then described how he had been expelled from certain regions in Spain and how he was now cruising in those waters in search of a land where he might settle. He then asked Gurguit for some small region in Britain which he might occupy, so that he need no longer continue this hateful wandering over the sea. A year and a half had passed since he had been expelled from his homeland and had set sail across the ocean with his comrades. When Gurguit Barbtruc learned that these men came from Spain and were called Basclenses, and when he understood just what they wanted of him, he ordered his representative to go with them to the island of Ireland, which at that time was a completely uninhabited desert. He granted the island to them. They have increased and multiplied there and they still hold the island today.[24]

Geoffrey also records how Brutus passed through Phoenicia and Mauritania in his wanderings, taking into his company in northern Spain a fellow Trojan called Corineus, after whom Cornwall was to be named (17). The connections between Britain and North Africa transcend genetics and are discernible in both literature and legend.

Later, during the Saxon incursions, Geoffrey writes, the British grow restive under the rulers Vortiporius (Vortiporn, king of Dyfed), Malgo (Maelgwn Gwynedd) and Keredic (first king of the Alt Clud) who succeeded Constantine and Conanus, the last of the Romans.

> They sent to Ireland for Gormund the King of the Africans, who had gone there with an enormous fleet and conquered the people of that country ... Gormund, accompanied by 160,000 Africans, came over to Britain ... he drove the King from city to city and then forced him to take refuge in Cirencester, where he besieged him. Isembard, the nephew of Louis King of the Franks, went to join him there and made a treaty of friendship with him. The terms of the treaty were that, as a token of his friendship for Gormund, Isembard should renounce his Christian faith ... Gormund then fought Keredic and chased him over the Severn into Wales.
>
> Once this inhuman tyrant Gormund, with his countless thousands of Africans, had destroyed almost all the island, as I have described already, he handed over a considerable part of it, called Loegria [England], to the Saxons, whose treason had been the cause of his landing. Such Britons as remained sought refuge in the western parts of the kingdom: in Cornwall and Wales.... Many priests fled in a great fleet to Armorican Brittany [170–71].

We perceive from this sequence of events that the Africans were already entrenched in Ireland and then descended on the island of Great Britain, where they joined together with their German allies the Saxons and caused the Britons to flee to Little Britain on the Armorican peninsula of western Gaul. We know this migration occurred in two stages, one in the fifth century and one a century later in the time of Gildas. The earlier timeframe corresponds to the heyday of the Vandal kingdoms in Spain and North Africa, providing a relative chronology. Under their king Genseric, who succeeded his brother Gunderic, the conqueror of Andalusia, the Vandals fell on Africa and by 439 had established a kingdom that embraced the entire Roman province. In 455, they sacked the city of Rome. Their kingdom was exterminated in the Vandalic War of 533–34, in which Justinian managed to reconquer the Africa province for the Eastern Roman or Byzantine Empire.

True Origins of Sepharad

Gormund is a Vandal name. We learn from Geoffrey's account that he and his Africans were not Christians, for Gormund attempts to force his Gaulish ally Isembard, perhaps a Burgundian or Visigoth, to "renounce his Christian faith." Although the later *chanson de geste* calls Gormund a Saracen, the Islamic religion had not yet come into being in Gormund's day. It seems more possible that Gormund was either an Arian or a Sephardic Jew.

The word "Sepharad" or "Sfarad" has been derived from a Vandal or Visigothic word meaning "dark" (Gothic *svarts, svard,* German *schwarz*). Rabbinical traditions associate it with a Hebrew word in Obadiah 1:20, but this etymology is probably an interpolation.[25] In the chapter titled "Realms of Silence," Shlomo Sand has several pages canvasing the history of the Himyarite, Cyrenaican, Phoenician, Carthaginian and Berber proselytes in North Africa. The Church Fathers Tertullian and Augustine, both from Africa, were very much concerned about the strength of Judaism in Carthage, the old Phoenician capital. Many of the Sephardic Jews who later spilled over into Spain, says Sand, were probably semi-converts or in an intermediary state between paganism and Judaism.[26] The poet Commodianus, who was probably from fifth-century Roman Africa, "attacked the numerous proselytes and mocked their switching and changing of religions and the blatant inconsistency of their worship" (201).[27]

> The advance of the church was temporarily halted by the Vandal conquest. These Germanic tribes from Europe dominated North Africa between 430 and 533 CE, where they established an Arian Christian kingdom. There is next to no information about the situation of North Africa's Jews during the Vandal century, but it is known that relations between the Arians and the Jewish believers were much better than between the latter and the consolidating Orthodox Church [201].

On the strength of these connections and in view of the timeframe, we would suggest that Gildas and his immediate forebears might have belonged to the "half-Jews" criticized by Commodianus, possibly semi-converts or Arians or Pelagians.

Gildas is said to have been a son of Cauus (Caius, a Roman name), whose father was Rhydderch Hael, a descendant of the first king of Alt Clud, Ceredig Guletic (the Coroticus to whom Patrick wrote a letter). Ceredig's other successors were Erbin, Cinuit, Gereint and Tutagual. They were related to the kings of Gwynedd and Rheged, including Urien, whose Latin name, Urbigenus, means "city-born" or Roman, another indication of Romanitas. As for Tutagual, Rydderch's father, Adamnan gives his name as Tothail. So much for the kings of Alt Clud, all of whom are nothing but names with the exception of a few bare mentions culled from British legend by Norman Davies (46–60).

We suggest many of these kings were Visigothic in origin, regarding themselves as heirs to the power that had passed from Rome to the Goths. Tothail (also rendered Tothael and Tothwalla) incorporates the name of a Visigothic sibship, as reflected in Totila, king of the Ostrogoths in Italy who was a relative of Theudis, king of the Visigoths and swordbearer of Theodoric the Great (d. 552). Rydderch, whose name also appears as Rydderig, becomes in later literature Roderick, a name shared with the semi-legendary "last king of the Goths" before the arrival of the Arabs. In France and Spain, it became one of the most prolific of Sephardic surnames. Varieties include Rodric, Rodrig, Rodrich, Rodrigue, Rodrigues, Rodriguez and Rodriques. According to Faiguenboim's dictionary, it is today the third most common Sephardic Jewish surname.[28] In medieval Wales, it was widely used, appearing at a frequency of 1–2 percent in fifteenth-century records. Forms included Rhydderch, Roderick, Rothero, Prothero, Rotherough, Ruddock, Rutherch and Ruddz (an abbreviation).[29]

Gildas' Vision

Once we can place Gildas in the Arian Christian and Sephardic Jewish tradition of Visigoths ruling the crumbling western provinces of the Roman Empire, defending its legacy from true barbarians such as the Vandals and Anglo-Saxons, the point of view and lessons of his history fall into focus and become clear. Gildas rolls out a knowing and rhetorically polished critique of British society, capped by a scalding attack on its leaders for giving in to corruption and luxury. His history is a declamation in three parts, cataloging the achievements and depravities of kings, abbots and warlords who are supposed to represent the forces of *Romanitas*, as that ideal was best practiced by the Visigoths of the Kingdom of Toulouse and other civilized client states. The obvious intent is to provide, in the ancient mold of historians, a perpetual memory of good and evil deeds, things to emulate and things to avoid. He begins with the accomplishments of the Romans and groans of the Britons about 450, the colony's last plea for help before being enveloped by the barbarian Saxons. Gildas, in other words, is a true historian, with well-crafted themes and a hard-won right to describe the events of his day. It is shame he is nowadays so often dismissed as overblown and preachy.

Rome at this juncture still derived a lot of value from the British grain supply, showing that even if imperial authority had evaporated, the towns and countryside were safe and productive under petty dukes, ex-military leaders and local magistrates (*decuriones*). Among the sins for which Gildas excoriates his fellow Britons are those of materialistic excess and luxurious living. He lauds by name heroes such as Aurelius Ambrosius, whom he describes as a leader of the resistance to the Saxons. He mentions the victory at the Battle of Mons Badonicus (Bath), a triumph attributed to King Arthur in later literature. Part two consists of a scathing castigation of five British kings, Constantine, Aurelius Conanus, Vortiporius, Cuneglas and Maelgwn. Part three is a similar invective against the clergy of the time.

In British myth and historical tradition, not only Ireland but also Cornwall is the stronghold of Africans. Mark, the king of Cornwall in Arthurian legend and jealous husband of Isoud or Isolt of Ireland, is portrayed in the Tristan romances as dark-complexioned, rich and of fiery southern temperament. Mark or Marcus is a frequent name in Jewish genealogies, particularly among English Jews. Was this in memory perhaps of the soldier in Roman Britain proclaimed emperor by the army there sometime in 406, in the last death rattle of imperial rule? The legendary Mark's sister is Elizabeth, a Hebrew name. Their royal residence is fixed in Tintagel on the north coast of the Cornish peninsula facing Ireland. This site's chief fame in medieval literature reached its apogee in the immensely popular cycle devoted to Cornwall and Tristram and Isolde.

Here again, legend and history seem to coalesce. A series of excavations in Tintagel in 1933 uncovered a forgotten chapter in southwest Britain's prehistory. According to Oliver James Padel at the department of Welsh history at University College of Wales, Aberstwyth, "The area of Tintagel headland teems with fragments of pottery of a type manufactured in

King Mark of Cornwall and Tristram (floor tile from Chertsey Abbey, Surrey) (© The Trustees of the British Museum).

the Mediterranean area (mainly in North Africa and Asia Minor); these fragments are dated between the mid fifth century and the late sixth."

> The importance of Tintagel as a find-site for this pottery cannot be overemphasized. Since being identified there, it has been found to occur at other sites within Dark-Age western Britain and Ireland, including other sites in Cornwall and Devon ... and South Cadbury in Somerset ... as far north as the Scottish Highlands.... Being imported from so far away, this pottery represents expensive, luxury, goods.[30]

Tintagel Castle was formerly believed to be a Celtic monastic community, but Padell and others have proved that it resembles no other ecclesiastical sites in Wales and Cornwall. "What is the pottery doing in Britain, at this and other sites?" The Welsh researcher believes, "It must

Tintagel Castle (Wikimedia Commons).

have been brought in the way of trade, and if an object for the trading connection is to be sought, then an obvious one would be Cornish tin" (231). This answer, however, does not explain the amounts scattered at other sites or why the pottery is concentrated in such impressive quantities at Tintagel. And so Tintagel has emerged as a whole new cultural complex.

Of great importance will be the inscriptions in the region in ogam (pre-alphabetic) and Tifinag (Berber) scripts. The word "Tintagel" is difficult or impossible to etymologize in Cornish. A better explanation than Padel's hypothetical "Cornish *din, 'fort' (variant *tin), plus *tagell, 'constriction': 'the fort of the narrow neck'" (231) might be one based on the Semitic elements *Thina* "bend of headland" plus *Ghayl* "place with water," a description which suits the natural topography (see photo).[31]

Gildas is the first of a long line of writers to identify the British with the Jewish people. To be sure, this is an old Christian typological device. The first Jewish Christians considered themselves members of Israel. Robert Hanning finds the figural use of New Israel and national adaptations of the term *praesens Israel* ("present-day Israel") in Orosius, Eusebius, Gregory of Tours and others.[32] But Gildas seems to take what might strike us at first blush as a rhetorical topos further. He compares St. Alban and the thousand townspeople the protomartyr won over to "the Israelites of old," alleging that Alban "opened a path across the noble river Thames."[33] In another passage, he quotes Psalm 44, a text central to the incipient rabbinical effort in Palestine and other places in the East to justify the Jewish people's defeat and exile by the Romans: "Thou hast given us as sheep to be slaughtered, and among the Gentiles has thou dispersed us (25)." Summarizing the progress of the Cymry up to their critical victory at Mons Badonicus, he writes (26):

> After this, sometimes our countrymen, sometimes the enemy, won the field, to the end that our Lord might in this land try after his accustomed manner these his Israelites, whether they loved him or not, until the year of the siege of Bath-hill, when took place also the last almost, though not the least slaughter of our cruel foes, which was (as I am sure) forty-four years and one month after the landing of the Saxons, and also the time of my own nativity.

Lost Sheep of Israel

At times, Gildas writes in an explicitly autobiographical vein. On a few occasions, he apparently drops any pretense and speaks of a Jewish background to British Christianity. Of his first studies, he says:

> These passages and many others I regarded as, in a way, a mirror of our life, in the Scriptures of the Old Testament, and then I turned to the Scriptures of the New; there I read things that previously had perhaps been dark to me, in clearer light, because the shadow passed away, and the truth shone more steadily. I read, that is to say, of the Lord saying: *I am not come but unto the lost sheep of the House of Israel.* And on the other side: *But the sons of this Kingdom shall be cast into outer darkness, there shall be weeping and gnashing of teeth.* Again: *It is not good to take the children's bread and cast it to the dogs.* Also: *Woe unto you Scribes and Pharisees, hypocrites.*
> I heard: *Many shall come from east and west and recline with Abraham, Isaac, and Jacob in the Kingdom of Heaven.*[34]

Here he seems to confess that before converting to Christianity he read only the Old Testament or Torah. He identifies with "the lost sheep of the House of Israel." Remarkably, he specifies that his own people are Canaanite, for he references the story of Jesus' rebuke of a Phoenician woman. Here is the version of the parable from Matthew 15:21–28:

> Then Jesus went from there, and departed into the borders of Tyre and Sidon. And, behold, a woman of Canaan[35] came out of the same borders, and cried unto him, saying, Have mercy on me, O Lord, thou Son of David; my daughter is grievously vexed with a demon. But he answered her not a word. And his disciples came and besought him, saying, Send her away; for she crieth after us. But he answered and said, I am not sent but unto the lost sheep of the house of Israel. Then came she and worshiped him, saying, Lord, help me. But he answered and said, It is not right to take the children's bread, and to cast it to the dogs. And she said, Truth, Lord; yet the dogs eat of the crumbs which fall from their master's table. Then Jesus answered, and said unto her, O woman, great is thy faith; be it unto thee even as thou wilt. And her daughter was made well from that very hour.

Perhaps one of the most suggestive clues to Gildas' roots, though, occurs in his vitriolic description of Constantine, the treacherous British leader who broke his oath of peace: "Of this so execrable a wickedness [violating the peace] Constantine, the tyrannical whelp of the unclean lioness of Damnonia, is not ignorant (28)." Gildas tells how Constantine falsely puts on the guise of an abbot and murders two royal youths who took refuge in a church. By calling Constantine the son of the lioness of Damnonia (*inmundae leaenae Damnoniae tyrannicus catulus*), he invokes the pedigrees recited about the kingdom of Damnonia (not to be confused with Dumnonia, or Devon in the south). He weaves these together with Old Testament references.[36] In Jacob's blessing of his children, "Judah is a lion's whelp" (Genesis 49:8), and the lion of Judah became the tribal emblem of all his descendants, especially those who also claimed to come from the House of David. In Moses' blessing of the patriarchs in Deuteronomy 33:22, we also read that "Dan is a lion's whelp." Gildas calls another British king who earns his disproval, Aurelius Caninus or Cynan or Conanus, a "lion pup" (*catulus leoninus*).

Gildas clearly regarded Britain's rightful rulers as Canaanite—we should say Semitic. Dan was originally assigned territory on the coastal plain, near Philistia, a neighbor both of the Judeans and of the Phoenicians. Later the tribe migrated to the northern extremity of the land where it destroyed and rebuilt the city of Laish ("lion" or "lionlike"), settling there and renaming the city Dan. In the eyes of Gildas and his contemporaries, the Damnonians were, accordingly, the children of Dan in Britain. By using the word "unclean" of Constantine's Danite mother, Gildas insinuates that her people were idolatrous—in other words, lapsed Jews.

Meaning of Romanitas

From a Welsh perspective, the western and northern regions of England preserved far more continuity with the past than the parts of the island that ended up in the hands of Saxons. More than a semblance of Romanitas survived. Yet the sense of loss audible in Gildas' jeremiads would become "the motive force of much of Welsh mythology," including Arthurian legend. It was primarily Welsh lineages that were commemorated in the king-lists and on inscribed stones. For instance, "the most powerful by 540 was that of Maglocunus, a ruler portrayed by Gildas as a man of impressive sinfulness ... the Maelgwyn Fawr or Maelgwyn Gwynedd of Welsh tradition (Davies 50)." Maelgrwyn was a descendant of Cunedda, who came to Gwynedd from among the Men of the North in southern Scotland and apparently was descended from Roman forebears and connected with Magnus Maximus. "There is a determinedly Brythonic, and indeed Roman, air to early Gwynedd (52)." The kingdom of Dyfed in southwest Wales, on the other hand, was of Irish origin, with North African and Vandal overtones. But both Dinas Powys (Dinas Pagus, Land of Pagans), or Glamorgan, and Gwent (from Caer-went) developed from a combination of the Roman settlements and the old traditions of the Silures and other southern Welsh tribes. The fourth-century Roman protector-general Magnus Maximus is rightly considered the father of the Welsh nation. All that was lacking was the adoption of a national identity as Cymry ("countrymen") or Cumbria (Latin Cambria). "The word *Cymry* evolved from the Brittonic word *Combrogi* ("fellow-countrymen") and was applied to the old northern kingdom of Rheged (Cumbria), straddling the border between Scotland and England (71)."

John Davies cites two surprising inscriptions that prove city life and exotic influences remained intact in at least Gwynedd during this time. One is a memorial to the son of Avitorius at Penmachno mentioning the consulate of Justinus, "a man who is known to have been appointed consul in 540 by the remnant of Roman power still existing in the West." The other, an epitaph carved for King Cadfan, who died about 625, exhibits the most up-to-date fashions in Roman lapidary lettering, and "the format of inscriptions provides evidence of links with France, northern Africa and the eastern shores of the Mediterranean." Moreover, the fort thought to have been the seat of Maglocunus, Degannwy, "has yielded fragments of glass and pottery from the Black Sea, Athens and Bordeaux" (55). Most of Britain, not just Cumbria or Wales, remained in control of British kings until the middle of the sixth century, and it was only in the following hundred years from 550 to 650 that the Saxons and related Germans won the areas that came to be known as East Anglia, Essex, Wessex, Kent, Sussex, Mercia and Northumbria.

Popular belief imagines the Welsh as an embattled, backward remnant forced into a small mountainous peninsula of western England. But the land possessed by these true Britons was once much more extensive. Northumbria swallowed most of the kingdoms of the Old North. Rheged was annexed in about 635, Carlisle by 685, and the kingdom of the Votadini ceased with the capture of Edinburgh by Oswy in about 638. The last of the Brythonic kingdoms of the Old North, Strathclyde, survived for four hundred years. It was not extinguished until 1018, when it became part of the Dalraidic kingdom of Scotland founded by the Irish. In broad outline, the story of Britannia was different from Gallia or Hispania. Here Romanized and semi–Romanized provincials lost the fight to the more wild and furious barbarians.

To Nennius, the shadowy author of the *Historia Brittonum*, his countrymen were *cives*, that is, citizens of a lost state. The word "Welsh" itself did not originally have a contemptuous connotation. "It would appear," maintains Davies, "that 'Welsh' meant not so much foreigners as peoples who had been Romanized; other versions of the word may be found along the borders of the empire—the Walloons of Belgium, the Welsch of the Italian Tyrol and the Vlachs of Romania—and the *Welschnuss*, the walnut, was the nut of the Roman lands" (71). Thus southeast Wales and the church of Dyfig, Illtud and David was "the cradle of the Celtic Church and the starting point of a movement which was to revitalize Europe" (72). A measure of the prosperity of Dinas Powys was that it was "a place where objects from Bordeaux, Athens and Alexandria were in use—and if pottery could be carried to the Vale of Glamorgan so also could ideas, books and students. Llantwit Major can be considered to be the axis of the Christianity of the Celtic-speaking peoples" (73–74). Samson, Paul Aurelian and Gildas studied there, and "indeed, almost all the leaders of early Irish monasticism had been trained in Wales (75)."

Latin, Greek and Hebrew

During these centuries only Irish, Welsh, Scottish and English monks kept the flame of learning and civilization alive in the West. The Carolingian renaissance dawning in the eighth century was due nearly exclusively to the mission to the court of Charlemagne led by Alcuin of York. The survival of ancient Latin texts was possible, similarly, only because of the British-styled scriptoria established at Corbie, Bobbio, Luxeuil, Fulda, Salzburg and elsewhere on the Continent. The Welsh, Irish and Northumbrians were supreme in every branch of learning and towered over the age in sheer intellectual force.[37]

Knowledge of and interest in Hebrew in Christian Europe followed British culture carriers wherever they went. With the same intellectual currents, there proceeded a trickling of Hebrew out of the British Isles. According to Faritius, the cellarer of Malmesbury Abbey and physician to Henry I (b. in Italy, died 1117), Aldhelm of Malmesbury (639–709), second abbot of this famous Welsh institution, had not only been a member of the royal house of Wessex but a speaker of Hebrew.[38] Not only do the Welsh bards, beginning with Taliesin (c. 534–599), claim Hebrew as their original written language,[39] but British monks on the Continent also exhibit an inexplicable knowledge of it. Of Radbert of Corbie, Manitius, usually doubtful of such claims, is forced to admit that he knew Hebrew idiomatically (as well as Greek).[40] Radbert came from unknown origins and was abbot of Corbie about 845. His baptismal name was Paschasius ("Easter"), suggesting that he was a convert. Corbie was a Benedictine abbey in northern France that sprang from Luxeuil, a powerhouse of scholastic learning founded by the Irish missionary Columbanus at the end of the sixth century. From the same source comes a knowledge of Hebrew preserved in an eighth-century Latin grammar with a provenance from

Bobbio, an abbey founded by Columbanus in 614. Bobbio became one of the greatest libraries in Christendom.[41]

An Irish monk in northern France, Smaragdus of St. Mihiel (Hebrew *eesmaragd*, "Emerald," of Semitic derivation, probably another *converso* name[42]) was so well versed in Hebrew that he contributed glosses to the Bible on the fine points of pronunciation with diacritical marks in rabbinical use at the time. Smaragdus' treatise on the inflection of Hebrew and Latin words endorsed the pronunciation of Aaron in three syllables, adopted in all subsequent Biblical scholarship. Smaragdus was familiar with Greek, too, but he knew Hebrew better. He produced the first of a genre that became more popular in the latter Middle Ages. His *Mirror of Princes* was modeled on Arabic court literature and addressed to none other than Charlemagne.[43]

Speech of the Western Isles

Familiarity with ancient Hebrew can be detected in the bizarre language called Hiberno-Latin. This playful, polyglot type of scholars' discourse was practiced from the sixth to the tenth century. The *locus classicus* for Hiberno-Latin is a text from the second half of the sixth century called *Hisperica Famina*. The title means, literally, "Relics of the Speech of the Western Isles." Manitius describes *Hisperica Famina* as "technically meaningless, but linguistically intriguing."[44] This verdict reminds us of how James Joyce—a latter-day devotee of Hiberno-Latin—defended his puns by quipping that they were both trivial and quadrivial. Hisperic Latin, then, has been judged by most to be a linguist's language, a mathematical puzzle. It has inspired a small cottage industry in academic circles, where it is usually approached as an invented language. But it does seem to have an organic basis. Those who study the history of school texts have demonstrated that it lifts archaisms from older Greek-Latin lexicons like the Hermeneumata of Dositheus. But what of the many "Hebrew loan-words," if that is what they are?

Few medievalists today doubtless recall Leo Wiener (1862–1939), a professor of Slavic languages and literature at Harvard. Born in the Jewish town of Bialystok in Tsarist Lithuania, he was a descendant of Aquiba Eger, grand rabbi of Posen, and Moses Maimonides, the preeminent Sephardic Jewish philosopher who codified Talmudic law in twelfth-century Almoravid North Africa. Leo's son, Norbert Wiener (d. 1964), is better known. The child prodigy grew up to become a professor of mathematics at MIT and the celebrated founder of modern-day cybernetics. The elder Wiener was not only a polymath, writing one of the first histories of feudal law as well as several books on the African influence on American Indian civilization, but also an old-fashioned savant, a prodigiously active philologist who translated the twenty-four volumes of Tolstoy's complete works in an astoundingly short time with "remarkable felicity and accuracy."[45] One of Wiener's more obscure works was a four-volume collection of essays on Arabico-Gothic culture of the early Middle Ages.[46] Among the arcane texts Wiener elucidated, fortunately for us, was the Hisperica Famina (in volume 1).

Wiener found Arabic to be the key to understanding Virgilius Maro the Grammarian, another baffling author of the early medieval period in western Europe. He assigned the writings to a date of around 750; current scholarship places the texts in the first half of the seventh century, if not before. Bernard Bischoff, a leading authority on Medieval Latin, believed Virgilius was a Spanish or southern French Jew living in Ireland and familiar with the Cabala, perhaps originally coming from Toulouse. If this is true, Virgilius' Semiticisms, whether they are inspired by Hebrew or Arabic, predate the Mozarabic culture brought to Spain and southern France by the Islamic conquest of 710 and relate rather to the living traditions of Visigothic Septimania.

We must apply an earlier date, then, to Wiener's detection of Arabicisms in Hisperic Latin, a timeframe falling well before the birth of Islam in the seventh century. For instance, in the poem called *Rubisca* (l. 12), Wiener notes that the bizarre Latin word *nedula*, glossed in Irish manuscripts as *alba* ("white") may be explained by Arabic *nadura*, which he renders perhaps over-imaginatively, "it was and became beautiful and fresh, or fine-skinned" (30). In line 32 of the same poem, he compares both Hebrew *šen* and Arabic *sinn* where the Latin text has *sennis*, glossed *dentibus* ("teeth"). He assumes that Arabic is more apposite than Hebrew and deduces that all these specimens of Hisperic Latin owe their "origin to Visigoths, or their friends, who based their studies on the old Spanish writers and the new Arabic poetry" created in mid-eighth-century Moorish Spain. But the bulk of Hisperic Latin, including the famous prayer for protection known as *Lorica* attributed to Gildas, is, as we have already seen, much earlier. It was associated not with Mozarabic Spain but mid-sixth-century Britain.

Conceivably, the exotic linguistic trophies prized by Virgilius and others did not all come from book learning. Some obviously stem from the living memory of Semitic languages, including Arabic, Hebrew and Berber. All these were apparently spoken in Britain until the sixth century, whereupon knowledge of them was preserved only in the esoteric traditions of Welsh and Irish-founded monasteries.[47] Wiener was wrong about his starting points but he was on the right path.

Between the withdrawal of Roman protection in 410 and the triumph of the Anglo-Saxons, the British Isles witnessed a half-friendly invasion by Visigothic and Vandal clients of Rome in a chapter of its history that has mostly been lost to us because of the lack of writings and records. Joining the Romano-Britons, the Vandals, Visigoths, Arabs, Jews and Berbers of North Africa, Iberia and the Midi brought their respective languages, cultures and religions in a jumble to the western half of Great Britain, where they blended with existing traditions, in particular the "Celtic" version of Christianity, already seeded there from the Mediterranean. In *pre–Islamic* Hisperic Latin, we find Arabicisms such as *gibron = gabrun* "homo," *ergla = rigl*, pl. *argul* "crura, legs" and *olla = allah* "deus, Allah." We also find a Semitic word for the moon (*gansia*), a long description of the Jewish ark of the covenant (Wiener 88) and the pagan belief in the evil done by a genii's darts, from which the *lorica,* an unusual device with Semitic and Celtic cognates, protects the wearer (70).

Anglo-Saxon Side of History

Nothing seemed to prevail against the new menace to civilization in Britain. The Anglo-Saxon presence in Britain had taken hold at first in the old Romano-German colonies, beginning with York, and its character was of a milder, more constrained sort as long as the empire held. After the brutal sixth century, however, it grew to cover all the eastern, "non–Welsh" parts of the country. But even this chapter in Britain's medieval past is not without its mysteries, and it is entirely unclear how penetrating or absolute the Anglo-Saxon culture was. If one were to maintain there were no Jews among the Anglo-Saxons one might be correct. But one would be wrong to argue there were no Jews in Anglo-Saxon literature and written tradition.

"Anglo-Saxon history is by no means a simple factual record, with a core of reliable and coherent evidence around which we can construct a chronicle of the times," begins the preface to one collection of texts.[48] Dates of chance literary works that survive, usually in fragments, are a particular problem. The greatest epic of these centuries, *Beowulf*, exists in a single manuscript from the library of the seventeenth-century antiquarian Sir Robert Cotton. It nearly perished when the Cottonian library burned in 1731. The tenth-century Exeter Book containing the largest known collection of Anglo-Saxon literature seems at times to have been used as a beer-mat and cutting board. It cannot be said that the English were very careful with their national treasures. Nevertheless, enough survives of Anglo-Saxon writing to form a picture of how their society regarded Romans, Jews, Britons and other non–Germanic people, including the intransigent Welsh.

Two dominant images of Jews emerge from reading Anglo-Saxon literature. On the one hand, they are portrayed as proud, exotic, sophisticated denizens of the Middle East, neighbors of the Egyptians, Greeks and Persians, and forerunners of Christian society. On the other, they are seen as a scattered, wandering race of dispossessed exiles. Importantly, in neither characterization do we meet with anti–Semitic stereotypes. Jews are humanized, idealized, made to fit into the heroic patterns of bardic song and learning. In *Widsith*, the oldest text to survive in any Germanic language, the minstrel enumerates "Israelites" and "Hebrews" along with Assyrians, Indians, Egyptians, Medes, Persians and Myrgings (Welsh) as among the peoples he impresses with "song swelling to the sweet-touched harp [and] men there of unmelting hearts, who well knew, worded their thought, said this was the best song sung in their hearing."[49] In Cynewulf's story of the discovery of the True Cross, Elene is a "stately queen" whose "proven band, a host in armour" is seeking "the Jewish fatherland." She summons the "heartsick Hebrews" in Jerusalem to reveal the hiding place of the cross, "but they were stubborn, harder than flint, nor would they confess aught of the mystery." She bullies them until their leader Judas capitulates and the Jews convert to Christianity. Jews are thus described as proud, and pious, and wise, and formidable enemies, but in the end it is a sympathetic and respectful portrayal. Judas is represented "though strengthless and feeble" as praying "in the Hebrew tongue," and makes a long, Judaic-sounding hymn of praise to the Holy One. By eventually accepting Christianity, these fictional Jews avoid the plight of their brethren as allotted to them by the Augustinian worldview, which we will shortly examine.

Jews, Christians and Pagans

In the religious epic *Andreas*, the Jews are again enlisted to authenticate the message of the Gospel. We hear the story of the resurrection of Abraham, Isaac and Jacob to spread the news of Christ's arrival. It is set largely in a ship on the sea piloted by God on a mission to rescue St. Matthew from the clutches of the Mermedonians, a cannibal people in Africa. In a fragment of a poem based on the book of Judith preserved in the same manuscript as Beowulf, the anagogical is carried even further. "Judith is unequivocally shown as the admired and beloved leader of the Israelites ... an epic heroine" (79). She is extolled as "the holy handmaid of heaven ... wise-mooded ... the illustrious lady" and "the bright, peerless handmaid of God," also "Judith the brave," the "brave handmaid of heaven," "eminent woman" and "Judith the lofty." The Hebrews are "warriors" and "heroes." They trounce Holofernes and his Assyrians in the best manner of an Anglo-Saxon war band:

> The mighty host came, then,
> The folk of the Hebrews, fought valiantly
> With keen-edged cutlasses, settled with sword-blades

> Their quarrels of old, with edges that gleamed
> Their long-standing hate; Assyria's glory
> From the work of that day waned mightily,
> Her pride was humbled [85].

In the Anglo-Saxon glorification of Jews we see none of the timidity and cowardice later attributed to them.

Studies of anti–Semitism and works on the persecution of Jews are so prolific and final it may be supposed that nothing can be added to the treatments of Judaism they offer for any given historical time and place. It has frequently been pointed out that anti–Semitism thrives even in periods like those of Anglo-Saxon England or Puritan Massachusetts where "there were no Jews." In addressing the subject here, though, it is perhaps useful to distinguish between anti–Semitism, which is, after all, essentially a nineteenth-century construct, and anti–Judaism. For the Latin West the chief architect of the medieval "witness doctrine" regarding the Jews was Augustine of Hippo (354–430). In his "Sermon against the Jews" and "Faith in Things Unseen," he formulated a church policy that justified God's preservation of the Jews and counseled Christians to be tolerant of them because of their special role in history. As Paula Frederiksen shows in *Augustine and the Jews*, his milder teachings were a reaction to the hatred and violence toward Jews espoused by the Manicheans and Greek theologians who promoted the more virulent dynamics that played out in the Eastern Church.[50] Even so, Augustine remained rigidly anti–Jewish.

Augustine's philosophy toward the Jews rested on two pillars. In answering the question why God did not save the Jews but allowed them to continue in blindness, he pointed to the Jews' piety and learning. "By never forgetting the Law, the dispersed Jews serve the Church. 'In their hearts they are our enemy; in their books our witness.'"[51] "You are not to slay them," Augustine preached, lest they someday forget your law.... For if they dwelt with that testimony of their Scriptures in their own land only, and not everywhere, then the church, which is everywhere, could not have them at hand among all the Gentiles as witnesses to those prophecies that were given in advance concerning Christ."[52] Not only were the Jews necessary as perpetual and ubiquitous "negative witnesses," ever-present and unchanging symbols of blindness punished sufficiently, but they were useful as interpreters of the Bible, even if only because they knew Hebrew. Their Old Testament stories were allegorized with Christological meanings and applied as lessons to Christians in equal measure to the New Testament.

The logic of the message "Do not slay them" in Psalms 59:12 was not always understood with Augustinian sophistication and subtlety. As Frederiksen notes, "Already in the first half of the seventh century, in Visigothic Spain, Isidore of Seville, himself a student of Augustine's work, was busy misinterpreting it. In a Christian society obsessively focused on anti–Jewish legislation, Isidore fails to refer to Augustine's theology of Jewish witness, and he even adapts several of Augustine's anti–Donatist arguments to justify anti–Jewish coercion. In Isidore's great work *De fide catholica*, Augustine's reading of Psalm 59:12 is conspicuously absent."[53] For many reasons, however, Britain did not go down the same road as Visigothic Spain. Its Celtic Church, for one, cherished the role of Judaism in biblical exegesis, and we have seen the admiration for Jews that carried over into Anglo-Saxon times.

Summing up, neither British (read Welsh) nor Anglo-Saxon society seems to have harbored strong anti–Semitic attitudes in the post–Roman period. Far from it. Jews, ex–Jews, converts and semi-converts played an integral part in the events of these centuries. They left straightforward literary records of their Jewish sympathies and background, if only we are willing to approach the testimony of Gildas and his contemporaries with impartiality and a fresh look. A major factor was undoubtedly Britain's "Celtic" brand of Christianity. But with the coming of Augustinian Christianity from Rome at the end of the sixth century, the dynamic changed.

Primates and Primitives

After surviving the catastrophic plagues, foreign invasions and bloody battles of the sixth century, Britain received the mission of Augustine, a Benedictine monk sent by Pope Gregory. Augustine became the first archbishop of Canterbury in the year 597. He is considered the apostle to the English and founder of the English Church. Britain became, as it had been for the Roman emperors, a jewel in the crown of the bishop of Rome. Until the High Middle Ages and Reformation, Britain was the *only* nation successfully colonized and subjected to the papacy outside of Italy.[54] If the account of the Welsh historian Theophilus Evans is to be credited, Augustine was no saint. Evans wrote *Drych y Prif Oesoedd* (Mirror of the Early Centuries) in 1716. It was translated into English by George Roberts and published as *A View of the Primitive Ages* in Llanidloes in 1834. According to Evans, Augustine in 601 encouraged the Saxons to carry out a massacre of 1,200 monks and scholars at the academy of Bangor-is-y-coed, or Bangor-on-Dee, in the ancient central Welsh district of Maelor. His account of this last stand of British religion against Catholicism is colored by romanticism and the anti-papist views of his day. But we have other sources for this important turning point in Britain's history.

Of the antipathy between the Welsh and the English, Bede plainly wrote, "The Britons for the most part have a national hatred for the English, and uphold their own bad customs against the true Easter of the Catholic Church."[55] But even the meek and learned apologist for Augustinian Christianity does not gloss over the Battle of Chester, giving us noteworthy historical details of this suppression of native religion. After the British religious leaders refuse to recognize Augustine, saying "if he would not rise to greet them ... he would have even less regard for them once they submitted to his authority," King Æthelfrith of the Northumbrians, who "might well be compared to Saul the king of Israel, except of course that he was ignorant of true religion," cruelly accomplishes the elimination of the "accursed" Welsh which the Augustinian Christians from Kent desired. According to Bede, Æthelfrith

> raised a great army at the City of Legions—which the English call Chester but which the Britons more correctly name Carlegion—and made a great slaughter of the faithless Britons. Before battle was joined, he noticed that their priests were assembled apart in a safer place to pray for their soldiers, and he enquired who they were and what they had come there to do. Most of these priests came from the monastery of Bangor, where there are said to have been so many monks that although it was divided into seven sections, each under its own head, none of these sections contained fewer than three hundred monks, all of whom supported themselves by manual work. Most of these monks, who had kept a three-day fast, had gathered to pray at the battle, guarded by a certain Brocmail, who was there to protect them from the swords of the barbarians while they were intent on prayer. As soon as King Æthelfrith was informed of their purpose, he said: "If they are crying to their God against us, they are fighting against us even if they do not bear arms." He therefore directed his first attack against them, and then destroyed the rest of the accursed army, not without heavy loss to his own forces. It is said that of the monks who had come to pray about twelve hundred perished in this battle, and only fifty escaped by flight.... Thus was fulfilled Bishop Augustine's prophecy that the faithless Britons, who had rejected the offer of eternal salvation, would incur the punishment of temporal destruction [153–54].

We see from this narration that Bede regarded the Welsh as extreme heretics, not even believing in or worthy of "the offer of eternal salvation" (Jesus Christ the Savior), and thus well rid of, even if at the hand of a pagan barbarian king ironically called Saul.

In the next chapter we will follow the fortunes of the new Anglo-Saxon dominions as they in turn withstand the onslaught of Saracens or Muslims from the south and Vikings from the north and east.

3

Saxons, Vikings and Muslims

As discussed in the previous chapter, many Jews likely remained in England and particularly Wales after the Roman withdrawal. North Africans or Sephardic Jews swelled their ranks. Their numbers probably continued to increase in the centuries after that, especially by in-migration along important trade routes. During this period, Celtic Christianity with its characteristic institutions spread from its center in Wales to Ireland and Scotland. A line of demarcation gradually took shape, dividing Britain in two as the Anglo-Saxon and Welsh petty kingdoms stabilized and reached a sort of détente. England evolved into the heptarchy of Northumbria, Wessex, Mercia, East Anglia, Essex, Sussex and Kent.

Waves of invading Norsemen in the eighth century altered this state of affairs, but the impact was mostly on the Anglo-Saxon east. As Peter Hunter Blair reports, "The first Viking attacks [fell] upon the exposed coasts of Britain. Lindisfarne was sacked in 793, Jarrow in 794 and Iona in 795, and even before [Saxon King] Egbert's accession, three Viking ships had come to land on the Dorset coast near Portland and killed the royal officer who went down to discover who the strangers were. Danes and Norwegians between them took possession of half of England from Essex, Suffolk and Norfolk in the southeast, to Lancashire, Westmorland and Cumberland in the northwest. They occupied Shetland and Orkney, as well as much of the Scottish mainland. They seized the western isles, established many settlements in Ireland and set up a kingdom on the Isle of Man. And with them they brought their language, institutions and social customs, as well as their heathen beliefs."[1]

The Norsemen moved on in their marauding fury to the European continent. In 834, they fell on the largest market town in the Rhine estuary, Dorestad, which had a mint. They bore off the moneyers working there and began minting coins of their own make back home in Scandinavia. In 841, they visited fire and the sword upon Rouen in a campaign of plunder and pillage through England and France. The Anglo-Saxon Chronicle laconically recorded, "In this year there was great slaughter in London, in Quentowic and in Rochester."[2] Quentowic was a flourishing merchant town with its own mint on the French side of the Channel near Calais. It now lay in smoking ruins.

The monasteries serenely pitched in isolated positions on unprotected British coasts or islands were the first victims of the Viking attacks, from Coldingham in the north to Thanet and Reculver in the south. Many stories were related by the frightened populace about the Vikings' ruthless indifference to Christian clergy, sacred books and places of worship. In one exuberant four-year voyage of devastation under Danish captains Bjorn and Hastein, they looted Arles, Nîmes and Valence in southern France and sailed into the eastern Mediterranean as far as Alexandria, Egypt. Finding Luna in southern France impregnable within its city walls, they sent messengers telling the townspeople that Hastein lay at death's door. They were heartsick, and soon they reported their leader was dead. They would fain only give him a proper Christian burial:

The townspeople agreed to provide one; a long procession of sorrowing Vikings followed the coffin to the graveside, where at the moment of committal the "dead" Hastein rose in his coffin, drove his sword through the officiating bishop and led his men on a riot of slaughter through the city streets.[3]

It was the usual practice of the Vikings to come in the spring and raid for the summer, putting the local men to the sword and carrying off meat, drink, gold, silver and women. They then returned "with these earnings to parents, wife and children, and ... saw to the roof, scratched the boar's back, whittled a toy sword, begat a new baby and waited on the next call to service ... Viking [raiding] was seasonal employment."[4] Occasionally, the Scandinavians would remain "enisled" offshore or in an estuary, so that they could start their spring campaigns even sooner. For example, Ragnar and his men sallied up the Seine and plundered Paris on Easter Sunday, March 28, 845.[5]

In 865, a horde of up to a thousand Vikings arrived in England under Ivar (Yngvarr, called the Boneless), Ubbi and Halfdan ("Half-Dane"). They came from Scandinavia and Ireland to avenge the death of Ragnar who, after wringing 7,000 pounds of silver out of the Frankish king Charles the Bald, was outdone in treachery by King Ella of Northumbria, who threw him into a snake pit.

To avoid imminent annihilation, the men of Kent bought their enemies off with England's first recorded Danegeld in 865. Despite this, over the course of the next five years the Vikings overran and ransacked the kingdoms of Northumbria, Mercia and East Anglia. In a flash, Deiria passed into Danish hands. In East Anglia the Norsemen captured King Edmund in 869. According to Abbo of Fleury, they beat him and tied him to a tree, and then they jeered at him, shot him full of arrows and finally beheaded him. He became St. Edmund in the afterlife. In 870, Halfdan attacked Reading and would likely have plundered all of Wessex, had not Alfred succeeded to the throne of his brother Ethelred and mounted an effective resistance. Mercia collapsed in 874. Rebecca Fraser's account of one Viking attack is specific as to what exactly the Vikings preyed upon when she writes of "the loss of nearly all of the priceless objects in the monastery Ubanes.... They carried many of the [coastal] inhabitants into slavery."[6] The monastic complex of Wearmouth-Jarrow near Newcastle where Bede had celebrated the glories of the English Church in burnished prose was wiped from the face of the earth a little over a century after his death.

As noted earlier, at this point the Viking depredations had already cast a spell of terror on the European continent. In 855, raiders in long-ships sacked Paris and "took up more or less permanent quarters on the Rhine, the Scheldt, the Somme, the Seine, the Loire and the Garonne. In 859, their kinsmen were creating havoc in Morocco and carrying off prisoners to their Irish bases."[7] Among the spoils were "negroes ... poor wretches, *fir gorm*, blue men, *blamenn*, black men (or merely men with dark skins)," the nation's first Black Irish.[8] The Vikings also found time to terrorize Moorish Spain, rampaging up the Guadalquivir to Seville before the emir Abd al–Rahman II pushed them back with heavy troops.

Settling Down

Having laid waste to all of eastern Britain, the Danes now turned to actual occupation of their new territories. Approximately half of modern Yorkshire was divided up by Halfdan among his followers. The Danes assimilated with the natives over time, and some of the indigenous people they joined with were clearly Jews. The Anglo-Saxon Chronicle in the tenth century refers to a fortress near York as Iudanfyrig, Jews Fort.[9] The Vikings' ally Ceolwulf in Mercia received half of that kingdom, with the other half parceled out to Danes. "In short the great shires of Yorkshire, Nottingham, Lincoln, Derby and Leicester had ceased to be part of the political realm of England … [although] Danish settlement … did not involve a systematic displacement of the English."[10] Watling Street, the ancient Roman trackway crisscrossing Britannia, served as the informal boundary between the Danes and English. The Anglo-Saxons to the south and west gradually acknowledged the Viking conquests and gave the abandoned territories the name Danelaw (*Denelagu*), "a kind of Denmark overseas, conquered, occupied and organized by Danes, and clearly distinguishable from the rest of England by race, law, language, personal names and place-names, and not least by social custom." Scandinavian vocabulary entered English with words like law, by-law, outlaw, husband, happy, ill, loose, ugly, sister, birth, die and even the pronouns they, them and their. Viking influence was indelibly fixed in place-names ending *-by, -beck, -breck, -fell, -gill, -keld, -mel, -rigg, -scale, -sough, -skeith, thwaite, -thorp* and *-toft*.[11]

And yet as the map shows, there were large areas of Britain which were little affected by the Viking incursions. Further, archeological finds from 700 to 1000 CE testify that trade between England and the Mediterranean, Middle East and India persisted and survived, strongly suggesting that many Jewish trade channels had remained intact. By 866, Saxon King Alfred recaptured London from the Vikings, destroying several Danish settlements in the process. Soon the city was reestablished as "the entrepôt of English national and international trade."[12]

Viking DNA Patterns

The DNA evidence regarding Viking settlement patterns in Britain resembles the linguistic picture. The Y chromosome structure of the British population indicates there was a strong Norwegian influence in the Orkney Islands north of the Scottish mainland and that the Orkneys were an important center of Viking activities between 800 and 1300 CE[13] Bryan Sykes in *Saxons, Vikings, and Celts* detects a high level of Viking genes in northern Scotland, especially Shetland, where the proportion is approximately 35 percent.[14] Despite these hotspots of Viking ancestry, however, other researchers report substantial Anglo-Saxon male population continuity in central England based on the analysis of eight British sample sets collected on an east-west incline across England and Wales.[15]

Overall, the male British population, excluding Orkney and Shetland, reflects relatively high incidences of DNA from southwestern Europe. British male DNA most closely resembles populations found in Spain, France, Germany, Belgium and Switzerland and is overall not much different from the genetic bedrock exposed in chapter 1. The Scandinavian genetic contribution seems to be largely limited to the Western Isles of Britain and extreme northern areas of Scotland.[16]

Rise of Islam

Leaving the Viking invaders, who are already well covered (perhaps to undeserved excess), let us now take a road much less traveled. This leads to North Africa and the Levant. Flowing from our initial research premise, and building on the instances established in the last

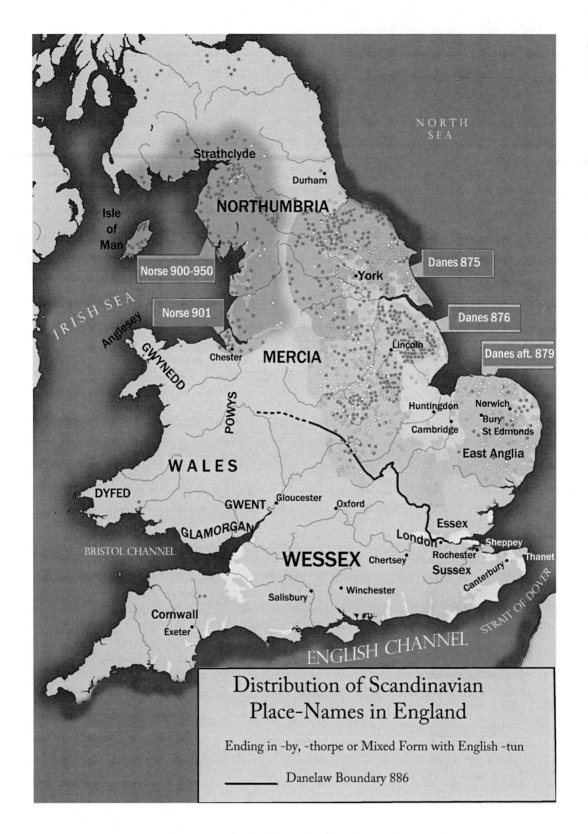

Strathclyde

Durham

NORTHUMBRIA

Isle of Man

Norse 900-950

Danes 875

York

Norse 901

Danes 876

Chester

MERCIA

Lincoln

Danes aft. 879

Anglesey

GWYNEDD

POWYS

Huntingdon

Norwich

Cambridge

Bury St Edmonds

East Anglia

WALES

DYFED

GWENT

Gloucester

Oxford

GLAMORGAN

Essex

London

Sheppey

WESSEX

Chertsey

Rochester

Thanet

Sussex

Canterbury

Winchester

Salisbury

Cornwall

Exeter

NORTH SEA

IRISH SEA

BRISTOL CHANNEL

ENGLISH CHANNEL

STRAIT OF DOVER

Distribution of Scandinavian Place-Names in England

Ending in -by, -thorpe or Mixed Form with English -tun

———— Danelaw Boundary 886

Anglo-Saxon England with Danelaw (map by Donald N. Yates).

Upon entering the Muslim-ruled areas of the world, Jews observed their religion under restrictions. Some chose to convert to Islam (Spencer Collection, The New York Public Library, Astor, Lenox and Tilden Foundations).

chapter, let us investigate more thoroughly what impact the Middle East had on Britain during the post–Roman centuries. This impact, we argue, is quite substantial and began almost by chance.

The Arab merchant Muhammad Ibn Abdallah of the Quraysh tribe in Mecca had taken his family to a spiritual retreat during the month of Ramadan in 610 CE—almost exactly two centuries after the Roman abandonment of England. On the seventeenth night of Ramadan, Muhammad was awakened by a divine epiphany which compelled him to begin writing works of scripture—a 23-year effort resulting in sixteen spiritual lessons known collectively as the Quran. The new religion born of his efforts was named Islam. Islam encouraged its followers to proselytize to the infidel and bring all the peoples of the world into submission to the one true God, Allah. Gerhard Endress aptly describes the miracle of Islam as "a legal arid government system which formed the foundations of the first community in the name of this God."[17]

That community was the *umma*, which still survives long after the Christian "City of God" collapsed and became little more than a theological notion. Unlike the Vikings, the Arabs did not ravage everything in their path and then return home. Their motives were not material plunder, but religious conquest. The modus operandi of their jihad or "holy war" was to proceed city by city, state by state, offering subjugated peoples the choice to convert to Islam (in which case they enjoyed full citizenship in the *umma*) or continue to practice their own religion and be subject to special taxes, fees and restrictions. As a result, Muslim countries have had Christian and Jewish minority populations ever since the original march of conquest.

People of the Book

Islamic law (the *shari'a*) placed the *dhimmis* or non–Muslim subjects in a special category if they were also People of the Book (*ahl al-kitab*). This included Judaism and Christianity, faiths based on revealed truth as enshrined in their books of scripture, but it sometimes was also extended to Zoroastrians and others. Muslims did not particularly care if Jews and Christians claimed a common "Abrahamic" origin, as they regarded their own religion as taking precedence over both Jews and Christian ("Abraham was not a Jew nor yet a Chistian," III:67.) "As the *dhimmis* had to undergo no specific restrictions in religious worship (only in its outward expression, such as processions and the use of bells) and no special burdens—the poll tax (*jizya*) levied on the *dhimmas* was not usually more onerous than the alms tax (*zakat*) of the Muslims—conditions were laid down which led to tolerant coexistence for centuries."[18]

Muslims were reminded of these regulations every day by the Quran (the "recitation"). We read, for instance, in sura 3, one of the most familiar chapters of the Quran:

> Do they seek for other than the Religion of Allah? ... Say: "We believe in Allah, and in what has been revealed to us and what was revealed to Abraham, Isma'il; Isaac, Jacob, and the Tribes, and in (the Books) given to Moses, Jesus, and the Prophets, from their Lord: we make no distinction between one and another among them, and to Allah do we bow our will [III:83–84].

In another passage (III:70) we read, "Ye People of the Book! why reject ye the Signs of Allah, of which ye are (yourselves) witnesses?" It was an attitude, then, of lenient reproof and of live-and-let-live. Both Jews and Christians were expected to keep a low profile, and not to have shops or dwellings near the mosque or main thoroughfare. They usually had their own communities under an official who preserved their rights to autonomy and protected their jurisdiction. One "catch" was that the death penalty was enforced on anyone who submitted to Islam and then apostatized. This double-edged sword seemed to keep many Jews from professing Islam, while large segments of the Christian population, especially on the land, seemed to make no declaration one way or the other but "go with the flow."

Usury and many of the prevailing customs of trade based on credit and investment were forbidden to Muslims. Jews became preeminent in occupations dealing with money as well as in the long-distance wine trade, alcohol also being taboo, not to mention a host of artisan crafts spurned by Moslems such as leatherwork and metalworking. Jewish physicians enjoyed unrivaled prestige.[19]

After the farewell pilgrimage and death of the Prophet Muhammad in 632 (Year One in the Muslim calendar), his successors the caliphs (*khilafa*, "succession") imposed the authority of an Islamic government in the whole of Arabia and dispatched Arab armies of conquest against Mesopotamia, Palestine and Syria. In a victory against the Byzantines, they seized Palestine within two years. Over a ten-year period the Muslims subjugated Egypt, Syria and Persia (modern-day Iran), leaving behind military settlements and the beginning of Islamic governmental institutions and financial organization. Damascus submitted to them in 635, Babylon in 641, Alexandria in 642. The first Arab campaigns in North Africa began in 647. Persepolis, the capital of the Persians and center of Zoroastrianism, fell in 650. Two years later, the Islamic army seized Armenia from the Byzantines.

The Umayyads

The caliphate of the Umayyads began in 661, less than thirty years after Mohammed's death. Damascus became the new Islamic capital at the beginning of a second major period of expansion. In 672 the Umayyad navy attacked Constantinople, which the Caliph lay siege to unsuccessfully for seven years. In 691, they built the Mosque of Umar or Dome of the Rock in Jerusalem.

As the 600s drew to a close, Muslim Arabs evicted the Byzantines from Carthage and became masters of Berber North Africa—a region that stretched from the Atlantic Ocean to the eastern shores of the Mediterranean Sea. They now controlled the key oceanic shipping routes from the Straits of Hormuz to Gibraltar. Soon Muslim armies vanquished the Gothic forces of Roderick and attacked southern Spain, gaining control of key ports along the Northern Mediterranean, such as Gades (Cadiz). To the east their reach extended into Bukhara and Samarkand in Central Asia. Here they established the Islamic provinces of Khwarazm and Transoxiana. In 719, Cordova became the residence of the Arab governors of Al-Andalus (Andalusia, "Land of the Vandals") and the push continued northward into France. Even Charlemagne was unable to stop the Islamic tide; Roland's horn sounded the note of retreat in the mountain passes at Roncesvalles in 778.

Wherever it spread, the leaders of Islam erected outposts manned by Arab army governors, local administrators, scribes, accountants, judges (*kadi*) and *mawali* ("clients"), along with tax farmers who ensured a regular flow of income. The next phase of Arab expansion under the caliphate of the Abbasids began with a coup d'état in Baghdad in 750 and lasted until the eleventh century, establishing Baghdad as the cynosure of world trade and intellectual innovation. Islamic merchants even had a trade colony on the coast of China.[20]

Influence of Judeo-Arab Civilization

Charles Talbot, a student of the history of medicine, puts into perspective the impact which the diffusion of Islam had upon the world outside of England. "About the time that St. Augustine landed on the shores of Kent to spread Christianity, Mahomet was born.... By the year 670 CE, when Theodore and Hadrian founded their school of studies at Canterbury, the Arabs had conquered most of the Middle East; and by the time Bede was writing at Jarrow, they had become firmly rooted in the south of Spain." Talbot writes:

> The period of the Danish invasions in England ... coincided with the prosperity of the Abbasides, Al-Mansur (754–775), Harun-al-Raschid (786–802) and Calif al–Mamun (813–833), under whom an enormous collection of Greek works was gathered together at Baghdad. Here, at the House of Wisdom, where the manuscripts were stored, a school of translators was established, so that all the important scientific writers of antiquity—Hippocrates, Dioscorides, Archigenes, Rufus of Ephesus, Galen, Oribasius, Philagrios, Alexander of Tralles and Paul of Aegina—were made available in Arabic translations. The translators were for the most part Syrians, but there were also Persians, Greeks and Jews, who all contributed to the diffusion of Greek science and literature. By the middle of the tenth century ... the Arabs had reached the height of their power.... Their [academic] output was sufficiently great to fill vast libraries, one of which, at Cordoba, had at least six hundred thousand volumes.[21]

This period of history is summarized from a Jewish perspective by the sixteenth-century Hebrew writer Joseph Cohen, who recorded that "in the year 4570 [810 CE] Christians and Moors found one another, and men of high station were brought low, and for Israel there was a time of trouble. For many Jews fled from the sword from Germany to Spain and England."[22] Cohen's specific mention of England shows that Jews were on the island of Great Britain in 810. Showing a solidarity between two branches of Sepharad, Spanish and British Jews on the edges of Christendom gave shelter and succor to their Ashkenazi brethren during the persecutions.

Jews accommodated themselves to Islam far better than the Christians did, and they lived far more willingly under Muslim governance than Christian rule. According to Arab historian Albert Hourani, "That they survived and flourished was due not only to the strength of their communal organization, but to their being able to occupy certain economic positions in the interstices of a complex society, and also to their not being identified with any of the states with which Muslim rulers were at war from time to time. The situation of Christians was not the same."[23]

Radanite Jews

The rise and spread of Islam from the Persian Gulf eastward toward India and China and westward through North Africa, the Iberian Peninsula and Gaul disrupted traditional trade channels, but simultaneously enabled new ones. Endress writes, "Stability, government backing of the currency, and thereby a functioning monetary economy and open frontiers within an orderly empire created the conditions necessary for a surge in trade" (87). These were times when Europe was in a complete economic meltdown, accompanied by periodic outbreaks of famine and cannibalism.[24] Endress denies that Islam's political or ethical attitudes were responsible for a decline of western Mediterranean trade, as the French historian Henri Pirenne had argued: "The sources suggest the opposite" (88). Under Islam, Jewish merchants, fluent in Latin, Greek, Arabic, Hebrew, Aramaic, Coptic and French, became the primary carriers of luxury goods such as ivory, gold, precious stones, silk and spices, as well as purveyors of scientific and technical knowledge, including papermaking, metallurgy and weapons manufacture. They were also intellectual cross-pollinators for various forms of monotheism, astronomy, medicine and philosophy, the entire legacy of Greco-Roman antiquity.

The Radanite Jews established trade routes traversing western Europe and central Asia to China. Several etymologies have been suggested for the word "Radanite." Many scholars, including Barbier de Meynard and Moshe Gil, believe it refers to a district in Mesopotamia called "the land of Radhan" in Arabic and Hebrew texts of the period. Others maintain that their center was the city of Ray (Rhages) in northern Persia. Cecil Roth and Claude Cahen espouse the theory that the word comes from the Rhone river valley in France, Rhodanus in Latin. They point out that the center of Radanite activity was probably in France, as all of their trade routes began there. Still other scholars speculate that the name derives from the Persian terms *rah* "way, path" and *dan* "one who knows," meaning "one who knows the way."

The activities of the Radanites are documented by Abu l-Qasim Ubaid Allah ibn Khordadbeh in *Kitab al–Masalikwal-Mamalik* ("The Book of Roads and Kingdoms"), composed probably around 870 CE. Ibn Khordadbeh describes the Radanites as sophisticated and multilingual. He outlines four main trade routes utilized in their journeys, all of which begin in the Rhone Valley of France and terminate in China. The commodities carried by the Radanites are primarily those having small bulk and high demand, such as spices, perfumes, jewelry and silk. But their goods also include oils, incense, weapons, furs, and slaves. Ibn Khordadbeh's account reads as follows:

> These merchants speak Arabic, Persian, Roman (i.e., Greek and Latin), the Frank, Spanish, and Slav languages. They journey from West to East, from East to West, partly on land, partly by sea. They transport from the West eunuchs, female slaves, boys, brocade, castor, marten, and other furs, and swords. They take ships from Firanja (France), on the Western Sea [Mediterranean], and make for Farama (Pelusium). There they load their goods on camel-back and go by land to al–Kolzom (Suez)…. They embark in the East Sea (Red Sea) and sail from al–Kolzom to al–Jar (port of Medina) and Jeddah (port of Mecca), then they go to Sind [Pakistan], India, and China. On their return from China, they carry back musk, aloes, camphor, cinnamon, and other products of the Eastern countries to al–Kolzom and bring them back to Farama, where they again embark on the Western Sea. Some make sail for Constantinople to sell their goods to the Romans; others go to the palace of the King of the Franks to place their goods. Sometimes these Jew merchants, when embarking in the land of the Franks on the Western Sea, make for Antioch (at the mouth of the Orontes); thence by land to al–Jabia (? al–Hanaya on the bank of the Euphrates), where they arrive after three days' march. There they embark on the Euphrates and reach Baghdad, whence they sail down the Tigris to al–Obolla. From al–Obolla they sail for Oman, Sind, Hind [India], and China. …
>
> These different journeys can also be made by land. The merchants who start from Spain or France go to Sus al–Aksa (Morocco) and then to Tangier, whence they walk to Afrikia (Kairouan) and the capital of Egypt. Thence they go to al–Ramla, visit Damascus, al–Kufa, Baghdad, and al–Basra (Bassora), cross Ahwaz, Fars [Persia], Kirman, Sind, Hind, and arrive in China. Sometimes, also, they take the route behind Rome and, passing through the country of the Slavs, arrive at Khamlidj, the capital of the Khazars. They embark on the Jorjan Sea [Caspian], arrive at Balkh, betake themselves from there across the Oxus, and continue their journey toward Yurt, Toghuzghuz, and from there to China.[25]

These were, in other words, epic journeys made by the Radanites, all connecting to the fabled Silk Road through Samarkand, the Tarim Basin and Dunhuang to Chang'an (present-day

Xian), capital of Tang Dynasty China. Through Central Asia, the Radanites had to negotiate their way through a welter of thirty-six languages.[26]

Jewish Ways of Doing Business

During the early Middle Ages, the Islamic governors of the Middle East and North Africa and Christian kingdoms of Europe often banned each other's merchants from entering port. Corsairs of both sides raided the shipping of their adversaries whenever opportunities arose. In this anarchic environment, the Radanites functioned as neutral go-betweens, keeping open the lines of communication and trade between the lands of the old Roman Empire and Far East. It is also important to remember that by the terms of Islamic commercial law, Jews and only Jews were positioned to conduct long-distance trade in the first place. "The Koran forbade lending money at interest, and the *shari'a* also prohibited commercial investment in goods, because transactions in cash-only allowed a fair division of the profit between the partners."[27] The mainstays of Jewish business became the *commenda* (partnership agreement), capital stock division for investors and traders, the *sakk* (an Arabic word that gives us "check"), promissory note or Hebrew *starr*[28] and letter of credit (Persian-Arabic *suftaja*).[29] Regulatory authorities differentiated between the wholesale dealer (*khazzan*) and long-distance trader (*raqqad*), but both these occupations were generally highly profitable and dominated by Jews.[30] Christians labored under the same restrictions as Muslims as far as loans, capital and credit were concerned, at least in their own countries.

Most of the sea-going ships, river-going barges and cross-country relay and carrier transports of the early Middle Ages were owned by Jews, or more properly Jewish trade consortiums and banking interests. Renee Doehaerd assembles records of the following signs of commerce during these centuries of political disintegration in western Europe: the strong, secure Arles market (196), Italian luxury goods factories, Paris merchant houses (186–87), ecclesiastical silk and brocade supply (192), precious stones from India, royal warehouses for oil, spices, dates, figs, almonds and other Eastern produce in southern France (193), furs and slaves from England and the north—(many intended to supply Islam's need for soldiers (197–98, 202, 206), Eastern wines from Gaza and Chios (194), Egyptian papyrus, the continuing metals trade in tin, copper and lead from England and Cornwall (200) and "warehouses [for Baltic and North Sea imports] in cities such as York, Cologne, Worms, Mainz and Duisburg" (201). She also makes note of one Anglo-Saxon merchant, possibly Jewish, by name—Botto[31] of Kent, who traveled through Marseilles in 790 (199).

As a result of the revenue they generated, these Jewish merchants enjoyed significant privileges under the Merovingians and Carolingians in Gaul as well as throughout the Muslim world, a fact that greatly vexed the local Church authorities. Several scholars conclude that the Radanites were instrumental in spreading Judaism and establishing Jewish communities along their trade routes.[32] We propose that they were central to the maintenance of Judaism in Britain in the centuries immediately after the fall of the Roman Empire until the arrival of Talmudic and Tosafist forms of Judaism after 1000. Let us examine the evidence available to support such a claim.

A seventh-century Anglo-Saxon chief, we learn, bought Egyptian wheat from a merchant fleet touching British shores and belonging to the church of Alexandria, in other words shortly before the fall of Egypt to the Arabs (642). He paid for it with gold "and a quantity of zinc, which was miraculously transformed into silver during the return journey:

another ship, loaded with tin, accompanied it."[33] The shipping company could only have been Jewish.

Archeological Finds, Manuscript Illumination

The Anglo Saxon Online Gallery site sponsored by the Cotswold District Arts Council and Corinium Museum in Cirencester provides documentation regarding the types of trade goods reaching England during the years 470–600 CE, when the Radanites were most active.[34] Significantly, its gallery of artifacts demonstrates that the incoming Germanic peoples (Angles, Saxons, Jutes) maintained the international trade patterns already in use.

> The materials and styles of the objects buried [in] Butler's Field Cemetery show us that [Britain] was not a community isolated from the rest of the world. Extensive trade routes linked the Cotswolds with Scandinavia and the Rhineland and stretched as far as the Indian Ocean. The large quantity of amber beads found in the 6th century graves show us that the trade routes concurrent with this first phase of burials were linked with the Baltic and Scandinavia. Strong links must also have existed with the Rhineland, because a number of metal bowls and cauldrons found were made and imported from there. By the seventh century, however, it is clear that the trade routes had changed. The second phase burials include cowrie shells and objects made with garnets and amethysts. These all indicate a change to the more southerly trade routes through the Mediterranean. These gave access to extensive routes through the Red Sea and on as far as the Indian Ocean.

What we learn from these archaeological reports is that, far from being isolated from distant cultures, Britain during its Anglo-Saxon period was in contact with persons and material goods from places as remote as Hindu India, Muslim and Jewish sections of the Middle East, pre–Viking Scandinavia and Russia—all dependent upon trading links with the Radanite Jews and their ilk.

Archaeologist Johanna Story at Leicester University adds further adumbrations to the overall picture presupposing a Radanite role in transporting these diverse goods to medieval England:

> Ideas about style, fashion and craftsmanship flow along the trade routes, indeed are carried on the trade routes, since merchants in the medieval world were concerned chiefly with the supply of luxury goods, not staple commodities.... Together with the flow of material culture came the intellectual luxuries—knowledge, learning and progress. So what sort of contacts, trading and cultural, took place, what evidence exists for them, and what is the student of the period entitled to conclude from the evidence?[35]

Story provides a detailed register or catalogue of the intellectual and material bounties arriving in Britain during this time period.

> Key evidentiary artifacts include Cuthbert's vestments, the so-called Nature Goddess and Rider silk, Coptic bowls, amethyst pendants from India and Ceylon and lapis lazuli from a mine in Afghanistan. Documents on East-West (or North-South) relations range from King Offa of Mercia's letters to Charlemagne to others describing the reception of Carolingian ambassadors at the court of the caliph of Baghdad. Offa's coinage contains a unique example of a gold mancus copied from a dinar struck in 774 by Caliph al–Mansur of Baghdad and dated 157 in the Arabic system. ... Sumptuous imported art can be found on the vine-scroll motif of the Ruthwell cross and on a panel in the monastery at Jarrow traced to Armenian prototypes. The Durham Gospel fragment dating from the mid-to-later-seventh century exhibits interlace patterns from Egyptian Coptic and Byzantine-Italian exemplars.[36]

Manuscripts as Luxury Goods

Story also draws attention to the Book of Durrow, ca. 675 CE, containing pages with carpet designs which are either Oriental or inspired by Roman mosaic pavements, as well as full-page portraits of the Evangelists echoing a Persian manuscript of the Diatessaron of Tatian, perhaps brought to Iona by Arculf, a pilgrim who had visited Jerusalem.

Story further notes:

> Within the Lindisfarne Gospels, ca. 690 CE, the celebrated feasts include one for St. Januarius, a saint of Naples, suggestive of a southern Italian origin. Text in two columns is also suggestive of a late antique Italian exemplar. There is a late antique model for the portrait of St. Matthew at his writing desk, which relates to a picture of the prophet Ezra in the Codex Ammantianus. Here there are details in the illustrated carpet: geometric design from Persia with an interlace from Egypt.... The colours include kermes, a red obtained from an insect that lives only in kermes oaks in the Mediterranean, and ultramarine blue, or lapis lazuli, obtained only from a single mine in Afghanistan....[37] Using Frankish masons and glaziers, Benedict Biscop built his church at Monkwearmouth [seventh century] in a distinctly Mediterranean style, plastered in and out, with a cement floor finished in pounded red brick."

We propose that Islam, just like Judaism, played a significant role in bringing these Middle Eastern influences to Anglo-Saxon Britain. The French historian Henri Pirenne, in a 1922 paper entitled "Mahomet and Charlemagne," famously stated, "Without Islam, the Frankish empire could never have existed; Charlemagne without Mahomet would be inconceivable." The Muslim lands were a benefit to European trade, not a hindrance.

Additional evidence of trade with the Middle East is provided by the materials found in the tomb of King Raedwald, ca. 621–630 CE, now on display in the British Museum: "Raedwald's helmet and armor were made in Sweden, while his drinking bowls were the product of Middle Eastern craftsmen."[38]

King Offa of Mercia

Perhaps the most compelling evidence of Middle Eastern influence within England is the coinage of King Offa of Mercia (757–796 CE), a predecessor to the English monarchs today, including Elizabeth II. What do we know of him? Coming to the throne after a period of civil wars, he first consolidated his control of midland peoples such as the Hwicce and the Magonsaete. After 762, he took advantage of instability in the kingdom of Kent to establish himself as overlord there. He was in control of Sussex by 771 CE. Three years later, Offa proclaimed himself king of the English. In the 780s he extended his power over most of southern England and regained control of the southeast. He also became the ruler of East Anglia. Offa frequently came into conflict with the Church, and in particular with Jaenberht, the archbishop of Canterbury. He died in July 796.

Conflated apparently with an ancestor named Uffi in Danish legend, Offa is extolled by the royal *scop* Widsith in a text that was probably composed shortly after 800. This song of praise to heroes mentions his most memorable accomplishment, the construction of Offa's Dyke:

> Offa ruled Angel, Alewih the Danes;
> He was of all these men the most courageous,
> Yet he did not outdo Offa in valour:

Before all men Offa stands,
Having in boyhood won the broadest of kingdoms;
No youngster did work worthier of an earl.
With a single sword he struck the boundary
Against the Myrgings[Welsh] where it marches now,
Fixed it at Fifeldor [Severn]. Thence forward it has stood
Between Angles and Swaefe [Celts] where Offa set it.[39]

A later Anglo-Saxon document claimed, "There was in Mercia in fairly recent time a certain vigorous king called Offa, who terrified all the neighboring kings and provinces around him, and who had a great dyke built between Wales and Mercia from sea to sea."[40]

In a time when coinage of any sort was rare, three gold coins of Offa's reign have survived. One is a copy of an Abbasid dinar of 774 and carries Arabic text proclaiming the phrase of Islam "There is no God but Allah." On the reverse side occurs the legend "Offa Rex." At the start of the eighth century, the primary circulating coinage in England was small silver pennies. Offa's light coinage can probably be dated to the late 760s and early 770s. A second, medium-weight coinage can be identified before the early 790s. However, the gold dinar is unique.

Some of Offa's coins bear the image of, and mention, his consort Cynethryth, the only Anglo-Saxon queen ever named or portrayed on coinage. Among these is a remarkable series of pennies struck by the moneyer Eoba. These may have been derived from contemporary coins of the Byzantine emperor Constantine VI, who minted a series showing a portrait of his mother, the later Empress Irene, but the purpose of the gold coin struck with Arabic writing is unknown.

Gold dinar of King Offa of Mercia with Arabic inscription "There is no God but Allah" (© **The Trustees of the British Museum**).

Eoba, as Yoba or Yoab or Jobe, is a Jewish name.[41] The name Offa seems to be Germanic, a pet form of Ulf, meaning Wolf; common variants in Frisian are Uffe, Ufe, Uffke, Uffko, Ufke, Ufko, Ufo. We must be careful not to be too literalistic in interpreting the evidence. All we can say for certain is that the use of Arabic on a Mercian coin of 774 demonstrates that Islamic influences had extended to the British Isles.

Apogee of Arabic Incursions or Not?

We are all familiar with the much-bruited turning point in the destiny of the West when the Christian armies of Charles Martel, Charlemagne's grandfather, vanquished the forces of the Umayyad Caliphate led by Abdul Rahman Al Ghafiqi, Governor-General of al–Andalus, at the Battle of Poitiers (or Tours) in 732. But what if the Battle of Poitiers was not the highwater mark of Islam in Europe? Alessandro Barbero, professor of medieval studies at the University of Piemonte Orientale in Vercelli, maintains, "Today, historians tend to play down the significance of the battle of Poitiers, pointing out that the purpose of the Arab force defeated by Charles Martel was not to conquer the Frankish kingdom, but simply to pillage the wealthy monastery of St-Martin of Tours."[42] Similarly, Tomaž Mastnak writes:

> Modern historians have constructed a myth presenting this victory as having saved Christian Europe from the Muslims. Edward Gibbon, for example, called Charles Martel the savior of Christendom and the battle near Poitiers an encounter that changed the history of the world.... This myth has survived well into our own times.... Contemporaries of the battle, however, did not overstate its significance. The continuators of Fredegar's chronicle, who probably wrote in the mid-eighth century, pictured the battle as just one of many military encounters between Christians and Saracens—moreover, as only one in a series of wars fought by Frankish princes for booty and territory.... One of Fredegar's continuators presented the battle of Poitiers as what it really was: an episode in the struggle between *Christian* princes as the Carolingians strove to bring Aquitaine under their rule.[43]

However important Poitiers was, it appears that Charles Martel might not have won it without the help of Jewish allies in Aquitaine. The duke of Aquitaine was placed in charge of protecting the Frankish lands against future Muslim incursions, and King Pepin and his sons set aside a domain on the Spanish Marches as a Jewish buffer state. Aquitaine, the time-honored link between southern England and the Continent, became the seat of a powerful, autonomous and long-lasting Jewish princedom under the Makhiri and Natronai.[44] Much of the background of this little-known medieval polity and center of diffusion for Jewish ideas is covered in our books on Scottish Jews and early American Jews and Muslims.[45]

Jewish Vassal State

The key figure was the Babylonian academy head (Gaon) and dynastic leader of the exile (Exilarch) Machir/Makhiror Al-Makhiri or Natronaiben Habibai (Hakhinai, Zabinai, Zabibai), also known as Theodoric, count of Septimania, Aymeri (Haim), Todros, Dietrich and Theodore. Makhir was crowned King of the Jews of the West in 768. His successors were privileged vassals of the Carolingians and ruled as legitimate princes of western Jewry.[46] Makhir had fled to Gaul via Palestine and Rome when the Abbasid revolution ended the rule of the Umayyads in Persia. His children and grandchildren intermarried with the Carolingian and Aquitanian nobility. Jewish princes in Narbonne were seen to occupy the same relationship to the Carolingian emperor as the Jewish-Persian exilarch to the caliph in Baghdad.[47] In a few generations a mythic Davidic lineage was remembered as a hereditary claim founded on blood and genealogy. The Carolingians accorded these Jews favored status. They dominated winegrowing in the valleys of the Rhone and Saone and Paris region, where they were treated not as foreigners but freemen. As Esther Benbassa notes, "A certain number of Jews managed the assets of bishops and abbots. Others were in the service of kings. They played an important role in East-West trade. They also practiced medicine. They were found, too, in trades such as the dyeing of fabric, and the tanning and currying of leather." She adds that "this picture is far removed from that of the Jew confined to commerce, particularly in money."[48]

In France, the territory of a Jewish commune was referred to in charters as *terra Hebreorum*, "land of the Hebrews."[49] The Jewish and Arab-controlled areas of the Midi were two huge regions where "during this period the Church underwent real eclipses ... and there were long vacancies in episcopal sees," according to medieval historian Jacques Le Goff. "The episcopal lists for Périgueux have a gap from 675 to the tenth century, for Bordeaux from 675 to 814, for Châlons from 675 to 779, for Geneva from 650 to 833, for Arles from 683 to 794, for Toulon from 679 to 879, for Aix from 596 to 794, for Embrun from 677 to 828, and for Béziers, Nîmes, Uzès, Agde, Maguelonne, Carcassone and Elne from the end of the seventh century to 788."[50]

Closer to England, in Brittany French Jews passed as Christians and were even involved in agricultural production, usually seen as an activity that precluded Jews. The bishop Hincmar of Reims in the ninth century wrote that Nantes had a count and residence in that Breton city where Jews held prominent positions not only in the supply of luxury goods but in managing country estates and the food supply.[51]

As late as the 1400s there were still Nesim (plural of Nasi, "prince") and Natronai (*geonim*, plural of Gaon) officially seated in Narbonne. "In no other Christian land," we read in one ecclesiastical history, "did the Jew enjoy such privileges. His right to hold land in *franc-alleu* was similar to that of the Christian; he was admitted to public office, and his administrative ability rendered him a favorite in such capacity, with both prelate and noble; his synagogues were undisturbed; and the Hebrew school of Narbonne was renowned in Israel as the home of the Kimchis [an important rabbinical family of scholars]."[52] Because of its large Jewish population, Toulouse and surrounding areas became the object of the first Inquisition when Innocent III declared a crusade against the Cathars and Albigensians in 1198. The "Spanish" Inquisition of 1485, along with measures taken earlier in the 1390s, was patterned after it.

Religious Practices

Aside from their refusal to bow to the authority of the Church, one of the main bones of contention in the eyes of authorities about Jews was home worship services—the Jewish and, one might say, crypto–Jewish, norm. This was already evident in a publicly staged dispute between Christians and heretics held in the cathedral of Narbonne in 1190.[53] Under zealots like Simon de Montfort, earl of Leicester, an estimated 100,000 to 200,000 people were massacred in the name of churchgoing and obedience to Rome.

It is important to point out that although Makhir imported the Talmud (essentially completed by the year 700), French Jews did not scrupulously follow it until after the twelfth century, when the forces of anti–Semitism were beginning to gather.[54] In the meantime came the flowering of Provençal culture situated between Islam and Christendom, with its Arabic-styled troubadour poetry, the mystical texts of the Cabala and a rebirth of the ancient learning and the sciences overflowing from Moorish Spain.

A similar type of adoptive Judaism evidently flourished in England, Wales and Scotland and was reinforced by French Jews under the Normans. If we fast-forward to the nineteenth century, Davis was the second best known Jewish name in England, borne by 1 in 32 of donors to Jewish charitable causes according to Joseph Jacobs' tally for the *Jewish Encyclopaedia*.[55] We have already noted the popularity of David and Davies in Wales. Davidson is one of the most common surnames among Scottish convert descendants.[56]

Finally a Name

In the chaotic centuries of the Vikings and Muslims, pockets of Jews must certainly have persisted even—and especially—in the British countryside. Because of their important economic roles, they unquestionably enjoyed some continued presence in towns and cities. This brings us to a record of a famous Anglo-Saxon scribe associated with a variety of Anglo-Caroline minuscule script known as Style IV. His name was Eadwig Basan and he was, according to his own signature, a monk. Eadwig's name occurs in the colophon of a Latin manuscript of the gospels preserved in Hanover and believed to have been written at Canterbury Cathedral "in the immediate environs of 1020," that is, several decades before the Norman Conquest. "The monk named Eadwig Basan wrote this book," proclaims the colophon.[57]

Of course, scribes sometimes copied the accompanying bibliographic information along with the literal text from the exemplar of the text set in front of them. There are instances of ancient scribes' names in editions of Vergil from late antiquity being perpetuated down to the advent of print and textual criticism. Sometimes the name of an early scribe or editor gets preserved as that of the author. It is possible that Eadwig Basan was the name of the scribe who copied the gospel-book at Canterbury Cathedral around 1020. Or he might have been the scribe who produced the exemplar upon which the Canterbury manuscript was based. Paleographer David Dumville in his study of English Caroline script distinguishes between Eadwig, the scribe mentioned in the colophon, and "Eadwig," the scribe who wrote the Hanover (Canterbury Cathedral) gospels. "Eadwig" (if not Eadwig) has a chancery hand that has been detected in ten other specimens "on purely paleographical grounds," dated between 1012 and 1023.

Where does the name come from? Dumville translates the Hebrew Basan as "the Fat," and explains it as a "monastic joke," finding the origin of the name in a learned, clowning type of biblical exegesis. Whether it is a reference to the scribe of the Canterbury gospel book of around 1020 or to the writer of its earlier manuscript model, however, the name stands as an intriguing record of a pre–Norman historical figure who was of Jewish *and* English culture. Basan is a common Sephardic surname surviving even today in Latin American countries and the Southwest of the U.S.[58] It is not unheard of in England. There it has a wide distribution throughout all counties in Victorian-era censuses.[59] Usually derived from the name of a mythic giant bird in Hebrew legend, the same surname is observed in the contemporary Moroccan food author Ghillie Basan and Jewish scholar Yehil Basan (1602–1625).

If we accept that Eadwig Basan was the literal name of the scribe about 1020 who copied the book and signed it with his own name (which seems the most reasonable conclusion to our minds), Eadwig Basan—quotation marks removed—had more than a flash-in-the-pan career. Dumville believes he was undoubtedly a royal chancery scribe at the court of the Wessex kings in Winchester. He personally drafted and engrossed a formal charter granted to Canterbury's Christ Church in 1018 by King Cnut, the new joint ruler of Denmark and England. After that, he retired or "was attracted into" the circle of Archbishop Lyfing, previously abbot of Chertsey (Surrey) and bishop of Wells (Somerset). The Cathedral School of Wells near Glastonbury was founded in Anglo-Saxon times and is one of the oldest extant schools in the world; in the seventeenth century the dean was Dr. Walter Raleigh, a nephew

Specimens of Eadwig Basan's writing from an eleventh-century manuscript in Hanover's Kestner-Museum juxtaposed with modern-day Times Roman font distantly derived from it (art by Donald N. Yates).

of the explorer Sir Walter Raleigh. At any rate, once at Canterbury, Eadwig (or "Eadwig") pioneered the sturdy, round script that became "a badge of Englishness," conspicuous in every book written in England in the half century before the Norman Conquest (150, 126–28, 135–36). It was "a scribal mark of Englishness ... which outlasted Anglo-Saxon England itself" (125–26).

Eadwig was probably a *converso*. One can speculate that his ancestry was seated in the old kingdom of Wessex and region of Wells. Again, the trail leads to Dorset and the West Country, a part of England that retained great continuity with its Roman and pre–Roman past during the unsettled centuries of the Vikings and Saxons. If it should ever be doubted that Jews rose to prominence in Christian society during the English Middle Ages, we can point to Eadwig Basan. It was this royal Anglo-Saxon-era scribe who fashioned the standard script called Anglo-Caroline Minuscule Style IV and helped create the clear, workmanlike typeface that is so widely used today.

Why Laws About Jews If No Jews

Other than Eadwig Basan, is there anything to refute the statement of Andrew P. Scheil, who wrote without qualification in 2004, "There were no Jews in Anglo-Saxon England"?[60]

Others besides us have pointed out that Jews play a conspicuous role in Old English literature, and that there are Anglo-Saxon laws mentioning Jews. Yet the unanimous verdict continues to be that these are false references. True Jews did not arrive in England until the Norman Conquest when William brought them over from Rouen.

A fresh cut is taken by Henry Straus Quixano Henriques in *Jewish Marriages and the English Law*. Henriques begins by citing the oft-quoted opinion of the English lawyer William Prynne (d. 1669), who wrote the tract *A Short Demurrer to the Jews*:

> I have deduced their introduction into England only from William surnamed the Conqueror, because I finde not the least mention of them in any of our British or Saxon Histories, Councils, Synods, Canons, which doubtlesse would have mentioned them, and made some strict Laws or Canons, against their Jewish as well as against Pagan Superstitions, had they exercised them here, as they would have done as well as in Spain, and other places, had they resided here.[61]

Henriques goes on to remark:

> But apart from Edward the Confessor's law, the authenticity of which Prynne disputes, there are contained in the *Liber Poenitentialis* of Theodore, who was Archbishop of Canterbury from 668 to 690 A.D., and the *Excerptiones* of Ecbert, who was Archbishop of York from 735 to 766 A.D., a not inconsiderable number of canons and regulations relating to the Jews: e.g. it was provided that a Christian woman committing fornication with a Jew should undergo severer penalties than if guilty of the same offence with a Christian (Theod. *Lib. P.*, XVI, § 35); and that if any celebrated the feast of Passover with the Jews, he should be expelled from every church (Theod., *Lib. P.*, XXX, § 4); and that if any Christian received unleavened bread or any food or drink from the Jews, he should do penance on bread and water for forty days (Ibid., XLII, § 1); and that if a Christian were to sell another Christian, although his own slave, to Jews, he was to suffer severe penalties until he redeemed him (Ibid., § 4; Ecb. *Ex.* 150). Again, mass was not to be celebrated in any place where the bodies of Jews or infidels were buried (Theod. *Lib. P.,* XLVII, § 1).

Henriques then discusses the twenty-fifth law of Edward the Confessor, previously regarded as spurious, but now accepted as an authentic part of pre–Norman law.

From these proofs we can now surmise without any doubt that the Norman Jews found other Jewish communities in place when they moved into William's newly conquered lands. Jews and ex–Jews were probably plentiful in the Welsh, Cornish and Scottish parts of the island. It is not true that "the history of the Jews in England is depressingly similar" to that in other countries, or that "any account of medieval Jewish history must begin to seem repetitive or to sound like special pleading."[62] We do not have a case of history repeating itself, but of the historians repeating themselves. The more interesting and compelling storyline in Britain is one not of anti–Semitism but philo–Semitism. This was a phenomenon that did not occur in the history of any other European nation.

With the coming of the Normans the national amnesia about Jews takes on a wholly different dimension.

4

Contextualizing the Normans

Most accounts of the Jews in Britain begin less than a thousand years ago—a full millennium after the starting point for this book. The formal entry of Jews into England is usually placed in the year 1066. That was the year when William the Conqueror not only invaded England but also introduced Jews from Rouen to assist in administering the new realm. This Year One has become virtually written in stone. We read in the *Jewish Encyclopaedia* of 1906, "William of Malmesbury ('Gesta Rerum Anglorum,' ed. Duffy, p. 500) distinctly states that William the Conqueror brought the Jews from Rouen to England, and there is no reason to doubt his statement." The author of this article, Australian-born Jewish scholar Joseph Jacobs, goes on to explain that William the Conqueror's motives were "to get the feudal dues paid to the royal treasury in coin rather than in kind, and for this purpose it was necessary to have a body of men scattered through the country that would supply quantities of coin." Never far behind the creation of a genesis event in Jewish history is the stereotype of financial motives, it would seem.

More recent writers mitigate the crassness of Jacobs' assertion and attribute William's actions to a policy of facilitating trade between his new kingdom and his continental territories. But this is still to take a limited view. Most are unwilling to entertain more than an exiguous and highly restricted presence for Jews in England. Theodore Steinberg, for instance, writes that "their Jewishness and their Frenchness made them doubly alien."[1] This statement may sound astute at first, but it makes many false assumptions. Another source states that "the King could turn to the Jews as his own private source of income and would tax them heavily for specific projects, e.g. the construction of Westminster Abbey, funding wars or crusades."[2] Few writers want to view William's relationship to the Jews as anything but exploitative and opportunistic.

But what if William himself came from Jewish ancestry? We have already observed that the British Isles were not, as many have supposed, devoid of Jews or lacking even in Jewish communities before 1066. Relations between Jews and Germanic peoples were not always as bleak and hostile as partisan authors today may depict them. To judge from Anglo-Saxon literature, the English regarded the Jews as no more alien than the Romans and others of Mediterranean origin. Jews and Gentiles, for one thing, lived in closer daily contact than most of us realize. Could modern commentators be viewing Jewish history through the lens of the nineteenth and twentieth centuries? Is there not more to the history of the Jews than a catalogue of persecutions and restrictions, entries and exits?[3] The cases of Britain and France are particularly rife with contradictions to the standard histories. At the center of their respective stories stands the enigmatic figure of William the Conqueror.

William I of England was known during his lifetime (ca. 1028 through 9 September 1087) as William the Bastard, a nickname that has followed him into posterity. The historical facts are confused, often by design. He was the only son of Robert I, duke of Normandy 1027–1035, and the grand-nephew of Emma, wife successively of two English kings— Ethelred the Unready and Cnut the Great— whence his claim to the throne. His mother was a concubine of Duke Robert variously identified as Herleva, Arlette, Arletta and Arlotta. She was said to be the daughter of a local tanner or clothier, whose name is given in a single source as Fulbert. Herleva later married Herluin de Conteville and had two sons with him—Odo of Bayeux and Robert, count of Mortain. Herluin and Herleva also had a daughter who married William sieur of La Ferte-Mace, and Herleva had another daughter, Adelaide of Normandy, possibly a child of Robert's. Herleva's two brothers, the Norman noblemen Osbern and Walter, figured prominently in William's life and career as supporters and protectors.[4] Her son Odo, half-brother of William, commissioned the famous Bayeux Tapestry glorifying the

William the Conqueror, engraving by Andre Thevet, Paris, 1584 (© The Trustees of the British Museum).

accomplishments of his noble house. This bare recitation of family members' names reveals a fundamental dichotomy discernible in the figure of Herleva. She supposedly came from humble origins, but her social skills were excellent. Her progeny quietly took over wherever they could.

Legends and Anecdotes

According to a legend still recounted by tour guides at the historic seat of the dukes of Normandy in the territory of Calvados, young Duke Robert spied Herleva from the roof of his castle tower and was overcome by her beauty. The ramparts of Château de Falaise still look down on the washing trenches cut into stone in the courtyard below. Herleva saw Robert on the tower as she was going about her dyeing and raised her skirts a bit, the tale goes, to attract his eye. Instantly smitten, the Duke ordered her brought to him through the back door. Herleva refused, saying she would only enter the Duke's castle on horseback through the front gate, not as an ordinary commoner. In a few days, dressed in the finest clothes her father could provide, and sitting on a white horse, Herleva rode through the front gate, head held high.[5] In this account, be it noticed, there is some ambiguity about Herleva's social standing.

An important glimpse into how William's contemporaries regarded the matter of his illegitimacy filters down from an anecdote related by Orderic Vitalis in about 1109–1113. In an interpolation to William of Jumièges' *Gesta* written forty years before, Orderic comments on an incident that occurred during the siege of the town of Alençon in Lower Normandy in 1051. As William's forces stood in array outside the walls, the citizens of Alençon taunted the young duke about his mother's family by flapping old leather clothes on the sides of the bridge where the shops were located.

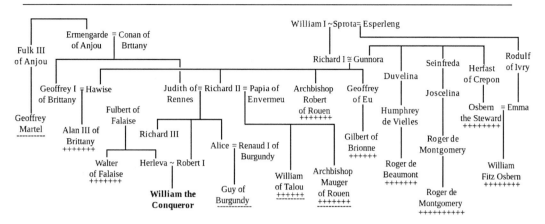

Norman genealogies (Wikipedia).

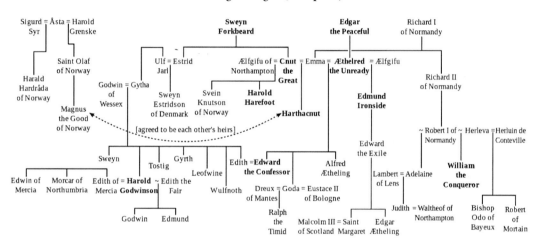

William the Conqueror's kinsmen and rivals (Wikipedia).

The defenders of the bridge, whether Angevins or disaffected Normans, received the Duke with the grossest personal insult. They spread out skins and leather jerkins, and beat them, shouting "Hides, hides for the Tanner." The Duke of the Normans had acted a merciful and generous part towards the rebels of Val-ès-Dunnes and Brionnes; but the grandson of Fulbert of Falaise could not endure the jeers thus thrown on his descent by the spindle side.... So now William swore, according to his fashion, by the Splendour of God, that the men who thus mocked him should be dealt with like a tree whose branches are cut off by the pollarding-knife. He kept his word. A vigorous assault was made upon the bridge.... The castle still held out. ... Thirty-two of the offenders were brought before him; their hands and feet were cut off, and the dismembered limbs were thrown over the walls of the castle, as a speaking menace to its defenders. The threat did its work; the garrison surrendered.[6]

According to Orderic, the audacious townspeople on the bridge may also have accused Herleva's "*parentes* (parents or kinsmen)" of being *pollinctores*, "undertakers, those who lay out a corpse," possibly an innuendo about the office of chamberlain (*cubicularius*) held by her father at the ducal court.[7] The exact Old French words of the jest are lost to us. Wace in the *Roman de Rou* ("Romance of Rollo," 1155–74) and Benoît in his *Chronique des ducs de Normandie* embroider the incident somewhat, but they fail to pass down anything about *pollinctores*. In 1185/6, King Henry II acknowledged the joke about his Norman predecessor's parentage when the Bishop of Lincoln observed the King using needle and thread to put stitches into a bandage. The Bishop wittily remarked, "How like you are unto your relatives at Falaise."[8] Fortunately, Henry did not take umbrage at the Bishop's allusion to William's origins. No hands or feet were lost.

Concubines and Consorts

In the Norman world, concubines were considered not only permissible but highly desirable, particularly if they sealed a pact of peace or legitimized succession. David Couch reminds us that "Ralph Glaber [985–1047] noted the fact that the Norman dukes were given to producing heirs with concubines, and shrugged his literary shoulders over this habit, comparing them with the biblical patriarchs of the Israelites."[9] This mention of Israelites by the earliest chronicler of the Normans may not be entirely decorative.

The first Norman concubine of note is the curiously named Poppa, consort of Rollo, William's great-great-grandfather and the founder of the Norman duchy. It is said she became his prize when Rollo sacked the city of Bayeux, slew her husband and carried her off, as was the Viking wont. Rollo was fresh from a tour of duty spreading terror in Ireland. He then launched a campaign of bloodshed in the Loire valley that led to his being granted lands by the reigning emperor, Charles III. This was the territory that became Normandy.

Rollo and Poppa are of course the distant ancestors of the present-day British royal family, and they seem to represent two strains and two tendencies in the nobility that became England's new peerage. Although Rollo nominally accepted Christianity in 911, he "perhaps reverted to paganism before his death, and a pagan reaction took place in western Normandy after the murder of his son, William Longsword, in 942."[10] Certainly, there was a pagan Danish side to the Normans. Viking blood in eleventh-century Normandy long remained true to type. We have already observed lapses and prevarications regarding religion under the Danish invaders and settlers in England's Danelaw. To the old members of the former Roman Empire like the Welsh and French, the Normans were nothing but maurading barbarians. Rolf's grandson, Richard I, earned the sobriquet *piratarum dux* ("Duke of the Pirates"). Richard II, William the Conqueror's grandfather, welcomed and harbored pagan Viking raiders and continued the family tradition of seizing prestigious local noblewomen as hostages or trophies. Pappa, a second by that name, though not of Scandinavian roots, and of unknown parentage was one. Another was Judith, daughter of Conan I of Brittany, a noble house deriving from Wales with many Jewish names in its genealogies. It is usually hard to judge at any given interval in the Normans' rise to prominence what exactly their religion was. Opportunistically, Richard II set up his brother Robert as archbishop of Rouen. Odo was ordered to baptize one of the Viking leaders, Olaf. The warlord then sailed back to Norway, where he became, after the necessary adjustments of history, the patron saint of Scandinavia. But the brand of Christianity Olaf spread, or imposed, used armed "missionaries" from Normandy, and there seem to have been other falterings in his faith. When it came time for Olaf's codification of Norway's new religion to be recognized by Rome, certain Viking preferences were found to be retained in it. St. Olaf's creed was singularly silent about the celibacy of priests.

And what about the maternal legacy of the Normans? Poppa's name has been taken either as a Latinate-derived term of endearment, meaning something like "babe" or "doll" (compare Old French *poupée*) or a variant of the Old Frisian warrior name Poppo, Poppe, Norse Papar.[11] Poppe was the name of a duke of Friesland slain in battle by Charles Martel. Genealogist and medieval prosopography expert Katharine Keats-Rohan tackles the thorny issues surrounding Poppa and claims that her name indicates descent from the Popponen. This Scandinavian family tended to bestow the name Poppo on the second son.[12] Keats-Rohan proposes that Poppa was a granddaughter of Heinrich of Thuringia and his wife Ingeltrude, daughter of Louis the Pious, and makes Heinrich a brother of Poppo II, Poppa's father being Berengar marquis of Neustria. If correct, such a scenario would give Poppa, despite her Danish-sounding name, a Carolingian descent through her father.[13]

And what of Poppa's mother? If she was Adelinda, this also confers Carolingian descent on Poppa. If, on the other hand, Poppa's mother was Cunigunde, she has Carolingian bloodlines both through Cunigunde's known father, Pepin, count of Senlis (c. 840), and Pepin's wife, a daughter of Theodoric, count of Vermandois (876). However it is reconstructed, Poppa's genealogy goes back in multiply intertwining fashion to Machir, the prince of Narbonne and King of the Jews in the West.

At any rate, Popa, Papia and related forms like Popet are well-established medieval Jewish names, deriving from *popa*, "venerable old priestess," possibly an amuletic name similar to Buba (Slavic "grandmother") or Vetula (Latin "old woman").[14] It seems odd that Rollo's ravished bride would have borne the female equivalent of a Danish warrior's name. Perhaps Poppa is simply a Danish accommodation to the original Old French Popa or Papia.

Carolingian Liaisons

Martel was the illegitimate son of Pepin, mayor of the palace of Frankish Austrasia under the declining Merovingian dynasty. In 732 at Poitiers, as we have seen, he scored a victory over the Muslims that allowed the Pepinid mayors of the palace to pursue reconquest of southern France in alliance with their vassals among the Narbonnais and Septimanian Jews. He was known as Martel ("the Hammer") for beating back the foe in battle, some comparing him to Judas Maccabeus, the savior of the Jewish state, others calling him the Frankish Joshua.

What is usually ignored is that Charles Martel's great-grandmother was a noblewoman named Itta, a Jewish name.[15] We do not know much about her, but her birth land was held at the time by the Visigoths. These Arian barbarians absorbed many Jews in adapting to the Romano-Gallic culture in the southwest of France. By 550 CE they moved on to seize most of Spain. Later, they helped make Arabic Spain a celebrated high point for Jewish civilization: "The Jewish community thrived demographically, thanks to local proselytizing and to the waves of conquest and immigration ... it also flourished culturally."[16]

Medievalists have generally brushed over her name as a form of Ida, pretending it is Germanic. In actuality, it derives from Yehudit (Judith). Ironically, this archetypal Hebrew feminine name runs throughout Carolingian, Angevin and Norman genealogies as well as the modern royal families of Europe such as the Bourbons and Hohenzoellerns. Charles Martel's grandfather Ansegisèle, son of Arnulf of Herstal, married Itta's daughter Begga (Rebecca), another name reflecting Jewish roots. Arnulf of Metz, who may himself have been of Jewish ancestry, took a wife named Doda (feminine form of David), a name that was still popular among Carolingian noble families three centuries later. Charles Martel, at any event, was indisputably the son of a Jewish father, as well as being Jewish through his direct maternal lineage.

The Frankish kings and their Pepinid successors typically selected Jewesses for partners. Charlemagne's last concubine was a Jewess known variously as Adeline, Adelaide or Adela. She is believed to be the *Ur*-mother of European royalty, the matrilineal ancestor, among others,

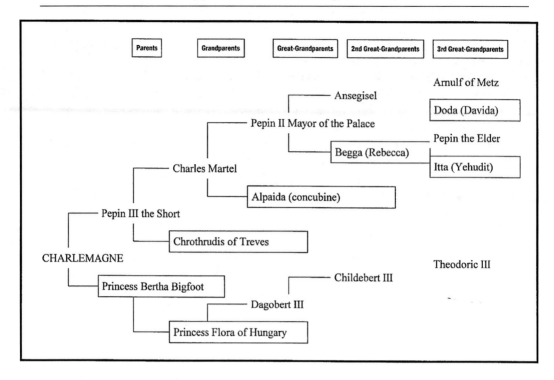

| Parents | Grandparents | Great-Grandparents | 2nd Great-Grandparents | 3rd Great-Grandparents |

Charlemagne's Jewish ancestors (Chart by Donald Yates).

of Marie Antoinette.[17] Here again history has bowdlerized the name in the interests of painting a pleasing Christian picture of royal genealogies. In all likelihood, her name was Adel. It is one that recurs over and over in Frankish and Norman genealogies, and it was intentionally twisted into many other forms. Einhard and the court chroniclers who followed him in the reign of Charlemagne's son Louis the Pious promoted an etymology deriving the name from Germanic *Adel* ("noble"), even twisting it into *Adelheid* ("nobility"), the origin of Adelaide, a name scattered through all the aristocratic houses of Germany, France, Belgium and England. The falseness of this Christian origin is proved by the popularity of the name among later Jews, both Sephardic and Ashkenazic, who developed the multiplicity of forms Ada, Edna, Eida, Ethel, Adela, Adeline, Dela and Etalka.[18]

Foundation of House of David

Thanks to the Davidic connections stemming from Machir, the Pepinid and Carolingian dynasties adopted the Lion of Judah as their military device, which inspired the beginnings of medieval heraldry. They self-consciously styled themselves a sacred royal line, the first in Europe.[19] The sovereigns of this new Israel were declared a second Moses, a second David and a second Solomon. Charlemagne adopted the nickname David in his circle of intimates, and his own portrait was used for that of the biblical king and psalmist by manuscript illuminators. As medieval scholar Alessandro Barbero observes, "Pepin brought into use the ritual recorded in the Old Testament, in which it is told that Saul took control of the kingdom by being anointed by the prophet Samuel. After him, David and Solomon took the throne by being anointed."[20] Rollo, then, drew on an ancient tradition.[21]

In the Norman state the rulers plainly did not despise Jews, and Jews had few official disadvantages in society. The Normans instead married with them and allowed them to live in the capital and everywhere else, in conformity with earlier practices stemming from the Jewish Midi. Norman Golb reports that "we have no reason to suspect that the Jewish population ever disappeared in the time of the Vikings or the early Normannic dukes; there is likewise no evidence that the new rulers ever vitiated its leadership before the start of the eleventh century. On the contrary, Rollo and his successors would have made use of the Jews to advance the economic stability and growth of the conquered land, just as their Varangian kinsmen did in the decades following the conquest of Kiev. It was apparently only with the new millennium that conditions took a turn for the worse."[22]

Let us now return to how William was insulted by the townsmen of Alençon. We suggest that the upshot of their ribaldry was to say, "Look who's come to town, the Jewish collector of old leather goods: here they are!" Old clothes collecting, like being an undertaker, was a déclassé occupation. In the former reference, one may also detect some rather sophisticated wordplay involving "investing," a common metaphor applied both to laying siege to a walled city and becoming clothed in the vestments of office in the feudal ceremony of investiture.[23] It would seem that the people of Alençon were poking fun at the family's precipitous rise in fortunes. They had gone from being undertakers and ragmen, the lowest of professions, to tailors or furriers, a bourgeois trade, and finally to noble aristocrats. Most modern commentators follow M. A. Deville in thinking of William's mother as the daughter of a burgher of Falaise.[24]

The Lion of Judah, whose ultimate source lay in the Judaic arms of Charlemagne's ally Prince Machir in the eighth century—heraldically styled "Gules, a lion rampant or"—was registered around 1243 by the Breton FitzAlan family when they succeeded to the earldom of Arundel, Great Britain's oldest extant title (created 1138). A younger branch of the FitzAlans went on to become the Stewart/Stuart family who later ruled Scotland. The lion rampant became a feature of the armorial devices of the rulers of England, Wales, Scotland and Ireland, as well as dukes of Norfolk and earls of Warwick, Leicester, Northumberland, Shrewsbury and Bedford, not to mention innumerable lesser peers of the realm, boroughs and other corporate bodies. The same emblem appears today in the official coat of arms of the city of Jerusalem in the state of Israel, various former provinces of southern France near its original homeland under the Jews of Narbonne and in the flag and arms of Leon, the ancient kingdom and present-day autonomous region of Spain (art by Donald Yates).

The Alençon burghers' jest was particularly biting in view of Herleva and her relatives' sudden elevation to privileged positions. We can understand how William may have been sensitive to such an issue, for he was invested by King Henry of France with the insignia of knighthood and duchy of his father Robert at the age of eight. His half-brother Odo became bishop of Bayeux in his teens.[25]

No doubt some of the townspeople who unwisely welcomed William's army with a display of vests and furs were themselves Jews. Alençon had an important Jewish community. Many of its Jews would have been engaged in the very profession they half denigrated, half flaunted.[26]

Falaise was also famous for its Jews and had a rabbinical court.[27] It possessed a Street of the Jews 300 meters long.[28]

The name Herleva itself may be a tell-tale sign of Jewishness. It was also the name of a cast-off mistress of William Longsword who married a miller. We have a masculine form of the name in Herluin, the name of the lowly squire to whom Robert later sent his mistress, William's mother. She married him and their children became part of the new Norman aristocracy. Leva may be the source of both Herleva and Herluin. It is a Jewish first and last name, borne by men and women, and it is said to be the name of a Norman family coming from Old Occitan. The etymology of "Leva" lies in a word for "import levy" which was transferred as a title to the collector of such duties. Leva Levi was a medieval Hebrew author of a work known as *Décisions rituelles*.[29] Harleva, then, appears to be the original form of the name of Robert's mistress, William's mother. Har (הר) is a Hebrew element preserved in numerous Jewish surnames, including Harlev ("heart mountain," compare Hertzberg), Harlew, Harlow, Hartov ("good mountain," Gutenberg) and Harpaz ("mountain of pure gold," Goldberg).[30] The learned city of Montpellier, site of Europe's first medical school, was called Har Gaash ("trembling mountain"), a Talmudic reference to Mount Gash in Joshua 24:30. This designation was abbreviated in the name of the renowned Harari family, who came from Montpellier. Harari was also the nickname for Jacob ben Makhir ibn Tibbon, an epigone of the Babylonian exilarch Machir.[31]

Now comes the pièce de la resistance in our argument that William's mother was Jewish. One legend about her contains her actual words on the occasion of going to bed with Duke Robert. The source is a compilation made in Norwich after the middle of the fourteenth century and passed down under the name of a semi-fictional English chronicler named John Brompton (fl. 1436).[32] We read that at Falaise

> the Dukes of that country had a palace, to which they resorted in times of peace for pleasure; and were wont to make it their constant residence in time of war, on account of its strength. At this castle Duke Robert was in the year 1022, and being a prince of a very debonnaire disposition, was present at a place where the young maidens of the town were dancing, and there he saw the fair Arlotta [Herleva], and being charmed either with her beauty or behavior, fell desperately in love with her. She was brought to his bed that night, and our gravest historians, such as Bromton [sic], and Knighton, tell us that when she had undrest herself, she tore her shift from the bosom down to the bottom, for which she gave this reason, *That it was neither decent nor fit, that what had touched her legs, should come near the mouth of her lord.*[33]

Apocryphal or not, this is a strange speech. The medieval sources attributing these words to William the Conqueror's mother upon the moment of his conception could hardly have been aware of the Jewish attitudes they reflected. According to Jewish law concerning what is clean (*kosher*) and unclean, anything below the waist was classified as unclean, whereas the mouth was associated with the holy (*kadosh*). Furthermore, the custom of *kilayim* (literally, "mixture, confusion") prohibited wearing cloth from mingled species of plants and animals such as linen and wool. The laws of spiritual purity extended even to separate washes for clothing worn below the waist. Jewish males were required in very strict communities to wear undergarments with fringes below the waist to avoid contact between the outer garments and the "dirty" lower body. There was, and is to this day in orthodox Judaism, a prohibition against kissing below the waist (a sin also in Muslim *halal*). In the religious context, we can see why Herleva would not allow Robert to brush with his lips even the upper part of her dress. The incongruous and unique details in this anecdote argue on the side of its having a basis in truth, of being "history as it occurred." It is doubtful that any of those who transmitted the tale were cognizant of the cultural significance of Herleva's words. The story as it is preserved for us therefore appears to be tacit proof that Herleva was a Jewess.

Jews in Medieval Normandy

The earliest written documentation we have of Jews dwelling in Normandy dates from 1007 CE when Robert, King of Sarefat (France), decreed that the Jews must convert to Christianity.[34] When some Jews refused to be baptized, Robert ordered them to be killed and their property confiscated. However, a wealthy and powerful Jew from Rouen, Jacob ben Jequthiel, intervened on their behalf. In a remarkable effort, Jacob ventured to Rome with his family, negotiated directly with the Pope, met with Roman Jews in service to the Pope, including Moses the Nasi, Abraham, and Sabbathai, and then returned to France, where he took up residence in Lorraine. Ten years later, Jacob and his family were invited along with thirty other Jewish families by Baldwin count of Flanders to come settle there. In approximately 1022, Jacob is said to have died "near the banks of the Arras River." His sons allegedly brought his body to Reims and placed it in the Jewish cemetery of that city.[35]

Golb questions some of the inconsistencies in the written account of Jacob's actions, but he concludes that the basic events and issues it describes are historically accurate. The papacy did have several Jews as advisers. This was apparently not an unusual situation. Reportedly Pope Alexander, 1060–1073, had some two hundred prominent Jews in residence in Rome and intervened on behalf of the Jews in France. Pope Alexander praised both Viscount Berenger of Narbonne and Prince Landulph VIII of Benevento for acting as guardians of the Jews in their territories. Further, the origins of the textile industry in the section of Flanders where Jacob and his fellow Jews were asked to settle by Baldwin coincide with the 1020–1030 time period.

Golb notes that Rouen, where Jacob ben Jequthel is said to have begun his journey, is spelled alternatively Radum, Radhum and Ruda by various chroniclers. Based on the Hebrew manuscript evidence, Golb proposes that not only was Rouen a Radanite capital, but also a seat of Jewish religious and political authority. He reminds us,

> A number of Latin and Hebrew medieval sources agree that in the time of the Carolingian rulers, a Jewish personage was appointed by imperial fiat to govern the Jews of Septimania. Latin sources refer to him as the *rex Judaeorum*, or "king of the Jews," while in Hebrew sources he is known as the *nasi*— that is, "chief dignitary" or "prince." Appropriately this ruler and his hereditary successors held office at Narbonne, the old capital of the Provincia Narbonensis. They possessed large land holdings granted by Charlemagne or his successors as perpetual allots. This dynastic line, the first of whose members was an eminent personality named Makhir, retained its power and wealth throughout the Middle Ages and until the beginning of the fourteenth century; many of its members were named Todros (Theodore) or Qalonymus. In establishing this office, the Carolingians clearly intended to stabilize and legally to protect the many Jewish communities in this part of their realm.[36]

We will show in chapter 10 how this same family became the Tudors of Wales.

According to tradition, Charlemagne transferred the Lucca branch of the eminent Qalonymus family to Mainz, Germany. Under Pope Boniface in the eighth century, this city became an archbishopric to which the lands of Germany were attached, and Charlemagne himself built a palace close by at Ingelheim am Rhein. As an Austrasian city of great importance, Mainz was the appropriate seat of authority for the region's Jewish leadership. "The family of Jewish dignitaries at Mainz was apparently still prosperous at the time of the First Crusade,

Normandy and surrounding provinces with principal towns (map by Donald N. Yates).

but nothing was written of it afterward, apart from individual scholars named Qalonymus who continued to live there."[37]

As provinces of the Frankish empire broke apart into smaller political units, a Jewish authority was established in each of the emerging territories or domains. A letter from the chief Jewish scholars of Rome to their colleagues in Paris, dating from the first half of the twelfth century, mentions the "four kingdoms" of Francia (Sarefat), Lorraine (Lothair), Burgundy and Normandy, "from which the Torah goes out to all Israel." Among the participants in the council of the eminent rabbinic figure Jacob Tam in 1165 were representatives of Normandy, the "sea-abutment" (Brittany), Anjou, Poitou and Lorraine. A similar council issued a decree on behalf of the communities of Sarefat, Anjou, Poitou and Normandy. Jewish records also speak of the "kingdoms" of Limoges and Anjou. These authorities, as Golb documents extensively, not only regulated the Jewish affairs of their realms, but also represented the Jewish communities before the royal or ducal authorities of feudal France's individual political territories. The *rex Judaeorum* at Narbonne represented the Jewry of Septimania, or of Septimania and Aquitania together, while in Austrasia the branch of the Qalonymus family that had been intentionally moved from Lucca to Mainz held this authority.

The northwestern realm of the Carolingian Empire was named Neustria—an area comprising most of what is today northwest France and parts of the Low Countries. The center of this area became Normandy after the Viking invasions. In view of the stable nature of Jewish communal life in Carolingian times, Golb proposes that there must have been a central Jewish authority in Neustria. Peter the Venerable offers important evidence to this effect in his allusion, circa 1140, to a *rex Judaeorum* ruling at Rouen. As one of the Carolingian Empire's main cities, Rouen would have been the logical choice for such a political figure. In 779 CE Charlemagne mentioned *Rodom* as being among his realm's ports and cities, and in 795 the emperor designated the archbishop to be governor of the city. In the edict of Pitres (864), which names certain Jews as royal minters, Rouen is designated as one of the empire's ten royal mints.

Golb's valuable reconstructions indicate that additional Jewish communities were present in Arles dating from the eleventh century, somewhere along the Bethune River, and in Aumale, Dieppe (including a family named Abraham engaged in the ivory trade with Africa), the textile weaving town of Montivilliers, Coutances, Fecamp, Le Fosse, Evreux, Pont Audemer, Bernay, Neuve-Lyre, along the principal rivers of the Eure, See, Alençon, Falaise, Theury-Harcourt, Ecouche, La Perrière and Caen, among others. The Jewish community in Caen, according to Golb, "was apparently continuous from late Gallo-Roman times until the expulsion of 1306" (83). Thus, we may be able to recreate Jewish ancestral linkages between France and England which date back to Roman settlement.

In the year 1066 Duke William crossed the English Channel from Normandy to Hastings with a heavily armed, well-trained Norman force and defeated King Harold Godwinson and the English Army. On Christmas Day of that same year, William "the Conqueror" was crowned William I of England in Westminster Abbey. Within months the Normans had begun to reshape all of English society—from the court system to taxation to land ownership. Rebecca Fraser writes, "By 1085, not only had all the land [in England] been redistributed, but the ... class responsible for royal business in the shires was now composed of all Norman Frenchmen, rather than Englishmen.... These Normans called up 'panels of inquiry' to determine what the boundaries, the ancient rights, and the labour obligations were for each estate, whether belonging to a lord or a churchman."[38] She explains:

> The Normans' claim to England was based on conquest. At the same time they were natural lawyers and immensely businesslike. They were obsessed with legitimacy and believed in doing everything by the book. The legal powers of the King of England were far greater than those of other western European monarchs. Although the Anglo-Saxon lord was entitled to hold his own courts to judge disputes over land in his domain, to punish thieves and to assess stolen goods, the English national custom [was] that those rights were granted by the king. The king and his officials were considered to be responsible for keeping the peace. Moreover, the King of England was entitled to raise taxes in every part of the country. When his instructions or writs came to the shire court, the English tradition was that they were to be obeyed [98].

Moreover, "On Christmas 1085, with the land transfer complete, the king was now in a position to send ... government officials to set up an enlarged version of the shire court in every county.... The Norman commissioners were to have no (personal financial) interests in the particular shire and the facts were to be checked by another group of commissioners" (99).

By 1086, the process of civil transformation was over. In a few short years the indigenous English population had lost control of England to the Normans. As one standard history makes clear, fewer than 250 persons controlled most of the land of England. These secular and religious princes, prelates and barons together with their vassals, dependents and retainers[39] "numbered some 10,000 people ... a foreign elite imposed on a nation of one to two million English." The Anglo-Saxon aristocracy with its thanes and earls and subordinate landholders was largely replaced. Further, soon after becoming king in 1066, William also began to transfer Jews from his French lands in Normandy, especially the area around Rouen, to England. Once in England, Golb notes, these newly arrived Jews found English Jews *already in residence*, having been present at least in York and Mercia since the 700s.[40] To repeat, then, there is no reason to believe that Britain has ever been without Jews.

Henry I, 1100–1135

The early twelfth century saw the appearance of the first national law courts, as well as the government department called the Exchequer, the precursor of the Treasury, under the reign of Henry I, William's youngest son. Fraser describes these institutions as follows:

> The Curia Regis, or king's court, had arisen out of the deliberations of the king with the leading barons in council.... With the reign of Henry I, the rapid expansion of legal training ... and of canon law in the separate Church courts, began to influence the development of the criminal law. A new professional class of lawyers grew up, better equipped to deal with legal problems along the lines of universal principle. Trained judges in London started taking the place of the king in determining the legal issues of tenants-in-chief or deciding disputes appealed from the shire or county court.... A new government department known as the Exchequer collected tax.... However, despite the increasing specialization and professionalism, the king's household continued to be the centre of government. The king's *chancellor* was head of all the clerks..., who performed the role of civil service, doing much of the scribal work needed by the king's business. The *chamberlain* was the other prize position at Henry's court. The chamberlain supervised the king's Treasury.... Other king's servants were the *steward*, who looked after the king's hall, and the *constable*, who looked after the outdoor servants, including, as his name suggests, the horses in the king's stable.

Fraser further elaborates on these offices introduced by the Normans.

> Out of these domestic positions would eventually grow the offices of state. Great lords would pay the king to take their sons into his household, because of the career opportunities it offered. A page in Henry I's household who showed willingness and ability in putting out the king's clothes or even his food might find his route to high office smoothed by being chosen to help the king's chaplain. He would then usually become a chaplain himself, opening his way to being part of the king's secretariat (117).

Acting perhaps under the counsel of his *converso* physician Petrus Alphonsi, who appears to have been one of the most important agents of this rationalization of government, Henry inflicted a selective *obliteratio memoriae* that destroyed many of the royal decrees and acts of his reign as well as his those of predecessors, particularly Anglo-Saxon records, now rendered dead letters. It is believed that the silence in the records about Jews during this time is due to Henry's administrative reforms.

They Came with the Conqueror—or Claimed To

William and his sons were not alone in drawing a veil over their Jewish origins. Practically the entire peerage and landed gentry of England followed suit at one time or another. Gradually, a claim to be descended from the Normans became a guarantee of being a "true-blooded Englishman." Says L. G. Pine, however, "All the boasts about descent in an unbroken male line from a companion of the Conqueror are to be taken with a very great deal of salt." He points out that William's pedigree itself became extinct in the male line in the third generation, and that few noble houses lasted many years before the head of the family left issue "an only daughter, his heiress, who married John Smith.... The Percys, a truly Norman family, were twice extinct in the male line; on the second occasion they owed their revival and the perpetuation of their name to the marriage of the Percy heiress to a wealthy man, Sir Hugh Smithson."[41] After reviewing the situation, Pine thinks, "The fact that so many people to-day can prove descent from our royal line—100,000 such descents are said to be in existence—demonstrates the solidity of British society" (46–47).

It also demonstrates the *solidarity* of British society. Pine's debunking exercises not only serve to strip away the pretensions of present-day Anglophiles; they also expose the repeated acts of disguise and denial through which the tangled branches and twigs, and indeed the very roots of British genealogy, have spread their enchanted mythology of national origins.

Of the families who claim to be Norman Dukes, all have signs of Jewish connections either early or late in their development, not to say midway or throughout it. "The Dukes of Richmond, Grafton, St. Albans and Buccleuch owe their Norman ancestry to the ancestresses' ability to capture the heart of Charles II. They originated respectively from Louise de Kerouaille, Barbara Villiers, Nell Gwynn and Lucy Waters" (57).

"The Beauforts derive from an earlier royal indiscretion. They stem from Charles Somerset, himself the illegitimate issue of John of Gaunt, son of Edward III" (57). The royal and ducal house of the Earls Marshall and heads of the College of Arms, the Dukes of Norfolk, "cannot be got back earlier than John Howard, a plain and honest yeoman of Wiggen Hall, St. Peter, in Norfolk, who in 1267 had by Lucy, his wife, a son, the 'lad of pairts,' Sir William Howard, Justice of the Common Pleas in 1297 (58–59)." Next in seniority among the Dukes are the Seymours, Dukes of Somerset. They emerge from the obscurity of Woundy and Penhow in Monmouthshire in the time of Henry III claiming origins from a place called St. Maur, near Avranches in Normandy. Pine remarks, "Their name is Norman, yet as regards affiliation to the original Norman settler, I wonder" (59).

The dissolution of the monasteries under the first Cromwell brought about the creation of the duchies of Bedford (the Russells) and Devonshire (the Cavendishes), as also the Marquesses of Salisbury and Exeter (the Cecils). "Nothing is more interesting," says Pine, "than the attempts to derive Russell from Rosel in Normandy, and to antedate the Cavendish history before they acquired their surname from their lands in Suffolk" (59).

The Osbornes ("a foreign name") were a family of respectable merchants in Tudor England. Sir Edward Osborne, Lord Mayor of London in 1583, was the great-grandfather of the first Duke of Leeds (60).

Concerning the Montagus, Dukes of Manchester, Pine admits that Montagu is a Norman name but tattles on them, revealing that their original style was Ladde, of Hanging Houghton in the parish of Lamport, in Northamptonshire. "The evidence of surnames is always dangerous," he adds. "Lord Swaythling's family name is Montagu, (originally Samuel); the supporters of his shield are soldiers of ancient Judea, not of Normandy" (61).

The forebears of the august Dukes of Wellington changed their surname from Colley to Wesley in 1728 and "were gentlemen in Henry VII's time, no more" (61).

The Dukes of Portland "are Dutch in origin, having accompanied William of Orange in 1688" (61–62). "We have left only Westminster, Rutland, Newcastle and Northumberland.... The name of Grosvenor is foreign, but traces of the conquest ancestry there are not" (62). The Dukes of Rutland (Manners) go back to a fourteenth-century figure from Etal in Northumberland and cannot be proven to derive from Mesnières, near Rouen. "The lack of details about his antecedents is, to say the least, significant" (62). The Dukes of Newcastle, the Clintons, have a "phony pedigree" from Saint Pierre de Semilly near Manche, arr. St. Lô, canton St. Clair, in Normandy. The first of that name was plucked by Henry I for his usefulness "from, so to speak, the dust of the earth" (62–63). The Percys round out the list of Norman ducal families, but even they had periodic shortages of male heirs and survived only through the strategy of marrying off females to related families, notably the dukes of Newcastle, Somerset and Northumberland. "The great Hotspur and all the other mediaeval Percys were Percys in the female line" (64).

The inbreeding of English dukes and earls is mirrored in the deceptive genealogies of thirty-nine "Norman" marquesses. "We know that Reading is of Jewish origin; the Marquessates of Salisbury and Exeter were the reward of an earlier immigration into England of another chosen people, in the case of the Cecils, the Welsh" (68). The Boteville brothers Geoffrey and Oliver cited as ancestors of the Marquess of Bath were originally Thynnes and "Poitevins, not Normans" (68). The Marquessate of Northampton came out of nowhere—or rather the West Country and Welsh borderlands.

Pine has chapters on England's Norman earls, viscounts, barons, baronets and landed gentry, as well as the Normans in Wales. Everywhere we look the story seems to be the same or similar. Space forbids us from reviewing these segments of the British peerage, but we will have occasion to revisit many of their names in that monumental record of theft called Domesday Book.

5

Who Was Jewish in the Conqueror's England

The transition from Saxon thanes to Norman barons was captured in a detailed survey of England's income-producing feudal properties made in 1086–7, twenty years or approximately one generation after the conquest. The undertaking filled all with such awe it was named Domesday, or Judgment Day, Book. Matthew Paris referred to it as "the great book which is kept in the Treasury at Westminster and is called Domesday, and is so named because, like the Day of Judgment, it spares no-one."[1] It survives in two volumes of parchment written in Latin in a single clerical hand. It was also called the King's Book and Great Book of Winchester after the location of the royal treasury where it was first kept. Domesday Book is "unmatched in its age, its scope and the consistent detail of its contents.... It has been in official custody ever since it was made, and is celebrated now as the first of the public records and an endlessly rich source of historical material."[2] Fulfilling the king's will, some seven or eight panels of bishops and earls made circuits of all England registering every customary fee and taxable possession in the realm, down to every demesne, field, factory, tenement town, pasture, wood, house, cottage, sheep, pig and cow. The commissioners listed valuations for thirty-one counties starting with Kent in Great Domesday. They added Essex, Norfolk and Suffolk in Little Domesday, the second, bulkier and more undigested of the actual volumes.

The canvassers worked from a strict questionnaire, described in a contemporary records as follows:

> They inquired what the manor was called; who held it at the time of King Edward [the annotation TRE, *tempore regis Edwardi*]; who holds it now; how many hides [standard unit of assessment to tax, an amount of land that could support one household] there are; how many ploughs in demesne (held by the lord) and how many belonging to the men; how many villagers; how many cottagers; how many slaves; how many freemen; how many sokemen [men subject to a lord in a given jurisdiction]; how much woodland; how much meadow; how much pasture; how many mills; how many fisheries; how much had been added to or taken away from the estate; what it used to be worth altogether; what it is worth now; and how much each freeman and sokeman had and has. All this was to be recorded thrice, namely as it was in the time of *King Edward*, as it was when King William gave it and as it is now. And it was also to be noted whether more could be taken than is now being taken.[3]

No other country possesses such an elaborate single official dossier from so far back. Many historians have remarked on its perfection, although the undertaking was left unfinished and was out of date even as it was being set down. Moreover, numerous copies, extracts, abbreviations, finding aids and spin-off compilations continued Domesday's work down through the centuries. One of its editors, Professor G. H. Martin, observes that Domesday Book "seems throughout to be the work not only of a single hand but also of a single mind."[4] The Domesday survey is "far more than just a fiscal record," for it presents a "detailed statement of lands held by the king and by his tenants and of the resources which went into those lands."

> It recorded which manors rightfully belonged to which estates.... It was moreover a "feudal" statement, giving the identities of the tenants-in-chief (land holders) who held their lands directly from the Crown, and of their tenants and under-tenants.... The compilation of such detailed information, however, required a survey wholly unprecedented in its scope and precision. The fact that the scheme was executed and brought almost to complete fruition within two years is a tribute to the political power and formidable will of William the Conqueror.[5]

One of the most important near-contemporary insights into the Domesday survey is that of a scribe of the Anglo-Saxon Chronicle. He tells us that at the 1085 Christmas court at Gloucester,

> William had much thought and very deep discussion about this country, how it was occupied or with what sorts of people. Then he sent his men all over England into every shire and had them find out how many hundred hides there were in the shire, or what land and cattle the king himself had in the country, or what dues he ought to have in twelve months from the shire. Also he had a record made of how much land his archbishops had, and his bishops and his abbots and his earls, and ... what or how much everybody had who was occupying land in England, in land or cattle, and how much money it was worth. So very narrowly did he have it investigated, that there was no single hide nor a yard of land, nor indeed one ox nor one cow nor one pig which was left out and not put down in his record. And all these records were brought to him afterwards against which there was no appeal.

Another important description of it was written within a few years of its completion by Robert, Bishop of Hereford, one of the ecclesiastics whom William brought to England. The king's men, he wrote,

> made a survey of all England; of the lands in each of the counties; of the possessions of each of the magnates, their lands, their habitations, their men both bond and free, living in huts or with their own houses and lands; of ploughs, horses and other animals; of the services and payments due from each and every estate. After these investigators came others who were sent ... to check the first description and to denounce any wrongdoers to the king. The survey was launched at William's Christmas court in 1085. Initially, each tenant-in-chief, whether bishop, abbot or baron, and each sheriff and other local official was required to send in a list of manors and men. There were already earlier lists of lands and taxes in existence, some dating from the Anglo-Saxon period, others from after 1066, which were kept both in the principal royal city of Winchester and locally in the shires. They too were drawn upon for the survey.[6]

William was evidently gratified to have such an exact record of his wealth, and he immediately began to sell off some of his new holdings based on the evaluations listed in Domesday, which was kept close by his side along with the Great Seal of England. But as G. H. Martin reminds us, "It is highly unlikely that he thought of such a venture himself." Prosopographer Keats-Rohan remarks, "The conquest of the most sophisticated state of its time by the most ruthlessly efficient entrepreneurs of the time ensured the future of England as the home of innovation in the science of government ... and was firmly rooted in pre-existing English tenurial structures."[7] There were notable lacunae—for reasons unknown neither London nor Winchester were canvassed—but the effort captured a snapshot of names, titles and place-names, one which has been surprisingly little used by genealogists. In property law and local history, "so lasting was the influence of Domesday Book as a blueprint for the feudal geography of England, that many of the great baronial holdings were to remain virtually unchanged throughout the middle ages."[8] Now let us consider who owned what and who owed what to

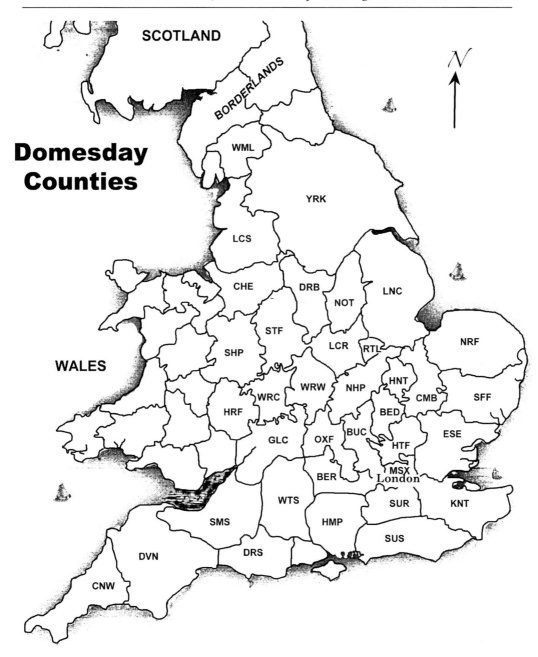

Domesday circuits with historical counties (map by Donald N. Yates).

CODE	Historic County	Code	Historic County	Code	Historic County	Code	Historic County
BED	Bedfordshire	ESE	Essex	LNC	Lincolnshire	STF	Staffordshire
BER	Berkshire	GLC	Gloucestershire	MSX	Middlesex	SFF	Suffolk
BUC	Buckinghamshire	HMP	Hampshire	NRF	Norfolk	SUR	Surrey
CMB	Cambridgeshire	HRF	Herefordshire	NHP	Northamptonshire	SUS	Sussex
CHE	Cheshire	HTF	Hertfordshire	NOT	Nottinghamshire	WRW	Warwickshire
CNW	Cornwall	HNT	Huntingdonshire	OXD	Oxfordshire	WML	Westmorland
DRB	Derbyshire	KNT	Kent	RTL	Rutland	WTS	Wiltshire
DVN	Devon	LCS	Lancashire	SHP	Shropshire	WRC	Worcestershire
DRS	Dorset	LCR	Leicestershire	SMS	Somerset	YRK	Yorkshire

whom in England both before and after the Norman Conquest. Let us also attempt to gain a better glimpse of the wealth managers who were responsible for creating this unusual record.

Jewish Names in Domesday

Before attempting to expand upon the geographical context of Jewish culture evident in the Saxon predecessor names and Norman and Breton successor names in all the counties covered by Domesday, let us make a superficial first cut and draw the reader's attention to some obvious Hebrew names from Keats-Rohan's comprehensive alphabetical listing. **Abraham the Priest** occurs in Gloucestershire—an archdeacon from Gwent in Wales. There are four lords named **Adam**, all Norman. Two, in Rochester and Kent, are tenants of Odo, bishop of Bayeux, King William's half-brother; one is a tenant of Bishop Remigius of Lincoln; and one is the son of Durand Malzor (a Sephardic Jewish name probably from the south of France). The Scottish Bruce ancestor Robert de Bruis is a Norman fief holder in Yorkshire. His son Adam married a woman named Jueta (Judith). **Adelina the Jester** (or Jester's Wife) is mentioned in Hampshire (a Jewish given name). Another female who held dower lands separately from her husband is **Adeliza**, widow of Hugh de Grandmesnil[9] and daughter of Ivo count of Beaumont-sur-Oise. She was reputedly a great beauty and drew income from several manors in Bedfordshire. **Aelueue** and **Wateman of London** were English and retained their tenancies in Middlesex (Wateman[10] is Arabic). There are two Englishmen named Azor (Arabic "Illuminated"),[11] one of whom was a butler or steward (dispenser) in the household of Edward the Confessor.

The earliest member of the **Bagot** (Splendors, Fortune)[12] family is found as a tenant of Robert de Rosny of Stafford; they seem to come from Calvados in Normandy. In addition to meaning simply "wealthy, lucky," the name is Arabic for "grape" and originally would probably have designated a vineyard owner, vintner, grape or wine merchant or more generally, an imbiber of wine.[13] **Ared the Falconer**, who succeeded to a tenancy of Bernardus Accipitrarius in Berkshire, was probably Arabic, like his name and craft. **David Latimer**[14] was an interpreter who was a tenant of fellow Norman William de Braose in Dorset; he was succeeded by his son Rainald, who was followed by his son John, official cupbearer to the overlord. **Farman**, a lord in Kent, whose name is derived from Arabic "order, decree,"[15] was the ancestor of the Fareman family of Wrotham. Several English thanes in Yorkshire bear the name **Gamel** (Hebrew letter). The name of **Gollan**[16] is found in Cambridgeshire as that of an Englishman. The Jewish female name **Golde**, "mother of Ulrich," occurs as that of an Englishwoman, and there are several further examples of **Golda**[17] in Caen (Normandy). The name of an accountant (*sacmannus*) of King William is **Golstan**; his origins are not clear but he received a grant in Essex.

Hosea occurs as Hose and Hussey. **Ieuitia** is a corruption of Judith, and this is the name of the wife of the mysterious foreigner Hervé *Bituricensis*, a major tenant-in-chief after the conquest, whose name may be the origin of English Wrenn. There is a "confused entry" (p. 281) about a "Frenchman" named **Isaac**, who predated the Normans and survived their protracted quarrels and side-switching in Suffolk and Norfolk. The fact that he named a son Roland suggests a southern French origin. At the end of his life, he endowed Eye Priory and retired there. There are many **Levins** (Leuuinus, Lewin), all Anglo-Saxon. **Manasser Arsic** was a great baron whose family had holdings in Oxfordshire, Somerset and the Boulonnais, that is, on both sides of the Channel, and were sometimes regarded as English, sometimes as Norman. **Moyses** is a Domesday tenant of the bishop of Coutances in Somerset, and **Morel** is the name of a similar benefice holder under the bishop of Thetford. Both are without question Jewish names. There are two persons named **Rabel**, a non–Norman, non–Frankish, non–

English name. One is an artist or jeweler in Norfolk; the other held a fee of Robert of Mortain in Cornwall. We find two **Salomons** and one **Samson**, the latter first a treasurer at Bayeux, then bishop of Worcester. Finally, **Simon** or **Simeon** crops up several times, its provenance being English, French or Flemish.

Cornwall was the southwesternmost county in England, the site of ancient tin mining and continuing trade with the Mediterranean. Here we find a man named Doda (the Hebrew diminutive for David) as one of the pre-conquest landowners whose holdings were regranted by William. Doda was allowed to keep his lands, suggesting that he was not seen as a Saxon threat to the Norman administration, but rather was a supportive Jew. Doda was reacknowledged as a thane of the kingdom and made a subtenant of William's half-brother, Robert, count of Mortain, first earl of Cornwall (Herleva's son by Herluin).[18] He was confirmed in his lordship of Carsella (Carsallan), the location of the china claypit of St. Austell, center of Cornwall's most important industry.[19]

In the same county are several other Jewish or Muslim-named landowners: Haslam (i.e., HaSalam in Arabic),[20] Rabel (who held Pengold or Penguol from Count Robert), Algar (Algeria),[21] Brian,[22] and even a priest named Boia. The last-named has a surname that is a Latin word meaning "fetter"; in Italian it came to designate a hangman. It is also a Romanian/Turkish surname and Sephardic Jewish name; for example, there is a prominent Hungarian historian surnamed Boia.[23] Our Anglo-Saxon Boia, who is listed as the priest who held Pendavid in Cornwall among other benefices or heritable fees in Domesday, may be the original form of the unusual surname Bowhay, which survives in Bowhay Manor in the parish of Exminster and of which there are hundreds of examples confined to Devon and Cornwall.[24]

The town names for Cornwall in the Domesday Book similarly indicate a partly Jewish and Muslim population: Tamar Valley, Hamelin, Pendavid, Talgar (locative form of Algar), Argentel, Moireis, Ottram, Hamet (Mohammed), Mingeli, Elhil Karsalan (Casella).

Cornwall

Persons		*Places*	
Algar	Argentel Lantmanuel	Neotes Hamotedi (Mawan)	Perran Zabuloe
Boia (the priest)	Chelenoch	Ottram	Polschat Karsalan
Brian	Hamet	Panguol Bernel	Rame Disart
Doda (pre-invasion)	Lege	Pendavid Hamelin	Roschel Elhil
Haslam	Legea	Pengelli Auta/Awta	Talgar Cola
Rabel	Mawan/Mawant	Pennahalgar Botonoan	Tamar Valley
Trelawni[25]	Mingelo	Penquaro	Tavistock
	Moireis	Peret	

Devonshire, home to several of the English privateers including Drake and Raleigh, whom we have discussed in another book as of likely Sephardic origin, offers a veritable cornucopia of Hebrew, Arabic and even Turkish names. Prominent landowners included Fitz Gamelin (Camel in Hebrew and Arabic),[26] Asgar (Hebrew),[27] Edeva (a Jewess),[28] the Gould (Gold/money) family,[29] Alfred de Epaignes (of Spain), Haimeric,[30] Solomon (Jew), Beatrix (Jewess),[31] her brother William Cheever and Tovi (Jew).[32]

With William Cheever (Willelm Chieure) we can set down the name of a Norman who was unquestionably one of "the King's Jews."[33] The brother of Ralph de Pomeroy and Beatrice, he appears to be identical with Guillaume de la Cheval, allegedly depicted handing William his horse in the Bayeux Tapestry (see illustration). King William dubbed him the Baron Knight Sir William Cheever, granting him the honor or fief of Bradninch and confirming him as a

hIC·MILITES·EXIERVNT·DEhESTENGA·

TAPISSERIE DE BAYEUX

William's knights leave the battlefield at Hastings, from the Bayeux Tapestry. This scene has traditionally been associated with William Cheever, one of the "King's Jews" and a major tenant-in-chief in Devon. (Etching by Victor Sansonetti) (Art & Architecture Collection, Miriam and Ira D. Wallach Division of Art, Prints and Photographs, The New York Public Library, Astor, Lenox and Tilden Foundation).

major tenant-in-chief with 47 properties, amounting to 23,000 acres, all in Devon.[34] Cheever is a medieval Jewish name related to Cooper, Kiefer, Küpfer and the like, used in the vernacular for Jacob, in Hebrew legend the first merchant and metallurgist. The name or title often came to mean "manager, handler, steward, caretaker, trustee" as in the Ashkenazic Shaeffer and variants.[35]

Our Cheever lived in the eleventh century and may have remained in Normandy as an absentee landlord, but he maintained a commercial empire spread across Devon, with interests in cattle, wool, farming, grain, mills, rental houses, fisheries and horse breeding, as is evident from the many entries in Domesday. Cheever's possessions include Ash Barton, Awliscombe (mill, 16 cattle, 287 sheep, 97 goats), Axminster (a royal Saxon college), Bradford Mill, Buckland Manor, Cadeleigh, Countisbury (Roman signal house and site of Wind Hill Battle with Danes 873), Cruwys Morchard (Morceth, estate), Exminster (fishery, 220 sheep), Mackham (Madescame), Matford Barton (shared between Alfred the Butler from Count Robert, half-brother of the conqueror and Ralph from William Cheever), Mildon (Mildedona, formerly held by Edith, Edward the Confessor's queen, who died 1075), Oakford (Alforde, mill, 200 sheep, 100 goats), Haccombe, Huntshaw, Ilkerton (Incrintona, 72 wild mares), Instaple Farm, Lympstone (Levestone, "Levi's Town"), East Lyn (houses, new mill, 34 cattle), Linton (old fishing village of Lynmouth), Pirzwell (Pissewelle, granted to Hamo), Radworthy in North Molton (on Exmoor), Rocombe (Rachun), Tedburn St. Mary (Teteborna, cob), Waringstone (Otria, Oteri), Yowleston House (Yoel's Town). Two of his most valuable estates were Woolacombe (previously held by King Edwin) with seven slaves and 12 villains as well as plowmen, and Bradninch with a mill, slaves, plowmen, pasture and woodlands. As the example of Matford Barton shows, Cheever divided some domains with William's other household retainers, and subtenancies were allotted to Hamo, William the Servant of the King, Jocelyn, Ralph, Warin and others.

Judhael of Totnes

Perhaps the most remarkable new tenant-in-chief is the Breton nobleman Judhael of Totnes,[36] whose name combines Juda, "Jew," with the theophoric suffix -el, and who owned approximately *half* the entire province.[37] Keats-Rohan has a lengthy entry on him; his enigmatic career and the tale of his powerful connections boil with intrigue and adventure (285–86). Originating in Brittany, where his father was the west Norman knight Alfred the Giant, he married the sister-in-law of Germond of Picquigny in the strategic fiefdom of Picardy and formed deft alliances with the counts of Flanders to the north. Despite or because of his Jewish ancestry and faith, Judhael's descendants married into several prominent Norman families, including those of de Braose,[38] de Beauchamp,[39] Chaworth,[40] Mowbray,[41] Grey,[42] de Laval,[43] Mortimer[44] and even the royal Plantagenet family. Notably, in the family genealogy a descendent in the late 1500s (Thomas Swinburne) marries a woman who is conspicuously Jewish, Hieronyma Chaytor. In the 1130s and 1140s, Judhael's son Alfred and a nephew, also named Judhael, "were close to Baldwin I de Redvers,[45] earl of Devon and "head of a network of western Normans in Devon" (Keats-Rohan 286). The Judhael or Totnes line, like that of the High Stewarts of Scotland, who were also Breton in origin, with their alternation of Walters and Alans, long preserved a naming pattern modeled on the High Priests of the Temple in Jerusalem. Without realizing its implications, Keats-Rohan astutely remarks upon it as having a "significance beyond what was customary in name-giving" (42).[46]

The de TOTNES Lineage (ca. 1000–1995)

34. Alured de TOTNES

33. Judael de TOTNES b. abt 1049 ; d. aft 1123
m. Guermond de PICQUAGNY b. abt 1013 ; d. abt 1085

32. Aenor de TOTNES b. abt 1081
m. Phillip de BRAOSE b. abt 1070 ; d. bet 1134 and 1155

31. William, 3rd Lord of Bramber de BRAOSE 1100–1192 m. Bertha de PITRES b. 1130

30. Bertha de BRAOSE 1151–1170 m. Walter de BEAUCHAMP 1173–1235

29. Walcheline de BEAUCHAMP 1194–1235 m. Joane de MORTIMER 1194–1268

28. William, 5th Baron Beauchamp de BEAUCHAMP 1215–1245 m. Isabel de MAUDUIT 1227–1268

27. William, Earl of Warwick de BEAUCHAMP 1237–1298 m. Maud FITZJOHN 1237–1301

26. Isabel de BEAUCHAMP 1266–1306 m. Patrick, Lord Kidwillyin de CHAWORTH 1250–1283

25. Maud CHAWORTH 1282–1316/1317 m. Earl of Norfolk Henry 1281–1345

24. Joan, Baroness Mowbray PLANTAGENET 1312–1349 m. John, 3rd Baron Mowbray de MOWBRAY 1310–1361

23. John, 4th Baronï Mowbray MOWBRAY 1340–1368 m. Elizabeth, Baroness Segrave SEGRAVE 1338–1368

22. Joan de MOWBRAY 1363–1402 m. Thomas GREY 1359–1400

21. Maud (Matilda) GREY 1382–1451 m. Robert OGLE 1373–1435

20. Robert OGLE 1406–1469 m. Isabel (Elizabeth) KIRKBY d. 1477/78

19. Ewyn OGLE 1440–1486 m. Eleanor HILTON 1450–1513

18. Ralph OGLE 1468–1512/1513 m. Margaret GASCOIGNE 1473–1515

17. William OGLE 1491–1542 m. Margery DELAVAL b. 1493

16. John OGLE 1525–1586 m. Phillis OGLE 1525–1626

15. Dorothy OGLE b. 1575 m. John SWINBURNE 1573–1604

14. Thomas SWINBURNE 1597–1666 m. Hieronyma CHAYTOR b. 1610

13. Nicholas SWINBOURNE b. 1640 m. ? b. 1640

12. John SWINBOURNE 1666–1729 m. Anne FISHER 1665–1729

11. Richard SWINBOURNE 1689–1766 m. Mary SMITH b. 1688

10. John SWINBOURNE 1717–1799 m. Mary SHEMMONS b. 1725

9. Thomas SWINBOURNE 1749–1819 m. Mary WALL 1749–1827

8. Samuel SWINBOURNE 1791–1843 m. Sarah BLUNN 1792–1837

7. Thomas SWINBOURNE 1817–1859 m. Hannah Divinish HATTON 1825–1857

6. James SWINBOURNE 1855–1913 m. Elizabeth Ann BECKETT 1856–1892

5. Leah SWINBOURNE 1878–1924 m. Charles RIGBY 1878–1922

4. Ruby Margaret RIGBY b. 1917 m. Albert James SIMPSON 1917–1969

3. Susan Mary SIMPSON b. 1945 m. Robert Frank TAYLOR b. 1943

2. Samantha Louise TAYLOR b. 1965 m. Kevin James HOY b. 1951

1. Jacob Samuel HOY b. 1995

Devonshire

People			*Places*
Aelfeva	Judhael of Totnes	Ralph de Pomeroy	Aissa
Aissa	Ludo	Ralph Pagnell	Bagetore
Alfred d Epaignes	Maaberia	Ralph U Halls	Bicatona
Ansger	Madona	Rbt. D'Aumale	Blacaploa
Ansketel	Mammeheua	Roger Fitz Payne	Brais
Asgar	Manelle	Roger Goad	Carmes
Ausa	Matingeho	Rowdona	Colacoma
Beatrix	Melewis	Selac	Colebrocha
Bernard	Molacota	Solomon	Coma/Cume
Bretel	Morin	Stocha	Dene/Dena
Countess Gytha	Most Man	Tacabeara	Hagintona
de Poilley	Nimeth	Tala	Hagitonal
Drogo	Niressa	Tavi	Hama
Duna	Offawilla	Tawi	Hame/Hama
Edeva	Oladona	Tochelei	Hamel
Escaga	Oliver	Torra	Hanoch
Eshipabroca	Oppaluma	Tovi	Hela
Falleia	Orrawa	Tuchel	Hocha
Flueta	Osbern de Sacey	Uluelie	Hola
Gould family	Paorda	Walter de Douai	Honesham
Haimerk	Pedahael		Lamaseta
Jacobescherche Wicca	Pola		Leia

People	*Places*
	Leuya
	Nimetona
	YudeFord

The towns in Devonshire at the time of the Domesday records are likewise frequently Judaic and Arabic in flavor: Nimeth (from Nimmes), Tala,[47] Manelie (apiary),[48] Orrawia (valley),[49] Aissa (high pasture),[50] Falleia (Arabic for "land"),[51] Uluelie (summit, peak),[52] Tawi (well),[53] Tavi, Molacota, Hama (Brackish Water),[54] Bagetore (depression), Nimetona (from Nimes), Dena (Arabic for "land, territory"),[55] Hagintona (Hagen's Town), Hanoch, Hocha,[56] Yude ford ("Jews Ford"), Leuya (Luwa, a province in Iraq).[57]

Somerset lies between Devonshire and Dorset and has no seaports, lack of them suggesting that the inhabitants were not transients or persons involved primarily in the shipping trades. However, the landowners listed in the Domesday records include several with Hebrew or Muslim names. Among these are Doda, Aeleva, Azelin, Vitalis (life, *Chaim*),[58] Bofa, Alfry, Leofa, Giso, Asser the tutor, Samson the chaplain, Manasseh the Cook, Dodman, Ida of Boulogne, Magtere, and Fitzgamelin.

Place-names recorded in Domesday include Aissa (again, "high pastureland"), Babacha, Babakari (*Bab* is Arabic for "gate/door"),[59] Babbig, Bagelie (Aqueduct),[60] Baga trepa, Brochelle, Baruch (Fort), Caffecoma (Well),[61] Gahers ("low-lying"),[62] Picotta (Place of Idols),[63] Carma,[64] Haia (extremity, refuge)[65] and Terra Teodrici (Land of Theodorich, Theodore). On the basis of this roister of Arabicisms in its place-names, Somerset can perhaps be identified as one of England's Sephardic heartlands. It was founded by Visigoths, Vandals and Berbers in the fourth to sixth centuries (see chapter 2). After the plague and famines of the mid–sixth century it became the Wasteland of Welsh legend. That more Arabs migrated to England after the establishment of Islam in the seventh century is suggested by names like Picotta, meaning Place of Idols.

Somerset

People		*Places*
Accheleia	Durand	Ailgi/Aili
Acha	Fastrad	Aissa
Aeleva	Fitzgamelin	Ascwei
Agelric	Fitzpayne	Babacha
Alfgeat the priest	Fulcran	Babakari
Alfred d'Epaignes	Giso	Babbig
Alfry	Haia	Bacoila
Alric	Hamet	Bagatrepa
Anketel	Ida of Boulogne	Bagelie
Ansketel	Kari Givela	Banuela
Ar	Leofa	Blachamora
Asser the tutor	Ludo	Brochelie
Azelin	Maghere	Brune
Bernard Pancevolt	Manasseh Cook	Caffecoma
Bofa	Mauger	Cameleia
Bretel	Megela	Camella
Bretel	Mera	Carma
Doda	Nigel	Cinioch
Dodman	Nigel de Gournai	Crucca
Drago	Nigel the Dr.	Cuma/Cumba

People	People	Places
Odo	Sowi	Duuelis
Ogis	Vitalis	Elleberia
Peret	Walter de Douai	Gahers
Peri	Will. Hussey	Lege/Lega
Rademar	Winegot the priest	Picotta
Raderar		Soche
Roger Arandel		Talanda
Sampson the Chaplain		Terra Teodrici
Siward		Torra

Hampshire county lies in the middle of the southern English coast, giving residents easy access to the Mediterranean sea lanes. A very interesting set of persons are listed as landholders for the county in Domesday Book. Notably, several of these persons are designated as ministers or assistants to the king (William I). Apparently they had been rewarded for their service to him with the honors of important agricultural and industrial holdings. We suspect that these Hampshire barons who were granted incomes close to the seats of trade and government in prime locations are mainly Jewish courtiers who had loyally served William. Among them are Adelina the jester, Vitalis the priest (Vitalis is the Latinized version of the Hebrew name Chaim, "life"),[66] Aubrey the chamberlain (Albericus, an important Breton suzerain),[67] Siric (Persian?) the chamberlain and Alfsi (also perhaps Persian) the valet. Additional persons owning land apparently having overtly Jewish or Islamic names are FitzAzor (son of Illuminated), Swarting ("black," cognate with *sephardi* and *sefart*), Durand, Shoflet (Peacemaker), Gerin, Osmelin and Alnoth.

The towns of Hampshire also have many Hebraic or Arabic names: Esselei (Assaeli, Wasteland),[68] Dena (Ruins),[69] Etham,[70] Hallege, Chenep,[71] Menes (Windy Place),[72] Abaginge, Haselie, Levintun (Town of Levites). Like those of Somerset, the naming patterns imply that Jews and Arabs arrived following the widescale devastation of the native populations, finding ruins, abandoned towns and unoccupied land.

Hampshire

People	People	Places
Adelina the Jester	Osmelin	Abagmge
Alfsi the Valet	Papald	Berardinz
Alfwy	Ralph Bloiet	Broc
Alnoth	Roald	Chenep
Aubrey the Chamberlain	Saewin	Copenore
Bernard Pancevolt	Seric	Dena
Bolla	Shoflet	Dene
Cola the Hunter	Siric the Chamberlain	Eccleswelle
Durand (of Gloucester)	Swarting	Egrafel
Durnand	Vitalis the Priest	Ellatane
Fitz Azor	Walter Tyrrell	Emelei
Gerin	Will. Mauduit	Esselei
Germanus		Etham
Godric Malf		Hallege
Guy		Haselie
Hergrand de Pont		Heche
Mauger		Herdel
Odo		Houch

People	Places
	Jvare
	Levintan
	Mene
	Menes
	Nonoelle
	Romesy
	Sidemaneston
	Sopellie

Sussex is a long, narrow county lying directly across the Channel from France (Gaul). We would expect it to have Jewish and Islamic influence, if such settlements existed, and it does. The names of Domesday landowners include Theodoric (Greek for "God-loving"; recall that this is the surname of the noble Jewish family of Todros mentioned in a previous chapter), Gozo (Ghaus, "succor"),[73] Ansketel, Roger Daniel, Tesselin, Lewes, Azor (Most Illuminated),[74] Lovell, Mauger. Its towns and villages also feature some Hebrew and Arabic names: Tangemere (Tangier by the sea), Dodimere (David by the sea), Seleisie (i.e., Selassie, "plain"), Ramelle, Polebenge (Polish town?), Loventone (Levin town), Hame (Chaim), Levitone (Levite town), Moham (Mohammed), Moreleia (village of the Moors).

Sussex

People		Places
Ansgot	Sasward	Dodimere
Ansketel	Tesselin	Durand
Arnold	Theodoric	Hame
Awin	Tosard	Hamelsham
Azelin	Will. De Braose	Harundel
Azor		Levitone
Gozo		Lewes
Ivo		Loventone
Lewes		Moham
Lovell		Morleia
Mauger		Poleberge
Morin		Rameslie
Nigel		Sasingham
Ralph Fitz Theodoric		Seleisie
Roger Daniel		Sifelle
Rozelin		Tangemere

Kent lies closest to France across the English Channel. It was the arrival point for the Romans when they expanded into England and served as an important shipping point from the time of the Roman occupation onward. Tenants here include Ansketel de Rots (Anschatel the Red), Hamo (Hebrew) the sheriff, owner of much land,[75] Adam fitz Hubert, also a large landholder, Abel the Monk (perhaps a convert), Nigel the Doctor, Vitalis the Knight and Edeva. The towns of Kent have names suggesting a strong Jewish and Islamic influence: Tongas,[76] Essamels ford, Palestrel, Ora, Acers (Acre), Eisse, Bogelei, Tarent, Addela, Dena, Maresc,[77] Castro, Alham, Mama,[78] Hammil, Hagelei and Levelant (Levite Land).

Kent

People	*Places*	
Abel the Monk	Acers	Gecham
Adam (fitz Hubert)	Addela	Gomersham
Ansered	Aigtessa	Hagelei
Ansgot	Alham	Hama
Ansketel de Rots	Bichelei	Hammil
Edeva	Bogelei	Langafel
Hamo the sheriff	Castro	Lasela
Hardes	Celca	Levelant
Maino	Dena	Maresc
Mauger	Dovera	Merlea
Nigel the Dr.	Ece	Ora
Ralph of St. Samson	Eisse	Ospak
Vitalis (Knight)	Esmerefel	Palestrei
	Essamels ford	Perie
	Estrei	Ripa
	Esturai	Romenel
	Ezilamenth	Tangas
	Ferlaga	Tarent

Essex county has many excellent sea harbors along its coastline, making it a natural shipping point to France, the Mediterranean and the Baltic. Persons granted land there in the Domesday book include those having the Hebrew or Islamic names of David, Hato, Sasselin, Hamo, Vitalis, Algar, Mauger, Serlo, Leofeva (a woman), Anchatel, Azo, Hamo the Steward, Gilbert Fitz Solomon, Rainam (Dreamer, Prophet) and Peverel. The towns and villages of Norman Essex similarly feature what appear to be Arabic/Hebrew-inspired names: Walla (Muddy), Hame, Turoca, Roda (Cemetery), Mosa (Barren), Angra (Eminence), Laianhagam, Lagtiefara, Assuuella, Aluiella, Asce (Black), Bura,[79] Monehala, Estra, Hecham (Stony), Atahoi, Samartuna (Samartown) and Smaltuna Ismael-Town).[80]

Essex

People		*Places*	
Adam, son of Durand Malzor	Mauger	Alulella	Hecham
Aethelgyth (woman)	Otto the Goldsmith	Angra	Laghefara
Algar	Peverel	Asce	Laianhagam
Ansketel	Pirot	Assuuella	Latners
Ascelin	Rainam	Ata hoi	Magghedana
Aubrey	Rich. Garnet	Bachencia	Monehala
Azo	Rob. Gernon	Baduuer	Mosa
David Eudo the steward	Roger Bigot	Bura	Pava Colun
Frado	Roger de Raismes	Cicchcnai	Polheia
Gil. Fitz Solomon	Sasselin	Cinga	Roda
Hamo	Serlo	Estra	Samartuna
Hamothe Steward	Tihel Le Burton	Ginga	Smaltuna
Jocelyn	Vitalis	Golghangra	Tacheleia
Leofeva (woman)	Walter Tirel Hato	Hacheleia	Turoca
		Hame	Walla

Suffolk also has coastal trading areas. Persons who were granted rents there recorded in Domesday are Coleman, Amund, William Pecche, Tihell, Lewin (Levin), Sasselin, William Gulaffra/Gulafa, Walter de Caen, Aedi, William, son of Satuala, Hatno de Valenis, Tela (a woman), Stanand Fitz Alwi, Anshetill, Ralph the Crossbowman (many crossbowmen were Jews), Anant, Vavassor, Otto the Goldsmith, and Tulca (pre-conquest holder). Places and villages have names that are clearly Hebrew or Arabic, such as Aketona (Ake-town), Hassa, Barnebei, Barro, Ben Agra, Benenhala, Begatone (Bega-town), Brochola, Bura, Burgata, Bukesalla, Capeles, Cambas, Damardestuna, Elga, Essel, Heia, Faraham, Babba. Also we find Hagala, Horam, Mealla, Saham, Almaham, Elmal Maham, Seilah, Wadgata and Washam. One place was named Cleope-tona (Greek?).

Suffolk

People		Places	
Adelm	Ovethel	Acle	Palegrava
Aedi	Pagan	Aketona	Saham
Algar	Picot	Almaham	Seilah
Aluric	Pirot	Atelega	Sellanda
Aluric the priest	Ralph Baynard	Balesheia	Uledana
Aluric Wanz	Ralph Pinel	Barnebei	Wadgata
Amund	Ralph the Crossbowman	Barro	Washam
Anant	Ran. Peverel	Begatona	
Anshetill	Rob. Gernon	Benagra	
Audoeno	Rob. Malet	Benenhala	
Berard	Rog. De Raismes	Brochola	
Coleman	Roger Bigot	Bukessalla	
Elmant	Sasselin	Bura	
Ermiot	Stanard Fitz Alwi	Burgata	
Eudo the Steward	Tela (free woman)	Cambas	
Frodo	Tiger	Capeles	
Fucred	Tihell	Cleapetona	
Fulcho	Tura/Tuka (pre-conquest)	Damardestana	
Hamo	Ulmar	Elamlmaham	
Hamo de Valenis	Vavassor	Elga	
Hervey Beruarius	Vavassors	Faraham	
Hervey de Bourgel	W. Hurrant	Gabba	
Hugh Fitz Gold	Walter de Caen	Hagala	
Jarnacot	Walter the Crossbowman	Hashetuna	
Jutichell the priest	Will de Noyers	Hassa	
Lewin	Will Gulafa	Hecham	
Milo	Will. Gulaffra	Heia	
Mundet	Will. Pecche	Hoi	
Osketel	Will. Scutet	Horam	
Othem	Will, son of Sahuala	Kanauadis	
Otto the Goldsmith	Will. the Chamberlain	Mealla	

Norfolk has excellent trading opportunities with Scandinavia and the Baltic, given its coastal location. Tenants noted in the Domesday survey include Eli, Agneli, Alfheah, Hagni (a pre-conquest holder), Azelin, Isaac, Ralph Fitz Hagni, Durand, Simon, Reinbald the Goldsmith, Berner the Crossbowman and Tihel Le Breton. The largest landowners are Tovi, Simon and Isaac, indicating that much of the county was in Jewish hands. Town names are strikingly Hebrew/Arabic: Benelai, Acre (Estate),[81] Alabei, Essebei, Aschebei, Asselai, Belaga, Cattetuna, Eccles, Faganaham, Toffas, Acra, Saham, Salla, Mora, Ragadona, Mateshala, Lena, Marsam, Lagaam, Golosa, and Hecham (a common name repeated elsewhere).

Norfolk

People		Places	
Alfheah (pre-conquest)	Reinbald the goldsmith	Acra	Heccles
Ansketel	Robt. Malet	Acre	Hecham
Azelin	Tihel le Breton	Alabei	Hocham
Berard	Wagen	Aschebei	Kanapatone
Berner the Crossbowman	Will. De Cailli	Asselai	Lagaam
Durand		Babinghelia	Lena
Eil		Becham	Marsam
Essebei		Belaga	Mateshala
Godric the steward		Benelai	Mora
Hagni		Cattetuna	Obuuessa
Hermer de Ferrers		Claia	Pagrava
Mary Isaac		Depedala	Ragadona
Mary Rober Bigot		Depham	Saham
Mary Simon		Eccles	Salla
Mary Tovi		Essebei	Slaleia
Ralph Baynard		Faganaham	Toffas
Ralph Fitz Hagni		Golosa	

Middlesex

People	Places
Edeva	Dallega
	Eia
	Hesa
	Leleha

We see in the south of England, particularly in Devon, Cornwall and Somerset or those counties lying below Wales, an abundance of place-names testifying to colonization by Semitic speakers. Nor are signs of Britain's pre–Saxon past insignificant in Essex, Suffolk and Norfolk. Let us go on and proceed with this tour of forgotten Britain with the northern, midland and border counties with Scotland and Wales in the next chapter.

6

More Domesday Jews and Arabs

We continue our survey of Jewish and Muslim names of persons and places. After covering the south and east of England, we move now northward and into the Midlands and back down along the Welsh marches (see map in chapter 5).

Lincoln county comprises a portion of Mercia, the kingdom ruled by Offa, who, as we have seen, relied on Radanite ties to build his wealth and power. If we are correct in our reading of history, we can anticipate finding several landowners of Jewish heritage, as well as many towns and villages carrying Arabic/Hebrew names, and this is just the case. One of the largest landowners in the county is Alfred (the Jew) of Lincoln, followed by Ralph Pagnell (Pagenel = Jew or Muslim), and Heppo (Jewish) the arblaster (crossbowman). A man named Offram (Arabic Affan, Uthman)[1] was a pre-conquest tenant who was permitted by the Normans to keep his entitlements, indicating, we surmise, a trusting of Jews and/or Muslims over Saxons, perhaps because of a common language. Other Lincolnshire personages include Simund (Simon), Gamelin ("Camel"), Almod, Aschel the priest (rabbi?), Algar (Algeria/North Africa), Hacon (Righteous), Basuin, Azor and Saswolo (Joy of Allah). Town and village names also reflect Jewish and Islamic culture, merged in some cases with Anglo-Saxon and bearing the Danish suffix -bi or -by: Levesbi, Salebi, Sisse, Sealebi, Suabi, Chime (Chaim), Waragbi, Muudle,[2] Salmundebi (Solomon), Halebi (Hale or Ali), Asebi, Aplebi, Aschebi, Aslachebi, Alesbi, Bechebi, Brune (Brown), Castre, Hazebi, Hagenbi, Hecham (yet again) and Hag (Chief).

Lincoln

People		Places	
Algar	Malger	Alesbi	Chime
Amod	Mary Alfred of Lincoln	Alfgare	Cotes
Aschil the priest	Mary Heppo the Arblaster	Apelia	Fendebi
Azor	Mary Ralph Pagnell	Aschebi	Frisebi
Baldwin the Fleming	Norman d-Arci	Asebi	Goldesbi
Bassain	Odo the Arblaster	Asgerebi	Haebi
Berengar	Offram (pre-conquest)	Aslachebi	Hag
Colsuan	Raymer de Brinou	Bechebi	Hagenbi
Count Judith	Raynald	Berebi	Halebi
Durand Malet	Rob. Malet	Bergebi	Harebi
Gamelin	Saswolo	Bolebi	Hecham
Gilbert Ghent	Simund	Brezbi	Hicham
Guy de Craon	Waldin the Engineer	Brune	Levesbi
Hacon	Wolo	Castre	Muuelle
Ivo Tailbois		Catebi	Sisse
King Offa		Catenai	Suabi

People	Places
Salebi	Warayebi
Salmundebi	

Yorkshire/West Riding/North/North Riding: Yorkshire County, just north of Lincoln, experienced large-scale population disruption, yet not displacement, with the arrival of the Viking Norsemen in the mid-eighth century, as we have seen (chapter 3). Prior to that time it had been part of Mercia and had trading relationships with Scandinavia and the Baltic. Thus we would anticipate finding place-names that bear evidence of an earlier Jewish or Muslim presence, with however slightly fewer persons of such descent settling there and becoming landowners, the exception being the city of York itself. Within the capital we would expect to find a cluster of E1b1b, G, and J1/J2 haplotypes reflecting either a continued Jewish presence from Roman and Anglo-Saxon times or arrivals after the Norman Conquest.

Major landowners include Nigel Fossard, Manbodo, Gilbert de Tison, Robert Malet, Ralph Pagnell/Pagenel, Alelm, Gamel, Enisan, Roselin, Chetel, Swan (pre-conquest holder, Aswan?), Hamelin, William Vavasour, Ramechil, and several persons named Gamel (Camel in Arabic and Hebrew). Towns and villages within Yorkshire include many with Jewish/Islamic names: Turalzbi, Aschelebi, Bagen-tone, Barnebi, Ballebi, Begun, Brachenel, Caton (Short), Asch, Aschel, Halsam, Holam, Aluengi, alia Geuedale, Morebi, Ferebi (Phoebus), Pagele, Rutha, Medelai, Massan, Nagel-tone, Asgozbi, Samaer, Suanebi, Tarne-tona, Warlavexbi, Bag-

Seal of Odo, Bishop of Bayeux, William's half-brother and one of the most powerful barons in the conquered realm as Earl of Kent. He is shown in his dual role as secular and ecclesiastical lord (Print Collection, Miriam and Ira D. Wallach Division of Art, Prints and Photographs, The New York Public Library, Astor, Lenox and Tilden Foundations).

bebi, Barnebi, Borel, Aschilebi, Feizbi, Alia Harneseuch, Harem/Haram,[3] Lillaia, Oure, Catala, Paghenale, Radun, Ruhale, Salebi, Sosacra, Tancreslei (Tangiers), Achum, Ascham, Amelai, Hageneuorde, Hallun, Hasele.

Yorkshire

People	Places	
Alelm	Alia Geuedale	Brachenel
Berengar de Tosny	Aluengi	Caton
Erneis de Buron	Asch	Ferebi
Gerbodo	Aschel	Halsam
Gilbert de Tison	Aschilebi	Holam
Nambodo	Ascri	Hornessi
Nigel Fossard	Babetorp	Morebi
Ralph Pagnell	Bagentone	Pagele
Rayner	Ballebi	Rasbi
Rob. Malet	Barnebi	Rosse
	Begun	Rutha
	Beureli	Turalzbi
	Bonnebi	

North Riding Yorkshire

People	Places		
Berengar de Tosny	Alia Atun	Carebi	Medelai
Enisan	Alia Hamelsech	Catune	Molzbi
Gamel	Alwardebi	Childala	Nageltone
Nigel Fossard	Andrebi	Danebi	Parva Merse
Ralph Pagenel	Ansgotebi	Dragmalebi	Quennebi
Rob. Malet	Asgozbi	Echescol	Sambura
	Ashilebi	Endrebil	Scalebi
	Bachesbi	Feizbi	Schirebi
	Baghebl	Halmebi	Semaer
	Barnebi	Harem/Haram	Sorebi
	Bergebi	Haxeby	Suanebi
	Bordalebi	Hobi	Tametona
	Borel	Ioletun	Tolesbi
	Bragebi	Laisinbia	Toscutun
	Brecca	Malmerbi	Warlavesbi
	Buschebia	Massan	Witebi

West Riding Yorkshire

People		Places		
Archil	Nigel Fossard	Acastra	Chichelai	Hallun
Baret	Orm	Achum	Chidale	Hamelesuurde
Berengar	Picot	Aitone	Denebi	Hangelif
Chetel	Ralph Pagnell	Alia Eurebi	Dodesuurde	Hasele
Countess Judith	Ramechil	Amelai	Eleslac	Haserlai
Geaf. Alselin	Rob. Malet	Ascham	Fereia	Lillala
Gerbodo	Rozelin	Camelesford	Fereleia	Marra
Hamelin	Swan (pre-conquest)	Catala	Feresbi	Medelai
Malger	Will. Vavasour	Catebi	Flatebi	Napars
Mary Gamel		Cattala	Gisele	Oure
Nigel		Cherebi	Hageneuorde	Paghenale

People	Places	
Radun	Sandela	Tancreslei (Tancred's lea)
Rihella	Scalchebi	Tateuuic
Ripeleia	Setel	Tohac
Ruhale	Sosacra	Wadelai
Salebi	Stollai	Wihala

Westmorland county lies north of York, near Scotland, and has several lakes and inlets. Yet here also we see the presence of E1b1b, G, and J1/J2 male haplogroups as well as evidence of Jewish/Muslim land ownership. Landholders include Haimo, Judicuel, Theobald the doctor, Cola, Azelin, Payne, Durand, Bernard, Vitalis the priest, Croc, Wado, Azor, Selo de Burcy, Odolina (a woman), Liseman, Algar and Grimbald the goldsmith. What is very important about this list is that it includes many Jewish landowners we encountered in the *southwestern* part of England. This may mean that William placed these very loyal vassals in key locations of his kingdom, because he knew he could trust in their support for his reign. One of these, Judicuel or Judicael the Huntsman, became implicated in the revolt in the North of England associated with the names of Ralph of Gael, a Breton king rewarded by the grant of the earldom of East Anglia, and the native English noble Hereward the Wake (Keats-Rohan 45–46). Though relatively fewer towns and villages carry Hebrew/Islamic names, some are still present in the North: Aisi, Vitel-tone (Chaim/Life), Imemerie, Laven-tone, Nigra Aura (black gold), Piri-tone, Smalebroc (Ismael), Benzelin, Sela, Tocheham, Troi, Waisel, Duene.

Westmorland

People		Places	
Aiulf the Sheriff	Nigel the Dr.	Atsi	Tocheham
Alfgeat	Odolina	Bezelin	Troi
Algar	Otho	Cosseham	Ulfela
Azelin	Payne	Duene	Viteltone
Azor	Rainer	Essage	Wadone
Berengar Giffard	Ranulf Flambard	Gare	Waisel
Bernard	Reg. Canute	Hame	
Cola	Saetic	Imemerie	
Countess Gyxha	Selo de Burcy	Iwis	
Croc	Theobald the Dr.	Lacham	
Durand	Vitalis the priest	Lacoch	
Goda (woman)	Wadard	Laventone	
Grimbald Goldsmith	Wado	Lediar	
Haimo	Wenesi's wife	Nigra Avra	
Irso	Will. Corrielian	Paueshow	
John the Usher	Will. De La Mare	Piritone	
Judicael	Will. Shield	Sela	
Leofgeat (woman)	Wulfric Waula	Smalebroc (Israel)	
Liseman		Ticoode	

Lancashire county lies just south of Westmorland and north of Wales on the western British coast facing Ireland. Landowners include Hamo, Dwan (Royal Court or Tribunal)[4] and Gamel de Pennington, and towns, Bagelei, Catun, Ellhale, Heleshale, Lea, Hessam, Magete, Rabil, Sorbi and Jalant.[5]

Lancashire

People	Places			
Dwan	Bagelei	Heleshale	Lea	Sorbi
Gamel de Pennington	Catun	Hessam	Magele	Torboc
Hamo	Chellet	Holand	Mele	
Roger de Poitou	Chenchebi	Hornebei	Rabil	
	Ellhale	Jalant	Rosse	

Cheshire, Shropshire and Herefordshire: These three counties lie along the Welsh border and were placed under the control of the so-called Norman Marcher Lords after the conquest in order to keep the "Celtic" Welsh (who we argue were in large part of Jewish and Arabic descent) under control. Yet distinctly Hebrew/Muslim landowners and towns are still present. In **Cheshire**, Landowners include Payne, Gamel, Eli (the *pre-conquest* holder), Hamo de Masby (Moses), Fitz Tezzo and Asgar. Towns include Shlulan, Walea, Hamede (Mohamed), Calmundelie and Aca-tone. In **Shropshire**, Landowners are Rainald the Sherriff, Picot, Thochi, Robert Pincerna, Nigel the doctor, Azelin and Roger Venator. Places include Halam/Halas, Walle, Achel, Achelai, Benehale, Beges-tan, Cavrahalle (Carvajal is the surname of a prominent Sephardic family in medieval Spain), Doden-tone, Dalelie, Melela, Melam, Papelau, Pole, Polelie, Quatone. The two town names containing *Pole* may indicate Polish Ashkenazi Jewish settlements resulting from trade through the Baltic. In **Herefordshire**, known to have a medieval Jewish community, major landowners include Bernard, Durand, Rog (Roq, Warrior) de Mussegros ("great Moslem?") and Nigel the doctor. Places include Elmelie, Walelege, Baisson, Camehop, Ewais, Hamenes Capel, Hulla (Knoll), Matma and Moches (Moshe).

Cheshire

People		Places	
Asgar	Hamo de Mascy (Moses)	Acatone	Creu
Drogo	Hugh de la Mere	Ascelie	Hamede (Mohammed)
Eli (TRE)	Payne	Boselega	Mera
Fitz Tezzo		Brosse	Schiuian
Gamel		Calmundelei	Walea

Shropshire

People		Places	
Avenel	Turgis	Achel	Madolea
Azelin		Achelai	Melam
Eddiet		Barbingi	Melela
Madoc		Begestan	Nene
Mary Rainauld the sheriff		Benebale	Obelie
Mary Will. Pantulf		Caurahalle	Papelau
Nigel the Doctor		Dalelie	Pole
Outi		Doden/Dodintone	Polelie
Picot		Ferlau	Posselau
Ralph the cook		Goldene	Quatone
Rayner		Hach	Rohalle
Rob. Pincerna		Halam/Halas	Saltone
Roger Venator		Lai	Walle
Thochi		Lau	Witehala
Toret		Luure	

Herefordshire

People	Places	
Bernard	Ascis	Hamenes
Durand	Baisson	Hasles
Nigel the Doctor	Bolelei	Hulla
Ralph de Tosny	Camehop	Matma
Rog de Mussegros	Capel	Moches (Moshe)
	Chabenore	Pelelei
	Elmelie	Sbech
	Ewais	Walelege

The Jewish presence in Herefordshire is a good example of an unknown pocket of crypto–Judaism in England.[6] Herefordshire is one of thirteen well-documented medieval Jewish communities in pre-modern Britain and may count as the second most important in England. It had the three essential ingredients, a royal castle, an adequate hinterland and a sheriff who exercised direct authority over the Jews and was responsible for their security in time of trouble. Hereford's Jewish community flourished from 1218 under Hamo and his family, who were among the wealthiest in land. The family possessions passed to Ursell until 1241 and Moses until 1253. Moses died and the family sank into insignificance due to royal indulgences given to their debtors.

From 1260 to the expulsion of 1290, Aaron le Blund, from London, dominated the Hereford community. A member of the Le Blund family was later to become mayor of London. Some of Hereford's Jews moved in from Oxford because of rising anti–Semitism stemming from the pope's preaching of a crusade in 1215. Dominican friars had a priory in Hereford aiming to convert Jews. But conversion sometimes went the other way. In 1222 a deacon adopted Judaism, was circumcised and married a Jewess. He was handed over to the secular authorities and burned at the stake. Shortly thereafter, the Hamo family's political fortunes declined on the local scene due to their alliance with the DeLacys in the Welsh conflict. As the tide swelled into a storm against those who continued to identify as Jewish in the 1200s, Aaron of Hereford bore the brunt of the crown's fondness for rewarding faithful service by forgiving debts owed to Jews. Forced contributions were extracted from both individuals and the community. Moses of Hereford contributed £3000 towards the building costs of Westminster Abbey at Easter 1272, and a further tallage of 5,000 marks was imposed. All Jews who could not provide security for payment were to be thrown into the Tower. Indeed, the whole Hereford Jewish community had been lodged there when it failed to meet its small contribution to the 500-mark tallage of Michaelmas 1259.

In 1275, Edward I issued a writ that "no Jew dwell or abide in any of the towns which the queen [Eleanor, his father's Provençal bride in 1236] has for her dower." The Jews of Worcester were moved to Hereford, the sheriffs supervising their deportation "doing no injury, either to their persons or goods." The Gloucester Jews showed no enthusiasm for residence in their designated Jewry at Bristol, where William Giffard and others had earlier come by night and attacked the Jews and broken into their houses. In consequence, some Gloucester Jews joined the Worcester community at Hereford. Nonetheless, an ostentatious Jewish marriage celebration took place in Hereford in August 1286 under Aaron. The Church was not happy, and excommunicated the Christians who attended. Finally, in 1290, Edward I sent secret orders to the sheriff that all Jews, with their wives, children and chattels, were, on pain of death, to quit the realm by 1 November, the feast of All Saints. The sheriff was to ensure they suffered no injury, harm, damage or grievance in their departure. The penalty for any Jew who remained behind was death. Most, we can assume, found ways to convert or go under cover.

Derby, Nottingham, Staffordshire: These three contiguous counties lie below Yorkshire in north-central England. Major landowners in **Derby** include the Peveral family, Saswala, Toli, Alfsi and Cola; towns in Derby include Eyam (Chaim), Ha Beni, Eisse, Hatun, Hosselei, Alia, Sandiacre, Salle, Segassale, Smalei (Ismael), Toxenai, and Ghivell. **Nottingham** landowners include Payne, Alselin, Wazelin, Haldane, Schegebi, Bernard and Algar; while among the towns are Ascom, Baburde, Stochas, Hamessel, Lambelia, Calun, Madressi, Ragenehil, and Walesbi. However it is **Staffordshire** that exhibits the highest level of Hebrew/Islamic landowners and town names, perhaps because it was part of King Offa's Mercian realm. Tenants include Payne, Cadio, Algot, Gamel the King's thane, Aelmar the King's thane, the Bagot family, Tanio, Nigel the doctor, Algar, Samson the King's clerk, Arni, Nawen, and Cadio. Honor and village names in Staffordshire include Badehale, Sinai Park (!), Bughale, Barra, Opeweas, Levin-tone, Rouuella, Rugehala, Ache, Pancriz, Pagin-town, Tamahore and Totehale.

Derby

People	Places	
Cola	Alia	Hatun
Peverel family	Badequella	Mareis
Saswala	Eisse	Salle
Toli	Eyam	Sandiacre
	Ghivell	Segassale
	Habenai (ha Beni)	Smalei (Ismael)
	Halen	Tixenai
	Hosselei	

Nottingham

People		Places	
Algar	Muscham	Ascam	Ragenehil
Alric	Payne	Baburde	Raveschel
Alselin	Salwin	Bonei	Stochas
Berenger de Tosny	Schegebi	Calun	Walesbi
Bernard	Walter d'Aincourt	Chinemarel	Watelai
Count Godiva	Wazelin	Hamessel	
Gilbert Tison	Will. Peverel	Lambelia	
Haldane		Madressi	

Staffordshire

People		Places	
Aelfric: King's thane	Gamel: the King's thane	Ache	Pancriz
Aelmar: King's thane	Henry de Ferrens	Aclei	Peleshale
Algar	Hervey	Badehale	Pinchetel
Algot	Leofnoth	Barra	Rischale
Arni	Nawen	Bughale	Rouuelia
Ascelin	Nigel	Cota	Rugehala
Bagot family	Offa (Mercia)	Levintone	Sinai Park
Baldwin	Payne	Madelie	Talc
Cadio	Picot	Opewas	Tamahore
Fragrin	Samson (from King)	Pagintone	Tammuorde

People		Places
Samson the clerk	Tanio	Totehala
Several Nigel		Wineshala

Leicestershire, Warwick and Worcester: These three adjoining counties lie due west of Lincolnshire in north-central England. Within **Leicestershire** we find the following Jewish/Muslim names of gentry: Selina, countess of Hunt, Payne, Mainou le Breton, Aelman, Feggi, William Lovett, Serlo. Places in Leicestershire with Jewish or Muslim names include Chetelbi, Ascebi, Essebi, Bageworde, Barhou, Catebi, Gadesby (Cadiz), Caiham, Haliach, Muselai (Muslim), Sawelle, Tochebi, Alebie. In **Warwick** county we again encounter Nigel, Aelfeva, Saswalo, Aelmer, Hascoit Musard, Algar, and Judhael, while finding Baron La Zouche,[7] Soto and Ansegis listed for the first time. Places in the county are named Guara, Wara, Haseleia, Hasselou, Museleie (Muslim for Peacemaker),[8] Pirio, Sucham, Thessale (Greek), Sowa and Ulveia. Finally, in **Worcester** we find among the taxpayers persons named: Darand, Aldeva (a woman), Payne, Nigel the doctor, Acard, Doda, and Urso the sheriff. Jewish and Muslim town names in this county include Achelenz, Belleom, Aelmelia, Hageleia, Hala, Hamme, Lea, Moor, Russwococ (Cliffs),[9] Heref Stoch and Tothehel.

Leicestershire

People		Places	
Aelmer	Meginta	Alebie	Muselai
Arnold	Oger	Ascebi	Saltebi
Askel	Payne	Bageworde	Sawelle
Buterus	Rainer	Barhou	Tochebi
Count of Melan	Ralph Framen	Bebi	
de Craon	Ravel	Caiham	
de Mowbray	Roald	Catebi	
Durand Malet	Rob. De Tosny	Chetelbi	
Feggi	Rob. the usher	Essebi	
Gauf. Alselin	Robert the Bursar	Gadesby	
Henry de Ferrers	Selina (Count of Hunt)	Goutebi	
Hugh Musard	Serlo	Grobi	
Ingold	Walkelin	Hadre	
Ivo	Will. Lovett	Haliach	
Mainau le Breton	Will. Peverel	Messecham	

Warwick

People		Places
Adolf (pre-conquest)	Leofeve	Alia Bichetielle
Aelfeva	Mary Aelmer	Arlei
Alfsi (pre-conquest)	Nicholas	Arue
Algar	Nigel	Guara
Ansegis	Nigel d'Aubigny	Haseleia
Baron La Zouche	Oslac	Hasselou
Brown	Ranulf	Muselcic
Count Godiva	Rob, the Bursar	Pirlo
Drogo	Salo	Seruelei
Hascoit Musard	Saswalo	Sowa
Hervey	Soto	Sucham
Johais	Stephen	Taschebroc
Judhael	Tonni	Thessale

People		Places
People		*Places*
Ulfketel	Will. Goizenboded	Ulveia
Wazelin		Wara

Worcester

People		*Places*	
Acard		Achelenz	Holowei
Aldeva (woman)		Aelmelia	Lea
Doda		Badesei	Ludella
Drogo		Bellem	Moor
Durand		Cochehi	Namele
Mary Ralph de Tosny		Elmerige	Pirian
Nigel the Dr.		Eslei	Russwococ
Payne		Hageleia	Sapie
Rob. Parler		Hala	Tothehel
Rob. the Bursar		Hamme	
Uiso the sheriff		Heref Stoch	
Walter Ponther		Holim	

Gloucester, Oxford, and Northampton: These three contiguous counties lie almost at the center of Britain; they are landlocked and have among the lowest levels of E1b1b, G, and J1/J2 in all of Britain. Yet here we still find Jewish/Islamic landowners and town names, albeit at a more modest occurrence than at other locales in England. In **Gloucester**, for example, the only identifiably Jewish/Muslim landowners are Alfsi, Ralph Pagnell, Azelin, Nigel the doctor, Hascoit Musard (Counselor), Durand the sheriff and Sigar de Chocques; yet there are some places with Hebrew/Arabic names: Omenie, Esselie, Camma, Dodesuelle, Hamme, Caroen (Cairouan in North Africa), Simondeshale and Moorcroft. In **Oxford** we actually find some names of Jewish/Muslim landowners not encountered previously: Ackem (Hebrew), Aba ("father" in Hebrew and Arabic) and Gadio, as well as some familiar Jewish names, Ansketel, Theodoric the goldsmith, Payne and Brian. Town names in this county include those of Teowe, Tovi, Perie and Haselie. **Northampton**'s seemingly Jewish/Arabic lords or tenants include Bondi (pre-conquest), Dodin, Azelin, Saswalo, Ansketel, Adam, David Sasgar and Simon de Pattishall. Places with Jewish/Muslim names are Asca, Badebi, Bracheli, Hecham, Falelau (Dry Land),[10] Hala, Hasou, Isham and Pirie.

Gloucester

People		*Places*	
Alfsi	Ketel	Atheliai	Hagenpene
Ansketel	Madog (pre-conquest)	Begelberie	Hamme
Azelin	Miles Crispin	Camma	Manegodesfelle
Bernard	Nigel the Doctor	Caroen	Moorcroft
Countess Goda	Ralph de Tosny	Dimoch	Omenel
Durand the Sheriff	Ralph Pagnell	Dodesuuelle	Omenie
Hascoit Musard	Sigar de Chocques	Esselie	Rawelle
Jocelyn le Breton	Will. Leofric	Goizenboded	Simondeshale

Oxford

People		*Places*
Aba	Alfwy	Bechelie
Adam	Ansgar	Haselie
Alfsi	Ansgered	Lewa

People		*Places*
Ansketel	Isward	Peregie
Aretius	Mainou	Perie
Brian	Miles Crispin	Tachelie
Brown the priest	Payne	Teowe
Columban	Rahere	Tobelle
Gadio	Ranulf Flambard	Tovi
Guy d'Oilly	Rich. Poynant	
Hascolt Musard	Theodoric the Goldsmith	
Hervey	Toli	
Ingelrann	Wadard	

Northampton

People		*Places*	
Adam	Lancelin	Asbi	Hasou
Ansketel	Mauger	Asce	Hecham
Azelin	Payne	Ascebi	Hisham/Isham
Bondi (pre-conquest)	Rotais	Asceli	Pascelle
Count Judith	Sasgar	Avelai	Pirie
David	Saswalo	Badebi	Wilebi
Dodin	Sibold	Bernac	
Durand	Simon d Pattishall	Brachelai	
Fulchere	Sweetman	Castre	
Gelder	Will. Peverel	Falelau	
Ivo		Hala	

Bedfordshire, Hertfordshire, Cambridge, Huntingdon: Also in central England are the counties of Bedford, Hertford, Cambridge and Huntingdon. Very few persons with E1b1b, G, and J1J2 haplogroups are found here and *prima facie* Jewish/Muslim landowners are sparse. In Bedford, however, we do turn up such names as William Lovett, Solomon the priest (!), Fitz Azor, Sigar de Chocques and Fitz Solomon listed as landholders or tenants. Several of these persons we have seen before and presume they are Jewish courtiers loyal to William. Town names suggesting Muslim/Jewish culture are not numerous but do include Dena, Golden-tone and Hagenes. Similarly, Hertford landowners seemingly Jewish include Adam (who was subtenant in several honors), Payne, Asgar, Lovett and Sigar de Chocques. Jewish/Muslim place names include Almeshou, Chaissou, Hailet, Parva Hadam, and Sele. In Cambridge, we find only Algar (Algeria), Judicael (a Breton discussed above in Yorkshire), Payne and Sigar, together with a few others, but again we interpret these as representing William's desires to maintain a Jewish presence across England. Hebrew/Arabic town names are also limited but include Eli, Haneia and Oure ("gold"). Huntingdon county, which is quite small, seems to have very few Jewish/Islamic landowners—Lunen, Golde and her son Wulfric—and only one or two town names indicating such heritage, such as Pirie.

Bedfordshire

People		*Places*
Ansketel the priest	Pirot	Cochepol
Azelina	Richard Bassett	Dena
Bernard	Ritz Solomon	Goldentone
Countess Judith	Robert de Tosny	Hagenes
de Alneto	Serlo de Rots	
Fitz Azor	Sigar de Chocques	

People		*Places*
Solomon the priest	Will. Peverel	
Tovi the Priest	Will de Cairon	
Will. Lovett		

Hertfordshire

People		*Places*	
Adam	Ralph Baynard	Absa	Haslehangra
Amalgar	Sigar de Chocques	Almeshou	Lufenele
Ansketel	Wigot	Caldecota	Offelei (Offa)
Asgar		Chaissou	Parva Hadam
Eudo		Escepehala	Sele
Hu. De Beauchamp		Hadam	Wachelei
Lovett		Hailet	Wakchra
Payne		Hamelamestede	Wara

Cambridge

People	*Places*
Aelmar	Ely/Eli
Earl Algar (Alqusa?)	Fugelesmara
Judicael	Haneia
Maxwell Fry	Hatelai
Payne	Helle
Pirot	Horsei
Rob. de Tosny	Oure
Sigar	
Walter Gropius	

Huntington

People	*Places*
Eustace the sheriff	Chetelstan
Golde and her son Wulfric	Pirie
Lunes	
Rohais (woman)	

Berkshire, Surrey, Buckingham, Rutland: The last four Domesday counties to be discussed all lie in central England in areas where haplotypes E1b1b, G, and J1/J2 are very infrequent. Supporting our thesis, there seem to be few occurrences of identifiably Jewish/Muslim landholders or town names—although some thin representation does seem present and we do encounter the names of Jews whose holdings we have noted earlier in other counties. Within Berkshire, tenants include Alfsi, Simon Aleyn, William Lovett, Alfward the goldsmith and Theodoric the goldsmith. Town names include Fareli and Bagenore. Among Surrey's likely Jewish/Muslim property owners are Hamo the Sheriff, Salie's wife and Theodoric the Goldsmith. Place-names include Aissela, Hallega and Essira (Assyria, Syria). Buckingham was especially sparse, with Mainou le Breton and Payne as landowners and Cicelai (Sicily) as a town name. Finally, Rutland County, which is situated nearest to Lincoln, has Alfred the Jew of Lincoln as a Domesday landowner, and Richale as a possible Jewish/Islamic place-name.

Alfred was one of two Breton vassals of Count Alan, said to have commanded the left wing of Britons and west Normans in William's victorious army at Hastings. With his brother Brien, Alan served as a guarantor of the new domain under their lord, Ralph de Gael, earl of

Norfolk. Alfred the elder was a native of Rennes in the borderland between Brittany and Normandy, probably from the seigneury of Montfort-Gael, who held lands in Lincolnshire even before 1066 (Keats-Rohan 141–42). He married a daughter of William Malet, another important Breton and likely Jew or crypto–Jew of the same ilk, who died fighting the rebel Hereward the Wake in 1071 (46). Unlike his fellow Bretons and their English sympathizers, his son Alfred of Lincoln remained loyal to the king, despite his kinship ties with Saxons and Britons, and became "a wealthy man whose family was to rise steadily during the following decades" (47).

Berkshire

People	Places
Alfsi	Bagenore
Alfward the Goldsmith (King's thane)	Benneham
Askell	Farelli
Henry de Ferreos	Peise
Leofeva	
Ralph de Tosny	
Raph de Bagpuize	
Simon Aleyn	
Theodoric the Goldsmith	
Will. Lovett	

Surrey

People	Places
Ansgot the interpreter	Aissela
Ansketel de Rots	Essira
Hamo the sheriff	Hacheham
Kelel Hunter	Hallega
Reginald	Hameledone
Salie's wife	
Tesselin	
Theo. the goldsmith (from the King)	

Buckingham

People	Places
Baldwin	Cicelai
Ketel	
Mainou le Breton	
Payne	

Rutland

People	Places
Alfred of Lincoln	Hameldun
Count Judith	Riehale
Gilbert de Ghent	Tie
Gleu	
Godfrei de Cambrau	
Jocelyn	
Rob. Malet	
Robert de Tosny	

Domesday lists less than 3,000 landholders, of whom Keats-Rohan isolates and identifies 2,477 individuals, some pre–Norman magnates reconfirmed in their holdings, others new Norman or Breton tenants-in-chief or their retainers. What emerges from this analysis of Jewish and Islamic personal names, surnames and place-names is a strong picture of rapprochement between "William's Jews" and Breton and native English Jews throughout the reorganized kingdom of England. A new multinational aristocracy crystallizes, one that brings to the fore, for instance, the De Vere family, earls of Oxford,[11] who were originally from Nantais in Brittany, or the Taisson family,[12] coming from Anjou. The Fitz Geroie family combined Breton, Angevin and Manceau elements. The Giffards[13] and their followers the Malets[14] (a name meaning possibly "messenger") were from Poitou. Walter "the Burgundian" was a tenant of Gotshelm de Claville[15] in Devon.

The entire social fabric of the land was re–Judaized. This process was already occurring in the Norman state, in which "migration to Normandy was proving attractive to men even from regions traditionally hostile to Normandy, such as Anjou" (Keats-Rohan 8). The groundwork had been laid by the marriage of William Longsword's sister to William of Aquitaine, one among several dynastic moves that proved key. The Normans increasingly linked themselves to the Carolingians and their Machir[16] blood. The greatest Norman barons in post-conquest England were Robert of Mortain, Hugh of Avranches,[17] Roger of Montgomery,[18] William of Warenne[19] and Alan the Red,[20] all related to William the Conqueror, though of different origins. "Three-quarters of those named in Domesday in 1086," according to Keats-Rohan, "left descendants traceable in 1166." It was not a clean sweep or replacement policy, however, but one built on England's preexisting culture and government, much of that Jewish and Muslim in character.

7

The Jews in England 1066–1290

We are now going to embark on a critical look at the documentation regarding the known—and unknown—Jews of England during the period 1066–1290, that is, from the time of the Norman Conquest through the expulsion of the Jews by Edward I in 1290. We envisage presenting several unorthodox, even forbidden, arguments. In particular, we will pursue the thought that the influence of Judaism on Norman religion and culture is much more pronounced than previously supposed. There were in all likelihood many Judaizers among the clergy, the nobility and even within the royal household.

We begin by noting that when the Vikings invaded and occupied France in 960, they were thoroughly pagān. There is no record of William's father, Duke Robert, often called Robert the Devil, having been baptized. He died on his way to Jerusalem in 1035, leaving his young only son and heir to accede to the throne as duke of Normandy. There was less than one century of Christian religious practice among the Normans at the time of their invasion of England in 1066. No well-educated or active Christian clergy was established in Normandy to transfer to England. However, there were persons and communities actively practicing Islam and Judaism both in Normandy and Brittany, as well as in England and Wales.

William himself was not raised in a religious, royal household. The illegitimate son of a tanner's daughter who was very probably Jewish, as we have seen, he displayed no marked religious affiliation during his reign. His full sister is named *Judith* (Yehudith, "Jewess"), a name that is inexplicable if we are to believe she and her parents were Christian. With this background, let us now turn our scrutiny to some of the social and political events of the years between 1066 and 1290.

Henry of Huntingdon: History of the English People 1000–1154

We begin with a historical narrative by Henry of Huntingdon, a Norman archdeacon in Lincoln, who began writing his *History of the English People* between 1123 and 1130 and continued it up until his death in 1154. The prologue to this work is remarkable enough to deserve being quoted *in extenso*:

> But why do we linger among strangers? See how sacred history teaches the moral code, giving the attributes of justice to Abraham, fortitude to Moses, temperance to Jacob, and prudence to Joseph, and showing their opposites—injustice in Ahab, feebleness in Oziah, intemperateness in Manasseh, and imprudence in Roboam. Especially, O good God, what a shining example of humility, that holy Moses, having joined with his brother in offering sweet-smelling incense to God, his protector and avenger against all his enemies, flung himself into the midst of terrible danger, and shed tears for the slanderous Miriam, and always laboured in prayer for those who wished him ill! What a beacon of

clemency that David, wounded and enraged by Shimei, would not have him slaughtered when he was alone, hard-pressed and weak, and he, David, was strongly armed and attended by his retinue; and later, when he was restored victorious to his throne, he would not permit vengeance to be taken on Shimei.... With these considerations in mind, therefore, I have undertaken to narrate the history of this kingdom and the origins of our people.... But as we can begin nothing without making an appeal to God, let us commence by calling on Him: O Adonai, our creator, shepherd, and defender, source, quickener, and end of all things, we pray Thee to favour this work and guide it to its close.... For whatever kings or peoples plan to do, if it is accomplished, it is by Thy action ... from Whom and by Whom and in Whom alone, all things exist.

It is unusual in our opinion for an ostensibly Catholic clergyman—a full four hundred years prior to the Protestant Reformation—to be calling upon *Adonai*, the Hebrew name for God, and referencing the Torah as his narrative text, rather than asking the guidance of, say, Jesus or the Apostles, or inspiration of the Holy Spirit. What is more, we are told that Archdeacon Henry read Psalm 78 every day at services. This psalm was, and is, a central piece of *Jewish* worship services.

Psalm 78

My people hear my teaching; listen to the words of my mouth.

I will open my mouth in parables, I will utter hidden things, things from of old.

What we have heard and known, what our fathers have told us.

We will not hide them from our children; we will tell the next generation the praiseworthy deeds of the Lord, his power, and the wonders he has done.

He decreed statutes for Jacob and established the law in Israel, which he commanded our forefathers to teach their children.

So the next generation would know them, even the children yet to be born, and they in turn would tell their children.

Then they would put their trust in God and would not forget his deeds, but would keep his commandments.

They would not be like their forefathers—a stubborn and rebellious generation, whose hearts were not loyal to God, whose spirits were not faithful to Him.

The men of Ephraim, though armed with bows, were turned back on the day of battle;

They did not keep God's covenant and refused to live by His law.

They forgot what He had done, the wonders He had shown them.

He did miracles in the sight of their fathers in the land of Egypt, in the region of Zoan.

He divided the sea and led them through; He made the water stand firm like a wall.

He guided them with the cloud by day and with light from the fire all night.

He split the rocks in the desert and gave them water as abundant as the seas;

He brought streams out of a rocky crag and made water flow down like rivers....

But they continued to sin against him, rebelling in the desert against the Most High.

They willfully put God to the test by demanding the food they craved.

They spoke against God, saying, "Can God spread a table in the desert?

When he struck the rock, water gushed out, and streams flowed abundantly. But can he also give us food? Can he supply meat for his people?"

When the LORD heard them, he was very angry; his fire broke out against Jacob, and his wrath rose against Israel,

For they did not believe in God or trust in his deliverance.

Yet he gave a command to the skies above and opened the doors of the heavens;

He rained down manna for the people to eat, he gave them the grain of heaven.

Men ate the bread of angels; he sent them all the food they could eat.

He let loose the east wind from the heavens and led forth the south wind by his power.

He rained meat down on them like dust, flying birds like sand on the seashore.

He made them come down inside their camp, all around their tents.

They ate till they had more than enough, for he had given them what they craved.

But before they turned from the food they craved, even while it was still in their mouths,

God's anger rose against them; he put to death the sturdiest among them, cutting down the young men of Israel.

In spite of all this, they kept on sinning; in spite of his wonders, they did not believe.

So he ended their days in futility and their years in terror.

Whenever God slew them, they would seek him; they eagerly turned to him again.

They remembered that God was their Rock, that God Most High was their Redeemer.

But then they would flatter him with their mouths, lying to him with their tongues;

Their hearts were not loyal to him, they were not faithful to his covenant.

Yet he was merciful; he forgave their iniquities and did not destroy them. Time after time he restrained his anger and did not stir up his full wrath.

He remembered that they were but flesh, a passing breeze that does not return.

How often they rebelled against him in the desert and grieved him in the wasteland!

Again and again they put God to the test; they vexed the Holy One of Israel.

They did not remember his power—the day he redeemed them from the oppressor,

The day he displayed his miraculous signs in Egypt, his wonders in the region of Zoan.

He turned their rivers to blood; they could not drink from their streams.

He sent swarms of flies that devoured them, and frogs that devastated them.

He gave their crops to the grasshopper, their produce to the locust.

He destroyed their vines with hail and their sycamore-figs with sleet.

He gave over their cattle to the hail, their livestock to bolts of lightning.

He unleashed against them his hot anger, his wrath, indignation and hostility—a band of destroying angels.

He prepared a path for his anger; he did not spare them from death but gave them over to the plague.

He struck down all the firstborn of Egypt, the first fruits of manhood in the tents of Ham.

But he brought his people out like a flock; he led them like sheep through the desert.

He guided them safely, so they were unafraid; but the sea engulfed their enemies.

Thus he brought them to the border of his holy land, to the hill country his right hand had taken.

He drove out nations before them and allotted their lands to them as an inheritance; he settled the tribes of Israel in their homes.

But they put God to the test and rebelled against the Most High; they did not keep his statutes.

Like their fathers they were disloyal and faithless, as unreliable as a faulty bow.

They angered him with their high places; they aroused his jealousy with their idols.

When God heard them, he was very angry; he rejected Israel completely.

He abandoned the tabernacle of Shiloh, the tent he had set up among men.

He sent the ark of his might into captivity, his splendor into the hands of the enemy.

He gave his people over to the sword; he was very angry with his inheritance.

Fire consumed their young men, and their maidens had no wedding songs;

Their priests were put to the sword, and their widows could not weep.

Then the Lord awoke as from sleep, as a man wakes from the stupor of wine.

He beat back his enemies; he put them to everlasting shame.

Then he rejected the tents of Joseph, he did not choose the tribe of Ephraim;

But he chose the tribe of Judah, Mount Zion, which he loved.

He built his sanctuary like the heights, like the earth that he established forever.

He chose David his servant and took him from the sheep pens;

From tending the sheep, he brought him to be the shepherd of his people Jacob, of Israel his inheritance.

And David shepherded them with integrity of heart; with skillful hands he led them.

As readers have no doubt gathered, this psalm is a detailed recitation of the history of the Jewish people, Israel. We propose that Henry and his family were to some degree crypto–

Jewish, having converted in the recent past to Christianity, or perhaps an intermediary form of it.

Bishop Alexander, at whose request the *History* was written, bears a Greek name popular among Jews, not a Christian saint's name, and his brother is named David. Bishop Alexander too was likely of Jewish ancestry. Also known as Alexander of Blois, lord of Banesbury or Bambury, and nicknamed "the Magnificent" for his luxurious lifestyle, he was related to the greatest statesmen of the time: Roger of Salisbury (his uncle), Nigel bishop of Ely (either a half-brother or cousin) and Richard fitzNeal, who succeeded his father as treasurer of the kingdom and bishop of Lincoln. Huntingdon calls Bishop Alexander "the second prince of the land after the King." Alexander's parents were Humphrey and Ada. When he died in 1148, he left Lincoln Cathedral his large library.

A Jewish Pope

To find Jews in ecclesiastical circles during this period we need look no further than the Vatican. According to the papacy's modern-day chronicler Eamon Duffy, one pope came from the ranks of the wealthy Roman Pierleoni family, "recently converted from Judaism." The German reforming pope Gregory VII (Hildebrand) struck a deal with the Pierleonis in the late eleventh century (he reigned 1073–1085).[1] Two generations later, Pietro Pierleoni, who had been born Jewish, circumcised and reared in their stronghold across the river from Rome in the Jewish quarter of Trastevere, with the powerful backing of the family, and now intermarried with the Normans of southern Italy, was elected Pope Anacletus II. He reigned 1130–38. Pietro had been sent to school at Cluny, the Benedictine monastery founded by William of Aquitaine, an heir of Machir. His great-grandfather was Baruch Judaeus.[2] In the fashion of America's Church of Jesus Christ of Latter-Day Saints, the Vatican retroactively baptized Pietro's ancestor to the year 988. Yet the Jewish pope's election caused a firestorm of anti–Semitism in its day.

Henry's Milieu

The facts concerning Henry of Huntingdon's origins are meager, but revealing. He was born between 1080 and 1085 in Huntingdon, now part of Cambridgeshire, two out-of-the-way counties registering intriguing levels of Jewish and Middle Eastern influence in Domesday, as we saw. He studied at Ramsey Abbey, a tenth-century foundation with even more ancient roots under the suzerainty of the Lords of Ramsey, major landholders in Lincolnshire and Cambridgeshire. Henry came into the honors and fees of his father Nicolas in Huntingdon and Hertfordshire. Clergymen, particularly in the British Isles at this time, routinely married, had families and passed down titles and possessions. Henry's father took him as a boy to be brought up by Robert Bloet, bishop of Lincoln, King William II's chancellor. Robert's successor, Alexander, became the literary patron of Henry, as well as of Geoffrey of Monmouth.

Although he was a French-speaking member of the Norman elite, Henry knew the English language, for he translated parts of the Anglo-Saxon Chronicle into Latin. He also used Bede, Caesar, Nennius (an omnibus collection that reworked several versions of a *Historia Brittonum* and an even earlier compilation by the Welshman Run map Urbgen),[3] Eutropius, Aurelius Victor, the rare *Historia Miscella* and most importantly, Geoffrey of Monmouth. Henry read the latter's monumental, trend-setting *History of the Kings of Britain* in draft at the monastery of

Bec. Both he and Geoffrey had mutual friends in Abbot Theobald and the learned monk Robert de Torigni.[4] All these figures were satellites spinning around the literary sun of one of the age's greatest patrons, Robert Fitzroy, earl of Gloucester, about whom we will have more to say later.

The first six books of Henry's *Historia Anglorum* are based on secondary sources, the last two on eyewitness accounts or his own observations. These take events down to the reign of Henry II in about 1155, when the chronicler died.[5] Henry also wrote eight books of epigrams, eight books of love poetry, eight books on herbs and a book of advice or mirror for princes. At Ramsey, he was a pupil of the polymath Albinus of Angers, a product of the top-flight humanistic program introduced from France by the Benedictine scholar Abbo (a Hebrew and Arabic male name) of Fleury (St.-Benoit-sur-Loire, near Orleans). Many of these cultural ties can be traced to Anjou, the cradle of the Plantagenets, who ruled England after the Normans. The first Angevin king was Henry II, the heir of the Empress Matilda and Count Geoffrey of Anjou, and Henry's queen consort was Eleanor of Aquitaine. We have encountered Anjou in a previous chapter as the province that attempted to wrest Alençon away from the young William, duke of Normandy. It was a major seat of French Jewry, whose counts carried forward the Makhiric royal line in France.

Ramsey Abbey was known as "Ramsey the Rich." Although it is not mentioned specifically by name in Domesday, it was one of the most venerable ecclesiastical institutions in Anglo-Saxon England. Its holdings of over 40,000 acres have to be reconstructed from an archaic tangle of fees and benefices where they are assigned to St. Benedict or St. Mary's and All Virgins, titles of the abbey. Its possessions stretched from Lincoln and Ely to Cambridge and London. Ramsey also had valuable fisheries and 32 burgesses in Huntingdon.[6] Its abbot had a seat in Parliament, ranking third among the prelates of the realm after Glastonbury and St. Alban's. It is one of the oldest of English monasteries, if not *the* oldest.[7] Ramsey's library was the largest in Britain. Astonishingly, it was the home of many Hebrew books.

Christian Hebraism and Conversos

The Ramsey Psalter, a masterpiece of medieval English manuscript illumination, was executed for an abbot of Ramsey in the fourteenth century. The psalter was probably presented to John of Sawtry who was abbot from 1285 to 1316, by his wine steward (cellarer) William of Grafham between 1303 and 1310. Because of its unusual illustrations, it has been singled out as a rare unique vestige of "Christian Hebraism" in England. Gothic manuscript expert Lucy Freeman Sandler devotes several learned articles to its "perplexing departures from contemporary formulas of psalm illustration."[8] She draws particular attention to the "unique sequence of miniatures referring specifically to the history of Ramsey Abbey," which she qualifies as rare literal illustrations based on Jewish rather than prevailing Christian Bible study, and to the "radical" historiation of Psalm 98 ("Sing unto the Lord a new song") featuring the Judean prophet Habakkuk, "expounded pictorially in terms of the history of the Jews during their days of Babylonian captivity," as well as other mysteries traced to the same milieu. The maker of the Ramsey Psalter, she writes, shared the evident belief, completely unorthodox in Christian circles, that it was Moses who wrote Psalm 90.

The Ramsey Psalter's treatment of conventional subjects is so extraordinary that Sandler wonders "what prompted the Ramsey artist or his adviser to a historical rather than a Christological interpretation" (128). Disturbed, she can find no answer. Nor can she cite any parallel for why in the Psalm of the King-Priest (old number Psalms 109, now 110) with the verse "The Lord above said to my lord, 'Sit at My right hand while I make your enemies your footstool,'" occurs the peculiar "artist understood the second lord, not as Christ, but as King David" (131). He was obviously "acquainted with the Hebrew interpretation" (132). Every other biblical commentary of the Christian Middle Ages adopts an allegorized pictorial program involving the Trinity in this context. One authority in the fourteenth century, Nicolas Trivet, specifically rejects the Ramsey Psalter's emphatic historicized interpretation of this Psalm as "Jewish nonsense" (132). Of course, we think it not nonsense but *avoteynu*, the practice of honoring "our forefathers."

Eliminating mainstream psalm illustrations and the rare crossover Tal-

God speaks to David in the Ramsey Psalter and promises him he will "become a priest forever, a rightful king by My decree" (Psalms 110:4) (Austria, Sankt Paul im Lavanttal (Kärnten), Stiftsbibliothek, Cod. S. Pauli in Carinthia 58/1 [HMML Pr. No 12,667]).

mudic or Tosafist scholars occasionally consulted by Catholic translators and exegetes (*litteratores Hebreorum* or Jews), Sandler, with "documentary backing," attributes the Ramsey Psalter's "daringly Hebraic" position in medieval English history to a small cell of Christian Hebraists in Huntingdon (133). Like others, she remarks on a Ramsey Abbey catalogue in the mid–fourteenth century that lists "sixteen or seventeen Hebrew books, including two Bibles, a psalter, glosses on the Bible and a Hebrew grammar" (133). According to a statement by the sixteenth-century antiquary John Leland, when the synagogues of Huntingdon and Stamford near Ramsey Abbey were destroyed at the time of the expulsion of the Jews from England in 1290, Prior Gregory of Huntingdon obtained money from the abbey to buy their books at auction and "very joyful home he returned" (133).

Gregory was also a Greek scholar, and has a Greek name. But there is a bit of a sticky widget here. He is believed to have lived around 1255, long before the expulsion of the Jews by Edward I in 1290. It is unlikely he alone was "the originator of the unique programme of illustrations in the Ramsey Psalter," completed fifty years after him (134). We may take Gregory together with Henry of Huntingdon as examples of Englishmen of Jewish religion *and* ancestry who spanned several centuries and moved increasingly toward what we would now call, in hindsight, crypto–Judaism. They were medieval English Jews.[9]

If correct, we must now venture the question of how and why would persons whose recent ancestors were Jews be found as clergy in the English Catholic Church. The readiest answer that comes to mind might be forced conversion. But to arrive at a more nuanced answer we will need to take the reader through the 300-year period of "official" Jewish residence in Britain.

Names in the Sources

We begin by listing the name of every English Jew whose existence is vouched for by written records during that time period (Appendix B: Post-Conquest and Angevin Jews).[10] This listing names a total of 72 Jewish women across the three centuries and 453 Jewish men over that same time span. Yet the Royal Tally of Jewish residents in England at the time of the expulsion was more than 15,000, and this did not even include children under age 12.[11] The discrepancy between the figures 524 *documented* Jews (72 female and 453 male Jews) versus more than 15,000 *tallied* Jews proves that most English Jews were not comprehended in any official records. As there were no periodic censuses, most Jews—and Christians—simply went about their lives, were born, raised, grew up, married, worked, had children and died in virtual obscurity. Generally speaking, only landholders were the objects of record keeping anyway—perhaps less than five percent of the population. Only if an individual was in some way remarkable or notorious, filed a lawsuit, was hanged or murdered, offered personal offense or service to a king or noble did his or her name enter the written record. This means that the *vast majority* of England's Jewish residents over those three key centuries lived in quiet and peaceful anonymity.

If they chose to convert to Christianity—whether sincerely or insincerely, by some *via media* or rationalization—probably little public notice would have been taken or made of it. Conversions garnered attention only when they concerned *significant* figures in a community, for example a priest who embraced Judaism and was killed for it, a wealthy Jewish financier who was baptized, or the child of a prominent Jew who chose to become a Christian. In some cases, Jews in the service of the king converted to Christianity and these cases were documented; in other instances, Jews converted and became prominent Christian clergy, and these too were duly recorded. But the overwhelming number of conversion events would have occurred *sub rosa*. The *conversos* simply blended into the town or village or parish's Christian community without becoming conspicuous. The story is the much the same in medieval Spain and France. Jewish sources do not emphasize "apostasy," as it is usually termed, but one authority states that fifty years after the first anti–Jewish violence in the Iberian Peninsula in 1390, "New Christians outnumbered those who continued to profess Judaism."[12]

Where Did They Go?

There is virtually no scholarly discussion of where the 15,000-plus Jewish residents of England went when they were ordered out of the country by Edward I in 1290. We submit, given the high E1b1b, G, and J1/J2 Y haplotype levels found on the Scottish borders and in Wales, that several thousand may have simply walked over the border and carried on their lives as before. Certainly the average Jewish family would have had no means to afford a ship to Calais, Rouen or New Rochelle. But the majority, we believe, simply *stayed in place*, declaring themselves to be Christian and forming a vast underground crypto–Jewish community. They were supported in part by their co-religionist kin who had converted in earlier years and were now part of the religious and political and economic infrastructure of England—the status quo. The elevated E1b1b, G, and J1/J2 haplotype levels in *exactly those places where pre–Expulsion communities are known to have dwelt* appears to be irrefutable testimony for their descendants' continued presence.

English society during this time would have supplied multiple economic opportunities as well as a fair degree of mobility for these converts. Nigel Saul, for example, comments on the pragmatic and secular nature of the Church: "Many of those provided with bishoprics in the fourteenth century were ambitious careerists. One of the most successful was William of Wykeham. Wykeham was essentially an administrator; after serving Edward III as clerk of the works at Windsor, he rose to be keeper of the privy seal and chancellor, and in 1367 he was rewarded with the see of Winchester."[13] Winchester, of course, had a large and persistent Jewish community. Such practical church appointments were a consistent policy of the English monarchs. According to Saul, "Once the process of [clerical] selection was taken over by the King, the way was open to the appointment of more political figures—of curia lists, civil servants and scions of the aristocracy. Rarely now were scholars or religious persons chosen as bishops.... By the 1360s, Edward III had an episcopate shaped largely in his image and amenable to his wishes."[14]

By 1300 the English economy was booming. Over five million gallons of wine were brought into the country annually from Gascony; hundreds of thousands of squirrel pelts were imported each year from the Baltic. Devon and Cornwall—two heavily Jewish areas—were mining and exporting 800,000 pounds of tin per year. The wool export trade—which had always been open to Jews—was equally profitable, reaching 40,000 sacks per year shortly after 1300. The silver penny coinage, often the work of Jewish moneyers, together with bills of credit and other instruments inspired by Muslim commercial ways, made such international transactions both easy and flexible.[15]

But even in the centuries prior to the Expulsion, there were many clerking and record keeping jobs in which Jews, typically both literate and mathematically competent, could serve. The royal mints, especially at Winchester, employed a number of moneyers and assayists to strike and test the coinage. Sheriffs were needed in each shire to collect the taxes and provide accounting services to the King. The king's court, the Curia Regis, also required literate record keepers.[16] Several of the Jews noted in records in commercial centers during the Angevin period were called *chirographs*, "pensmen."

By 1191, London had developed the position of mayor, a political and economic position that required managing the conduct of commerce within the city. This innovation soon spread to other English towns. Mayors were assisted by a coterie of aldermen; concurrently, craftspeople and tradesmen began forming guilds to organize their work and prevent competition.[17] While persons who were overtly Jewish would have been legally barred from such positions, those who were avowedly Christian and private Judaizers would not. An exact analog to this pattern can be found in post–1390 and post–1492 Spain, when *conversos* were freely admitted to the highest ranks of commerce and governance, including even the royal household.

It is important to keep in mind that there was *not* marked anti–Semitism in either France or England prior to the First Crusade in 1089. Large-scale anti–Semitic violence against Jews in England began only with the coronation of Richard I in 1190. In France, for example, we find Elias de la Fleche, a converted Jew, serving as count of Maine from 1092 to 1110. Elias' daughter, Erembourg, married the heir of Anjou province, Fulk IV, king of Jerusalem. The English King Henry I's physician was Petrus Alfonsi, a converted Sephardic Jew, as we have already noticed. Apparently, moreover, restrictions on Jewish occupations were not enforced with great stringency. Bartlett reports that a miller surnamed Gamel (a Hebrew or Arabic name meaning "camel") who lived near Oxford, was arrested for stealing "turves" (pieces of turf) from the manor of Culham, although milling was an occupation ostensibly closed to Jews, being part of the food production chain.[18]

We also find a Ralph (Rafael) Luffa serving as Bishop of Chichester from 1091 to 1123, and a Simon in that same position from 1204 to 1207. In 1201 Judhael de Mohun was the court justice in Somerset.[19] In southern Gloucestershire in 1191 there was a Symonds Hall.[20] Simon de Senlis (d. 1153), the earl of Huntingdon, was also likely Jewish. Importantly, this man was the resident earl when Henry of Huntingdon wrote his *History*, from which we quoted at the outset of this chapter. This area of England was probably one in which many secret Jews lived and practiced their religion in private with the tacit support of both the church and nobility in the region, both of which included *converso* Jews.

Between 1130 and 1160, the major commercial families in London include "the Dornhills, Blunds and Bucuintes (an Italian surname which translates as 'oily mouth') who each provided at least three sheriffs at London during this period [and] were not only money-lenders, landlords and sometimes aldermen within the city, but also officials of the royal household and lords of manors."[21] The Blund family was *known* to be Jewish.[22]

In 1215 London's mayor was Serlo the Mercer, according to Bartlett (344). Serlo is a Spanish or Occitan Jewish given name. Further, Bartlett—although stating that Jews were primarily involved in moneylending—acknowledges that they are documented during this time period engaging in several other trades, "selling wine, acting as doctors, serving as crossbowmen" (349). Bartlett goes on to remark on the literacy of the population that "the ability to write was relatively widespread among the Jewish population and French, Latin and Hebrew were all acceptable for drafting documents" (351). Jews owned land, manors, rental houses and collateral, such as corn, wool, silver, gold, lead, tin and coin.

Concurrently with this time period in England, the Jews of France flourished economically and intellectually. Norman Golb, for example, writes:

> It is not difficult to understand why a [Jewish] central school of higher learning was required in Normandy. In addition to Biblical study and ritual worship, the practice of Judaism necessitated, as a *sine qua non*, adherence to rabbinical law as expounded in the Mishnah and developed in the Talmudic corpus.... This gave rise to the necessity of schools of learning throughout the occidental diaspora ...
>
> Within this context, scholars of northern France developed a particular renown for their genius in the study and interpretation of the rabbinical law directly from the Talmudic sources. It was through the instrument of the Talmudic school that the study of Jewish law was developed and carried forward in France.... Available evidence indicates that large schools in the north ... were concentrated in the main cities, such as Reims, Troyes, Paris, and Rouen, which at the same time were the principal centers of Jewish life.[23]

Golb further states (147):

> It has been estimated that before 1137, approximately 2,000 Jews lived in Narbonne, which for centuries had been the capital of the old Provincia Narbonensis and since Carolingian times was the seat of the Machir-descended Rex Judaeorum governing that province's Jewish communities. In London at the time of the expulsion of the Jews from England 1290, there were approximately 2,000 Jews over twelve years old, but Joseph Jacobs reminds us that London's Jewry was only a "daughter of Rouen's."

Crusades and Anti–Semitism

With arrival of the Crusades initially preached by the Picard or Norman Peter the Hermit and promoted by Pope Urban II in 1096 came an explosion of anti–Semitism. Anti–Semitism had been largely muted in both England and France up to this time. Now many people wondered why they should travel all the way to the Holy Land to slaughter infidels when the Jews defied them, the Christians, and were a reproach to God in their own backyards. Although popes, bishops and secular lords always deplored these attitudes, rabble-rousers began to call for Jews to either *be converted* or killed. Theologians continued to temporize on the Jewish question. In both the First and Second Crusade there were massacres of Jews, as well as *mass forced conversions*, in northern France and the Rhineland. Attacks occurred in England in 1189 and 1190 following the Third Crusade.

The most flagrant anti–Jewish outbreak in the eyes of both English and Jewish historians occurred at York. Here is Bartlett's account (359):

> The violence was at its most horrible in York. Here "neither fear of a most ferocious king, nor the force of law, nor reason, nor humanity" restrained a savage attack, led by a group of nobles who were deeply burdened by debts to the Jews. Joined by bands of crusaders, they began the assault by forcing their way into the house of the recently deceased Jewish moneylender Benedict killing everyone in it and then setting it on fire. Most of the York Jews, like their fellows in Stamford and Lincoln, now took refuge in the royal castle (Clifford's Tower).
>
> Meanwhile, attackers continued to plunder Jewish property. Any Jew found outside the castle was offered the *choice of baptism* or death. The castellan immediately sought the help of the sheriff of Yorkshire, who arrived with a band of local knights and ordered an attack on the castle. A huge force of Christians now assembled outside the castle—artisans and apprentices from York, knights and others from the surrounding countryside, many clerics, including a rabid hermit dressed in white, "who strove to convince the others that they were doing godly work." The sheriff was aghast at what he had stirred up, but "once spirits are aroused, neither reason nor authority has any weight to stop them."
>
> The Jews in the castle had neither sufficient food nor weapons to undertake an effective defense. They did what they could, hurling down stones on the attackers, one of which killed the fanatical hermit, but, as the Christians brought up siege machines, they realized that there was no hope. One of their leaders, a learned Jew from overseas (possibly Rabbi Yomtob of Joigny), now addressed them: "God, whom you ought not ask 'Why do you do this?,' commands us now to die for His law.... So, since the creator now requires back the life that He gave us, let us render it to Him voluntarily with our own hands." Not every Jew was convinced by this appeal to the ancient Jewish tradition of self-martyrdom, but the majority preferred to die at the hands of their own family and fellows than to trust to the good intentions of the Christians. After setting fire to their property and to the castle itself the Jewish men slit the throats of their wives and children before undertaking their own suicide. Those who remained, now caught between the fire and the besiegers, promised to accept baptism: "receive us as brothers, who once were enemies, and let us live with you in peace and in the faith of Christ." One of the leaders of the Christian attackers, the indebted Yorkshire knight, Richard Malebisse, swore that they would not be harmed. As soon as they descended from the castle, they were all killed.
>
> Naturally, the royal government was incensed at the treatment the Jews of York had received. The sheriff and castellan were dismissed, while confiscation, fines and imprisonment were inflicted on those of the perpetrators who could be identified or apprehended. Under the shadow of royal protection, Jews returned to York. Within thirty years of the massacre, the Jewish community there was again one of the richest and most significant in England.

The full version of this narrative has been given because it captures details carried forward in virtually all accounts since its occurrence. Yet as Adler (131–133) observes, many details of it are *clearly false*. For example, the three sons of Jose—Aaron, Benedict and Samuel—were not killed. Adler writes, "Aaron became head of the York community and married Henna (Hannah), the daughter of Samuel Cohen, whose father Leo [was] a partner with Aaron in many of his financial transactions" (131). Aaron and Henna lived in Jose's house, which was rebuilt after the attacks.

Adler further states that by 1204—fourteen years later—"Jews reestablished themselves in York.... Gentilia, Peitavin of Eye and Isaac the son of Moses successfully claimed debts owing to the deceased Jose and Benedict, Isaac Blund [recall this family being in London above] and Hoppecol.... Its former prosperity was restored by the year 1219, as in that year Aaron and Leo were appointed by the King ... and were among the twelve wealthiest Jews of the Kingdom" (133).

In France during the previous century (1096), the Jews of Rouen had been similarly attacked by Crusader mobs. While several were killed, many others accepted conversion.[24] At this same time, William Busac, the count of Soissons, was reputed to be a Judaizer. Crusaders were also said to have taken Jewish children during the Worms pogrom and sent them to Christian religious houses for conversion.[25] Mass forced conversions of Jews were recorded in Cologne, Speier, Mainz, Metz, Trier, Regensburg and Prague. However, many of these converts continued to practice Judaism in secret, much as would happen in Spain in both 1390 and 1492.

Ironically, the Crusades had positive results for Jews in England and France. The Norman Empire expanded from 1089 to 1150 to include large-scale settlements in Sicily, Malta and Palestine. During lulls in the fighting in the Holy Land (and these were both frequent and lengthy), the English and French established trade arrangements with the Muslims and Jews dwelling there, bringing back medical knowledge, and astronomical, philosophical and mathematical documents, in addition to spices, gold, jewels, silks, cotton muslins, artworks, embroidery and architectural motifs. As Rebecca Fraser observes:

> The social intercourse with the Arab world which the Crusades encouraged transformed western Christendom. In a great many respects the Arab culture was far in advance of the Christian. Western Europe benefited enormously from contact with scientific Arab medicine, which very slowly undermined the superstitious practices of the West. Arab science and mathematics introduced the zero and the decimal point, while the Arab use of spices showed the West how to preserve food. In European architecture the *ogee* or narrow twisting arch so characteristic of the thirteenth century was a direct transmission from Arab architecture.[26]

Reverse Influx of Jews and Arabs

As we have argued elsewhere, individuals and groups of Muslims and Jews emigrated from the Holy Land to England with the returning Crusaders.[27] For instance, Elias Ashmole's name was a corruption of Ishmael, one of the most familiar Hebrew names to Muslims. Many of his associates seem to have belonged to Ismaili Islam. Ismailism is a branch of Shia that traces its origins to Mohammed's lifetime. The Ismailis derive the origins of their creed directly from Mohammed and his descendants through his daughter Fatima tuz–Zahra. Among the earliest religious leaders of this form of Islam were Ali, Mohammed's cousin, and his two sons. Names associated with this branch of Islam—from its origins—include Uthman, Rashid, Muawiya, Hasan, Husayn and Yazid. In the Domesday chapters we encountered instances of these.

Who might some other of these Levantine Arabs or Jews in England be? The unnamed ones probably include the merchants who supplied "90 lbs of pepper, 28 lbs of cumin, half pound of galingale, 3 lbs of cinnamon, one pound of cloves, half a pound of nutmeg, 2 lbs of ginger, ... 1,450 lbs of almonds, 1,500 dates, five baskets of figs, 60 silk cloths from Spain" for a feast held by King John in 1211—all of these items coming from areas under Muslim control.[28] They also are likely to include the influential teachers of the arts and sciences Alexander

Neckam (1157–1215) and William Occam (1288–1348), who appear from nowhere in the 1200s and who had enormous impact on the cultural and intellectual life of England. Neckam and Occam bear Arabic and Hebrew surnames respectively—Nachuam and Acham.[29] Alexander Neckam's mother, Hodierna (Latin for "Today's Woman"), supposedly served as wet nurse to King Richard the Lion-Heart, whose mother was Eleanor of Aquitaine, so he would have grown up in the royal household. He was sent to school at St. Alban's. That he knew Hebrew rather intimately is shown by the introductory chapter to his work on the natural sciences, *De naturis rerum*, in which he discusses in detail the vocalization and use of Hebrew words in Genesis from the Torah.[30]

Adler (208) mentions four Jews living in various parts of England by the year 1223, all of whom were designated Le Turk (meaning from Turkey/Byzantium). These included Solomon Le Turk of Gloucester, Jacob Le Turk of London, Moses Le Turk of Exeter and Samuel Le Turk (whose place of residence is not given). There was even a Master Omer (a Sunni Islamic name)[31] who had a "chapel" in Canterbury in 1264.[32]

Documented Conversions

Although we propose that the vast majority of Jews converting to Christianity in England were undocumented, due to the social status of the converts (and also likely due to their desire not to have records made of their former religious affiliation), there are also several documented cases of public conversion. Adler (33) describes the following cases: "In 1234 a Canterbury Jew was baptized and took the name Augustine; in 1180 a Jewess became Christian and took the name Isabella; seven additional men (unnamed) converted in 1180; Samson of York converted in 1180. In 1232 several Jewish women entered the Domus Conversorum in London; a woman named Joietta became a Christian, as did a Jewish girl named Rose and a woman Guliana." On page 84, he notes that "a Jew named Isaac converted, but continued his financial dealings," which, in theory, should have been forbidden to Christians. Notable also is Adler's mention (152) of Elias Le Blund of London, who despite being Jewish was one of the City's foremost merchants, a sheriff and mayor. In Bristol, bordering the counties of Somerset and Gloucestershire with a large Jewish population, as we have discerned from their place-names, a school for converted Jews was opened in 1154, although no records exist of its attendees (183). In 1239 a Domus Conversorum was opened in London and attracted "a large number of converts" (282). Many of these converts entered church service.

One French Jew named Martin was ordained as a priest after his conversion. Even earlier, in 1096, a London Jew was baptized and became a monk at Westminster Abbey. In 1144 Theobald of Cambridge took holy orders, while two other converts, Warin and John, entered Oxford University. In 1247, ten men and seven women converts were allocated to abbeys and priories throughout England (288–289). Most were christened with new names after their sponsors, as was frequently the case years later in Spain. Yet, as in Spain, we must question the sincerity of these conversions, for most seem to be undertaken merely to obtain the social and legal privileges available to Christians. For example, when Nicholas and his wife Maud converted, he took up residence in London as a goldsmith and "continued his commercial relations with his Jewish friends" (293). Once the public conversion had been registered, the new Christian was free to continue his or her life as before, without the constraints of being Jewish. The result was a large number of privately Jewish persons now working in all areas—and at all levels—of the religious and economic spheres in English society.

Beginning of the Psalms in the Xanten Bible written by Joseph ben Kalonymus about the same time as the Ramsey Psalter, in 1294. According to legend, the monks of Ramsey under Oswald were the first to outfit service books with illuminated or historiated initials. One of the oldest surviving examples is Harley 2904, a psalter produced between 980 and 1000 now in the British Library. Its type of illumination became standard in English scriptoria, just as Eadwig Bassan's contemporaneous hand served the same function on the side of writing styles. Between painting and calligraphy the contributions of English Jews and ex–Jews were not unimportant in the history of the book (Spencer Collection, The New York Public Library, Astor, Lenox and Tilden Foundation).

Converts who entered the royal household were often markedly successful in their careers. For example, Roger le Convers (Roger the Convert) became the royal sergeant-at-arms. Much trusted by King Henry III, he paid no taxes on his London property, and he received an estate in Essex and many gifts. In 1260, Roger began assisting other Jewish converts in London to enter royal service. One of these, John Le Convers, also served as a royal sergeant-at-arms. Like the convert Henry of Winchester, he acted as paymaster to the army. Other prominent converts include Phillip the crossbowman, Nicholas le Convers, and Robert, who became jeweler to the queen. Another convert, Sir Adam de Chesterton, served as a king's justice, built a church in Cambridgeshire in 1268 and had business relations with Isaac Pennas, a Lincoln Jew. Notably, some of these converts were later accused of Judaizing, a charge that was also commonly made about the *conversos* of Spain in the 1500s (Adler 1936, 304).

The result of this socially motivated conversion to Christianity during the 1066–1290 period and beyond was a continuous infusion of private Jews into the royal administration and church. As a result, we have prominent churchmen such as Abbot Samson (1182–1210) of Bury St. Edmunds. Abbot Samson famously exhorted his delinquent monks, "I have nourished and brought up children and they have rebelled against me," an admonition taken from the book of Isaiah.[33] Simon of Sywell taught law at Oxford in the 1190s; Gerard, archbishop of York (1100–1108), owned and read a Hebrew psalter. We shall document in chapter 10 that the architect of the divorce between the English Church and Rome was himself a converted Jew who dwelled for a time in London's Domus Conversorum.

Beautiful Deaths

As a coda to this forgotten episode in English history, one might ask what Jewish authorities thought of the wholesale desertion of their ancient faith they witnessed around them on a constant basis. Studies of martyrdom in French and English Jewish tradition suggest that rabbis painted a purposefully drastic picture of these events. Shira Lander has reviewed the construct of martyrdom embedded in Jewish services such as the *Av Harachamim*, calling on God's mercy for the sake of those "who laid down their lives for the sanctification of the divine name," and prayers titled *Avinu Malkeinu* "for the sake of those who were killed for your holy name," as well as the Yizkor recitation of memorial prayers for the martyrs.[34] Lander concludes that all of these liturgical commemorations of martyrdom owe their roots to a period following the persecutions of the eleventh- and twelfth-century Crusades, a formative period for the development of Jewish martyrology. "It is clear that the role of martyrdom in Jewish traditions correlates directly to communities' contemporary experiences. In times when persecution is either imminently feared or experienced, martyrologies flourish. These generally appear first in narrative form and then subsequently are interpreted theologically through poems."

Susan Einbinder agrees, commenting that there is a gap of a millennium between the rabbinic martyrdom accounts and those produced in the wake of the Crusades, in other words, from the Hadrianic persecutions of the second century to the outbreak of new anti–Jewish activities in 1096.[35] In this context, new material was created from the experiences of the first Crusader persecutions. Einbinder proves that the new vernacular narrative tools employed elsewhere by troubadours and secular poets were trained on the pressures of conversion because apostasy loomed so seductive in Crusades-era France and England. "In this social climate, martyrology re-emerged as a medium for competition with Christianity, and the experience of actual Jewish persecution served as a trump card against the vast and powerful network of Christian martyrologies, *menologia*, *martyria* (pilgrimage martyr shrines), and martyr-intercessors."[36]

> The poems of the twelfth century portray the victims of the marauding and murderous Crusaders as pure, unblemished sacrifices offered to God. One poem even likens a father to a ritual butcher, "making the ritual blessing to sanctify the slaughter." Another relies on the powerful image of the sacrifice of Isaac to convey both steadfast faith and voluntary death. Whether murdered or suicides, victims all enact *kiddush hashem*, the sanctification of God's name.[37]

The trope of sacrifice was carried to ever new heights, so that when the Talmud was burned in Paris in 1242, poems described this event as a martyrdom of Torah itself. It was the murder of the very soul of the Jewish people.

French Jewish compositions about martyrdom served as a bulwark to stem the tide of conversion of a youthful, scholarly elite to Christianity as well as to enhance the prestige of the rabbinic elite defining it. The constructors of this genre were unwilling to acknowledge lapsed Jews as true Jews, reserving the highest status under halakhic law for Jews who died rather than submit to forced conversion. How many persons actually chose martyrdom in real life as opposed to the numbers of heroes in popular literature who meet death with the Shema on their lips is debatable. What regrets the "ex–Jews" experienced one can but speculate. History does not record any dramatic returns to Judaism. The doors were closed not only by the Christians but the Jews themselves.

In ending, we return to the point at which we began this chapter, with allusions to the Hebrew Bible and key events of Jewish history. We quote a portion of the coronation prayer recited for English monarchs from 1075 to 1225 (Bartlett 126).

> Almighty and Eternal God, creator of everything, ruler of angels and King of Kings, who made Abraham, your faithful servant, triumph over his enemies, who brought many victories to Moses and Joshua ... who raised David, your serving boy, to the height of the Kingdom, and who endowed Solomon with wisdom and the ineffable gift of peace, heed our humble prayers, we beseech thee. Multiply the gift of your blessings on this your servant, whom we in obedient devotion have chosen as king, and surround him always and everywhere with the power of your right hand.

In the next chapter we will take "A Necessary Excursion to Wales" to see how England's immediate neighbor dealt with the changing face of Judaism.

8

A Necessary Excursion to Wales

Walter Map, one of the towering literary figures of the Latin Middle Ages, received his unusual surname as a boy entering school in England. Born near Herefordshire on the Welsh Marches in 1140, the backward lad went on to become a professor in Paris and celebrated author of witty, rambling memoirs (*De nugis curialium*, The Trifles of Courtiers). His fellow pupils applied to him the derisive epithet of the day for the Welsh, whose language no Englishman, then as now, could understand, including their resounding, double-barreled names. There is a proverb: "As long as a Welshman's pedigree." The Welsh word for "son" is *map* (shortened to *ap, ab* or *p/b*), cognate with Scottish *mac*, used in the same way to designate parentage and ancestry in a patronymic system. We are informed that "a Welshman, as a sign of his free status, would know the names of his male ancestors for several generations, perhaps six or seven, each generation divided by ap."[1] Walter accepted the name in good fun (his schoolmaster was Gerard the Maiden), and even transferred it to the name of the property Mapesbury with which he was rewarded in later life, now a posh London suburb in NW2.

Walter's countryman Giraldus de Barri, born in Pembrokeshire 1147, was dubbed "the Wildman" (*Silvester*), because he came from the uncouth fastnesses of Cambria, a region that was beyond the pale of civilization in the eyes of the Normans. He is known to posterity as Gerald of Wales, author of early topographical descriptions of England, Wales and Ireland.[2]

But the greatest figure swept to center stage by the awakening Anglo-Norman interest in things Welsh was unquestionably Gruffud ap Arthur, better known as Geoffrey of Monmouth, one of the major writers of British historiography and the inventor of Arthurian literature (about 1100–1155). We have encountered him already as a literary friend of Henry of Huntingdon in the splendid retinue gathered around Alexander of Lincoln (chapter 7). Huntingdon read drafts of Geoffrey's monumental *History of the Kings of Britain* as it was being written between 1136 and 1139.[3] In a dedicatory letter to Alexander, their common patron, Geoffrey even hinted that rumor of some borrowings had reached his ears and he hoped he would be given proper credit for all his Welsh material. He wasn't, but the whole world now reads Geoffrey's, not Henry's, account of English history. Thanks to this crypto–Jewish clerical circle in twelfth-century England, British history was "Welshified" and to some extent also Hebraized.

So let us now explore these cultural currents swirling around the Normans and Bretons pulling along their strange neighbors and go on a long-overdue excursion westward. Wales comprises the central western bulge of Great Britain adjacent to the English counties of Gloucestershire, Herefordshire, Shropshire and Cheshire, between Cornwall, Somerset and Devon on the south and Lancashire and Cumberland on the north. Much of the so-called marches or borderlands separating Wales and England, as well as the southwestern counties stretching as far as Land's End in Cornwall, together with an Old North reaching as far as Strathclyde in Scotland, belonged, of old, to Wales. As with Scotland, historians have stressed

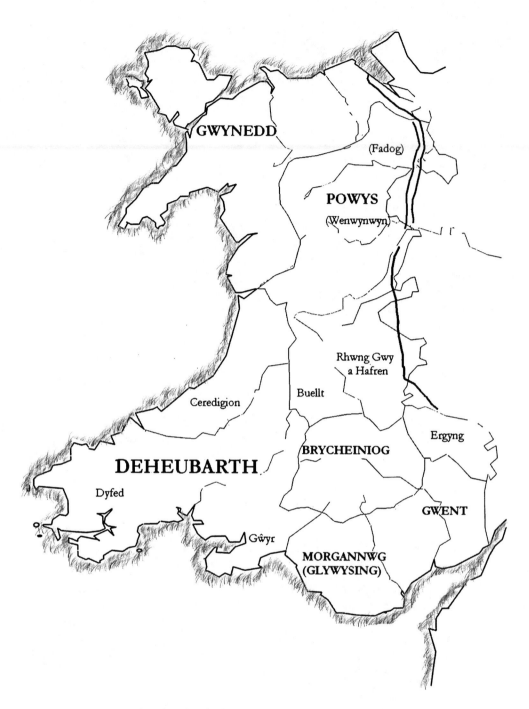

Map of Medieval Wales (gray lines represent rivers) (Wikimedia).

its Celtic and Gaelic culture and ancestry. But just as with its northern neighbor, we intend to puncture this widely accepted myth. In fact, Wales is dotted with locations exhibiting high levels of E1b1b, G, G2, J1 and J2 DNA, and has corresponding place-names and "saints" (holy men) indicating an important substratum of both Jewish and Muslim ancestry beneath its Celtic veneer. This new thesis simply bears out what study after study of human populations demonstrates: It is dangerous to write a people's history based solely on cultural inferences.

Relying on linguistic clues alone, we would have to assume that Haitians originated in France and that Greenlanders all came from Denmark. The French, moreover, would all become descendants of the Romans.

Even more so than in the case of Scotland, Wales has little history in the sense of what has been written down, or what records have been kept of events, places and personages. In fact, it has hardly any written monuments at all until around 1300 CE, a timeframe which corresponds closely to the Jewish expulsion from England. Historical sources continue to be scanty for the period extending from 1300 to 1530, the date when Henry VIII took the throne and when, as we shall document, many more Jews found their way to England (chapter 9).

When the Saints Came Marching In

Let us begin our survey of Wales by taking a look at the local and national saints (holy men and women) recognized in Welsh religious lore. Despite the fact that very few ancient Christian religious objects, writings, or carvings are to be found in Wales, the Welsh have a time-honored list of saints greatly outstripping that of neighboring England. We propose that early Wales did have religion—it was just not the Christian religion. A list culled from various sources presents the Welsh saints with their relative dates who we suggest were possibly Jewish or Muslim. As can be seen from their names, these are all of Arabic, Berber, Hebrew, Egyptian and Spanish origin.

Welsh Saints

Afan (cousin of St. David)	(500s)
Aneirin	(600s)
Armael (Hebrew)	(500s)
Asaf (Arabic)	(600s)
Bueno (Good, Spanish)	(700s)
Cadoc (Arabic)	(500s)
Cadwaladr (Arabic)	(600s)
Dewi/David/Dafyd (patron saint of Wales)	(500s)
Dogmael (Hebrew)	(500s)
Eilian (Aemilianus)	(500s)
El Lyw (Arabic)	(500s)
Elvis	(500s)
Gildas (Romano-Berber)	(d. 570)
Ishmael (Muslim/Egyptian)	(600s)
Kea (Gaius)	(400s)
Libio ("man from Libya")	(500s)
Lionio (Leon/Lion)	(500s)
Manaccus ("from Man")	(500s)
Odeceus (Odysseus, Greek)	(600s)
Perran (the patron saint of tin miners)	(400s)
Ruan (Ru)	(500s)
Samson (Hebrew)	(500s)
Sulien (cousin of Saint David, Berber)	(500s)

We have already witnessed in chapter 2 how a great settlement of North Africans came to Wales and joined forces with the Romano-Cambrians to repel the Saxons in the fifth and sixth centuries. They included apparently the first Sephardic Jews in Britain. Some of the Roman names in Wales' prehistory, like Gildas, clearly belong to a transitional period in North

Africa's history when it was seized by the Vandals and reconquered by the Byzantines. The father of Gildas in Pictish regnal lists is Caw or Cauus, a form of Gaius.[4] He seems to have spawned the figure of Kay, the close companion of Arthur in Welsh legend.[5] Eilian appears to be a Welsh saint's name with a similar background and time of origin.[6]

Others in this list of saints have unambiguous Arabic names and seem to relate to the period when North Africa was under Moorish or Arab rule. Asaf is a common Arabic name meaning "eminent."[7] El Lyw is strict Arabic for the Lion (or Warrior, Fighter).[8] Cadoc comes from Qaid, "commander," and it is noteworthy that he is called "an abbot who was said to be king," was descended from a Roman, Maximus, and was son of Gwynd Lyw (White Lion).[9] Arthur's son in legend was Amr ("an old Arabic name"),[10] and his sister was named Anna (Hannah, Jewish).[11] Ruan seems modeled on Ru, the mythological king.[12] Cadwaladr is also Arabic, and more specifically North African; he was king of Gwynedd in the seventh century, as well as being remembered as a holy man.[13] Afan, the cousin of the saint David, is the well-attested name Affan from the Quraish tribe of Mecca, a founding dynasty of Islam: An Affan was father of the celebrated Sunni caliph Uthman (d. 656). The name means "modest."[14]

To the list of Arabic names entering Britain in the sixth and seventh centuries we may also perhaps add Taliesin and Aneurin, the two court poets or bards whose compositions figure among the oldest preserved in the Four Ancient Books of Wales. Taliesin (or, as it is often spelled in English literature, Talliesin) is supposed to mean "radiant brow" but cannot be analyzed into Celtic language word-elements. It seems instead to be a corruption of an Arabic name, of which there are many beginning with Tal-, "appearance, countenance."[15] The name of Taliesin's adoptive father Elffin ap Gwyddno (Elvin son of the Goth) may be a clue to the events overtaking the kingdom of Cardigan after the barbarian wanderings and cataclysms of the mid-sixth century. Elffin's name cannot be explained in Old or Middle Welsh. As for Aneurin, no Celtic etymology can be offered for this poet's name either. It seems to be a corruption of Noori, "luminous," an epithet of Allah.[16] It also is remarkable that Taliesin, Aneurin and the other early Welsh bards do not address the God of Christianity, Jesus, Mary or the other "regular" saints, such as we may find them in other early medieval poetry, but rather only their own holy men, occasionally also an unnamed "Most High." In a song titled "The Praise of Lludd" in The Great Book of Taliesin (52), the bard raises the battle hue of the Britons, promising a bloody fight and prophesying, "There will be an adventuring of Everyone to Adonai."[17] Taliesin, notoriously, makes fun of monks.[18]

It is also worth noting at this early point that there were kingdoms within Wales named David/Dyfed and El Fael (Arabic, "The Land").[19] We propose that these "saints" were not martyrs or missionaries in the usual sense but Berber and Arabic-affiliated leaders spreading the gospels of Judaism and Islam to the inhabitants of western Britain.

Little knowledge has been disseminated about the Berber people, not least because their language has never been a literary or historical one. Since the first century of Islam, it has stood in the shadow of Arabic. Michael Brett and Elizabeth Fentriss, the authors of a book on their culture, describe the cult of the dead as one of the distinguishing characteristics of the Berbers in antiquity.[20] The Roman geographer Pomponius Mela reported that the Augelae (modern Awjila in Libya) considered the spirits of their ancestors to be gods, swearing by them and consulting them. After making requests, they slept in their tombs to await responses in dreams. Herodotus in the fifth century BC noted the same practice among the Nasamones, who inhabited the deserts around Siwa and Augila. He wrote:

> In the matter of oaths, their practice is to swear by those of their countrymen who had the best reputation for integrity and valour, laying their hands upon their tombs; and for the purposes of div-

ination they go to sleep, after praying, on the graves of their forebears, and take as significant any dream they may have.[21]

These practices continue among the Welsh and Irish; a thousand examples could be adduced from folklore and Arthurian legend. Welsh *cyfarwyddiaid* and *penceirddiad* (professional entertainers and chief poets) were expected to know about the graves and magical properties of Arthur, his son Amr, his brother Madog, Gawain, Bedever, Kay and all the kings of legend.[22] The tomb of Amr, Arthur's son, whom he slew and buried himself, was a tumulus called Llygad Amr located near the spring where the river Gamber arises in Herefordshire. It was said to be sometimes six feet long, sometimes twelve.[23]

Among the modern Berbers the cult of wandering or cell-bound holy men (*marabouts*) persists in the form of Maraboutism, widespread in northwest Africa, especially in Morocco. In bardic tradition such as the tales called the Mabinogion, there are said to be three saintly lineages in Welsh history, those of David and Caw being two of them. The Welsh took their saints with them to Brittany, and it has been pointed out that a large proportion of the place-names in both countries consists of two elements, one denoting a settlement (*trev-* or *lann-*, for instance), the other the name of one of the early saints.[24] The Berbers worshipped their kings, too, the first of whom was Battus, a word that means "king" or "pharaoh" in the Libyan language.

What Is *Known About Welsh History?*

If one goes to Google or Amazon or the New York Public Library and searches for Welsh history books, one is chagrined to discover a rather small set. In fact, only *one* history of Wales is widely accepted by scholars; it is *A History of Wales* (1993) by John Davies.[25] We will work our way through Davies' *History* now, pointing out the signs which confirm an Islamic and Judaic presence in the country from Roman times forward.

Davies (29) reports that "there were at least 13 [military] campaigns in Wales and its borders between 48 CE and 79 CE" conducted by the Roman army. Legionary fortresses, capable of holding 5,300 soldiers, were built at Deva (Chester) and Isca (on the river Usk, modern-day Caerleon, a word that means "City of the Legion"). The bounds of Roman control incorporated a large area lying between Chester, Caerleon, Carmarthen and Caernarfon. Yet Davies (31) comments that after 170 CE, "the only forts that provide unmistakable evidence of the presence of *soldiers* are those of Caernarfon, Caerhun, Caerows, Castell Collen, and Forden." The soldiers manning these forts were not from Rome, but rather recruits and mercenaries from conquered territories in the Rhineland and Danube regions. Thus, the soldiers likely were not the source of the E1b1b, G, G2, J1 and J2 haplotypes now found in Wales, as Appendix A makes clear.

Caerleon, the headquarters of the Second Augustan Legion—the Legio II Augusta—was established on the frontier of Britannia by Julius Frontinus in 74 or 75 CE to subjugate the Silures. Of mixed origins empire-wide, the Legio II Augusta had been summoned from Strasbourg on the Rhine frontier to form part of the original expeditionary force under Vespasian that reduced most of southwest Britain, remaining in Exeter until brought forward to Caerleon. However, with the soldiers came tradespeople, merchants, craftsmen and the like, who supported the garrison and the population surrounding it. As Davies (31) writes, "In Caerleon, a legion of 5,300 men with money to spend was a magnetic attraction. Outside the walls of the fort, a *vicus* developed—a township where people from far and near settled in order to profit

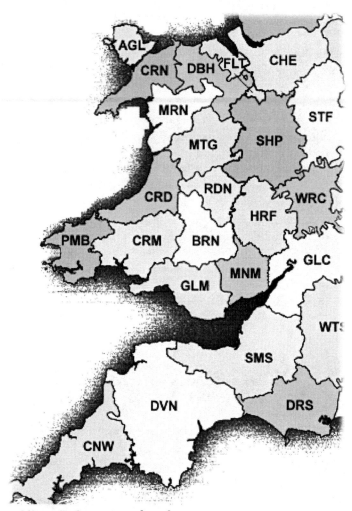

Historic Counties of Wales
AGL Anglesey
BRN Brenockshire
CRD Cardiganshire
CRM Carmarthenshire
CRN Caernarfonshire
DBH Denbighshire
FLT Flintshire
GLM Glamorgan
MNM Monmouthshire
MRN Merionethshire
MTG Montgomeryshire
PMB Pembrokeshire
RDN Radnorshire

Bordering Counties (Marches)
CHE Cheshire
DVN Devon
GLC Gloucestershire
HRF Herefordshire
SHP Shropshire
SMS Somerset

Historic counties of Wales and neighboring shires (map by Donald Yates).

from the money of the soldiers. By about 100 CE, the *vicus* at Caerleon had a population of around two thousand.... Smaller *vici* arose on the outskirts of the auxiliary forts—at Caernarfon, for example" (31). Since the military contingent at the Caerleon fortress seems to have withdrawn from that settlement after 170 CE, according to Davies (31), these Middle Eastern and North African genes must be regarded either as vestiges of Wales' native genetic patterns of DNA or traces of a selective inflow of foreign genes that persisted, that is, people who stayed.

The Roman occupiers of Wales not only maintained a military presence but also engaged in various manufacturing activities, all of which required skilled persons from outside the local population, who were untrained in these activities. For example, the town of Holt produced tiles; in Dolaucothe, gold was flushed from rock, requiring a large workforce. Ariconium was the center of iron mining and smelting. And the city of Viroconium was established as the *civitas* of Wales. It grew to be the fourth largest city in Roman Britain by 200 CE, and another *civitas* is believed to have been situated at Carmarthen. A mental overlay of the DNA landscape of Wales with these centers of population and manufacturing shows a close correspondence of Semitic haplotypes. We believe that *this* is the historical origin of the first Jewish presence in Wales.

Christianity was not strongly accepted in Wales—or in England or Scotland, for that matter—during the 300–500 CE time period. In all, Davies (36) reports that only one "pewter bowl bearing a Christian monogram" has been found in all of Wales dating from this epoch. There are, as he further acknowledges, very few written records surviving from the 400–600 CE period in Wales. One was written by a monk named Gildas between 500 and 550, as we saw in chapter 2, and other sources for the period, dating from 1250 CE, are copies of presumed earlier texts. All told, only about 25 *sentences* included in the cache of annals collected at St David's Cathedral (ca. 960) refer to the 447–600 CE period.

However, the 960 CE collection *does* have some genealogical material pertaining to the early Welsh kingdoms that came into existence in the post–Roman era. Davies (48) comments that "most of them [the royal lineages] could claim some degree of association with the Roman order." One of the most prominent of these lineages and kingdoms was that of David/Dyfed, which had at one time seven constituent "bishoprics" or religious centers. We propose that these were not Christian ecclesiastical units, but rather Jewish, and that the Kingdom of David and its ruling family were Jewish. Recall, by way of an analogy, that Adler mentions that the Jewish communities in England and France also had several so-called bishoprics.

During the mid-sixth century, the embers of Roman culture in Wales still glowed and were not completely out. Tablets with Latin inscriptions from that era have been unearthed. An epitaph for King Cadfan (ca. 625) of Gwipead shows linguistic links to "France, northern Africa, and the eastern shores of the Mediterranean" according to Davies (54). These cultural patterns, we propose, reflect the Jewish communities then actively trading with Gaul, North Africa, and Greece. An excavated fort at Degannwevy dating from the same time period "yielded fragments of glass and pottery from the Black Sea, Athens and Bordeaux, as has Doras Emrys" (54). Davies reports that several other archaeological sites produced similar artifacts dating from the 500s. This may be attributable to trade with merchants of the Radanite Jewish channels or it could signal the existence of continuing trade using the southern sea routes to North Africa and the Mediterranean. In other words, ongoing trade could have continued directly from Wales to North Africa and the Mediterranean region using sea lanes, rather than the Gallic Radanite overland routes.

By the 600s there are Welsh rulers named Cadwallon and Cadwaladr, Arabic names meaning "first born" and "first born son."[26] Cadwaladr's name is preserved in the traditions associated with Geoffrey of Monmouth, Holinshed and others, as the last British (read Welsh) king. That these glaring facts have not been noticed by earlier British historians or antiquarians is no doubt due to "[the] desire to stress the Teutonism of the English nation [by] nineteenth-century historians such as Freeman and Green.... They could turn to Gildas and Bede for support.... The central myth of British imperialism was the racial superiority of the English" (64).

In her study *The History of White People*, Princeton professor Nell Irvin Painter devotes several chapters to the English and American construction of white supremacist theories. She anatomizes the white Anglo-Saxon myth in detail, explaining how nineteenth-century figures like Emerson, Carlyle, Jefferson and others associated the "true" English with traits of brutality, freedom, masculinity and political power. From the time of the ancient Greeks, strong, handsome, intelligent, blond, blue-eyed and essentially manly northern Europeans invariably sat atop a heap of other genetically determined races shading off to the weak, servile, ugly, stupid, passive, female and black. Painter demonstrates that the model of whiteness was begrudgingly and belatedly expanded in Britain and the United States to include Irish, Italians, eastern Europeans, Jews and, most recently, Hispanic persons. Arabs,

Latter-day Taliesin Dylan Thomas (1914–1953) was born in the Uplands area of Swansea, Glamorgan, Wales. He had the curly hair and other physiognomic features of the Silures, as remarked upon by Tacitus and as evidently embedded in Welsh DNA, notably the North African type E1b1b (pencil sketch by Mervyn Levy, 1938) (© National Portrait Gallery, London).

North Africans and other Middle Easterners, however, are still waiting their turn. "The fundamental black/white binary endures," writes Painter, "even though the category of whiteness—or we might say more precisely, a category of nonblackness—effectively expands."[27]

Further underscoring the very probable transport of people and goods directly between Wales and North Africa is the occurrence of a plague in Wales toward the middle of the sixth century. Archaeology writer David Keys in his book *Catastrophe* has three chapters on the fallout from cataclysmic events that began with the eruption of a mega-volcano in Indonesia in the year 535/536. Keys maintains that "many of the modern states of western Europe owe their genesis to the climatic and epidemiological turmoil of this period ... famines in China, snow in Mesopotamia, the first emergence of plague in East Africa, and the darkening of the sun, as reported in Constantinople" (105, 107). Not for nothing were they called the Dark Ages. The bubonic plague that broke out in Egypt in 541 as part of the global chain reaction of events was carried in grain, rats, corpses and ships to the shores of Britain. The "great death" (*mortalitas magna*) swept away half the aristocracy of Ireland in a few days and caused "the birds and wild animals to become so tame as to allow themselves to be taken by hand." "In Wales, the *Welsh Annals* also reveal that in 547 (corrected to 549 by some modern historians) the king of Gwynedd, a powerful monarch called Maelgwn, died of the plague"—probably in the north coastal site of Deganwy (109).

Other places struck by sudden devastation were Tintagel on the north Cornish coast, Cadbury Congresbury, a hill fort with extensive Mediterranean wares in its excavation record in north Somerset, the Porthmadog/Borth-y-gest area at the northeast corner of Cardigan Bay with its great citadel of Dinas Emrys, a Cornish settlement involved in the mining and export of tin embracing Chun, Killibury, Grambla and St. Ives, High Peak and Mothecombe in Devon, and the formidable Roman city of Viroconium or Wroxeter (109–112).

Davies (67) notes that this plague did *not* strike in England "perhaps because they [the English] ... lacked contact with the shores of the Mediterranean." If this is correct, then it would imply that the primary trade channels with Wales began in North Africa and followed a path west and north, avoiding coming through the Straits of Gibraltar, and instead leaving from, say, western Morocco and continuing up to the southwestern coast of Wales. The presence of a Welsh saint named Libio (i.e., man from Libya) in exactly this time period provides support for this argument. We have already witnessed how the name Gildas points to Berber North Africa.

We have also established how Tintagel on the north Cornish coast, the mythical place of King Arthur's origins, was built up and then abandoned by its North African founders, Vandals and Berbers (chapter 2). In this context, we may now revisit the deadly plague from Africa that struck Wales. The Welsh Annals record that Maelgwn (considered the founder of medieval Wales by historians) succumbed to the plague in 547 or 549 and many other casualties followed, especially in areas with sea connections to the Mediterranean. Cadbury Congresbury on the river Yeo in Somerset is suspected to have been hard hit, as well as the great citadel of Dinas Emrys and the north Welsh coastal site of Deganwy and Porthmadog/Borth-y-gest area at the northeast corner of Cardigan Bay.[28] Wroxeter (Viroconium) "appears to have suffered a major drop in population followed by a complete reordering of the city's property boundaries."[29] The plague with its attendant scourges recurred several times in the sixth century, so that by the beginning of the seventh, up to 60 percent of the population was dead in southwest Britain, "perhaps up to 90 percent in some areas ... normal life virtually collapsed, much agricultural land went out of use, and—as archaeological record testifies—many towns and villages became depopulated and deserted."[30]

The modern chronicler of this global catastrophe, David Keys, believes a folk memory of the sixth-century plague in Britain gave birth to the concept of the Waste Land in Arthurian romance, Welsh Triads and other bardic literature. He notes that Arthur is said to have died in either 537 or 542.[31] The Welsh Annals for 537 state that at the battle of Camlann in which Arthur and Medraut fell, mass deaths occurred at the same time in Britain and Ireland. Reminding us that the literary backdrop for the "great pestilence" in the Grail romances and other literary accounts is the Somerset and South Wales area, Keys suggests "this corresponds with what was probably the case (due mainly to the plague) in the real world of the sixth century" (115). When Geoffrey of Monmouth came to write of these events, he describes how, some years after Arthur's death: "All the settlements were smashed to the ground with a great force of battering rams. All the inhabitants were destroyed by flashing swords and crackling flames. Those left alive fled, shattered by these dreadful disasters."[32] The toponymic landscape we investigated in the Domesday chapters covering Somerset and Devon in particular certainly reflects these upheavals, with Arabic place-names like Asla (Waste Land), Dimnah (Ruins),

Marmas (Graves), Roda (Cemetery), Mosa (Barren) and the ubiquitous and eloquent Hecham (Stones). The decimations and replacements of population in the seventh century fundamentally altered the course of Welsh and English history, with many more ramifications and effects on their society than the Anglo-Saxon invasions or intercourse with Gaul and Italy.

If our reasoning is correct, this would suggest that the western sea route might have been independent of that established by the Radanite Jews through Gaul, because, for the Radanites, the shortest, most efficient route to Britain would be directly across the English Channel to Kent. It also supports the hypothesis that a North African population with high levels of male E1b1b and mitochondrial U was already present in Wales during this time period, people capable of carrying on trade with North African ports and carrying, if legends be true, Mediterranean DNA to begin with. At any rate, North African genetics and epidemiology were only reinforced during these centuries.

"A Merchant's Country"

We have seen how values from the Mediterranean world coalesce in the figures of Welsh saints, who are often "abbots" and holy men as well as kings and rulers. Welsh bardic tradition is also very mindful of the role of merchants in the idyllic picture it paints of a society threatened by natural and human forces of invasion. In "The Omen of Prydain the Great," Taliesin envisages the Celts unified by "the holy banner of David" and speaks of Cynan and Cadwaladr as

> Two tenacious chiefs; profound their counsel.
> Two that will overcome the Saxons, with the aid of the Lord.
> Two generous ones, two treasurers of a merchant's country.
> Two fearless ones, ready, of one fortune, of one faith.
> Two exalters of Prydein of bright armies.[33]

In the same composition, the bard specifically mentions accounting officials (Cechmyn, managers of the Exchequer) together with the multitude of "merchants" in the court of Cadwaladr. These important professionals are called into battle with all the others to defend Britain: "May David be a leader to the combatants."[34]

Keys (helped by Arthurian specialist Elspeth Kennedy of Oxford University) concludes after surveying *The Perlesvaus, The Quest for the Holy Grail* and other literary texts, that "in terms of the period in which the action is set, in terms of the locations where the action takes place, and in terms of the mixture of famine, groin-area injury [Arthur's mortal wound], pestilence, depopulation, and war, the idea of the Waste Land may have been partially derived, through oral and lost written accounts, from the real famine-hit, plague-ridden, war-torn, depopulated Waste Land of mid- to late-sixth century southwest Britain" (117)—to which we add the towns and seaports of Wales.

Saint David

Only by turning our understanding of history topsy-turvy can we comprehend the significance of Dewy/David (Arabic Daoui). It is the Welsh name par excellence. Wales' patron saint lived probably from 530 to 589, about the same time as the historical Arthur. The River Dee is "David's River" (Welsh *Dyfrdwy*). David came from the royal house of Ceredigion (Cardigan), in the west-central part of the country that today has the highest proportion of native Welsh speakers and remains most untouched by English ways. Of all the Welsh saints of the period, he is the most famous, yet as Davies (73) remarks, "There is virtually no contemporary evidence relating to [him]." A biography of David appears only in 1090 CE—over 600 years after he is supposed to have lived.

If we consider only the name, Cardiganshire has the highest incidence of the surname Davies (22.5 percent). Other forms are Dewydd, Dewi, Dafydd, Deio, Dyas, Dyos, Davis, Dakin and Daykyn.[35] Daniel (Deiniol) and Solomon (Salmon) are also early Welsh saints whose names enjoy some degree of popularity down to the present. This high incidence of Hebrew names might tempt one to assume "that Wales had a high Jewish population, as surnames such as Samuel, Joseph, Isaac, Mordecai, and even Israel, may readily be found." One genealogist goes so far as to say "that the taking of Old Testament names had a general appeal throughout Wales."[36] Even Moses is not unheard of. But to dismiss the phenomenon as the vogue of Calvinist and Baptist denominations is to skirt the issue of why such names were favored by the Welsh throughout their history. We will see many instances in the course of our present inquiry where Welsh surnames and forenames appear to be indicators of Jewish and crypto–Jewish sympathies. This orientation is understandable fully only if the Welsh preserved many elements of British history elsewhere lost and retold that history with a philo–Semitic tendency.

Davies' *History* then moves on to the 800–1282 period. Around 800 a distinctive series of marriages began occurring in the royal lineages of Wales. Davies here makes a fairly important statement for our present thesis: "A manuscript discovered at Bamberg, Franconia [produced during the reigns of Merfyn and Rhodri in the ninth century] says that Irish visitors to court were presented with a cryptogram which could only be solved by transposing the letters from Latin into Greek (82)." Why is this significant? Because very few persons in the British Isles at the time knew both languages. However, Jews associated with Alexandria, Egypt, Berber North Africa, Constantinople and the Radanite trade channels were fluent in both Latin and Greek. Thus, the cryptogram may have served to distinguish Jews (and Egyptians) from non–Jews. Alexandria gained its name through Greek conquest ca. 300 BCE and was named for Alexander the Great. Much of the population spoke Greek until the coming of the Arabs in the seventh century. In its heyday, one-quarter of the city was Jewish, and these Jews also used Greek as their primary language, even in the synagogue. During these centuries, Greek-speaking Byzantium was the pinnacle of civilization. Rome (where many of the popes were Greek) was a struggling, parochial Italian village.

A holy man named *Asser* (a Hebrew/Arabic given name, a Jewish tribe, also signifying one from Assyria) was requested to come to Wessex in 880 CE to assist King Alfred. In 942 CE an insurrection of the Welsh against English rule was led by a man named Idwal ab (son of) Anarawd, both of whose names are Arabic or Muslim.[37] Another Welsh nobleman of the same time period is named Rhydderch ap Hy faidel. *Hy fayed el* is an Egyptian name. In a much later day, Mohamed Abdel Moneim Al-Fayed is an Alexandrine shipping magnate who became a furious Anglophile. After acting as financial consultant to the rulers of Brunei and Dubai, Al-Fayed bought the Ritz hotel in Paris, a Scottish castle, a football team and Harrods department store in London. His son Dodi was killed in the same car crash that took the life of Diana Princess of Wales on August 31, 1997.

Let us continue. Davies reports that within the royal elite of Wales there was "a readiness to marry close relations" (91)—an accepted pattern among both Jews and Muslims of the period, but a practice strictly forbidden by the Christian church, where marriages between cousins were illegal. Usually, medieval canon law enjoined strictures that included annulment, disinheritance, excommunication, public penance and even death against unions impeded by at least a fourth degree of kinship.[38] In 1039, Davies (97) mentions, a powerful Welsh king, Gruffudd ap Llewellyn, gained additional territory "after he killed *Iago ab Idwal*, the great grandson of Idwal ab Anarawd. Iago is, of course, the Romanesque spelling of Jacob."[39] Thus we glimpse a pedigree from Anarawd through Idwal to Iago carrying forward Hebrew and Arabic names. Cases like this can (and will) be multiplied as we delve into Welsh genealogies.

With the arrival of the Normans in 1066, Wales was vulnerable to attack, and by 1086 Norman castles had been established along the entire Welsh border by the so-called Marcher Lords. The affected lands were those in Chester, Monmouth, Cydweli, Denbigh, Ewas, Wigmore, Radnor, Bulth, Caerleon, Glamorgan, Newport (Gwnlliwg), Brecon, Abergavenny, Pembroke, Chepstow, Gower, Maelor (Bromfield and Yale), Oswestry, Chirk, Powys (Wenwynwyn), Rhuthun and Cemais. Through an intricate succession of male and female rights, as charted by Davies, emerged the baronies of Mortimer, Marshal, Clare, De Burgh, Despenser, Beauchamp, Neville, Bohun, Breos, Montgomery, Brotherton, Cantilupe, Owain, Grey, Audley, Mobray, Arundel and Tudor that dominated the scene in the pre-modern era.[40] Additional campaigns into Wales were undertaken by the Normans under Henry I (1109), with the former Kingdom of David being styled now the County of Pembroke. In 1105 Henry I settled a "colony of Flemings" in southern Dyfed/David (Davies 111), which may have contained Jewish colonists valued as tradesmen, financiers and merchants, as well as Sephardic Jews from the North African settlements.

Developments during the Industrial Age brought minor movements of skilled and non-skilled workers from other parts of England, while at the same time it concentrated Welshmen from the hills and mountains into the cities. Though Wales rose in rebellion several times against England—usually led by Welsh royal princes named David—ultimately the country was absorbed into the realm of subsequent Normans, Angevins, Yorks and Lancaster kings, while retaining a good deal of its characteristic "Welshness." In the twenty-first century, Wales (Welsh name Cymru or Cumbria) enjoys a measure of quasi-sovereignty. Welshmen all over the world, including a sizable South American colony in Chubut, Argentina, take pride in the resurgence of their instantly recognizable culture with its distinct language, literature, schooling, television and filmmaking, customs, holidays, art and music.

The story of Wales is clearly an inchoate and incipient one. Having given this sketch of its history, let us next descend several levels down to a rapid survey of its surnames and see if any of them, aside from those of the famous, bear tokens of its exotic past. We will italicize those that appear to betray Semitic roots.

The fundamental rule in Welsh genealogy is a patronymic naming system built on the use of *ap*, *ab* or *B-*, meaning "son of," the equivalent of Scottish *mac*. Thus, from the age of the Welsh princes, the forenames Dafydd, Gruffydd, Hywell, Llywelyn, Madog, Morgan (the name of the Welsh arch-heretic and bane of the early Church fathers, Pelagius, "sea-borne"), Owain and Rhys all survive to provide surnames of some consequence, and we have Anarawd, Bleddyn (supposedly "son of Blaidd," the Welsh name for "wolf"),[41] Bowen (ab + Owen), Price (ap + Rhys), Bevan, Protheroe ("son of Roderick," a common Spanish and Provencal name), Powell (ap + Howell) and Pugh (ap + Hugh). The *ap* system gradually decayed, so that someone whose name was David ap William became David William or Williams. Parish registers usually ignored Welsh customs and forms and standardized every name they could, often rendering them in Latin. Female names that were sometimes perpetuated as family names include Annis, Catling, Margerison, Sibly, Gwen, Gwenlan, Gaenor, Lowri, Ellyw, Elizabeth, Magdalen, Jonett, Eleanor and Alice (11–13).

Some of the names of illustrious ancestors that did not make the grade into perpetuity are Anarawd, Cadfael, Cydifor, Cynfyn, Elystan, Idnerth, Iestyn, Neffyd, Peredur, Selyf, Tudwal, Tyfid and Ynyr. Among common forenames used in the thirteenth century, at a point just before Welsh culture was engulfed by Anglicization, were Cynddelw, Cynwric, Ednyfed, Einion, Gronow, Heilyn, Iorwerth, Ithel, Madyn, Rhirid, Tedwared, Tudur and Wasmihangel. Less common were Cediro, Ednowain, Gwion, Gwrgenau, Hwfo, Ifor, Seisyll and Trahearn. Other than Tudor, which we will examine in Chapter 10, few of these, "sadly for researchers," as the genealogist authors lament, gave rise to modern surnames.[42]

Befitting a nation apart, Welsh surnames exhibit a high concentration. A favored few account for the vast majority. This goes counter to the situation, say, in England or France. Jones (Jonas) in Wales is the name of 14 percent of the population, while Smith, the most common English surname, is borne by only 1.37 percent of the population there (4). Other common Welsh names, in addition to David and Davies and others already mentioned, are Lewys (Lewis), Morus (Morris, Morse), Madog (Maddocks), Maredudd (Meredith), Philip (Phillips), Rhydderch (Roderick), Roger (Rogers) and Watkin (Watkins—10). Popular also were Adda (Adam), Bateman, Bebb, Brown (appearing in records as Bron, Broun, Brown, Brun), Connah (Cwna), Cunnick (Cynog), Daniel (Deiniol), Ellis (Elisa, Elissa, Eliseus, Elias, Ellice, Helis, all common across north Wales), Esau (Esay, Carmarthenshire), Evans (Ieuan, from Latin Johannes), Fenna, Games, Gammon, Gibbs, Gwalchmai, Haines, Hamer, Harris, Hopkins, Hoskins, Howe, Hussey, Isaac, Ithell (Iudhael, Ithael, Ithel), Jacob, James, Jehu, Job, Lloyd (*llwyd*, meaning gray/brown, perhaps also "panther"), Mason, Meyrick (Meurig, Mauricius, Maurice, Maurice, Morris), Nash, Newell (Noel, Nowell, Nevill), Oliver, Profit (from the word for prophet), Prosser (ap Rosser, south Wales), Salmon (Solomon), Samuel (Samwell), Sheen ("fair, handsome"), Sheldon ("wayfarer, stranger"), Tannatt, Warlow ("warlock, wizard"), Wigley and Yorath (Iorwerth).

We have deliberately left for last a consideration of Arthur, the mythic "Celtic" hero who first appears in the unsettled interregnum in the aftermath of the Romans, and around whom galvanized the whole dream of British singularity and unity during the High Middle Ages, when chivalry and courtly love became the watchwords of European civilization and refinement.

Starting with the name itself, considered purely from a genealogical and onomastic viewpoint Arthur is a rare name in Wales. Rowlands and Rowlands point out that it hardly enters into the patronymic surname system of Wales (72), although it is used by Henry VII for his eldest son and enjoys a checkered career in the English aristocracy subsequent to the Tudors. These writers also mention that "in 1574 Arthur ap Morys appears in the Mgy Muster in Newtown hundred," and note that "some families of this name may have originated in England, perhaps especially from Somerset (Doddrell) or Cornwall (White)" (ibid).

In Welsh, Irish, Mannish and Scottish regnal lists, Arthur is listed among kings of the Britons between Uther Pendragon and the last kings of Gwynedd, Maelgwyn, Cunedda, Cadwallon and Cadwaladr.[43] There are four figures of the sixth and seventh centuries who bore the name, however, and it is difficult to sort out which of them might have been the king elevated to Knights of the Round Table fame by Geoffrey of Monmouth (who, as we saw, himself bore the name and may have had a special interest in it). The earliest allusion to the name occurs in a Pictish record saying that Gwawrddur, a warrior in the troop gathered by the sixth-century ruler of Edinburgh (Land of Gododdin), was to be praised, "although Arthur he was not."[44] This demonstrates that the Arthur we know from subsequent literary fame was already a national hero in the 500s, the period of barbarian invasions that suits all the other pieces of

King Arthur in correct classical armor, etching in John Dryden's *King Arthur*, London, 1735 (© The Trustees of the British Museum).

evidence.[45] Arthur is strangely absent in the White and Red Books (as he is in Gildas) but makes a furtive showing in the *Black Book of Carmarthen* (with "no influence" seeping over from Geoffrey or the French romances).[46] Arthur is closely associated with Cornwall, "bear" (*arth*) of the host, "most strong in valor," and "head of the battalions of Cornwall."[47] In addition to being a warrior and king, he is also a bard.

The origin of the name Arthur has been endlessly debated.[48] It is almost certainly not "Celtic," neither from a P nor Q dialect, and cannot be traced further back than post–Roman times. The center of gravity for its appearance is the sixth century. In 1998, archeological excavations at sixth-century Tintagel brought to light a find subsequently dubbed the Arthur Stone, mentioning the name Artognou, claimed to be cognate. Although the reading is questionable, perhaps this inscription and milieu are on the right track. Arthur's name has become something of a grail quest for modern researchers. Other theories derive the name from Artorius (Roman or Messapic), Arnthur (Etruscan), Arcturus (the "bear star") or *Arto-uiros* in Brittonic ("bear man").

Perhaps the Gordian knot of the difficulty can be cut if we consider that many of the names in early Welsh history have Arabic and North African roots. Camlann, for instance, the site of Arthur's final deadly battle with the usurper Mordred, has resisted all efforts to etymologize or locate it. This unidentified place in England has a name that is supposed to mean Crooked Glenn.[49] We suspect it may be a corruption of the common Arabic place-name Khamilah, "area of dense trees, low or depressed area with good pasturage."[50] Camelot, the fabled capital city of the Round Table, appears to be little more than the plural of the same term.

Arthur's father is Uther Pendragon, the epithet following his name meaning Chief, or Head, of the Warriors, or Dragons.[51] We have already seen how Arthur's son is Amr, a pre–Islamic tribal name that is meaningless in any Brythonic language. *Ar-* is a common prefix in Arabic and North African naming conventions, meaning "the." Ar-Rumi, for example, the name of an early Arab poet, means "the Greek." Ar-Rahman is "the Most Gracious," Ar-Rabi, "the Master," and Ar-Rashid "the Right-Minded."[52] Many of these are traditional names of God's servants in pre–Islamic religion. If we take Arthur's name as Semitic or Arabic perhaps it is a corruption of his father's name: Ar-Uthr. As to what Uthr might have meant originally, however, we will not venture an opinion here.

Whatever the truth, these speculations would be beside the point after Arthur became a literary figure in the inventive hands of his descendant, Geoffrey of Monmouth. Ever since Geoffrey's blockbuster Norman romance, Arthur and his kin have become synonymous with Welsh and Breton history. The new national storyline with its Celtic, Welsh, Jewish and North African elements had a timeless plot that unified Britain, envisaged the Saxons as defeated and, in a strange reversal of the Vandal sack of 410, went to the very gates of Rome to conquer the known world.

We will close this chapter by giving the full text of one of the anonymous songs from *The Black Book of Carmarthen*.[53] In it can be traced the intertwining motifs of Judaism, saints' cults, warrior ethos, bardic pride, distant trade, nature worship and pagan animism that composed the religion of the Welsh, and indeed British people throughout the centuries.

> Hail, glorious Lord!
> May church and chancel bless Thee!
> And chancel and church!
> And plain and precipice!
> And the three fountains there are,
> Two above wind, and one above the earth,

May darkness and light bless Thee!
And fine silk and sweet trees!
Abraham the chief of faith did bless Thee.
And life eternal.
And birds and bees.
And old and young.
Aaron and Moses did bless Thee.
And male and female.
And the seven days and the stars.
And the air and the ether.
And books and letters.
And fish in the flowing water.
And song and deed.
And sand and sward.
And such as were satisfied with good.
I will bless Thee, glorious Lord!
Hail, glorious Lord!

9

The Irony of It All: English Jews and Muslims 1300–1450

When we left our English Jews in 1290 they had been ordered to either convert or leave the country. D'Blossiers Tovey, the author of one of the earliest comprehensive histories of Jews in Britain, relates, "What Countries the *Jews* retir'd to upon this occasion, is neither mentioned by their own Historians or ours." He speculates, based on the banishment of Jews in France and other countries following the English expulsion, that "several" must have been "recalled ... on Account of their USEFULNESS IN BUSINESS."[1]

Since the arrivals and departures of individual Jews were recorded in detail in the Netherlands, France and Germany prior to 1290, the silence of English records is very suspect. There is only one record of a single boatload of 160 Jews foundering off the coast of England and losing all on board (Adler 1935). This represents 1 percent of the estimated total 16,000 Jews in England at the time. We are left unable to account for the other 99 percent. For so many carefully regulated aliens of the realm to have vanished into thin air is unprecedented in Jewish recordkeeping. Since there are no written notices of English Jews arriving in other countries, we may assume (1) the majority of the 16,000 men, women and children constituting England's Jewry simply converted to Christianity, at least in the public's eye, and became lost to history as Jews, and (2) those who wished to practice their religion more openly without strictures moved toward areas where there was little governmental interference or even migrated over the borders of Wales and Scotland. Relatively high amounts of their descendants' DNA types are still to be found today in the Welsh Marches, Scottish Borderlands, Cornwall and Devon, as well as Scotland and Wales themselves.

A similar stratagem was adopted by Spanish Jews in the 1490s as they fled to Navarre and onward across the Pyrenees to Bayonne in southern France, to lax western cities along the Spanish-Portuguese border, to the Majorcas and other way-stations leading to freedom. "Most of the Jews found refuge in neighboring Portugal," although they were expelled from that kingdom too in 1496, the law being "commuted" in 1497 to forced conversion.[2]

Saul's account of English history states, "The English people had achieved a great deal by 1300 CE—much land had been brought into productive use, and a dense commercial network extended everywhere.[3] *But the expansion was ending by 1300* [our emphasis], and the next 50 years saw a series of catastrophes.... A disastrous series of wet summers in 1315, 1316, and 1317 caused a famine. At least half a million people died.... In 1348–9 the Black Death killed about half the population.... The plague recurred in the 1360's and there seems to have been no sustained rise in births to replace the losses.... In 1377, the poll tax suggests a [total] population of about 2.5 million, less than half the figure in 1300."

We would suggest, based on historical evidence concerning Jewish populations in other

Cities, towns and counties with Jews before 1290, according to Hyamson, *The History of the Jews in England*, 1908 (map by Donald Yates).

countries in which the Black Death occurred (e.g., France, Switzerland, Italy, Germany, the Netherlands), that the secret Jews remaining in England—and those dwelling in the Welsh and Scottish borderlands—died in fewer numbers than did the English population as a whole. Both bubonic plague and typhoid are spread by contaminated drinking water, coming into contact with infected vermin and handling infected corpses of the deceased. Although Jews certainly succumbed once infected, they were less likely to become infected because of their ritual practices of hand washing and food preparation. These hygienic activities likely led to lower mortality among those persons in England still privately following Judaic practices.

For the surviving population of Britain, the 1400s saw an upswing in economic fortunes. Saul (169) reports, "Enterprising individuals seized the opportunities for making money from new products or new methods.... In the fifteenth century [i.e., 1400s], cloth became a major export. Key figures ... were the clothiers based either in industrial villages or small towns in the southwest, East Anglia and ... the West Riding section of Yorkshire. These men invested ... [and] responded to the growing demand by coordinating the work ... and marketing the finished product.... In a few generations, England, once an exporter of raw materials, now supplied European markets with manufactured goods."

The reader has no doubt already observed that the areas where this industrial revolution originated are, in fact, those where Jewish populations had been present—and where crypto–Jewish populations remained. Hyamson's map says it all (see map). And then, socially, politically and culturally, a very interesting phenomenon occurs: "The aristocracy ... showed a remarkable capacity to adapt to the new reality.... There was much intermarriage among the gentry with London merchant families, and [they] accepted a stream of recruits from the merchants, lawyers, entrepreneurs and war captains" (170–171).

Roberts et al. (207–208) provides a largely supportive account of this period of English history:

> The rise of the great clothier, the entrepreneur who purchased wool from the farmer ... carried it to the weaver ... the fuller, the dyer ... [then placed] the cloth on packhorses to be carried off to market. Such an enterprise required great sums of capital, willingness to take risks, freedom from guild regulations, and laborers who would work for wages.... Baronial families ... avoided bankruptcy by marrying the daughters of rich merchants or by participating in trade.... Bristol [prospered] with its trade to Ireland and Spain.. But the most prosperous town of all was London.

The Calais Staple

The pattern for this transformation of the English economy had begun even earlier, however, with the establishment of the Calais Staple in France in the late fourteenth century. In Calais, a group of English merchants, most with offices in Bristol, London and York, established a cooperative trade entrepôt with the French and Dutch. Another set of English entrepreneurs, chartered by Edward III, were located in London and organized under the title Company of Merchant Adventurers of London. Their primary continental trading outlet was Antwerp (Harris 1974). The "mayor" of the Antwerp Staple was William De la Pole, about whom we will have much more to say shortly. Other financial players during this time period include Emery de Frescobaldi, the Bardi and Peruzzi families of Italy, the treasurer Baron Zouche of the venerable Breton de la Zouche family, Bernard Ezii, Henry Picard and Tideman de Limburgh (Harris, 1974).

Of the English-based enterprise, Harris reports:

> The Company of Merchant Adventurers of London brought together London's leading overseas merchants in a regulated company, in the nature of a guild. Its members' main business was the export of cloth, especially white (undyed) broadcloth. This enabled them to import a large range of foreign goods. The company was chiefly chartered to the English merchants at Antwerp in 1305. Henry IV's charter (1407) was in favor of the English merchants dwelling in Holland, Zeeland, Brabant, and Flanders. Other groups of merchants traded to different parts of northern Europe, including merchants dwelling in Prussia and the Hanse (whose election of a governor was approved by Richard II

of England in 1391), and the English Merchants in Norway, Sweden and Denmark (who received a charter in 1408). The members were trading capitalists. They were probably mostly composed of London mercers. The company also had members from York, Norwich, Exeter, Ipswich, Newcastle, Hull, and other places. The merchant adventurers of these towns were separate, but affiliate, bodies. The Society of Merchant Ventures of Bristol were a separate body, chartered by Edward VI in 1552.

A Case Analysis: York, Beverley and Hull

We now take a closer look at these merchant adventurers by examining Jenny Kermode's 2002 study, *Medieval Merchants: York, Beverly and Hull in the Later Middle Ages*, which lists 1400 individuals. We intend to build an argument that this group of merchants and entrepreneurs was crypto–Jewish. One clue to this is their trade channel, which as Kermode notes, "could extend from Iceland to North Africa and the Middle East" (2). Trading to such lands required not only language skills, including, for instance, Arabic and Hebrew, but also business contacts with whom a network of commercial contracts and credit could be established.

York, as the reader is probably already aware, had a robust and wealthy Jewish population prior to 1290. In 1377, its residents numbered some 14,000–15,000 persons, of whom, we propose, many of the most prosperous were crypto–Jews. Kermode notes that York was both wealthy and worldly, "one of the largest, and most indulgent, consumer populations in the north [of England] ... [there was] an unusually large conglomeration of highly specialized craftsmen ... with at least 50 guilds active in the 14th and 15th centuries.... York had been a center for textile and leather workers [a largely Jewish craft] since the early thirteenth century." Crafts such as York's leather and glass industries underscore an important rationale for why most Jews were not expelled from England; they tended to be concentrated in crafts essential to the local economy. The list of imports into the York consumer economy is also instructive as to ethnic origins: "imported dyestuffs ... and wine, almonds, liquorice, Mediterranean fruit and spices, silks and brocades" (8).

By intermarrying with the local aristocracy, the most successful of the merchant families became landed and ennobled or gentrified. Kermode (17) writes, for example, "the Coppendale Family of merchants had prospered in Beverly [near York] since the early fourteenth century [i.e., 1300s]; [they] owned armour, [and] were licensed to crenellate in 1366." The De la Pole family arrived in Hull, near York, in the early 1300s—notably from "parts unknown." As their surname signifies, their proximate residence was in Poland, a provenance which would suggest they might be Ashkenazi Jews. The De la Poles built an enormous palazzo in Hull that became known as Court Hall. Soon they were known as Pool(e) or De La Poole, becoming increasingly Anglicized. A remote descendant was Reginald Lane Poole (1857–1939), a British historian who was keeper of the archives at the University of Oxford.

These same northern merchants were usually chosen by the king to serve as royal tax and customs collectors and some were even sent on important diplomatic missions. Jews in Spain and France often filled similar positions because of their ability to supervise large sums of money and their multilingual negotiating skills. We have already noticed how the Catalan convert Petrus Alfonsi (born Moses Sephardi) became one of Henry I's chief advisors. Another Jewish physician who became an outright convert and even proselytizer was Abner of Burgos. As Alfonso de Valladolid, he published polemical books both in Spanish and Hebrew after a high-profile conversion in 1321. But for every case like Moses and Abner, there were hundreds of others during these centuries illustrating how Jews either remained Jews or chose some *via media*. Isaac Golluf, the son of the Jewish director of the treasury for King Juan I's wife Violante,

Merchant Adventurers' Hall in Fossgate, York, at the center of the city, built after 1357 (Photo by Elizabeth Caldwell Hirschman).

apostatized as Juan Sanchez de Calatayud in 1389 "with the stipulation that he would nonetheless inherit his Jewish father's estate." David Gitlitz, the historian of Spanish crypto–Jews, remarks of him: "His conversion sparked that of a number of followers. This group of converts appears to have been motivated by neither coercion nor religious conviction, but rather by political or economic opportunism."[4]

Henry IV brought two Jewish physicians from Italy to England. On December 27, 1410, he issued a safe-conduct for Helias Sabot, a Hebrew who was a doctor of medicine at Bologna. On February 18, 1412, he issued letters of naturalization for the physician, David de Nigarellis, who had come from Lucca.

The distinguished fourteenth-century Venetian-born poet Christine de Pisan bears a convert name. She was the daughter of Tommaso di Benvenuto da Pizzano or Thomas de Pizan, named for the family's origins in the town of Pizzano, southeast of Bologna. Probably coming from Jewish ancestry, Thomas became a physician, court astrologer and Councillor of the Republic of Venice. Several book-length studies have been devoted to the phenomenon of court Jews,[5] and historians are evincing a growing interest in their counterparts the so-called port Jews.[6]

Perhaps even more remarkable about our early English converts and semi-converts is the fact that merchants' widows and wives in York, Hull and Beverley often held jobs in their husbands' businesses and even engaged in trading and crafts on their own, becoming barber surgeons, chap women (peddlers), cloth sellers, cooks, fish mongers, iron mongers, parchment makers and vintners, among other occupations (Kermode 2002). This leeway given to females continues the precedents we have already observed in Jewish communities in England prior to 1290 whereby women actively engaged in business and banking. Such activities within Christian communities were virtually unknown. Some Jewesses, such as Isolde de Acastre, left large fortunes when they died.

From the 1300s into the 1400s the trade network of the York, Hull and Beverly merchants greatly expanded. Ships came and went from Dieppe and Rouen, Spain, Portugal, Bayonne, Castile, Italy, Sweden, Norway, Skandia, Iceland, Prussia, Poland, Hungary, southern Germany, Lithuania and Russia. All these locales had openly or secretly Jewish mercantile cells.

Below are listed the names of several of the most prominent merchant/entrepreneurs in these three northern English cities. Several are clearly Jewish.

Prominent Traders in York, Hull and Beverley

John Asseby	John de More	William Ithun
John Bagot	Nicholas Ellis	Robert Kelam
William Barnaby	Simon Eyre	William Kyam
Thomas Bernard	John Ferriby (Pharaby)	James Malpas
John Beseby	Will. Ferrour	Will. Pakone
John Brisco	John Fisshwyke	William Sallay (Salle)
Elias Casse	Stephen Gildhouse	Jordan Savage
Philip Cassel	Thomas Glasyn	Robert Shackles
Nicholas Catton (Arabic)	John Goldbeter	Henry Tutbak
Adam Coppendale	Richard Green	John Vavasour
Robert Crosse	John Gregg (Gray)	William Vescy
Henry Damel	John Gyll	Robert Yarom
John de Acastre	John Hagg	
John de Ake	Ralph Horne	

De la Pole Family

As it turns out, the history of the De la Pole family is quite extraordinary. A brief biography of Michael De la Pole, junior (1330–1389), the first nationally prominent member of the family, may be excerpted from an indifferent source, one unaware of any possible Jewish implications, as follows:

Michael De la Pole (c. 1330–1389) was an English financier, Lord Chancellor of England, and Earl of Suffolk. He was the oldest son of William De la Pole (d. 1366) and Catherine Norwich, daughter of Sir Walter Norwich. His father was a wool merchant from Hull who became a key figure during the reign of Edward III; after the collapse of the Bardi and Peruzzi Italian trading families, Michael De la Pole, senior emerged as Edward's chief financier. Michael enjoyed even greater popularity at court than his father, becoming one of the most trusted and intimate friends of Edward's successor, Richard II.

He was appointed Chancellor in 1383, and created Earl of Suffolk in 1385, the first of his family to hold any such title. However, in the late 1380's his fortunes radically altered. In 1386 he was impeached on charges of embezzlement and negligence, a victim of increasing tensions between Parliament and Richard. Yet, even after this disgrace, he remained in royal favour. De la Pole fled to Paris in 1387. He remained in France for the remainder of his life. De la Pole's descendants were key players in the political life of the next two centuries.

Now the question arises how a family whose surname, De la Pole, means "of/from Poland" in French managed to ascend to such dazzling social and political heights. Indeed, how and why did a Polish family become merchants in Hull, England? The answer—as odd as it is— serves to prove our central thesis for the present chapter, that British Jews after 1290 either moved across the border or accepted Christianity. In the De la Poles' case, they did a bit of both.

The De la Pole family originated in Wales from a royal lineage, that of Gwennonwen Ap Owen, prince of Powys, one of the Welsh states that took shape during the Middle Ages. Owen De la Pole (Owain ap Gruffudd ap Gwenwynwyn) surrendered the Powys Wenwynwyn (southern Powys) to Edward I in 1283, receiving it back as a marcher lordship, a position he held until his death after 1285 or 1286. Owen was born around 1234 and married a woman named Hawise le Strange in 1242. Their three children, Owen ap Griffith, Margaret, and Llewelyn ap Griffith, all were surnamed De la Pole, implying that this branch of the family must have migrated to or taken refuge in Poland. Importantly, protective privileges were granted to Polish Jews by King Boleslaw V in 1264. This was the same timeframe in which the De la Pole family seems to have left Wales and ventured to Poland.

Subsequent generations are provided in summary form below. Owen and Hawise's daughter, Margaret, married a Norman nobleman, Fulke Fitzwarin, in 1277, but we have no information on the locality. The younger son, Llewelyn, married a woman named Margaret Verch Maredudd Goch, but, again, we do not know the locale. The oldest son, Owen, said to be Prince of Powys, married his maternal first cousin, Joan Corbet, who was also his paternal second cousin, a practice unheard of except in Jewish and Islamic lineages. Owen is stated in the genealogy to have acceded to the throne of Powys in 1289, one year prior to the act or decree of English Jews' expulsion. Owen's oldest son, William De la Pole, somehow moved across England to Yorkshire. We speculate here that he may have been joining the large and prosperous Jewish community in York. Here William married a woman, Elina Rotenheryng, who has a Jewish/Ashkenazic surname. Their son William De la Pole (II), a wool merchant in Hull, became financier to King Edward III. He was married to Catherine of Norwich. Michael De la Pole, William De la Pole's eldest son, was named first earl of Suffolk in 1385 by Richard II. He also served as chancellor of England in 1383 and managed the king's finances.

Bodleian Bowl's Significance

That there were relations between English and Polish Jews is proved by the existence of a thirteenth-century brass pot with a Hebrew poem reportedly fished out of a moat in Suffolk or Norfolk around 1693 and now in the collection of the Ashmolean Museum in Oxford. D'Blossiers Tovey tells how it was purchased by the last earl of Oxford, Aubrey de Vere, who died in 1703, and its inscription was read by a master of Oriental languages at the university (249–51). In the 1960s another brass pot of the same shape, also dated to the thirteenth century, with the same or similar inscription, was excavated in Haymarket in London and is now dis-

Bodleian Bowl (Art by Donald Yates).

played in the Fitzwilliam Museum in Cambridge. The purpose of these pots, which seem to come from the same foundry but are found in disparate locations, is not well understood, but they were the offering of the Jew Joseph, son of Rabbi Jechiel. Joseph's father "exercised his functions in the Jewish community of the Polish town of Kowel, or Kahwell in its ancient spelling," according to a Hebrew paleography expert.

As the genealogy shows, the De la Pole family has a pattern of marrying first cousins. Walter De la Pole, for instance, marries Elizabeth Bradeston. The first record of a christening does not occur until John De la Pole in 1466. The De la Pole family's genealogy is regularly punctuated with Jewish surnames such as Lovet, Lovell, Layer, le Bruyn, Cheney, Foix and Hussey. Notable also is the family's marriage into the royal house of the Plantagenets, who regarded themselves as heirs of the kingdom of David.

Margaret PEVEREL (married dau. of Edmund Peverel of Castle Ashby)
  Children:
  1. John De La POLE (Sir)

John De La POLE (Sir)
  Born: ABT 1341
  Died: BEF 1389, Chrishall, Essex, England
  Father: William De La POLE
  Mother: Margaret PEVEREL
  Married: Joan COBHAM (dau. of John Cobham and Margaret Courtenay) 21 Oct 1362
  Children:
  1. Joan De la POLE

Joan De La POLE
  Born: ABT 1373
  Died: 13 Jan 1434
  Father: John De La POLE (Sir)
  Mother: Joan COBHAM
  Married 1: Robert HEMENGALE (Sir) 1380
  Married 2: Reynold BRAYBROOKE (Sir)
  Children:
  1. Joan BRAYBROOKE (b. AFT 1395–d. 25 Nov 1442) (m. Thomas Brooke)
  2. Nicola BRAYBROOKE (m. Sir Thomas Chaworth)
  Married 3: Nicholas HAWBERKE (Sir)
  Married 4: John OLDCASTLE (B. Cobham) 1409
  Children:
  1. Joan OLDCASTLE (b. ABT 1416)
  De La POLE FAMILY
  Griffith Ap WENNONWEN
  Born: ABT 1234
  Died: AFT 27 Feb 1285/6
  Father: Gwennonwen Ap OWEN (Prince of Powis)
  Mother: Margaret CORBET
  Married: Hawise Le STRANGE 1242
  Children:
  1. Owen Ap Griffith De La POLE (Prince of Powys)
  2. Margaret De La POLE
  3. Llewelyn Ap Gruffydd De La POLE

Margaret De La POLE
  Born: ABT 1253
  Died: 11 May 1336

Father: Griffith Ap WENNONWEN
Mother: Hawise Le STRANGE
Married: Fulke FITZWARIN (Sir) 25 Feb 1277
Children:
1. Hawise FITZWARIN (b. ABT 1276) (m.1 Ralph De Gousille—m.2 Sir Robert De Hoo)
2. Fulke FITZWARIN (d. BEF 6 Jun 1336) (m. Eleanor De Beauchamp)
3. William FITZWARIN

Llewelyn Ap Gruffydd De La POLE
Born: BEF 1257
Died: AFT 1289
Father: Griffith Ap WENNONWEN
Mother: Hawise Le STRANGE
Married: Margaret Verch MAREDUDD GOCH

Owen Ap Griffith De La POLE (Prince of Powys)
Born: ABT 1257, Powys, Wenwynwyn, Montgomeryshire, Wales
Acceded: 16 May 1289, Powys Castle
Died: 1292/3
Father: Griffith Ap WENNONWEN
Mother: Hawise Le STRANGE
Married: Joan CORBET (b. ABT 1253) (dau. of Robert Corbet and Catherine Le Strange)
Children:
1. William De La POLE (Sir)
2. Hawis "Gadarn the Hardy" De La POLE
3. Owen De La POLE
4. Lewis De La POLE (Sir)
5. Griffin De La POLE

Hawis "Gadarn the Hardy" De La POLE
Born: 25 Jul 1290
Died: 1353
Father: Owen Ap Griffith De La POLE (Prince of Powys)
Mother: Joan CORBET
Married: John De CHERLETON (B. Powis) 26 Jul 1307
Children:
1. Isabel De CHERLETON (b. ABT 1338–d. 10 Apr 1396) (m.1 John De Sutton—m.2 Richard Lefisher)
2. John De CHERLETON (B. Powis)

Lewis De La POLE (Sir)
Died: 1294
Father: Owen Ap Griffith De La POLE (Prince of Powys)
Mother: Joan CORBET
Married: Sibilla?

William De La POLE (Sir)
Born: ABT 1275, Kingston upon Hull, Yorkshire, England
Died: BEF Dec 1329
Father: Owen Ap Griffith De La POLE (Prince of Powys)
Mother: Joan CORBET
Married: Elena ROTENHERYNG
Children:
1. William De La POLE (Sir)
2. Richard De La POLE (Sir)

Richard De La POLE (Sir)
> Born: ABT 1311
> Died: 1 Aug 1345, London, Middlesex, England
> Buried: Holy Trinity, Hull
> Father: William De La POLE (Sir)
> Mother: Elena ROTENHERYNG
> Married: Joan ?
> Children:
> 1. Joan (Margaret) De La POLE
> 2. William De La POLE
> 3. John De La POLE (Sir)
> 4. Margaret (Joan) De La POLE
> 5. Elizabeth De La POLE (Nun)
> 6. Agnes De La POLE

Joan (Margaret) De La POLE
> Born: 1333, Wyverton, Nottinghamshire, England
> Father: Richard De La POLE (Sir)
> Mother: Joan ?
> Married: Thomas CHAWORTH
> Children:
> 1. William CHAWORTH (Sir)
> 2. Thomas CHAWORTH

Margaret (Joan) De La POLE
> Born: 1335, Wyverton, Nottinghamshire, England
> Father: Richard De La POLE (Sir)
> Mother: Joan ?
> Married: Ralph BASSETT

William De La POLE
> Born: ABT 1316
> Died: 26 Jun 1366, Chrishall, Essex, England
> Father: Richard De La POLE (Sir)
> Mother: Joan ?
> Married 5: John HARPENDEN

William De La POLE (Sir)
> Born: ABT 1302, Linby, Nottinghamshire, England
> Died: 21 Jun 1366
> Buried: Carthusian Priory, Hull
> Notes: The Complete Peerage vol. XII p 1. pp. 434–437.
> Father: William De La POLE (Sir)
> Mother: Elena ROTENHERYNG
> Married: Margaret (Catherine) De NORWICH (b. ABT 1306–d. 1382) (dau. of Walter De
>   Norwich and Catherine De Hadersete)
> Children:
> 1. Michael De La POLE (1° E. Suffolk)
> 2. Edmund De La POLE (Sir)
> 3. Walter De La POLE (Sir)
> 4. Thomas De La POLE (Sir)
> 5. Blanche De La POLE (B. Scrope of Bolton)
> 6. Catherine De La POLE
> 7. Margaret De La POLE
> 8. Isabel De La POLE

Thomas De La POLE (Sir)
Died: 24 Nov 1361
Father: William De La POLE (Sir)
Mother: Margaret (Catherine) De NORWICH

Blanche De La POLE (B. Scrope of Bolton)
Born: 1328
Died: 1378
Father: William De La POLE (Sir)
Mother: Margaret (Catherine) De NORWICH
Married: Richard SCROPE (1° B. Scrope of Bolton)
Children:
1. Roger SCROPE (2° B. Scrope of Bolton)
2. William SCROPE (1° E. Wiltshire)
3. Stephen SCROPE (Sir)
4. Richard SCROPE

Catherine De La POLE
Born: ABT 1341
Father: William De La POLE (Sir)
Mother: Margaret (Catherine) De NORWICH
Married: Anthony DICKINSON (b. ANT 1350–d. 1396) (son of Hugh Dickinson and Judith Robinson)
Children:
1. Richard DICKINSON (b. ABT 1377)

Margaret De La POLE
Born: 1321
Died: 1366
Father: William De La POLE (Sir)
Mother: Margaret (Catherine) De NORWICH
Married: Robert De NEVILLE of Hornby (Sir) 1344, Hornby, Lancashire, England
Children:
1. Thomas NEVILLE of Hornby (Sir)
2. Joan NEVILLE
3. Margaret NEVILLE

Isabel De La POLE
Father: William De La POLE (Sir)
Mother: Margaret (Catherine) De NORWICH
Married: Robert BRADESTON (Sir) (son of Thomas Bradeston, 1° B. Bradeston, and Isabel ?)
Children:
1. Thomas BRADESTON (2° B. Bradeston) (b. ABT 1352) (m. Ela De St. Lo)

Edmund De La POLE (Sir)
Born: ABT 1337
Died: 1419
Father: William De La POLE (Sir)
Mother: Margaret (Catherine) De NORWICH
Married 1: Elizabeth HANDLO (dau. of Richard Handlo and Isabella De St. Amand)
Children:
1. Elizabeth De La POLE
2. Catherine De La POLE
Married 2: Matilda LOVET (d. 1393) (dau. of John Lovet) (w. of *Andrew Sackville*)

Children:
3. Walter De La POLE

Elizabeth De La POLE
Born: 14 Jul 1362
Died: 14 Dec 1403/4
Father: Edmund De La POLE (Sir)
Mother: Elizabeth HANDLO
Married: Ingleram Le BRUYN (b. ABT 1360) (son of William Le Bruyn and Alice Layer)
Children:
1. Maurice Le BRUYN (Sir) (b. 1386–d. 1466) (m. Elizabeth Radford)

Catherine De La POLE
Born: ABT 1370
Died: 16 Feb 1430/1431
Father: Edmund De La POLE (Sir)
Mother: Elizabeth HANDLO
Married: Robert JAMES (b. ABT 1375) ABT 1400
Children:
1. Christina JAMES (b. ABT 1400) (m. Edmund Rede)

Walter De La POLE
Born: 1371, Sanston, Cambridgeshire, England
Died: 1444
Father: Edmund De La POLE (Sir)
Mother: Matilda LOVET
Married: Elizabeth BRADESTON (b. ABT 1373–d. 1429) (dau. of Thomas Bradeston, 2° B.
    Bradeston, and Ela De St. Lo)
Children:
1. Margaret De La POLE

Margaret De La POLE
Died: 1426
Father: Walter De La POLE
Mother: Elizabeth BRADESTON
Married: Thomas INGOLDSTHORPE (b. ABT 1401–d. 1422) (son of John Ingoldesthorpe and
    Elizabeth De Borough)
Children:
1. Edmund INGOLDSTHORPE (Sir) (b. ABT 1421–d. 1456) (m. Joan Tiptoft)

Michael De La POLE (1° E. Suffolk)
Born: ABT 1330
Acceded: 6 Aug 1385
Died: 1389
Buried: Carthusian Priory, Hull
Notes: Lord De la Pole, The Complete Peerage vol. XII p1 .pp. 437–440
Father: William De La POLE (Sir)
Mother: Margaret (Catherine) De NORWICH
Married: Catherine De WINGFIELD BEF 18 Oct 1361
Children:
1. Michael De La POLE (2° E. Suffolk)
2. John De La POLE (Canon of York)
3. Anne De La POLE
4. Margaret De La POLE
5. Elizabeth De La POLE

6. Thomas De La POLE (Sir Knight)

7. William De La POLE

8. Richard De La POLE

Anne De La POLE
Born: ABT 1378, Suffolk, Suffolk, England
Father: Michael De La POLE (1° E. Suffolk)
Mother: Catherine De WINGFIELD
Married 1: Gerard LISLE (son of Warin De Lisle, B. Lisle, and Margaret Pypard) 1373, Kingston Lisle, Berkshire, England
Married 2: Robert THORLEY ABT 1395, Snitterfield, Warwickshire, England
Children:
1. Margaret THORLEY (B. De La Warr) (b. ABT 1396–d. by 24 Nov 1433) (m. Reginald West, 2° B. West of Oakhanger / 7° B. De La Warr)

John De La POLE (Canon of York)
Died: 1415
Buried: Wingfield Church, Suffolk
Father: Michael De La POLE (1° E. Suffolk)
Mother: Catherine De WINGFIELD

Thomas De La POLE (Sir Knight)
Born: 1363, Hull, Yorkshire, England
Died: 31 Mar 1415/6 / 1433
Father: Michael De La POLE (1° E. Suffolk)
Mother: Catherine De WINGFIELD
Married: Anne CHENEY
Children:
1. Catherine De La POLE

Catherine De La POLE
Born: ABT 1416
Died: ABT 14 Oct 1488
Father: Thomas De La POLE (Sir Knight)
Mother: Anne CHENEY
Married 1: Miles STAPLETON of Ingham (Sir) ABT 1440
Children:
1. Elizabeth STAPLETON
2. Joan STAPLETON
Married 2: Richard HARCOURT of Wytham (Sir Knight) BEF 1477, Stanton Harcourt, Oxfordshire, England
Children:
1. William HARCOURT

Michael De La POLE (2° E. Suffolk)
Born: ABT 1361/2, Hull, York, England
Acceded: 1398
Died: 18 Sep 1415, siege of Harfleur
Buried: Wingfield Church, Suffolk, England
Notes: The Complete Peerage vol. XII p 1. pp. 441–442.
Father: Michael De La POLE (1° E. Suffolk)
Mother: Catherine De WINGFIELD
Married: Catherine STAFFORD (C. Suffolk) 1383
Children:
1. Elizabeth De La POLE

2. Michael De La POLE (3° E. Suffolk)
3. William De La POLE (1° D. Suffolk)
4. John De La POLE (Sir)
5. Alexander De La POLE
6. Thomas De La POLE (Clerk)
7. Phillippa De La POLE
8. Isabel De La POLE (B. Morley)
9. Catherine De La POLE (Abbess of Barking)

Phillippa De La POLE
 Father: Michael De La POLE (2° E. Suffolk)
 Mother: Catherine STAFFORD (C. Suffolk)
 Married: Hugh BURNELL (3° B. Burnell) (b. ABT 1347–d. 27 Nov 1420)
 Children:
 1. Edward BURNELL (d. 25 Oct 1415, at Agincourt)

Isabel De La POLE (B. Morley)
 Born: 1395, Cotton, Suffolk, England
 Father: Michael De La POLE (2° E. Suffolk)
 Mother: Catherine STAFFORD (C. Suffolk)
 Married: Thomas MORLEY (5° B. Morley)
 Children:
 1. Robert MORLEY (6° B. Morley) (m. Elizabeth De Ros)
 2. Elizabeth MORLEY (m. John Arundell)
 3. Anne MORLEY (m. John Hastings, 9° B. Hastings)

Elizabeth De La POLE
 Born: ABT 1406, Cotton, Suffolk, England
 Father: Michael De La POLE (2° E. Suffolk)
 Mother: Catherine STAFFORD (C. Suffolk)
 Married: John FOIX (E. Kendal) (b. ABT 1404)

Thomas De La POLE (Clerk)
 Died: BEF 15 Jul 1433
 Father: Michael De La POLE (2° E. Suffolk)
 Mother: Catherine STAFFORD (C. Suffolk)

Michael De La POLE (3° E. Suffolk)
 Born: 1394
 Acceded: 1415
 Died: 25 Oct 1415, Agincourt
 Notes: The Complete Peerage vol. XII p 1. pp. 442–443.
 Father: Michael De La POLE (2° E. Suffolk)
 Mother: Catherine STAFFORD (C. Suffolk)
 Married: Elizabeth MOWBRAY BEF 24 Nov 1403
 Children:
 1. Catherine De La POLE (Nun at Bruisyard)
 2. Elizabeth De La POLE
 3. Isabel De La POLE

Catherine De La POLE (Nun at Bruisyard)
 Born: 6 May 1410
 Father: Michael De La POLE (3° E. Suffolk)
 Mother: Elizabeth MOWBRAY

Elizabeth De La POLE
> Born: 22 Jul 1411
> Died: BEF 1422
> Father: Michael De La POLE (3° E. Suffolk)
> Mother: Elizabeth MOWBRAY

Isabel De La POLE
> Born: 4 Jun 1415
> Died: BEF 1422
> Father: Michael De La POLE (3° E. Suffolk)
> Mother: Elizabeth MOWBRAY

William De La POLE (1° D. Suffolk)
> Born: 16 Oct 1396, Cotton, Suffolk
> Acceded: 2 Jun 1448
> Died: 2 May 1450, Dover
> Buried: Carthusian Priory, Hull
> Notes: Knight of the Garter. Served for 24 years in the wars. In command at the victory of Verneuil, and at the siege of Orleans. Taken prisoner by Joan of Arc. Assassinated 1450, murdered in an open boat and his head was cut off and thrown on the beach. The Complete Peerage vol. XII p 1. pp. 443–448.
> Father: Michael De La POLE (2° E. Suffolk)
> Mother: Catherine STAFFORD (C. Suffolk)
> Married: Alice CHAUCER (d. 1475) (dau. of Thomas Chaucer and Maud De Burghersh) (w.1 of Sir John Philip—w.2 of Thomas Montagu, 4° E Salisbury) 11 Nov 1430
> Children:
> 1. John De La POLE (2° D. Suffolk)

John De La POLE (2° D. Suffolk)
> Born: 27 Sep 1442
> Died: 1491
> Buried: Wingfield Church, Suffolk
> Notes: Knight of the Garter.
> Father: William De La POLE (1° D. Suffolk)
> Mother: Alice CHAUCER
> Married 1: Margaret BEAUFORT (C. Richmond/ C. Derby) 1449 ANNULMENT 1452
> Married 2: Elizabeth PLANTAGENET (D. Suffolk) BEF Oct 1460
> Children:
>   1. John De La POLE (1° E. Lincoln)
>   2. Geoffrey De La POLE
>   3. Edmund De La POLE (4° E. Suffolk)
>   4. Humphrey De La POLE (Rev)
>   5. William De La POLE (Sir)
>   6. Richard De La POLE (5° E. Suffolk)
>   7. Edward De La POLE (Archdeacon of Richmond)
>   8. Dorothy De La POLE
>   9. Catherine De La POLE (B. Stourton of Stourton)
>   10. Anne De La POLE (Prioress of Syon)
>   11. Elizabeth De La POLE

John De La POLE (1° E. Lincoln)
> Born: ABT 1462
> Christened: 13 Mar 1466
> Acceded: 13 Mar 1466
> Died: 16 Jun 1487, battle of Stoke
> Notes: During the last year of the reign of King Richard III, he was designated heir to the throne,

being Richard's closest adult male relative in the Yorkist line. After Richard's defeat at the Battle of Bosworth in 1485, Lincoln was reconciled with the new king, Henry VII, but soon became impatient for power and tried to achieve it by supporting the claims of the boy pretender, Lambert Simnel. Lincoln was killed at the Battle of Stoke in 1487, at which the rebel army was defeated.
Father: John De La POLE (2° D. Suffolk)
Mother: Elizabeth PLANTAGENET (D. Suffolk)
Married: Margaret FITZALAN (C. Lincoln)
Children:
1. Edward De La POLE

Edmund De La POLE (4° E. Suffolk)
Born: 1471
Died: 4 May 1513, beheaded
Buried: Church of the Minories, without Aldgate
Notes: Knight of the Garter. On accepting the accession of Henry VII he surrendered his claim to the Dukedom of Suffolk. Degraded 1500. Beheaded 1513.
Father: John De La POLE (2° D. Suffolk)
Mother: Elizabeth PLANTAGENET (D. Suffolk)
Married: Margaret SCROPE (C. Suffolk)
Children:
1. Anne De La POLE (Nun) (b. ABT 1497)
2. Elizabeth De La POLE (b. ABT 1498–d. AFT 1513, plague)

Elizabeth De La POLE
Died: AFT 1489
Father: John De La POLE (2° D. Suffolk)
Mother: Elizabeth PLANTAGENET (D. Suffolk)
Married: Henry LOVELL (B. Morley)

William De La POLE (Sir)
Born: ABT 1494
Died: BEF 20 Nov 1540, Tower of London, London, England
Father: John De La POLE (2° D. Suffolk)
Mother: Elizabeth PLANTAGENET (D. Suffolk)
Married: Catherine STOURTON (B. Grey of Codnor) BEF 8 Jun 1501, Stourton, Wiltshire, England

Richard De La POLE (5° E. Suffolk)
Died: 24 Feb 1524, battle of Pavia
Buried: St. Augustine, Pavia
Notes: styled himself the E. Suffolk, the "White Rose." The Complete Peerage vol. XII p 1. p. 453–454.
Father: John De La POLE (2° D. Suffolk)
Mother: Elizabeth PLANTAGENET (D. Suffolk)

Catherine De La POLE (B. Stourton of Stourton)
Father: John De La POLE (2° D. Suffolk)
Mother: Elizabeth PLANTAGENET (D. Suffolk)
Married: William STOURTON (5° B. Stourton of Stourton)

Anne De La POLE (Prioress of Syon)
Died: AFT 1495
Notes: Prioress at Syon Abbey.
Father: John De La POLE (2° D. Suffolk)
Mother: Elizabeth PLANTAGENET (D. Suffolk)

Edward De La POLE (Archdeacon of Richmond)
Acceded: 6 Jan 1484
Died: BEF 8 Oct 1485
Father: John De La POLE (2° D. Suffolk)
Mother: Elizabeth PLANTAGENET (D. Suffolk)

Humphrey De La POLE (Rev)
Born: 1 Aug 1474
Acceded: Leverington, Cambridge
Died: 15 Feb 1513
Father: John De La POLE (2° D. Suffolk)
Mother: Elizabeth PLANTAGENET (D. Suffolk)

William De La POLE of Harrogate
Born: 1302
Died: 1337, Harrogate
Married: Amy ?
Children:
1. Michael De La POLE of Harrogate
2. Richard De La POLE
3. Edmund De La POLE
4. William De La POLE

Michael De La POLE of Harrogate
Born: 1330
Died: 1343, Rothbury
Father: William De La POLE of Harrogate
Mother: Amy ?
Married: Isabelle DANYERS 1338

Richard De La POLE
Born: 1286
Died: 1338
Father: William De La POLE of Harrogate
Mother: Amy ?

Edmund De La POLE
Born: 1288
Died: 1337, Hull
Father: William De La POLE of Harrogate
Mother: Amy ?

William De La POLE
Born: 1336
Father: William De La POLE of Harrogate
Mother: Amy ?
Married: Phillippa HUSSEY 1338
Children:
1. Anne De La POLE
2. Guy De La POLE (Sir)
3. Phillippa De La POLE
4. George De La POLE

To place an elegant finial on the chronicles of the De la Poles, and to bring the transformations of British Jewry down into recent times, it is likely that this medieval Welsh/English line also produced the famous American rabbi David de Sola Pool. Born in London on May 1885, David married in Jerusalem Tamar Hershenson, the daughter of Chaim Hirschensohn, a Zionist settler from Pinsk in the Polesia section of Belarus. In 1907, David became the minister of Congregation Shearith Israel in New York, the oldest synagogue in British America, also founded by Sephardic Jews, a position he held for 63 years, until his death in 1970. Over his long career, he edited service books for both Sephardic and Ashkenazic rites, was president of the American Jewish Historical Society in New York and wrote *Why I Am Jewish* (1957). David's parents were Eliezar Pool, a Dutch Jew, and Abigail Davis, an English Jew; they were married at Bevis Marks, the oldest English synagogue. His grandfather was Solomon Pool, born about 1820 in Rotterdam, the son of Eliezer Pool. There the genealogy stops, but many Pools and Vanderpools are recorded in the Netherlands around 1800, and they typically formed unions with other members of the Sephardic trading aristocracy.[7]

Cardinal Reginald Pole, descended from a Polish Jewish family (Print Collection, Miriam and Ira D. Wallach Division of Art, Prints and Photographs, The New York Public Library, Astor, Lenox and Tilden Foundations).

Bardi and Peruzzi Banking Companies of Florence

To turn now to a parallel situation, in the early 1300s Florence was an independent city-state in Italy. Two of the primary banking companies in the city were the Bardi and the Peruzzi, both of which made loans of substantial amounts to the English Crown. Prior to this time, the Riccardi of Lucca and the Frescobaldi banking houses had also made substantial loans to the English Crown. Ultimately, all four companies were bankrupted by the failure of England to repay the loans. As Unwin (1918) comments: "Four great companies of Italian merchants had been ruined by dealings with English Kings—the Riccardi of Lucca under Edward I, the Frescobaldi of Florence under Edward III and the Bardi and Peruzzi under Edward III" (10, online version).[8]

Lists of Names of Merchants of the Societies of the Bardi and Peruzzi of Florence, Trading in England, during the Reign of Edward III (Compiled from Calendars of Patent and Close Rolls). Merchants of the Society of the Bardi of Florence Trading in England during the Reign of Edward the Third

Clavo Angelini	Bartolommeo de' Bardi
Alessandro de' Bardi	Bartolommeo di (Sir) Rodolfo de' Bardi (fn. 1)

Bindo di Gianni de' Bardi (fn. 1)
Filippo de' Bardi
Gualtiero di Filippo de' Bardi (fn. 1) (fn. 3)
Pietro di (Sir) Rodolfo de' Bardi (fn. 1)
(Sir) Rodolfo di Giovanni de' Bardi (fn. 1) (fn. 4)
Taldo di (Sir) Rodolfo de' Bardi (fn. 1)
Bauchino Belchari
Pietro Bene
Francesco di Bocci, or Boschi (fn. N)
Giovanni Boletti
Gherardo Boninsegni
Tano Cecco (fn. 2)
Lottieri di Colino
Dino Forzetti
Giovanni di Francesco
Manetto Franzesi
Andrea Gherardini
Alessandro Gianni (fn. 3)
Filippo Gianni (fn. 3)

Lottieri Gianni (fn. 3)
Giotto di Giocchi (fn. 4) (fn. 5)
Giotto Ubertino di Giocchi (fn. 1) (fn. 5)
Francesco Grandoni
Roberto Infangati Rinuccio
Ubertino Infangati (fn. 1)
Francesco Lapi
Niccolo Marini (fn. 1)
Niccolo Marsi (fn. 2)
Pietro Maso
Perotto Matr (fn. 1)
Giovanni di Mevane
Cione Migliori (fn. 6)
Jacopo Niccolini
Pietro Rinieri
Rinucci (fn. N)
Giotto Roberti (fn. 1)
Tommaso Tedaldi
Taldo Valori (fn. 7)

In 1345, at the time of the failure of the Bardi and Peruzzi, the Company of the Bardi under Sir Ridolfo di Bartolo Bardi was thus composed:

Filippo Bardi
Ridolfo di Bartolo Bardi
Gherardo Boninsegni

Angiolo di Gherardo Lanfredini
Lapo Niccoli
Taldo Valori (fn. 1)

The above subscribed to the "arrangement" arrived at on 6 September 1347.

The following were the "Syndics" appointed by the Commune to assist the Creditors of the Bardi.[9]

Piero di Lippo Aldobrandini
Giovanni Arnolfi
Pegolotti Francesco Balducci
Naddo Bucelli
Paolo di Cecco Gianni

Silvestro di Manetto Issachi
Jacopo di Piero Machiavelli
Silvestro di Rinieri Peruzzi
Silvestro di Ricciardo Ricci

Merchants of the Society of the Peruzzi of Florence Trading in England during the Reign of Edward the Third

Arrigo Accorsi
Piero Aldobrandi
Tommaso d'Arnoldo de' Bagnesi (at one time representative
of the Company in Genoa)
Giovanni di Tano Baroncelli (Representative in London)
Riccardo Baroncelli
Piero Bernardini
Piero di Bernardino Dini (priore)
Guido Donati
Riccardo Fangni

Bonfantino di Vanni Fantini
Jacopo di Gherardo Gentili (priore)
Jacopo Gherardi
Giovanni Giuntini
Baldo Orlandini
Piero di Simone di Giovanni Orlandini
Neri Perini
Andrea di messer Amideo Peruzzi
Bonifazio di Tommaso Peruzzi (priore, direttore, 1336–1340, died in London, 1340)
Dionigi di Giovanni di Giotto Peruzzi
Filippo di Tommaso Peruzzi

Jacopo di Filippo Peruzzi
Ridolfo di Tommaso Peruzzi
Roberto di Tommaso Peruzzi
Tommaso d'Arnoldo Peruzzi (priore, direttore,
    1300–1331)
Zanobi di Tano Raugi (priore)

Giovanni Ricoveri
Piero Simone
Angelo Soderini
Giovanni Stefano
Riccardo di Geri Stefano
Stefano Uguccioni

Listed are those merchants who held office in Florence at any time, or were Directors of the Company[10] and the members of the Society of the Peruzzi from 1336 to the time of the failure, who subscribed to the "arrangement" of 6 September 1347. Pacino di Tommaso Peruzzi was Head of the Company.

Gherardino, and Giovanni di Tano, and Gherardo di Michi Baroncelli
Stefano d'Uguccione Bencivenni
Francesco Forzetti
Baldo di Gianni Orlandini
Berto di Messer Ridolfo Peruzzi
Bonifazio and Pacino di Tommaso Peruzzi
Donato, and Bartolomeo di Giotto Peruzzi
Donato di Pacino Peruzzi
Niccolo, Ottaviano, Andrea, and Napoleone d'Amideo Peruzzi
Pacino, Lepre, Sandro, and Giovanni di Guido Peruzzi
Tommaso di Messer Filippo Peruzzi
Ruggeri di Lottieri Silimanni
Geri di Stefano Soderini
Giovanni, and Guccio di Stefano Soderini
Filippo Villani (brother of the Chronicler)

The following were the Syndics appointed by the Commune to assist the creditors of the Peruzzi (474–76).

Braccino Feri
Manetto Filicaia
Filippo di Giovanni Macchiavelli
Zanobi di Ser Piero Ognano

Sandro di Simone Quarata
Vanni Rondinelli
Cambino Signorini
Ugolino Vieri

As the lists given above illustrate, there were both Jews and Muslims working with the Bardi and Peruzzi companies. An example of how these foreigners interfaced with local English Christians and Jews and crypto–Jews comes from an Arabic document contemporary with the earliest dated Hebrew manuscript written in England, assigned with great certainty to the year 1189. Leading Hebrew paleographer and codicologist Malachi Beit-Arié wrote a book-length study on this Hebrew biblical manuscript in which one of the appendices, by Zefira Entin Rokéa, deals with a related document in the library of Corpus Christi College at Oxford. This is an Arabic financial record written in Sephardic Hebrew script containing accounts of payments made to a Jew by various members of the English nobility and clergy. Beit-Arié identifies the Jewish payee as Solomon ben Isaac, whose Hebrew seal from the middle of the twelfth century was discovered in Edinburgh some years ago.[11] Solomon ben Isaac is believed by some to have been a Sephardic Jewish businessman visiting England, but he may have lived there for that matter. Whether he was a visitor or resident, he clearly had far-ranging dealings with religious, governmental and commercial authorities. Before these rare manuscripts came to light, it was generally believed that English Jews wrote no Hebrew books in England but imported them from France and elsewhere. It was also doubted that there was any substantial business correspondence between English centers of commerce and Sephardic Jews and Muslims.

For comprehensive lists of English merchants who came from Jewish ancestry or had Jewish associations during this time, see Appendix C: London Merchants.

10

Enter the Tudors 1450—1550

We now want to take the reader on a speculative journey. The Tudor family, which counts among its members the British monarchs Henry VII, Henry VIII, Mary I and Elizabeth I—some of the most powerful in the history of the country—originated in Wales. Penmynydd, a village on Anglesey, claims to be the birthplace of the Tudor dynasty. The Welsh surname Tudor (Tewdwr) is widely used in north Wales. In the form Tudur it is found in that region in frequencies "reaching 2 percent in Rhos and Rhufoniog and 1 percent in four other northern areas, including Powys Fadog."[1] In chapter 8, we presented a case that Wales was heavily populated from the 500s and 600s forward by persons who were of Jewish and Muslim ancestry. The Tudor origin-place of Anglesey (Mon in Welsh), we noted, has an extraordinarily high incidence of the Mediterranean/North African DNA type E1b1b (30 percent), a leading Jewish haplogroup. There were, in addition, persistent Jewish remnants in all likelihood left from the Roman occupation of Britain. We have seen how Wales' first saints bear the Jewish names Aaron, Alexander, David and Solomon, among others, and how the background of these saints was assigned by tradition to Caerleon in south Wales. The question naturally arises whether the Tudors came from like ancestry.

To begin with, the family name of Tudor itself points to Jewish ancestry. Elizabeth I famously bore a Hebrew name, one she boasted of herself,[2] and Henry VIII's older brother was named Arthur, perhaps more than a bow to chivalric fashion. Tudor, like the Welsh Tewdwr (sometimes written Thoedor), is derived from Theodore, in Greek Theodoros. The Greek meaning is "the gift of the Lord," and in Jewish tradition the name appears as Todros, Todras, Todres and Todris, adopted as a translation of Netaneil or Nathaniel.[3] The periodic reappearance of the names Nathan, Agnes (Nest) and Japeth in the Tudor "royal line" lends strength to the supposition that originally the Tudors were Greek-speaking Jews, perhaps from Byzantine North Africa shortly before its fall to the Moslems.

Significantly, Theodore is a name repeated over and over again in the Makhiri family of Jewish princes in Narbonne and Toulouse in southern France, beginning with that princedom's founding by Machir. Also known as Al-Makhiri, Aymeri, Ha-Makhiri, Makhiri, Natronai, Theodoric (his Frankish name, given to him after he married his sister to Pepin the Short), the Exilarch, Nasi and King of the Jews, this refugee from Baghdad was regarded as a descendant of King David, whose descendants were to be judges and rulers over all nations.[4] Among the *nesim* or princes who bore the name Todros in the Jewish state in France were Todros ben Makhir, Todros ben Moses, nephew of Kalonymos the Great (ca. 1170), Todros Bonmacip son of Kalonymos, Todros the father of Kalonymos and Todros son of Kalonymos the Great, who composed liturgical poetry in Hebrew. We have seen above how the descendants of Machir intermarried with the Carolingians and introduced the Lion of Judah and other Davidic appurtenances of empire to French and Flemish noble lines, perpetuating in the process

Occitan Jewish names like Ada, Adela, Edna, Itta (Judith), Alexander, Folk (Raphael) and Natan.

The agreed-upon facts regarding the origins of the Tudor family may be summarized as follows. The earliest named progenitor of the family was Marchudd ap Cynan, Lord of Brynffenigl, in Denbighland, North Wales, who lived in the mid–800s. The family estates overlap with the high concentrations of E1b1b male haplotypes found in North Wales and are also coterminous with early Roman fortresses and post–Roman settlement in the North Wales region. The arms of Marchudd consisted of "Gu, a Saracen's head, erased at the neck, argent, environed about the temples with a wreath of gold and argent." This emblem is still held by Marchudd's present descendant, Lord Mostyn, according to *Burke's Peerage.*[5] We are told that Marchud was father of Karwedh ap Marchudd, Lord of Brynffenigl, whose son, Jafeth ap Karwedh, Lord of Brynffenigl, was father of Nathan ap Jafeth, Lord of Brynffenigl, who had two sons, Edryd and Edwin, and an unnamed daughter, wife of Madoc Crwm, Lord of Llechwedd Issaf, founder of a noble house in North Wales and Powys. These facts would strongly suggest a Muslim background for the family, or Jewish antecedents who lived under Islam.

Given names for the sons of the lineage include Arseth, Jafeth, Nathan, Karwedh, Einion, Ddu and Levan. These would argue for a Jewish or Hebrew ancestry for the family. A Tudor Walensis occurs in Domesday Book (1086) as the pre–Norman suzerain of a Welsh district apportioned to Roger de Montgomery and has been identified as Tudur ap Rhys Sais.[6] Of Rhys ap Tudor (in other words, the "inverse" of the Judaic-styled patronymics), Welsh tradition records:

> Rhys ap Tewdwr had an only daughter, Nest,[7] who had a son by King Henry the First, Robert, Earl of Gloucester. By marriage with the daughter of Robert Fitzhamon [also a Jewish name], he succeeded to all his possessions in South Wales; and as the son of Nest, the only daughter of Rhys, was regarded by the Welsh as representing in some degree the princes of South Wales. He died in the year 1147.[8]

Skene's mention of Robert of Gloucester points to the exact moment when things (and people) Welsh were coming to the fore in the Norman world. Robert was the eldest illegitimate son of Henry I, a half-brother to the Empress Matilda, and he nearly became king of England. Significantly, it was the era when, as we have already witnessed, Henry of Huntingdon was writing his Hebraic-styled history, lifting large sections of it from Geoffrey of Monmouth, also known as Gruffud ap Arthur (chapters 7, 8).

The family were large landowners also in Denbigh in North Wales, especially around the area known as the Four Cantrels, and rose to prominence when one of its senior members, Ednyfed Fychan, became steward to Prince Llywelyn in 1215, remaining in that position until 1240. Ednyfed represented the prince in dealings with Henry III, as well as negotiating other Welsh state business. This stewardship role continued in the family until 1282. Upon the conquest of Wales by English king Edward I, the family switched its loyalty, and became supporters of the English monarchy through the reign of Richard II (1399).

The name floats up in records elsewhere in England as well. It occurs in Shropshire in 1221, and in 1287, shortly before the fatal decree of expulsion, there is a David ap Tudir mentioned in the assizes of Cheshire. The *Christian* Tudor enumerated as one of the freemen of Canterbury, to judge from his name, may have been a convert.

Sir Owen Meredith Tudor (Welsh *Owain ap Maredudd ap Tewdwr,* ca. 1400–1461) was descended from a daughter of the Welsh prince Rhys ap Gruffudd, Lord Rhys, and was the grandfather of the first Tudor king, Henry VII. After losing the Tudor lands to the English in the uprising of Owain Glendwr (Shakespeare's Owen Glendower), this Owain moved to

London and entered the service of Queen Catherine of Valois as her major-domo after the death of her husband Henry V of England. Owen and Catherine married, perhaps secretly, and among their children was Edmund Tudor, 1st earl of Richmond (1430–1 November 1456). Edmund married Lady Margaret Beaufort, and fathered Henry Tudor, the future king. It has frequently been pointed out that if Owen Tudor had elected to use his father's name, Maredudd, instead of the ap Tewdwr part from his grandfather when he became English, the rulers of England following the last of the Lancasters and Yorks would have been of the House of Meredith. He apparently had a reason for preferring Tudor. In addition to having a sort of éclat, unlike Meredith, Theodoros had precedents in Jewish history. Having been equated with Theodoric, Dietrich and Thierry, it was a name synonymous with heroes and rulers, celebrated throughout history, legend, epic and romance.

We now enter the latter half of the fifteenth century having identified a Jewish and Islamic presence in England connected with trade to and from the Continent and extending throughout the Mediterranean. Surprisingly, as we have documented, North Africa has also played a significant role in British history, especially from a Welsh point of view. With the last of the Crusades being fought in the previous century and the Ottoman Turks advancing Islam throughout Central Asia and North Africa, attention had drifted away from anti–Semitism at a national level toward the formation of global liaisons that enhanced wealth and capital and, derivatively, intellectual curiosity and exploration.

Rebecca Fraser observes of the period, "Instead of fighting suicidal wars among themselves, the European Kingdoms had begun to turn their energies outwards, exploring the unknown. By 1460 the Portuguese King, Henry the Navigator, had discovered the north-west coast of Africa. In 1481 Bristol merchants sailing west into the Atlantic hit on what ... may have been Newfoundland ... Edward IV supported the printer William Caxton ... enabling him to set up a press in the shadow of Westminster Abbey in 1476.... What people read was no longer controlled by the church.[9] There now circulated ... the uncensored literature of the Greeks and Romans.... It was the beginning of what is known as the Renaissance ... the humanist movement took hold in England."[10] It was perhaps indicative of the new liberality in thought and action, that Edward III's mistress, Jane Shore,[11] was the wife of a London merchant and very likely a Jewess. During this same time period the four great Inns at Court were constructed, housing lawyers, law scholars, legal students, and judges, as well as the court rooms where the common law was both created and enforced.

Earlier Documentation of Jewish Presence

Cecil Roth provides commentary on recognized Jews in England during the 1290–1609 period in which the decree of expulsion was in force, noting that no human law is absolutely observed in human society. Among these are the following episodes in Jewish history. In 1309, it was requested by Edward II that a Jew come to England to provide unspecified "services" to his majesty. As noted in the previous chapter, the House of Commons complained that the Florentine and Lombard financiers (the Riccardi, Bardi and Peruzzi Associations) "harbored Jews and Saracens in their midst."[12] Names suggested in Roth include Benedict Zacharie, David Jacobi of Lucca and Solomon de Alman (Alemane = Germany), goldsmith of Norwich. In 1410 Henry IV requested Elias Sabot, a Jewish physician, to travel from Italy to attend him. Sabot brought ten associates with him (the number necessary to form a *minyan*). Another Jewish physician, Samson de Mirabeau, was called to London to attend the mayor's wife a short time later.

Yet these represent the few public records of Jews coming into England from outside the country. As we have already proposed in the previous chapter, there were many secretly Jewish families living in England continuously since the Expulsion of 1290, in addition to others who trickled in later like the Welsh/Polish De la Pole clan. These persons congregated in the traditional Jewish urban strongholds of York, Lincoln, Norwich and London, and as merchants and traders in those regions of England where they had dwelt since the Roman settlement— the southwest coast, Bristol, Devon, Cornwall and southwestern Wales. As in the 1290–1450 period, this is where we find them.

Roberts et al. (223) write that "between 1490 and 1510 tin production in Cornwall and Devon, which had been stagnant, doubled. This came about because shaft mining replaced open cast mining, a change that meant the triumph of the capitalized entrepreneur.... Costly equipment ... became necessary that only a rich merchant or enterprising landlord could furnish." Notably, this increase occurred at exactly the time when *converso* and Muslim Spaniards were exiting Spain to seek shelter from the Inquisition and the fall of Muslim Granada. Since these are exactly the persons who had perfected shaft mining engineering, the "sudden" appearance of this new technology—together with ready sums of capital—should not be surprising.[13]

Bristol as a seaport expanded its size and reach under William Canynges (Turkish).[14] Canynges "owned 3000 tons of shipping and employed 1000 carpenters and workmen" according to Roberts et al. (223). Canynges was mayor of Bristol for five terms and served twice in the Parliament. His ships traded with Iceland, Finland and Denmark, as well as traveling to the Baltic ports. Canynges rebuilt the Bristol Church of St. Mary and became Dean of Westbury in 1469. Bristol receives scant attention in Cesarani's collection of essays on port Jews—evidently, modern researchers' scrutiny of records does not extend beneath the veneer of English-sounding names. The situation is better in Matir's work on Muslims in Elizabethan England, for he notes that the Privy Council complained in 1625 of "three or four" Turks and Moors in Bristol, as well as "ten in Baronet Seymor."[15]

Henry VII, the first of the Tudor kings of England, was a strong supporter of the Bristol merchants and traders. He helped them fund the 1496 and 1498 voyages of John Cabot (Giovanni Caboto—born in Genoa, Italy, and a citizen of Venice)[16] which led to the discovery of Newfoundland. Caboto's son, Sebastian, engaged in similar voyages from Bristol, sailing into Hudson's Bay in 1508. The Bristol merchants—together with their Sephardic kin and business partners in Portugal—were hoping to find a western route to the Spice Islands and the East Indies. The Italian financiers behind the Tudor entrée into the New World have recently been studied by Francesco Guidi-Bruscoli of the University of Florence.[17]

A Case in Point: The Cely Family

We take a closer look now at the business dealings of England's crypto–Jewish population during the Tudor era of Henry VII. The Cely family (whose name was likely originally Uzille, pronounced "ooseelee," from southern France) apparently lived in Cornwall, prior to moving to London and becoming wool merchants. Malden (1900, vii) writes, "The whole family and their connections were continually passing backwards and forwards between England, Calais and Flanders." They had a helper/servant named Josce Parmenter (Jewish given name and Calabrian Italian surname).[18] The great historical value of the Cely family is a cache of letters that were discovered in recent times; these essentially are the traders' business correspondence between 1475 and 1488 and provide a remarkable picture of the London-Calais Staple during the reigns of Edward IV and Henry VII. In the introduction to the book containing the letters, Malden states that "the members of the Cely family were prosperous men. They own land, they buy hawks and horses, they give rich presents, they turn over 2,000 lbs. of wool a year, and negotiate with rich gentlemen for their daughters in marriage."[19]

The list of people with whom the Celys did business in Calais (often spelled Callez, Calles or Caleys in the correspondence) is indicative, we propose, of their private status as Jews. A partial listing is given below:

Cely Trading Partners in Callez and Elsewhere

Wylliam Adam (Jewish)	James Holland
Thomas Arnolde	Thomas Horne
Richard Awode	William Jaccson
Barbell Berneught	Deryck Jacobson
Aleamus Bolonys ("Bolognaise," i.e. from Bologna)	Assche Laybacar
	Robard Lollay
Hewe Brone	Benyngne DeCasonn ("Lombard")
Nicolas Brystall (Bristol)	John, Domynco and Bartholomeo ("Lombards")
Anthony Corsy ("spaynarde")	
Rychard Cortes	John Jacope ("Lombard")
John Cossyn	Lewys More ("Lombard")
John Dangell (d'Angel)	Collard Messedawzth
John Danyell	Robard Lyncolln
John Dave	Gysebryght Moresson
Robarde Dawtie	Peyrs Morres
Jacob de Bloke (Black)	Adam Moy
Deago DeCastro ("Spaniard")	Gilbert Pamar
Gyllam de la Four	Joysse Parmenter
John de Lopys (Lopes) (Sephardic)	John Perys (Peres)
Romenett DeSall	John Reynolds (Moer)
Gabryell de Sarte ("genovo")	Thomas Samson
Gomers de Sore	Peter Sauley ("genovo")
John Doo	Robard Solle
Harry Franck	Thomas Spycer
Petyr Geneways (Genoese)	John Spynyell (Spanial)
Andrew Goodes/Good	Jacob Tymanson (Lombard??)
Jacob Gyesbryght	Jacob van de Base
Tamas/Thomas Hadam (Muslim)	Danyell van de Rade
Jacob Harman	Jacob Williamson
Ryscharde Herzon	

What we see from this listing is documentary evidence that the Celys were actively trading with Sephardim in Portugal and Spain, such as Cortes, de Lopys, Spynyell, Jewish members of the Bardi and Peruzzi banking associations of Florence, such as Peter Sauly, Gabryell de Sarte, and some Jewish traders from the Netherlands and its surrounding region, such as John Danyell, Ryscharde Herzon, John Perys, Tamas Hadam, Assche Laybacar, Deryck Jacobson, Jacob Harman, Robarde Dawtie (= David), Jacob Tymonson, Thomas Samson and a possible Muslim or Arab, Richard Awode.

This should not be surprising since the purpose of the Calais Staple from Edward IV to Henry VIII was to generate revenue for the English Crown. Further, at this point the Catholic Church was deeply corrupt, widely viewed as spiritually insolvent, and reduced to selling pardons for sin (termed "indulgences") to raise money for the papacy. Capitalism had effectively trumped religion in the value system of most European monarchs. We turn now to considering the Jewish experience under Henry VIII, the ruler who would separate the English Church from Roman authority forever.

Henry VIII, Thomas Cromwell and the Ultimate Revenge

In 1232 CE Henry III opened the Domus Conversorum in London. The purpose of the Converts' House was to provide a way station for English Jews who wished to convert to Christianity. As already discussed, such public acts of conversion could open the doors to opportunities, especially in the Church and royal household, where learned men, eager to advance their fortunes, could progress rapidly. In 1509 a very interesting English Jew arrived at the Domus seeking to become a Christian—Thomas Cromwell, who would have been twenty-one years old and ready to start a career in government service. Thomas was the son of Walter Cromwell (1463–1510), who is said to have come from Germany and worked variously (or concurrently) as a clothworker, blacksmith, and tavern keeper.

Thomas was initially employed by the Frescobaldi banking association of Florence as a cloth dealer at Syngsson's Mart in Middelburg, the Netherlands. If the Cromwells were originally German, Thomas would likely have been fluent in German-Dutch. We suspect that the family's name was originally Kromellin (an Ashkenazi Jewish surname) and was anglicized to Cromwell upon immigration. Thomas Cromwell was said to also be fluent in Latin, Italian and French. In 1514, he returned from the Netherlands to England, where, despite his layman status, he was put in charge of important church business by Cardinal Thomas Wolsey. In 1519 he married Elizabeth Wyckes, a clothier's daughter, and they had a son, Gregory. Cromwell studied law at the Inns of Court and became a member of Parliament in 1524.

By the late 1520s Cromwell was assisting Cardinal Wolsey to liquidate thirty Catholic monasteries in order to raise money for Wolsey's projects constructing public grammar schools and building the stonework of Oxford University. In 1529, Henry VIII, seeking to divorce Catherine of Aragon and marry Anne Boleyn, summoned Parliament. Cromwell was appointed by Henry to become his primary Parliamentary Counselor and soon, by 1532, had become Henry's chief minister—all in all, a meteoric rise for a former Jewish merchant.

We believe that one of the reasons—

Thomas Cromwell, the most powerful advocate for reformation of the Catholic Church under Henry VIII, was a Jewish convert to Christianity (Print Collection, Miriam and Ira D. Wallach Division of Art, Prints and Photographs, The New York Public Library, Astor, Lenox and Tilden Foundations).

despite his obvious managerial and political talent—which permitted Cromwell to advance so rapidly was the personal awareness of both Wolsey and Henry VIII, that he had earlier been a Jew—and therefore, his loyalty would be fixed upon his employer's welfare, rather than concern for church property or rules. Indeed, it would be a remarkable avenue of revenge upon the Catholic Christianity which had, in 1492, expelled the Jews from Spain and pursued them to the Netherlands, for a former Jew to assist in dismembering the Church.

Cromwell was perhaps the primary political architect in the separation of Britain from the Roman Church and the assertion of the sovereignty of the British monarch as supreme head of the Church in England. He played an important part in the English Reformation. The Parliamentary session of 1532, Cromwell's first as chief minister, clearly foretold a change of course. As is appreciated by commentators, many sources of papal revenue were cut off as ecclesiastical legislation was transferred to the King. During the next year came the legislation of the English Reforma-

The Princess Elizabeth became Queen Elizabeth I in 1558. Her reign supported the first British colony in the New World, Roanoke, which included Sephardic Jewish settlers (Print Collection, Miriam and Ira D. Wallach Division of Art, Prints and Photographs, The New York Public Library, Astor, Lenox and Tilden Foundations).

tion, the Act in Restraint of Appeals of 1533. This prohibited appeals on religious issues to Rome, and opened the way for Henry's divorce to proceed without the need for the Pope's permission. This radical law was drafted by Cromwell himself and its famous preamble declared:

> Where by divers sundry old authentic histories and chronicles, it is manifestly declared and expressed that this realm of England is an Empire, and so hath been accepted in the world, governed by one Supreme Head and King having the dignity and royal estate of the imperial Crown of the same, unto whom a body politic compact of all sorts and degrees of people divided in terms and by names of Spirituality and Temporality, be bounden and owe to bear next to God a natural and humble obedience.

When Cromwell used the label "Empire" for England, he did so in a special sense. Henry of Huntingdon had been the first to use the term to imply a mandate of world conquest and quasi-religious standing. This is also the meaning elaborated by Geoffrey of Monmouth in his account of how Arthur built an "empire" that rivaled, and indeed once attempted to conquer, Rome. In the thinking of all these men, the Kingdom of England is declared an Empire in and of itself, free from "the authority of any foreign potentates." This means that England now was an independent sovereign nation-state and no longer under the jurisdiction of the pope.

Cromwell was the most prominent of those who suggested to Henry VIII that the king make himself head of the English Church, and he advanced the Act of Supremacy of 1534 through Parliament. In 1535 Henry VIII appointed Cromwell as his first "Vice-regent in Spirituals." This gave Cromwell the power to act as supreme judge in ecclesiastical cases and provided a single unifying institution over the two provinces of the English Church (Canterbury and York). As Henry VIII's vicar-general, Cromwell next presided over the Dissolution of the Monasteries, which began in the winter of 1536. Henry next named Thomas as Baron Cromwell on July 9, 1536 and as Earl of Essex on April 18, 1540.

At this juncture, the nephew of the architect of the dissolution, Sir Richard Williams, chose Ramsey Abbey as the seat for his estate. On March 4, 1540, we learn, Ramsey Abbey along with the sum of £4,663 4s 2d was granted to Sir Richard Williams, alias Cromwell, in consideration of his good service, for a fee of £29.16s. The oldest abbey in the realm, home, as we have seen, of Henry of Huntingdon and locus of a Judaizing cell evident in Hebrew books and the Ramsey Psalter, was then simply turned into a quarry, the lead from the roofs being melted down into fodders and ingots for sale to the highest bidder. Gonville and Caius College in Cambridge was built from the stone and Kings and Trinity were partly rebuilt. Sir Richard was the son of Morgan Williams, a Welsh brewer at Putney, who married Thomas Cromwell's elder sister Katharine. In 1518 Williams had married Frances, daughter of Sir Thomas Murfyn, sheriff of the City of London. He became a favorite of King Henry VIII and was knighted in 1537.

Cromwell was now at the height of his political power—but also the man most hated by all those clerics and nobles remaining loyal to the Catholic Church. Conspiring against him, they played upon Henry's volatile temperament and religious conservatism. Cromwell was ordered beheaded by Henry VIII on July 28, 1540, at the Tower of London. Quite notably, the charges against him did not have to do with his encouraging the king to hurriedly marry Anne of Cleves (whom Henry had immediately disliked), the reason which most historians give as the rationale for his fall from grace. Rather, Cromwell was charged with "selling export licenses illegally, granting passports and commissions without royal knowledge, freeing people suspected of treason (these were almost universally Protestants), that he was base-born ... and most significantly, he was charged with heresy ... Cromwell, it was charged, had encountered and spread heretical literature, allowed heretics to preach [and] released them from prison."[20] In other words, Cromwell was guilty of displaying his Jewish roots and supporting those Jews who had adopted Protestantism. Notably, upon the scaffold Cromwell professed to die "in the traditional faith." Our interpretation of this statement is that at the moment of his death Cromwell chose to die as a Jew.

Despite Cromwell's fall, the religious reforms he had helped set in motion proceeded onward. Humanism received official government sanction at Oxford in 1535, "when the government issued royal injunctions that suppressed the study of canon law, encouraged the study of Greek, classical Latin, and Hebrew, mathematics and medicine." One of the most obvious reasons for this shift, largely ignored by traditional historians, was the dispersion of hundreds of thousands of Sephardic Jews out of Spain and Portugal and across Europe and North Africa from 1492 onward. Whether openly practicing Judaism, or more commonly pretending publicly to have embraced Christianity, these new Christians/Marranos/Anusim flooded into the commercial, legal, banking, academic and shipping sectors of the European economy.

As Roth writes:

> In 1512, the great Marrano mercantile and financial house of Mendes, which controlled the coveted pepper monopoly ... established its Antwerp branch. Its operations, carried on largely through New Christian agents, speedily spread across the North Sea. Ultimately, it became entrusted with the loan transactions of the English treasury. When, in 1532, proceedings were taken on a charge of Judaizing against Diego Mendes, the head of the Antwerp establishment, Henry VIII personally intervened on his behalf.[21]

Among the secret Jews in England at this time were Alves Lopez (recall "St. Elvis" of Wales and "de Lopez" who traded with the Cely family), Christopher Fernandes (New Christian/Marranos often took Christian first or last names as "cover"), Antonio de la Rosa, Dionysius Rodriquez, Manuel Brudo (a man who switched aliases between Isaiah Cohen, Diego Pires and Pyrrho Lusitano), Gaspar Lopes, Antonio Brandao and Henrique Nunes. Most lived either in London or Bristol.

In February 1542, a scant one and a half years after Thomas Cromwell's execution, action was taken to expel several of these suspected Judaizers from England under orders of Henry VIII. We suspect that Henry, once freed from being fettered to Rome, now saw the Protestant Reformation, largely fueled by New Christians/Marranos, as the greatest threat to his power. With Elizabeth I, after the Marian reign of terror, and increasingly with her successor James, however, a turn of the screw would bring the Marranos back, and under Oliver Cromwell and the later Stuarts, Jews would "return"—in all senses of the word.

11

Philo-Semitism 1550–1700

The period we explore in the present chapter came in like a lion and went out like a lamb. It began with the reign of Elizabeth I, whose long-lasting policies of canny statecraft, commercial empire and religious toleration rose in triumph over the wreckage of the Spanish Armada. By the end of it, the English nation had become the first to chop off a royal head and introduce a commonwealth (1649), Jews had been readmitted (1657), and the Restoration and Glorious Revolution had brought back a Parliamentary monarchy leading to what is celebrated as an Augustan Age. The United Kingdom of Great Britain was formally constituted by the Acts of Union of 1707, putting the religious wars behind the people and marking an end to strife between England, Wales and Scotland. All this happened virtually imperceptibly or, as Edward Gibbon might have said, "insensibly."

The readmission of the Jews under Oliver Cromwell was a fateful moment for the English, one that can be seen to offset England's two other dubious firsts, the blood libel case involving the accusation of ritual murder against the Jews of Norwich in 1144 and expulsion of Jews in 1290, two centuries before the Spanish. Adopting a *sub specie aeternitatis* perspective, Winston Churchill, in his *History of the English-Speaking Peoples*, writes of King Edward I's royal decree as follows:

> Edward saw himself able to conciliate powerful elements and escape from awkward debts, by the simple and well-trodden path of anti–Semitism. The propaganda of ritual murder and other dark tales, the commonplaces of our enlightened age, were at once invoked with general acclaim. The Jews, held up to universal hatred, were pillaged, maltreated, and finally expelled from the realm. Exception was made for certain physicians without whose skill persons of consequence might have lacked due attention. Once again the sorrowful, wandering race, stripped to the skin, must seek asylum and begin afresh. To Spain or North Africa the melancholy caravan, now so familiar, must move on. Not until four centuries had elapsed was Oliver Cromwell by furtive contracts with a mon-eyed Israelite to open again the coasts of England to the enterprise of the Jewish race. It was left to a Calvinist dictator to remove the ban which a Catholic king had imposed.[1]

As to the particulars claimed in Churchill's version of history, we have seen that Jews were by no means "held up to universal hatred," especially by the British, nor were their numbers small. We have even proved that most Jews at the time probably converted or pretended to and melded with their neighbors; certainly none sailed away into the sunset on ships, as romantically imagined of Rebecca the Jewess in Scott's *Ivanhoe*.[2] Words like "sorrowful, wandering race" belong to what has been called the "lachrymose" version of Jewish history. That Churchill calls "the" Jews a "race" says more about outmoded Victorian concepts of white domination and social Darwinism than it does about Jews. "Moneyed Israelite" plays into the worst stereo-types. "Calvinist dictator" seems a summary and demeaning epithet for such a complex per-sonality as Oliver Cromwell, who was the duly appointed head of government for England,

Ireland, Scotland and Wales for a decade, generally admired in the eye of historians today. Churchill seems to have everything wrong.

As cultural historian Gertrude Himmelfarb adumbrates in *The People of the Book*, anti–Semitism and its "opposite" philo–Semitism are both perilous concepts. Both terms debase Jews, "'objectifying' them, making them not subjects in their own right but the objects, if not of hatred and contempt, then of pity and pathos" (1). But to say that philo–Semitism is nothing but "anti–anti-Semitism" is an even more dangerous proposition (27). The voluminous literature on anti–Semitism labors as much as its opposite in the shadow of the Holocaust. Both approaches privilege the study of Jewish history as something driven by historical miracles—the Zionist Movement, the establishment of the state of Israel, the Balfour Declaration made by England's foreign secretary Arthur James Balfour to Baron Rothschild in 1917. The question remains why Britain served as an intellectual forge of philo–Semitism in the first place. Is it possible to tell the story of English philo–Semitism from "the inside out," as it were, not as some shadow-play of two stereotypes, the admired, often biblical Jew and the contemporary Jew, a people described by one seventeenth-century Englishman as "most rebellious, disobedient, gainsaying, stiff-necked, impenitent, incorrigible, adulterous, whorish, impudent, forward, shameless, perverse, treacherous, revolting, back-sliding, idolatrous, wicked, sinful, stubborn, untoward, hard-hearted, hypocritical?"[3] In short, how much of the Other did Englishmen of the time glimpse in Jews, and how much sameness? What might be the reasons for their passionate opinions on the question?

The background to philo–Semitism lies in English Hebraism. This was an interest in the Hebrew language and Jewish religion that began to flourish in Tudor England. It was Henry VIII who established the Regius Professorships of Hebrew at Oxford and Cambridge in 1536. Lists of the persons who held these chairs at the two universities provide some insights.[4] As the notes suggest, the tradition of English Hebraism reflected in the monarchy's university chairs started with an Anglo-Norman family from Yorkshire, the Wakefields, and was cross-pollinated by Sephardic Jews and converts from the Continent. The Wakefields can be traced back to the twelfth century in the West Riding of Yorkshire and beyond into Anglo-Saxon times. The same patterns of collaboration we have witnessed in trade are evident in these intellectual currents. Eventually, these professorships drew native appointees from all over England, Scotland and Wales. Many of the early appointees were active on the committee that translated the King James version of the Bible.

Regius Professors of Hebrew at Cambridge University, 1524–1800

until 1538	Unofficially, Robert Wakefield, Hebrew advisor at Henry's court
1540 Thomas Wakefield	Born at Pontefract, West Yorkshire like brother, knew Hebrew and Arabic naturally
1549 Paulus Fagius (Buchlin)	Born in Rheinzabern, Rhineland, learned Hebrew at university in Strasbourg
1550 Johannes Immanuel Tremellius	Italian Jewish convert, Protestant
1569 Antoine Rodolphe Chevallier	Born in Normandy, became Calvinist
1572 Philippe Bignon	Born in France, taught at Geneva
1575 Edward Lively	Englishman, learned Hebrew from John Drusius (Driesche), a Dutchman; one of translators of the King James Bible
1605 Robert Spaldinge	English
1607 Geoffrey Kynge or King	English
1608 Andrew Byng	York

c. 1622	Robert Metcalfe	Beverly, Yorkshire
1645	Ralph Cudworth	Somerset
1688	Wolfram Stubbe	Grandson of John Stubbs of Buxom, Norfolk
1699	James Talbot	Middlesex
1705	Henry Sike	Born in Bremen 1668; hanged himself
1712	Philip Bouquett	French Huguenot from La Rochelle
1748	Thomas Harrison	From ancient Harrison family
1753	Charles Torriano	Lombards in London since 1500s
1757	William Disney	Norman surname[5]; Kent
1771	William Collier	Welsh?
1790	John Porter	Portuguese?
1795	Henry Lloyd	Welsh

Regius Professors of Hebrew and Oriental Studies at Oxford University, 1524–1800

1524	Robert Wakefield	Unofficially, "King's Reader," self-taught
1540	John Shepreve or Shepreth	Unofficially, student of Wakefield's
1546 or 1547	Thomas Harding	Born at Combe Martin on north Devon coast
1548	Richard Bruern	Bruern—the name of ancient abbey in Oxfordshire. Associates were Peter Soto (Spanish Jew), White and Saunders
1559	Thomas Neale	Born in Gloucestershire, educated at Winchester
1569	Thomas Kingsmill	Hampshire. Went insane and took on Thomas Hooker of Exeter, Devon.
1591	John Harding (I)	From Southampton. Astrologer. Helped translate King James Bible.
1598	William Thorne	Wiltshire
1604	John Harding (II)	Second term
1610	Richard Kirby	From an old English family
1621	Edward Meetkirke	Son of Dutch ambassador to England, born in Aldersgate, London
1626	John Morris	Abingdon
1648	Edward Pococke	Chieveley in Berkshire, family from Hampshire, name is Jewish
1691	Roger Altham (I)	
1697	Thomas Hyde	Shropshire
1702	Roger Altham (II)	
1705	Robert Clavering	Scottish? Worked with Philip Levi, a converted Jew
1747	Thomas Hunt	Somerset, specialized in Arabic
1774	Richard Brown	Scottish?
1780	George Jubb	York
1787	Benjamin Blayney	Gregynog, Montgomeryshire, Wales

A connection with the old Domus Conversorum emerges in the figure of Philip Ferdinandus, a learned Polish Jew who became a recipient of its benefits at about the same time as he is found teaching Hebrew at Oxford, Cambridge and Leiden. He died in the Domus in 1600, and three years later we find an Elizabeth Ferdinando, evidently his widow.[6]

The interest in learning Hebrew between medieval and modern times in England can be followed also in *The Discovery of Hebrew in Tudor England: A Third Language*, by G. Lloyd Jones. Here we are told that its cultivation, especially by women of the aristocracy, "indicates that the Hebrew Bible was not regarded solely as the province of scholarly theologians."[7] Among England's Hebrew adepts were Lady Jane Grey (the Nine-Day Queen, Henry VII's great-granddaughter), her cousin Francis Willoughby, a Dorset coalfield owner and industrialist, James Whitelocke from a London mercantile family, Elizabeth Cary neé Tanfield Lady Falkland (author of *The Tragedy of Mariam, the Fair Queen of Jewry* in 1613, the first English play by a woman born in Oxfordshire),[8] the daughters of Sir Anthony Cooke (English Jewish surname), tutor to Edward VI and descendant of a lord mayor of London and high sheriff of Essex, and Mary Sidney, sister of the poet Philip Sidney. Elizabeth herself "was not unacquainted with Semitic languages" and observed certain Hebrew religious customs such as Shabbat evening candle-lighting.[9]

Born in obscure circumstances at Salvington, West Tarring, Sussex, John Selden (1584– 1654) rose to become England's foremost scholar of Jewish law. He is remembered as "Renaissance England's Chief Rabbi," although he did not profess to be Jewish and indeed was generally hostile or lukewarm to Jews, as shown in his tract "Of the Jews Sometime Living in England."[10] His father was a minstrel who played the violin, an instrument brought to England by Spanish Jews in the 1540s.[11] In London he came into the employ of Sir Robert Bruce Cotton of Huntingdon (related to the Bruces of Scotland and Montagus or dukes of Manchester), the antiquary whose 1000-book library later became the basis of the British Library. The Dutch legal scholar Hugo Grotius called Selden "the glory of the English nation," Ben Jonson lauded him as a "monarch in letters," and John Milton referred to him as "the chief of learned men reputed in this land." Selden left a legacy of writings on Noahic or natural law that was to bear fruit with John Locke and others. The on British poets and intellectuals of the seventeenth century whom he influenced includes Jonson, Milton, Andrew Marvell, James Harrington, Henry Stubbe, Nathanael Culverwel, Thomas Hobbes and Isaac Newton. Selden is representative of a generation of English philo–Semitists who obviously could tolerate, but not be very fond of, Jews. Selden's Jews exist in the "disembodied realm of Jewish law and legal exegesis," divorced from the contemporary ones who are praised for their "commercial acumen and collective cohesion."[12]

It was widely believed throughout Christendom that Jews exuded a peculiar ethnic smell which was removed by baptism and replaced by the perfume of sanctity. (The Jewish pope Anacletus II took care to have his great-grandfather deodorized by Vatican historians shortly before his election.) Sir Thomas Browne, the physician son of a silk merchant from Upton, Cheshire, assumed the task of refuting this belief in his encyclopedia *Pseudodoxia Epidemica* (Enquiries into Common and Vulgar Errors) in 1646, about the time Menasseh ben Israel was petitioning Cromwell for the Jews' readmission to England. In Chapter 10 of his work, titled "Of the Jews," and beginning "That the Jews stink naturally," Browne marshaled a series of arguments to lay this old canard to rest. Among them was that "there are at present many thousand Jews in *Spane*, *France*, and *England*, and some dispensed withall even to the degree of Priesthood; it is a matter very considerable, and could they be smelled out, would much advantage, not only the Church of Christ, but also the coffers of Princes." Note that even before the readmission of Jews, Browne estimates their numbers as significant and includes England in his list. If one could not smell a Jew, one could certainly not detect a crypto–Jew.

As the Puritans consolidated their winning positions in the religious wars, popular and learned interest in Jews exploded in the phenomenon of millenarianism, the belief that the coming transformation of society would bring the conversion of Jews as a precondition to the Second Coming of Christ. According to preachers of the day, this event could only take place in England, where the Word of God was taught in its purest form. About this time the expressions "Judaizer" and "judaizing" entered the English language, but these terms were not always pejorative.

Millenarianism went hand in glove with the gradual decision to extend toleration to foreign Jews, culminating with their "back door" reentry under Cromwell sealed by the famous legal case of the Sephardic merchant Anthony Robles. But its roots, again, go back to Tudor times. At the center of the movement was Thomas Brightman, a virulently anti–Catholic Cambridge clergyman born in Nottingham in 1562, who wrote an influential commentary on the New Testament book of Revelation called *A Revelation of the Reuelation* in the 1590s.[13] Brightman articulated a whole way of looking at the world based on "our Brethren, the Jews." This was not just philo–Semitism in the sense of "tolerating" the Jews but also in its original meaning of "loving" them. A close friend was George Meriton (or Meryton, died 1624), the dean of Peterborough and York, who grew up in Hertfordshire under the roof of Admiral Thomas Howard, the earl of Suffolk and son of the Earl Marshall and fourth Duke of Norfolk. Duke Thomas Howard, the favorite and second cousin of Elizabeth I, was executed for treason in 1572. The family tree of the Dukes of Norfolk is a cornucopia of British crypto–Judaism beginning allegedly with Hereward the Wake.[14]

The "background to the background" for philo–Semitism can be studied in the national martyrologies created by John Foxe (1517–1587), whose name is linked both to the Howards and Thomas Brightman. Foxe was the religious instructor for the earl of Surrey's children, Thomas, who succeeded to the dukedom; Henry, afterwards Earl of Northampton; and Jane who became Countess of Westmoreland. He came from Boston in Lincolnshire, where, in 1551, one Henry Foxe, a merchant, was mayor. The surname is similar to German Fuchs, a medieval Jewish adaptation of Phoebus or Feibos and seen on many ghetto trade-signs.[15] Foxe's Book of Martyrs, properly *Actes and Monuments*, was published first in Latin in Strasbourg in 1554, and later in English beginning with a gigantic folio of 1800 pages in 1563. This encyclopedia provided devotional reading for generations and propagated the sense that England was an elect nation.

Going through several editions with Foxe's friend, printer John Day, the Book of Martyrs was eventually ordered to be placed in every Anglican church. It inculcated into the faithful a national epic of suffering and dedication to the pure faith echoing the history of Israel in the Old Testament. The English martyrs originally ran from Wycliff to Cranmer and the Protestants burned as heretics by Queen Mary. John Foxe died in 1587 but his compilation took on a life of its own, being updated with Puritan, Quaker, Methodist, Huguenot, New Christian, Baptist and Pilgrim Father chapters. In general, Jews are viewed favorably throughout. They are portrayed as deserving of the Englishman's sympathies and even as admirable because they are persecuted by the same barbarous forces of papacy and Inquisition. Everyone knew that Jews could be counted on in England, for had they not justified the very existence of the Anglican church's separation from Rome by deciding that Henry's Levirate marriage to his brother Arthur's widow was, technically, illegal?[16]

Marian Persecutions

Under Queen Mary I, the Inquisition returned for several years to England, although most scholars do not see in it a particularly "Spanish" shape.[17] Many clerics and preachers fled to the Continent and waited out the reign of terror. Others, often simple folk, were hauled before the courts and have entered the pages of Foxe's martyrology as Marian victims. The heresy trials during Mary's occupation of the throne took place under the last papal archbishop of Canterbury, Reginald Pole, a member of our Welsh De la Pole family. They have not been studied in detail for what they might reveal about Jews or Jewish sympathizers, particularly in the records of less prominent individuals. Even Pole, who reputedly lost the papacy to Julius III by one vote in 1549, was not above suspicion.[18] When Mary died, the nation turned a page and had little appetite for studying her ill-advised attempt to make England Catholic.

The expectation that Jews would be converted at the end of the world was ultimately based on Paul's claim in Romans 11:26 that "all Israel will be saved," a teaching that Luther took note of. But the belief played out differently in England as opposed to Lutheran countries. Among the English writers who championed the theme were John Bale, a native of Cove in Suffolk (*The Image of Both Churches*, 1547), the Essex preacher Arthur Dent (*The Plain Man's Pathway to Heaven*, 1601) and Andrew Willett from Ely in Hertfordshire. The latter's *De universali et novissima Judaeorum vocatione* (On the Recent Universal Calling of Jews) appeared in 1590. Willett married Jacobine Goad (the "Good Name" of Davidic descent) and named one son Jacobus and one daughter Jacobine, the male and female forms respectively of Jacob, a name restricted to Jews at the time. Another of his sons, Thomas, became the first mayor of New York (New Amsterdam) and was captain of Plymouth Company in 1647; among his children were David, Sara, Rebecca and Esther.

Brightman's role for the Jews as returning kings of the East and England's destiny in the end times were taken up by the jurist Henry Finch, who in 1621 published a work entitled *The World's Great Restauration, or Calling of the Jews, and with them of all Nations and Kingdoms of the Earth to the Faith of Christ.*

If Judaism was a projection, it was also decidedly an introjection. Most Englishmen of the day accepted it as an article of faith that the Phoenicians and Jews colonized Britain. In 1549, John Bale, the same philo–Semite we saw above, published *The Laborious Journey and Search of John Leland*, inaugurating the English tradition of antiquarianism aimed at placing Britain on a par with the Romans, Greeks and Jews. It was addressed to Henry VIII. By time of the Restoration, we encounter Aylett Sammes (Jewish names), *Britannia Antiqua Illustrata: Antiquities of Ancient Britain Derived from the Phoenicians* (London, 1676). The likely Jewish-descended Robert Sheringham (born 1602 in Guestwick, Norfolk) suggested a Talmudic origin of some of the New Testament parables. He taught Arabic and Hebrew in Rotterdam during the royalists' exile. His *Joma: Codex talmudicus* (1648) was a Latin translation of and commentary on *Yoma*, that part of the Mishnah and Talmud on the observance of high holy days. *De Anglorum Gentis Origine Disceptatio* (1670) was Sheringham's contribution on the origins of the English language and people. It agreed with Samuel Bochart (a Sephardic surname[19]), a Rouen-born scholar who knew Arabic, Hebrew, Chaldean and Syriac. Much earlier, Sir Robert Cotton (1570–1631) had begun amassing antiquarian notes on the local history of Huntingdonshire. Later, we have Milton's *History of Britain* (1670), the Shropshire schoolmaster William Burton (died 1657), the naturalist Robert Plot, the first keeper of the Ashmolean Museum (he came from the village of Borden in Kent), and Edward Lhwyd, its second keeper.

Edward Lhwyd was born about 1660, the illegitimate son of Edward Lloyd of Llandforda, near Oswestry, Shropshire, and Bridget Pryse of Gogerddan, Cardiganshire. Lhwyd produced the first serious comparative study of the Welsh, Scots and Irish Gaelic, Cornish, and Breton languages and for this achievement is today regarded as the father of Celtic linguistics. His study was published in *Glossography* (1707), the first volume of his projected series *Archaeologia Britannica, giving some account additional to what has hitherto been publish'd, of the languages, histories, and customs of the original inhabitants of Great Britain: From collections and observations in travels through Wales, Cornwal, Bas-Bretagne, Ireland and Scotland.* Unfortunately, Lhwyd died before he could continue this work.

Judaizing an Old English Tradition

Lest we think that these preoccupations with the Jews' place in history were idle intellectual adventures or Puritan cant, we have several clear cases of judaizing in England during these times—that is, judaizing by Englishmen, not Marannos or acknowledged ex–Jews. In Scotland, as we have detailed in our book *When Scotland Was Jewish*, the line between Jew and Protestant was not hard and fast. Indeed, George Buchanan, the tutor of the young Mary Queen of Scots, was arrested and tried by the Inquisition while giving guest lectures at the University of Coimbra in 1549 and 1550. He admitted that many of the charges of judaizing were true and was imprisoned in the monastery of São Bento in Lisbon to repent of his errors. In 1552 he was given his freedom and he sailed for England.

A forerunner of the English denomination of Protestantism was Lollardism, a name of uncertain meaning given to the followers of John Wycliffe in the fourteenth century. A very early Lollard, John Seygno, whose surname appears to be Jewish,[20] asserted that the Sabbath should be celebrated according to the manner of the Jews, and that it was sinful to eat pork. Later, William Fuer (another foreign name) of Gloucester, who recanted his opinions in 1448, stated firmly that only the true Sabbath should be observed. In 1472 the Lollards of Lydney, also situated in Gloucestershire or South Wales, argued that the authority of the Old Testament was preferable to that of the New. It was widely held that the Gentiles were the "children of unpromise" and Jews, the "children of promise."[21]

A murkier case for crypto–Judaism involves Richard Bruern, who was appointed Regius Professor of Hebrew at Oxford in 1548 and denounced as a Jew. He was derided as an "emanation of the Hebrew choir of angels" (*Hebraei radius chori*). Bruern scandalized many of his contemporaries with what has been called his Rabelaisian career.[22] Apparently of good, old-fashioned rural Oxfordshire origins, he hopscotched from one plum appointment to another, leaving a trail of whispers about his religious and sexual mores. Among the charges that kept surfacing were eating the Pascal lamb at seders, conjuring with familiars, homosexual inclinations and seducing members of the cleaning staff of Eton College. One of the witnesses called to testify at Eton reported "in his manner in the churche, that tho he knele, he never preyth, but always his mouth open." Another "iudgeth him to be a Jewe or pagan rather than a christen man by his behaviour in church," and a third deposed that he had heard Bruern say repeatedly in Queen Mary's reign that neither her religion nor that practiced under King Edward was "right."

Two Oxford men, Alford and Thomas Barnard, tried to have Bruern prosecuted at Christ Church, where he had inherited a prestigious stall, specifically alleging Judaistic practices, "but he managed to stop these moves" (324). Breuern, in fact, "went from strength to strength," appearing as a witness at the trial of Stephen Gardiner, Mary's grand inquisitor, replacing Peter Martyr in the first stall at Oxford's Christ Church and being made a canon of Windsor at the royal chapel. At Oxford Breuer was found guilty of homosexual conduct with Roger Marbeck, who was sixteen years his junior. Roger was the son of the organist John, who had been tried for heresy under Mary Tudor in 1453. But Oxford did not send Bruerne down. Roger Marbeck survived the scandal, inherited Breuer's stall and after what is described as an unhappy marriage became Elizabeth's physician and first registrar of the College of Physicians in London.

To return to the story of Richard Brightman, the father of English philo–Semitism was careful to distance himself from Bruern and his circle at Oxford and Windsor:

> But what (will ye say) dost thou turne *Jewe*? God forbid. That they may renew the Temple, restore the Ceremonies, and possesse the land in times past, promised and given as an earnest of the heavenly. (These things are eternally buried, not worne out by time, but utterly abolished by Christ.) But I speak of restoring to their country, wherin they shall worship Christ according to his Ordinances: which is not contrary to Religion everyone knoweth, and all the Prophets seem to foretell it with one consent.[23]

Once public discourse had won itself free to this stance, it was all about bringing toleration to Jews and allowing them to convert if they wished but not forcing them, as it was felt that the compulsion of the truth, and the tide of history, was sufficient for that purpose.

Readmission a Pseudo-Event Like Expulsion

The "readmission" of the Jews did not occur by royal decree but rather as a consequence of making the issue a nonissue. The literature on this turning point in British Jewry is voluminous.[24] We cannot go into great detail but hope at least to prove that the Hebraicization of the culture did not occur *before* there were "real" Jews in England, as assumed by Himmelfarb and every other commentator or chronicler. There have always been significant numbers of

Jews in English society. It is simply not credible that an engaging national debate on the subject took place in a vacuum. True, the dynamics played out in a completely different way in England than in the Netherlands and France. And in Germany, nothing like it was witnessed until the nineteenth century.

Timetable for the Condition of Jews, 1655–1702

October 31, 1655: Humble address from Menasseh ben Israel to Oliver Cromwell. A fortnight later, on November 13, he submitted a petition for the readmission of Jews to England

December 1655: Whitehall Conference to discuss the petition. Dissolved by Cromwell before it reached a decision

Oliver Cromwell, etching based on a sketch made from life in 1652 by Samuel Cooper, Cromwell's favorite artist. While sitting for his portrait, Cromwell coined the phrase "warts and all." Samuel Cooper (1609–1672) came from a related crypto–Jewish family and was called "the most famous limner in the world for a face." His three-by-four-inch picture of Cromwell from 1657, known as the Harcourt Miniature, fetched the equivalent of nearly $1 million at auction in 2007, making it the most valuable painting for its size anywhere (http://www.telegraph.co.uk/news/uknews/1553848/Cromwell-miniature-sells-warts-and-all.html) (Print Collection, Miriam and Ira D. Wallach Division of Art, Prints and Photographs, The New York Public Library, Astor, Lenox and Tilden Foundations).

1656: Although no formal agreement on readmission, Jewish residents of London began living openly as Jews

December 1656: First synagogue established after Readmission

February 1657: First cemetery acquired in Mile End

October 14, 1663: Samuel Pepys visits the synagogue on Simchat Torah

1664: Bylaws (Ascamot) of new community agreed

August 22, 1664: Jews granted royal protection

January 1667: Jews allowed to swear in court on the Old Testament

1671: Start of practice of presenting each lord mayor with a gift

February 1674: Jews indicted for holding a service, but the king stopped the proceedings against them

1677: Court venue changed to avoid a Jew having to give evidence on a Saturday

1692: Establishment of first Ashkenazi synagogue

February 2, 1697: Site acquired for first Ashkenazi cemetery

1697: Jews admitted as brokers on the Royal Exchange

September 20, 1701: Bevis Marks Synagogue inaugurated

1702: Great Synagogue founded

What did Englishmen think of "real Jews" when they were able to see them again after more than three hundred and fifty years? One famous account comes from Samuel Pepys, the diarist, who along with his wife visited the Marrano synagogue in Creechchurch Lane (later Bevis Marks) on October 14, 1663. After mentioning that it was through a connection with Daniel Rawlingson,[25] Pepys makes these notes, which we give in their entirety for their unusual eyewitness value; visits by even prescreened Gentiles like Mr. Rawlinson's party would be banned the next year:

> Thence home and after dinner my wife and I, by Mr. Rawlinson's conduct, to the Jewish Synagogue: where the men and boys in their vayles [prayer shawls], and the women behind a lattice out of sight; and some things stand up, which I believe is their Law, in a press to which all coming in do bow; and at the putting on their vayles do say something, to which others that hear him do cry Amen, and the party do kiss his vayle. Their service all in a singing way, and in Hebrew. And anon their Laws [Torah scrolls] that they take out of the press are carried by several men, four or five several burthens in all, and they do relieve one another; and whether it is that every one desires to have the carrying of it, I cannot tell, thus they carried it round about the room while such a service is singing. And in the end they had a prayer for the King [Charles II], which they pronounced his name in Portugall [Portuguese]; but the prayer, like the rest, in Hebrew. But, Lord! to see the disorder, laughing, sporting, and no attention, but confusion in all their service, more like brutes than people knowing the true God, would make a man forswear ever seeing them more and indeed I never did see so much, or could have imagined there had been any religion in the whole world so absurdly performed as this. Away thence with my mind strongly disturbed with them, by coach.[26]

Actually, this was not the first opportunity Pepys had of observing a Jewish service. On December 3, 1659, he attended the funeral of Antonio Ferdinando Carvajal. Caravajal was one of the wealthiest Marranos in London, and his cousin was the rabbi of the fledgling Sephardic congregation. He fell victim to the same heroic surgical procedure for bladder stone removal performed by Dr. Thomas Hollier that was, happily, Pepys' salvation.

Other than betraying what might be a coy lack of understanding of Jewish customs, Pepys' entry reveals little about his own religious beliefs, which we know to be in the deist column. Like many of his contemporaries he was a latitudinarian. "At Cambridge," we are told, "he took the sacrament only 'once or twice'—he was not sure which—and then not again for more than ten years."[27] For Pepys, then, the interest in Jews seems to be purely commercial and practical.

Two Kinds of Jews

By the end of the period we have surveyed, two kinds of Jews were popularly identified in the English mind. First came the biblical ones, often referred to as Israelites, and second, the Marranos of Amsterdam and London, who labeled themselves "Jews of the Portuguese Nation" or "people of the Hebrew nation." B. Netanyahu has written a learned study maintaining that crypto–Jews dissembling their faith in Spain and Portugal were no longer entitled to be recognized as Jews by the rabbinical authorities, then or now.[28] This is an extreme position, but one generally followed by those who studied the Marranos' descendants in France, England, the Netherlands and the New World. No one has even thought to train a microscope on English Jews or converts or sympathizers in the time before Sephardic Jews "returned" to England. Unless they happen to be a Disraeli or Einstein, the narrowly sectarian school of Jewish studies

The York Minster Tree of Jesse window on the south wall of the nave dates from 1310. Part of it contained the oldest stained glass in England (mid-twelfth century). Depicting the branching generations of the House of Judah beginning with King David, it was extensively restored and repaired over the centuries, as it was regarded as a sort of British national family tree (see Elisabeth Reddish, "The Fourteenth Century Tree of Jesse in the Nave of York Minster") (After William Peckett repainted parts of it in 1789, the three quatrefoils above the window were outfitted with a Star of David and Templar device consisting of the divine plummet and Eye of God surmounting the whole. No better symbolism for England's continually self-renewing philo–Semitic history could have been chosen) (Photo by Jim Poyner).

is not interested in ex–Jews. Thus, Lloyd P. Gartner, in reviewing the progress of Anglo-Jewish historiography, rightly notes that "there has been no study of the relations between Anglicanism and the other main churches and the Jews."[29] Even the word "philo-Semitism" has been generally omitted from English dictionaries. Significantly, the term is *verboten* in the Encyclopaedia Judaica.[30]

And what about Muslim studies in England? The word "Orientalist" begins to appear in England in the later eighteenth century. We have noticed that several of the professorships at Oxford and Cambridge include Oriental languages in addition to Hebrew, that is, Turkish, Arabic, Chaldee, Persian, Urdu and Hindu. Orientalism as a state of mind and deprecating cultural term was largely to become defined by Englishmen. The beginnings of Islamic studies can be placed in the same Oxbridge setting. Thomas Bedwell (1563–1632) at Cambridge is cited as the scholar who introduced the study of Arabic into England and western Europe. The incumbent of the first Arabic Chair at Oxford was

Samuel Menasseh ben Israel, etching, 1636 (© The Trustees of the British Museum).

Edward Pococke (1604–1691). "Himself a theologian," writes Gerhard Endress, he "made the pre–Islamic history of Arabia and the dogmatic theology of Islam better known through his *Specimen Historiae Arabum* (1650), and his Arabic-Latin edition of the concise *History of the Dynasties* of *Barhebraeus* (1663), admittedly a compilation by a Christian writer, nevertheless added to the few sources then known a significant summary of Arab history until the Mongol invasion."[31] Later, the English translation of the Quran by George Sale in 1734 placed Islam in a totally different light. In 1784, William Jones, a Welshman, founded the Asiatic Society of Bengal to encourage Turkish and Persian studies, and at Fort William College in India the employees of the East India Company learned Islamic culture and languages from native teachers.[32] A groundbreaking work on the Persian contribution to civilization was Sir John Malcolm's *History of Persia* (1815).

In surveying this period of "Judaism without Jews," it is to be hoped we have not only dispelled the notion that England was devoid of Jews, and that they rushed in to fill a void after Cromwell, but also that we have argued with some success that the architects and promoters of philo–Semitism, natural law and millenarianism drew on ancestral memories of Jewishness that were peculiarly British. In some cases, crypto–Judaism was so strongly embedded in the debate that we are left only with a ghostly recognition of it, like the smile of the Cheshire cat. Certainly, one cannot complain that true individuals are lacking in these developments, that all the figures are stereotypes or ideals divorced from "real" Jews. There were obviously as many types of Jews, ex–Jews and crypto–Jews as there were varieties of social mobility, birth, parentage, privilege, education and wealth. The vast majority lived completely unremarkable, perhaps even largely unselfconscious, lives. In the next chapter, we will study the career and writings of one of these, Daniel Defoe, who, if he was not a Jew, as we shall see, should have been.

12

Daniel Defoe and Robinson Crusoe

Much is known about Daniel Defoe, the creator of the first English novel, *Robinson Crusoe*, originally published in 1719. But as the scholar John Richetti remarks in his biography, much is also unknown. "Despite several centuries of literary and biographical criticism ... and of repeated biographical investigation ... the inner man, the personality, the actual Defoe, remains an elusive and even a mysterious figure."[1] In this chapter, we intend to show that Defoe's ancestry was Jewish and that many of his social concerns, religious beliefs, attitudes, activism and artistic aspirations were those of a self-conscious British Jew of the seventeenth and eighteenth century.

The author's family name was Foe, at least in its latest manifestation.[2] Daniel added what his detractors referred to as a "Frenchified aristocratic prefix" in 1695, when he was a young man in his thirties. It was a time shortly after he had become established in his business career as owner of a Dutch brick factory in the town of Tilbury in Essex.[3] The facts of Daniel Defoe's genealogy are set forth in the adjoining chart. The first mystery we are confronted with is the absence of a birth record. He was the third child and only son of James Foe, a merchant and citizen of London living with his wife Ailce[4] in the Broad Street Ward of Cripplegate (also called Jew's Gate), a commercial district in the heart of the Old City, today's Barbican Center. Jewin Street, now covered by Defoe House, was the only place where Jews were allowed to be buried. Daniel's two older sisters were Mary, born 1657, who would marry Francis Barham and later the natural philosopher Robert Davis, and Elizabeth, who would become the wife of James A. Maxwell, a Quaker. Both siblings have birth records, but the parish register of St. Giles Cripplegate lists their births in a distinct manner as "borne but not christened."[5] Biographers and commentators are at pains to explain the reason why, or to suggest an explanation for their brother's lack of a birth record. The precise birth date of September 30, 1660, sometimes given for Daniel Defoe is based on a chain of conjectures from his fiction and not on actual records.[6] We can only be sure that he was born in 1660, a pivotal year marked by the return of Charles II and end of the Cromwellian period.

Of Daniel Defoe's ancestry, most writers today are content to say that his grandfather was a yeoman farmer from the little village of Etton in the East Midlands, and that the Foes can be traced back to sturdy rural English stock. That this is not the whole story, however, is suggested by some of the names in the Foe family tree. To begin with, Daniel was not an ordinary English given name in the time when the author's grandfather Daniel Foe was born, in 1598, nor in his grandson's day either. In the nineteenth century it was still so distinctly Jewish that George Eliot used it for the title character of her novel *Daniel Deronda*, about an English gentleman who gradually awakens to the fact of his Sephardic Jewish ancestry and becomes a Zionist. Rose, the name of Daniel Defoe's grandmother, is also Jewish.[7] We do not know her maiden name, but after the death of her first husband Rose Foe married Solomon Fall (Jewish

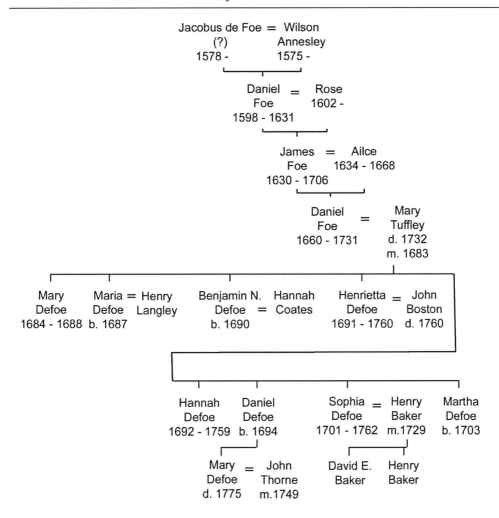

Daniel Defoe's genealogy (Donald Yates).

first and last name) of Maxie, Northamptonshire, and after being widowed again in 1641, she moved to Huntingdon, where she married Thomas King, a widower with two children, one of whom became the wife of her eldest son, Daniel, in 1643.[8] Daniel Junior died on the family farm in Etton in 1647, but his older brother Henry went to London and became the apprentice of the saddler John Levitt ("Levite"). James, Rose's youngest son by her first marriage to Daniel Foe, born 1630, followed Henry to the city at the age of fourteen and was apprenticed as a chandler to the same John Levitt, a member of the Butchers' Company trade guild.[9]

Defoe wrote in one instance that his grandfather was a country gentleman who rode to the hounds, giving the good ones names from one political party and the bad ones names from the opposite faction. He also boasted an armorial device with three griffons. But at the same time, he claimed kinship with Sir Walter Raleigh, the quintessential crypto–Jew.[10] Biographers have been eager to validate his assertions about his grandfather Daniel Foe but skeptical of the Raleigh connection. If true, says one of them, "the strain must have been thin indeed by the time of Defoe's birth."[11] Yet only a little over a century separated the Elizabethan Protestant explorer-courtier from the enigmatic journalist and author of *Robinson Crusoe*. Moreover, the chronicles of the Raleighs, Grenvilles (now Granvilles), Champernouns, Gilberts, Drakes, St. Legers, Zouches, Hawkins and Carews were by no means finished.

A clue to Defoe's real ancestry emerged in the nineteenth century when a descendant in America came forward with a family heirloom described as the chair in which Defoe wrote *Robinson Crusoe.* We will tell this charming story in the words of Joseph T. Richards as reported by a local historian of Cecil County, Maryland, Alice E. Miller. This writer starts by recounting the history of Blue Ball, an old inn near the Quaker site of Brick Meeting House. Andrew Job established it in about 1710 and went to Philadelphia, returning with a bond-servant, Elizabeth Maxwell, the runaway niece of the novelist Daniel Defoe.

The Story of Elizabeth Maxwell

Until she was eighteen, Elizabeth lived in London. Her mother was born Defoe. She was the sister of Daniel. The brother's desire to reform the realm by writing pamphlets criticizing Her Majesty's Government got him into trouble. To escape arrest in 1705, he fled to Mrs. Maxwell's home and lived in seclusion for years.

His niece, Elizabeth, became his pupil from her fifth year, and enjoyed her uncle's company and stories. When she was eighteen, she became engaged to a young man of whom her mother did not approve. The bar to their marriage made the girl despondent and she felt that she must cut herself off from all of her accustomed association with her friends. After a few months of this isolation, Elizabeth heard that a ship was about to set sail for America from a wharf near her home. Without a word to anyone, she ran aboard just in time and was off. After long weeks on the voyage, she made port in Philadelphia.

Such unceremonious passage as this was not unusual in those days, apparently, and these young people did not hesitate to sell themselves as bond servants to those who paid their passage money. So Elizabeth and a group of her fellow passengers came up for sale soon after landing. In the crowd around the auction block she saw a man wearing a broad-brimmed hat of the Quakers. She had known these people at home to be kindly, and so she asked this man to pay her passage money and to take her as a servant for the required seven years.

This man was Andrew Job. He had five sons, but no daughters. His wife needed help in her housekeeping. So Andrew paid Elizabeth's fare, and started home with her. He lived at East Nottingham, some fifty-five miles away ... near the Brick Meeting House, now the village of Calvert....

Elizabeth served out her seven years, but during all that time she did not write home. At the end of her time of service, she married one of the five sons, Thomas Job.... Then she wrote home, telling her mother the whole story.

Months passed. Finally a letter from Uncle Daniel. Then she learned that her mother's anxiety for her safety could never be satisfied, for she had died years earlier.

Her uncle told her further that by her mother's will "in case she should ever be found alive" she was to have a good property and her mother's furniture. Daniel said that he would send the furniture to her and asked that she preserve it carefully, because it had "come to the family from their Flemish ancestors who had sought refuge under the banner of Queen Elizabeth from the tyranny of Phillipe [sic]."

He went on to apologize for the wooden seats in the two chairs, explaining that he had worn out the cane seats and had replaced them with wooden ones.

It is interesting to know that at least one of these chairs is still to be seen at Nottingham.

The eighty-year-plus-old man telling this amazing tale ends by speculating that Defoe's loneliness after his niece's sudden flight may have set his mood for writing *Robinson Crusoe* in 1719.[12] The Defoe chair passed into the keeping of the Historical Society of Delaware, and a longer version of its provenance appeared in *Scribners Monthly* in 1876.[13]

What we learn from this lore is that the original Foe family was not English, but "Flemish." If the founding forefather joined the forces of the Protestant English campaigning against the Catholic king Philip II, this was probably at the beginning of the Anglo-Dutch War when

Elizabeth I sent Robert Dudley to lift the siege of Antwerp by the Duke of Parma in the summer of 1585. Droves of Sephardic Jews in exile from Spain and Portugal in Flanders took the side of the English, Dutch and French, leading eventually to the independence of the Netherlands and the partition of Flanders between Catholics and Protestants. Daniel's eponymous ancestor Jacobus de Foe, born 1578, was undoubtedly one of these new Flemings sworn to resistance against the Spanish. The family name, we believe, was Foa, an armigerous Sephardic line named for their ancient seat of Foix in the Aquitaine region of France.[14] Defoe apparently even alludes to this ancestry, tongue in cheek, when he writes of noble descent from "the De Beau Faux."[15] Defoe's editor Henry Morley mentions it in attempting to account for Defoe's fluent foreign language capacities and business trips: "He had connections in Spain, and it may even be that his family had Spanish origins, and at some former time had anglicised the name of Foà into Foe."[16]

Chair of Daniel Defoe (Scribners Monthly 1876).

Curiously, Defoe's enemies accused him of being Dutch. John Tutchin fired off the dunce's poem called "The Foreigners" in 1701 aimed at William III's favorites Hans Willem Bentinck, first earl of Portland, and Arnold Joost van Keppel, first earl of Albemarle. In it, he represented England as Israel, saying of its autocratic Stuart monarch that he had "all their Plagues ... crammed in the Single Person of a King," and calling Holland a country lying "due east from Judah's Shoar.... Its Natives void of Honesty and Grace, A Boorish, rude, and an inhumane Race ... born in Bogs."

> Let them in foreign States proudly command,
> They have no Portion in the Promis'd Land,
> Which immemoriably has been decreed
> To be the Birth-right of the *Jewish* Seed.

Evidently, in this political allegory, Scotland and Ireland are the realm of Hiram and the Phoenicians, "ye *Jewish* Nobles" are the English peerage, and Sanhedrins are the Houses of Parliament. The Puritan doctrine of equating the destiny of the British with that of the people of Israel was so ingrained by this time that it passed for an article of political faith. But the radical Whigs were probably not prepared for what came from the pen of a verifiable Jew. Defoe responded with "The True-Born Englishman: A Satire," lampooning the very notion of any purity of race. This effort won him a stipend from the king and led to his being tapped as a secret agent by Robert Harley, earl of Oxford. Defoe even adopted "True-Born Englishman" as his ironic *nom de plume*, publishing his collected works to date under that name in 1703 and 1705.

Defoe's existing portraits are highly burnished, revealing little about his appearance other than a pronounced sharp nose. But a "wanted" description put out after one of his skirmishes with the law paints a distinctly foreign picture of him:

He is a middle Sized Spare Man about 40 years old, of a brown Complexion, and dark brown coloured Hair wears a Wig, a hooked Nose, a sharp Chin, grey Eyes, and a large Mould near his Mouth, was born in London, and for many years was a Hose Factor in Freeman's-yard in Corn hill, and now is Owner of the Brick and Pantile Works near Tilbury-Fort in Essex.[17]

From Defoe's genealogy readers will also notice that his first naturalized English ancestor Jacobus de Foe marries Wilson Annesley. She must have been a member of the distinguished

Nottinghamshire family of that name. The pedigree includes Robert Annesley, high constable of Newport, Buckinghamshire; his son the English and Irish statesman Francis Annesley, 1st Viscount Valentia; Charles II's Keeper of the Privy Seal Arthur Annesley, 1st Earl of Anglesey (1614–1686); and most fittingly Defoe's family pastor, Samuel Annesley (1620?–1696), a prominent Dissenter, from the Warwickshire branch. Samuel Annesley served as chaplain to Robert Rich, the earl of Warwick, son of the first earl and Lady Rich, Penelope Devereux, countess of Devon, sister of Robert Devereux and the "Stella" of Sir Philip Sidney's love poetry. Annesley came, then, from a carefully endogamous set of forbears. Contemporaries called him "an Israelite indeed."[18]

Daniel Defoe (Print Collection, Miriam and Ira D. Wallach Division of Art, Prints and Photographs, The New York Public Library, Astor, Lenox and Tilden Foundations).

The designation Dissenter had a loose— and shifting—meaning. Today, we might apply the term "Presbyterian" to the majority of seventeenth-century Dissenters. But when it first came into usage the word described those, like Annesley, who feared that the 1662 Act of Uniformity introduced by Charles II would lead to a suppression of Scripture for private devotion, as well as disenfranchisement of all but Church of England adherents in public office. The new monarch flirted with absolutism in religion as in politics. With Nonconformists panicking, Defoe was made by Pastor Annesley to copy the entire Bible by hand. Looking back in middle age, he wrote in a characteristically flippant manner:

How many Honest but over-frighted People, set to Work to Copy the Bible into Short-Hand, lest when Popery come in, we should be Prohibited the use of it, and so might secure it in little Compass? At which Work, I my self then, but a Boy, work'd like a Horse till I wrote out the whole Pentateuch, and then was so tyr'd, I was willing to run the Risque of the rest.[19]

Is Defoe being less than disingenuous here? One wonders if there might not be more to the fact that he stopped with the part of the Bible that constituted the Hebrew Torah, which would have sufficed the needs of a crypto–Jewish congregation.

Defoe lived, and wrote, dangerously, and he defied anyone to look into his conscience. Before the novel *Robinson Crusoe* appeared in 1719, his best-known publication was *The Shortest Way with the Dissenters* (1702). This pamphlet parodied extremist Anglican views and was conceived in the same spirit as Jonathan Swift's *A Modest Proposal*. Just as Swift was to suggest that a solution to the economic troubles of the Irish lay in poor families selling their children as food to rich gentlemen and ladies, Defoe urged leaders of the Church of England to adopt the simple expedient of forced mass emigration and selective execution of Dissenters. If anyone disagreed with the Queen, it was obvious what must be done: "Those of the contrary Opinion to Hers, must be Extirpated, must be cut off Root and Branch; and like the *Jews* by *Edward* the First's Sanguinary Laws, Dispers'd, Banish'd, and Kill'd; and render'd Extinct they and their Posterity." Defoe extended the same logic to Occasional Dissenters, the "Apples" swimming merrily downstream with the "Horse-Turds."

It was a satirical ruse that backfired. The high-toned Anglicans and Tory members of Parliament were not amused. They burnt Defoe in effigy, swore out a warrant for his arrest and appointed a vicious special prosecutor. John Richetti wrote of the incident:

> From the appearance of that pamphlet Defoe is in nearly constant dialogue with his enemies, and his work is a series of fierce polemics, ferocious attacks and counter attacks. Defoe is an author whose life was changed by one piece of writing.... Defoe became a wanted man who was forced for the rest of his life to survive mainly as an embattled writer and political operative rather than a prosperous merchant and manufacturer who dabbled in writing.... Defoe would return obsessively to the misunderstandings of his writing that landed him not once but twice in jail and once in the pillory, and his polemical journalism, notably the *Review*, would be to an important extent based on a continuing complaint, a life-long grievance, that he was misunderstood and misrepresented by both friends and enemies.[20]

Robinson Crusoe's *Literary Position*

Then and now, *Robinson Crusoe* has been one of the most widely read works of realistic fiction in the world, one seen as canonical for British literature and definitive of what makes an Englishman English. Deceived by its perfection of concept, one is tempted to approach it in an autobiographical fashion, to fall under its "art-of-no-art" spell. Defoe's contemporaries received *A Journal of the Plague Year*, as a journalistic report rather than a literary work written thirty years after the events. At one and the same time, *Robinson Crusoe* belongs to historical romance (although appealing more to masculine tastes), journalism, inspirational books and topical nonfiction conceived on an epic scale. With its plain and simple style and edifying moral reflections it also easily falls into the category of children's literature. The critic J. M. Coetzee sums up its unique place by writing:

> Like Odysseus embarked for Ithaca, like Quixote mounted on Rocinante, Robinson Crusoe with his parrot and umbrella has become a figure in the collective consciousness of the West, transcending the book which—in its multitude of editions, translations, imitations, and adaptations ("Robinsonades')—celebrates his adventures. Having pretended once to belong to history, he finds himself in the sphere of myth.[21]

It is easy to forget that *Robinson Crusoe* is a fake memoir. Defoe encourages his readers to equate Robinson Crusoe with himself. In *Serious Reflections* (1720), he responds in the persona of Crusoe to cavilers and quibblers charging that his character's life story was made up, simply a romance, that Crusoe was not even a real person. Much as he answered his political enemies he has Crusoe say:

> I *Robinson Crusoe* being at this Time in perfect and sound Mind and Memory, Thanks be to God therefore; do hereby declare, their Objection is an Invention scandalous in Design, and false in Fact;

and do affirm that the Story, though Allegorical, is also Historical; and that it is the beautiful Representation of a Life of unexampled Misfortunes, and of a Variety not to be met with in the World, sincerely adapted to, and intended for the common Good of Mankind, and designed ... to the most serious Uses possible.

Farther, that there is a man alive, and well known too, the actions of whose life are the just subject of these three volumes, and to whom all or most part of the story most directly alludes, this may be depended upon for Truth, and to this I set my name.... So I can affirm that I enjoy much more Solitude in the Middle of the greatest Collection of Mankind in the World, I mean, at *London*, while I am writing this than ever I could say I enjoy'd in eight and twenty years Confinement to a desolate Island.[22]

Such artistic bravura led the Victorian commentator William Minto to say of Defoe that "he was a great, a truly great liar, perhaps the greatest liar that ever lived."[23] Without placing either Robinson Crusoe or its author on the couch of psychoanalysis, or committing them to the rack of literary criticism, let us nonetheless have a look at this masterpiece with eyes newly opened by what we have learned of Defoe's Jewish ancestry and the strain of English philo–Semitism examined in the last chapter.

Robinson Crusoe finds the prospects of a "middle station of life sliding gently through the world" unappealing as a young man and defies his father to go to sea. A violent storm, and warnings by the captain, do not deter him. He is ashamed to go home and boards a ship to Africa, returning with success. Taking off again, he has bad luck and is captured by Moors in Sallee (Rabat, Morocco). He escapes from this predicament with the slave Xury (Horry, Arabic), and they are rescued by a Portuguese ship. A Scotsman hails him, and the Portuguese captain treats him with the utmost kindness, calling him Seignor Inglese (Mister English). Next, he ventures to Brazil, where he becomes the owner of a sugar plantation. Hoping to increase his wealth, he joins with other planters and undertakes a trip to Africa in order to bring back a shipload of slaves. Another terrific storm strikes and he is thrown forth as the sole survivor of a shipwreck on a remote, deserted tropical island. After spending fifteen years on the island, Crusoe finds a man's naked footprint on the beach. This electrifying event occurs about halfway through the book.

York, Lisbon, Brazil

Robinson Crusoe tells us that he was born "of a good family" in 1632 in York, a city we have frequently encountered in the present study. His father is "a Foreigner of Bremen, who settled first at *Hull*," the headquarters of the powerful De la Poles, as we have seen. The North Sea port of Bremen, along with Hamburg and Amsterdam, was one of the most important strongholds of the Marranos before their gradual resettlement in Protestant England, Dutch Brazil and New York. The original family name, we learn, is Kreutznaer ("Crusader"), a detail that introduces further suspicion of a *converso* background. His mother's family, moreover, is Robinson ("Reuben's son"). Kreutznaer is changed to Crusoe "by the usual corruption of Words in *England*," although Crusoe, it is to be noted, evokes with its two syllables Defoe's own name and is evidently the same as Caruso, a Sephardic surname documented in Ottoman Turkish Hungary and São Paulo, Brazil.[24]

British Jewish connections surface overtly in the society Crusoe falls into in Brazil. "I had a Neighbour," he says, "a *Portugueze* of Lisbon, but born of *English* parents, whose Name was *Wells,* and in much such Circumstances as I was (36)." Through a network of Jewish and crypto–Jewish merchants and brokers in Brazil, Lisbon and London, Crusoe is able to recover his money and goods and invest them in a sugar plantation. He will rely on the same transnational system of bills of exchange, letters of credit and proxies to sell that plantation in Lisbon after his escape from the desert island.

The Wellses or Welleses were established merchants in London from medieval times (Appendix C). It appears from this reference that "Portuguese" is used as a synonym for Jewish, as is frequently the case in English. In the annals of American Jewry, we see that the rector T. B. Wells of Devon married Anne Elizabeth Jonas, daughter of Abraham Jonas of Exeter and Lucy Orah Seixas of a distinguished Sephardic London family, and there is also a Lulu Wells in the colonial Jewish Hart family records.[25] Mary Wells, daughter of Richard Wells and Frances White, was the wife of Joseph (George) Yates (an English Jewish name) of Buckland, Oxfordshire/Berkshire, one of the founders of Maryland, known as "the Surveyor."[26] In the same colony, Thomas Wells married Elizabeth Howard, a relative of the dukes of Norfolk. The De Welles of Essex and Staffordshire are a venerable West Country family that can be traced back to an Adam de Welles of Devon, Walter de Welles in the twelfth century and even before that, to a pre–Norman Ragemer de Welles. They intermarried over several generations with the Mowbrays and Ashtons.[27] Thus, if the name of Wells mentioned by Defoe was not that of an actual person, it certainly had a rich historical resonance and appropriateness. We have observed above that the cathedral city of Wells in Somerset is the site of one of the Jewish and Middle Eastern DNA hotspots in England.

Defoe does not give any of the ten slaving expedition partners' names, only to say that some of them came from San Salvador. At the time of *Robinson Crusoe*'s action, this designated the Jewish colony of Bahia or Pernambuco. The first synagogue in America, Kahal Zur Israel, was erected in nearby Recife in 1636. After the Dutch conquered this province with the help of the Marrano-organized Dutch West India Company in 1630, Portuguese Jews streamed into it. The Church complained of how many of them became "circumcised and openly professed the Jewish faith." A contemporary Dutch observer reported that these Jews, now openly so, "had a vast traffic beyond all the rest, they purchased sugar mills, and built stately houses in the Receif…. They were all traders."[28] In 1654, the Dutch were forced to cede the area back to Portugal, not, however, before issuing in Amsterdam the famous "Patenta Honrossa," the first document of its kind granting equality to the Jews in the Western Hemisphere. The colony at Recife dispersed to Amsterdam, London, Barbados, Jamaica, Surinam, New Amsterdam, Newport (Rhode Island), Martinique, Guadeloupe, Hamburg, Nevis and Curaçao.[29]

Alexander Selkirk

The germ of the idea and many of the embellishments for *Robinson Crusoe* came to Defoe from his reading the story of Alexander Selkirk, a Scotsman from Fife who spent four years marooned on the uninhabited archipelago of Juan Fernandez far off the coast of Chile. Accounts of Selkirk's adventures were rife in the London press. Just as Robinson Crusoe's ancestral name had been Robinson Kreutznaer, Selkirk's name had been altered from the original form of Selcraig. At the time Defoe wrote, another famous son of Fife, John Law, was head of the Royal Bank of France, mastermind of the ruinous South Sea Bubble that engulfed the finances of half of Europe.[30] Both Selkirk and Crusoe are protagonists who suffer from the sin of hubris, courting disaster in the pursuit of adventure. Defoe transferred the scene of punishment for his obstinate prodigal son to the Caribbean, near Curaçao about eighty miles off the coast of South America. He incorporated many of Selkirk's trials and tribulations—feeding on stale biscuits, fish and goat's meat, an island overrun by cats, forgetting human speech—but made the story all his own with the addition of cannibals, pirates, and the manservant Friday, not to mention overarching themes of far greater depth and complexity.

Most importantly, Crusoe is an Englishman, standing for everything English and representing, in the words of one commentator, an "unabashed propaganda for the extension of British mercantile power in the New World and the establishment of new British colonies."[31] Thus, Crusoe builds a little England on the desert isle, complete with storerooms, record keeping, fenced fields, animal pens, cheese making and even that emblem of British imperialism, the umbrella. Creating makeshift imitations of *le confort anglais*, he still pines for peas and carrots from an English garden and "English shoes." As the years go by, he cannot get out of his mind needles, pins, threads, English ale, ink, brass kettles, a spade and a proper tobacco pipe.

Despite all the handicaps of his situation, Crusoe works hard and steadily with great diligence and determination and contrives, by the time of the book's turning point, to achieve no small measure of contentment and ease amid his wild surroundings. He becomes the very picture of an English milord, albeit out of place and wigless. "To think," he says, "that this was all my own, that I was King and Lord of all this Country indefeasibly, and had a Right of Possession; and if I could convey it, I might have it in Inheritance, as completely as any Lord of a Mannor in *England* (101)." He even has a second home and a pleasure craft for cruising about his estates, to say nothing of pots of money, although none of his treasure is spendable given his circumstances.

> There was my Majesty the Prince and Lord of the whole Island; I had the Lives of all my Subjects at my absolute Command. I could hang, draw, give Liberty, and take it away, and no Rebels among all my Subjects.
>
> Then to see how like a King I din'd too all alone, attended by my Servants, Poll, as if he had been my Favourite, was the only Person permitted to talk to me. My Dog who was now grown very old and crazy, and had found no Species to multiply his Kind upon, sat always at my Right Hand, and two Cats, one on one Side the Table, and one on the other, expecting now and then a Bit from my Hand, as a Mark of special Favour [149].

Cultivating His Garden

Crusoe prides himself on the fact that his compound is secure and secluded. His "Wall" of thickly planted canes is so stout and grown up "that there was not the least Appearance to any one's View of any Habitation behind them (153)." His crops of barleycorn are "duly cultivated and sow'd," with plenty of land adjoining them to expand into.

> Besides this, I had my Country Seat, and I had now a tolerable Plantation there also; for first, I had my little Bower, as I call'd it, which I kept in Repair; *that is to say*, I kept the Hedge which circled it in, constantly fitted up to its usual Height, the Ladder standing always in the Inside; I kept the Trees which at first were no more than my Stakes, but were now grown very firm and tall; I kept them always so cut, that they might spread and grow thick and wild, and make the more agreeable Shade, which they did effectually to my Mind. In the Middle of this I had my Tent always standing, being a piece of a Sail spread over Poles set up for that Purpose, and which never wanted any Repair or Renewing; and under this I had made me a Squab or Couch, with the Skins of the Creatures I had kill'd, and with other soft Things, and a Blanket laid on them, such as belong'd to our Sea-Bedding, which I had saved, and a great Watch-Coat to cover me; and here, whenever I had Occasion to be absent from my chief Seat, I took up my Country Habitation [153].

Outwardly, Robinson Crusoe's progress is clearly a fable for the course of historical developments on another island, that of Great Britain, founded on simple agrarian values of thrift, ingenuity and prudence. In the end Crusoe reaps rich rewards following his escape and return to civilization. But what do we learn of his spiritual awakening or of any religious salvation—his inner life?

The first half of the tale is solely concerned with Robinson Crusoe. It is not until page 154 out of 301 that the narrative abruptly changes with the "Man's naked Foot on the Shore." This is also the midpoint of his absence from all society, being the fifteenth year of his existence as a castaway. The whole first half of the book is as meditative as the second half with its cannibals and pirates is action-packed. The events of Crusoe's inner life are recounted—literally *accounted* for—in the same bald empirical style, and to our mind they are just as revelatory of an English Jewish disposition. Here, if anywhere, we may follow Defoe's true thoughts and beliefs, uninhibited by any social conventions, unconstrained by any predetermined outcome, for in his solitude Crusoe sets down a record that purports to be pure self-confrontation and confession.

Neither Defoe nor Crusoe actually says what religion he professes. We know from his extensive output that Defoe came to reject both the Dissenter label and the establishmentarian Anglican choice. At the same time, he did not apparently like the deists either, regarding them as too liberal on many issues. He attacked the deists' doctrine of cultural inclusiveness and relativity, being unwilling to accept papists, Africans and Turks on the same footing as Englishmen and other Europeans. Jews occupied a special position in his cultural writings. In *An Essay upon Literature; or, An Enquiry into the Antiquity and Original of Letters* (1726), Defoe adamantly insisted that the prevailing deist theory attributing alphabetic priority to the Egyptians, Chaldeans or Phoenicians was ill founded, and that it was the Hebrews who received letters first. He went on to argue that the profane and modern uses of letters belonged preeminently to England as a chosen nation and people.[32]

Business and Religion

Crusoe comes to a religious awakening by dwelling on his many reasons to be grateful to God. He begins by repenting of his reckless ways and recalling the wise words of his father. Rather stolidly, he starts by drawing up a sort of bookkeeper's ledger "to set the good against the Evil, that I might have something to distinguish my Case from worse, and I stated it very impartially, like Debtor and Creditor, the Comforts I enjoy'd, against the Miseries I suffer'd (67)."

> Upon the whole, here was an undoubted Testimony, that there was scarce any Condition in the World so miserable, but there was something *Negative* or something *Positive* to be thankful for in it; and let this stand as a Direction from the Experience of the most miserable of all Conditions in this World, that we may always find in it something to comfort our selves from, and to set in the Description of Good and Evil, on the Credit Side of the Accompt [68].

Making a business of religion, however, will not entirely suffice, no more than making a religion of business. Crusoe must have an emotional experience. Ten months into his solitude, he picks up a Bible and reads the words, "Call on me in the Day of Trouble, and I will deliver, and thou shalt glorify me (Psalms 50:15)." Sadly, he reflects that the idea of deliverance was as remote and impossible-seeming to him as the promise of being fed was for the Children of Israel, who asked in disbelief *Can God spread a Table in the Wilderness?* (Psalms 78:19). Then he does something, he says, for the first time: "I kneel'd down and pray'd to God to fulfil the Promise to me, that if I call'd upon him in the Day of Trouble, he would deliver me (96)." The next day upon wakening, Defoe realizes *God had deliver'd me, but I had not glorify'd him* (97). From this experience onward, he becomes more and more grateful for his lot and the events that befall him. His prayers are consistently those of thanksgiving, not petitionary, and they are addressed to God, not Jesus. Jesus is mentioned only a handful of times in the entire book. One of these occurrences is at the moment of religious ecstasy just described, where Crusoe, oddly, invokes the title *"thou son of David"* (98).

On this very day, the fastidious Crusoe mysteriously loses track of time, underscoring the extraordinary and otherworldly nature of his experience. "I knew not how I should lose a Day out of my Reckoning in the Days of the Week, as it appear'd some Years after I had done.... But certainly I lost a Day in my Accompt, and never knew which Way (96)."

Subsequent tests of Crusoe's faith, like his temptation to judge the cannibals inhuman and preemptively fall on them and wipe them out, or the false hope of rescue with a second ship appearing, only serve to confirm him in his homespun, personal religion. After a dead boy's body washes up, he reflects that

> it gave me more and more Cause to give Thanks to God who had so happily and comfortably provided for me in my desolate Condition; and that of two Ships Companies who were now cast away upon this part of the World, not one Life should be spar'd but mine: I learned here again to observe, that it is very rare that the Providence of God casts us into any Condition of Life so low, or any Misery so great, but we may see something or other to be thankful for; and may see others in worse Circumstances than our own [188].

Ingratitude toward God and his own father is, in fact, decides Crusoe, "my ORIGINAL SIN" (195).

When it comes to imparting the principles of religious knowledge to Friday, Crusoe falls into several difficulties, particularly when it comes to explaining the Devil, Hell, nature of Christ and the Last Judgment. We do not know how ironic or satirical Defoe was being in presenting the simplifications of either Crusoe or Friday. Eventually Crusoe claims, "The Savage was now a good Christian, a much better than I ... a much better Scholar in the Scripture Knowledge, than I should ever have been by my own private meer Reading (221)."

Religion is far from being simply a nice thing to have in Crusoe's world, one of the status-conveying appurtenances of a civilized life. It may be a private affair, but its influence is deep. We see what an important role it plays in *Robinson Crusoe* when the redeemed hero at the end of his adventures vacillates about the prospect of returning to Brazil and resuming his life there as a "naturalized" citizen-planter:

> But I had some little Scruple in my Mind about Religion, which insensibly drew me back, of which I shall say more presently. However, it was not Religion that kept me from going there for the present; and as I had made no Scruple of being openly of the Religion of the Country, all the while I was among them, so neither did I yet; only that now and then having of late thought more of it, (than formerly) when I began to think of living and dying among them, I began to regret my having profess'd my self a Papist, and thought it might not be the best Religion to die with [287].

Lineaments of the Crypto-Jew

We can detect in Crusoe's words the eternally recurring quandaries of the crypto–Jew— evasion, dissembling, prevarication, temporizing, loneliness, rationalization, denial, hypocrisy, doubt, guilt, pride, defiance and a transcendent firmness. At first, Crusoe pretends religion is "not the main thing that kept me from going"; it was not knowing "with whom to leave my Effects behind me." He writes letters to the "good Padres," his two trustees and his former partner, and settles his affairs in Lisbon. Then he sells his cargo, turns his profits into bills of exchange and departs for England. When he reaches London, "the Center of my Travels," and has all his rewards and effects about him, he comes back to the subject of faith.

> But now another Scruple came in my Way, and that was Religion; for as I had entertain'd some Doubts about the *Roman* Religion, even while I was abroad, especially in my State of Solitude; so I knew there was no going to the *Brasils* for me, much less going to settle there, unless I resolv'd to embrace the *Roman* Catholick Religion, without any Reserve; unless on the other hand, I resolv'd to be a Sacrifice to my Principles, be a Martyr for Religion, and die in the Inquisition; so I resolv'd to stay at Home, and if I could find Means for it, to dispose of my Plantation [303].

The contextual details show that Crusoe's religion, and by transference Defoe's, is something lived, a historically and socially specific type, not simply a philosophy imbibed from reading and education, some theological taste or airy doctrinal variety. It is neither Puritanism nor deism, nor something in between, and it is more than just natural law. Popery and the Inquisition hardly appear as colorful, irrelevant foreign institutions. What they represent is an ancestral memory, a clear and present danger, a factor of great moment and import.

With Daniel Defoe we reach the end of our survey of Britain's early Jews and related peoples, including a surprising number of Muslims in its history. From the eighteenth century Jews would be defined increasingly by themselves rather than by non–Jews. They would be distinguished into multifaceted ethnic, religious, social and geographical categories. Muslims, Turks and other Middle Easterners were to face a long period of being Orientalized and excluded from the dominant white colonial culture. British Jews and crypto–Jews blended and lost much of their "otherness," often transforming into Jewish Britons or simply British *tout court*. British Jewry became indistinguishable in the triumphant spread of English and British or American-styled global culture. That it was a single continuous, self-aware community from the start, not the on-again, off-again, embattled proposition of popular books and encyclopedias of Jewish life, we hope these investigations have substantiated in a way that can lead at least to fresh perspectives on the phenomenon.

Epilogue

So what if the Tudors came from distant Jewish origins? What of it if the De la Poles had Jewish ancestors? What significance did it have for Cromwell's public virtue or flaws or place in history, even if he was conscious of his Jewish ancestry, even if that Jewish ancestry were proved beyond a shadow of a doubt? What does it matter if one-tenth of the historical surnames or place-names mentioned in the book actually and unequivocally do reflect Hebrew or Arabic roots? Or if a small percentage of DNA in the English gene pool is North African, Middle Eastern or Phoenician, as seems undeniable?

Since the appearance of the first two installments in the series of three that concludes with the present volume, we are familiar with these and other pointed criticisms of our work. Lest we be accused of conducting false scholarship and writing bad history, we are happy to answer some of those charges in bidding farewell to a genealogical mystery that impinged on us both in a personal way more than ten years ago. Why did our parents, grandparents and their elders dissemble our families' Judaism—often so successfully it could not be discovered either then or now—while flaunting elements of it in apparent faithfulness to their true identity? How much guilt or regret did they feel?

To answer this question, and assuage our own shock and alienation, we had to proceed backwards through the generations as with any well-founded genealogical search. We followed the clues wherever they led us. We wrote our books deconstructing our ancestry and cultural heritage backwards, beginning with the Melungeons of present-day Appalachia, following on with the Scots-Irish background in *When Scotland Was Jewish* and gaining a closer view of the general phenomenon with *Jews and Muslims in British Colonial America*. This left tackling the linchpin of crypto–Jewish history in England and Wales for last. Ireland, the other island, would receive a "pass" from us as being simply too challenging. It was relevant but significantly outside the scope of our inquiries, besides being problematical in more ways than one. Chiefly, our competencies simply did not extend to knowing Gaelic languages, a fundamental requirement. We have never opened that door.

The response of many to our publications is that they indulge in speculation. But one speculates about the future, not the past. We have no interest in speculating about our ancestry. It is what it is. We know some of it, perhaps a good deal of it, and we know what we don't know about it. We are deadly serious about genealogy. While neither of us is an essentialist in these matters, we do not believe you can have "relatively true" results in family trees. Who would want to claim that a certain person is "probably" his father? On a basic level, a person is either your ancestor or not. An individual is either a Jew or not, even if they (or their ancestors or descendants) converted, or concealed their origins, or kept their faith private, or were reticent publicly about their identity, or changed their name. An ex–Jew is not the same as a non–Jew. Strictly speaking, you cannot be a Jew and not be a Jew. The same governing logic can be extended to other subjects of historical investigation (Covenanters, republicans, deists, Scotsmen). Otherwise, everything is a quagmire.

We do not deny that our books are full of arguments. They are also full of facts. At the core of our assertions is the repeated act of instantiation. For instance, we argue that Gildas was probably connected to North Africa in some way or other on the strength of the finding that his name is neither British nor Celtic nor Latin but Berber. This is a fact. The argument is strengthened by his Late Latin rhetorical literary style being similar to that of other North African authors of the time. That Gildas was perhaps akin to one of the "half–Jews" criticized by the Roman African writer Commodianus, possibly either a semi-convert or an Arian and Pelagian, is a further stage of argumentation. We can cross-check such inferences by recourse to other things we know about Gildas, his being called in the manuscripts, like other pagan and non–Christian authors, a *sapiens* or philosopher, and his authorship of a poem dated to the early sixth century penned in an arcane high-brow *patois* full of Visigothic, Arabic and Jewish coinages, the so-called Hisperica Famina genre of writing. Gildas, we submit, came from a Sephardic Jewish background. Even if he converted to Celtic Christianity, he or his parents or immediate forebears were, in all likelihood, Jews. The same argument or a similar chain of arguments, deductive or inductive, underlies all our other identifications of Jews and crypto–Jews, Arabs or Muslims and crypto–Muslims, in English and Welsh history. Some portions of evidence may be stronger than others but it is all of a piece. The arguments are intended to be cumulative in their force and to show that English Jewry, like other western European varieties, was Sephardic in nature, from its beginnings under the Roman Empire to the open return of Jews instigated by Menasseh ben Israel and the Marranos of Amsterdam in the seventeenth century.

Our work has been research-driven rather than theory-driven. We have assembled the data and established instances of groups and individuals with Jewish ancestry in continuous evidence in English history. Presumably many of these carried Jewish sympathies and culture and mentality, to varying degrees, but that must belong to the next phase of investigation. Restricting ourselves to groundwork, we stop short of analyzing the data and going to the next phase of generalizations and inferences. We refrain necessarily from writing the detailed biographies and longitudinal studies that might be indicated by this first cut—a monograph on the crypto–Jewish beliefs and practices of Oliver Cromwell or a sweeping chronicle of the Tudors as a Jewish dynasty. Here we *will* venture into speculation and hazard the guess that such books *will* be written in the future by others. There is, in our opinion, an *embarras de richesse* to contemplate and digest. Were the English Reformation and Commonwealth shaped in large measure by the Jewish sensibilities of the Tudors and Cromwells? Has there always been an anti–Roman, anti–papist thread in British Christianity? Why was England in the forefront of emancipating Jews in the nineteenth century and establishing the state of Israel in the twentieth? Was it Jewish genes in the mercantile and banking class that helped ensure the international success of the British Empire? These and other larger questions we have left alone, feeling honored to do the basic research and help spur others to join the fray.

It is a strange circumstance, but English history has invariably been the privilege of Englishmen to write (less rarely, American men). The same observation cannot be made of French history or Italian. Think of Carlyle's history of the French Revolution, or Jakob Burckhardt's work on the Italian Renaissance, or Denis Mack Smith's *Italy: A Modern History* (1959), translated into Italian as the two-volume *Storia d'Italia dal 1861 al 1958*. But whether written by native sons or not, English, German, French, Italian and Spanish histories tend to fall into the nationalistic vein both as to their focus and purpose. From the beginnings and especially for the past two centuries, all have characteristic preoccupations and biases. Whether it is to celebrate the freedom of the misty Germanic forests of Tacitus and the German school that follows that ancient author, to purvey the imperial values of the Gallo-Romans and Carolingians (French historiography), or dissect the Tory and Whig dialectic of English history, European historians have been Eurocentric and nationalistic. They are usually fixed on discussing politics and diplomacy, and you can almost smell the odor of a pipe somewhere about them.[1] According to Norman Davies, author of the encyclopedic *Europe: A History*, "In the longer term, the definitive history of Europe will probably be written by a Chinese, a Persian, or an African" (Oxford 1996, 35). Davies, who is of Welsh descent, acknowledges the fatal prejudices in English historians when he notes that the only survey of British history to give proportionate attention to all four peoples (England, Scotland, Ireland, Wales) was written by an Anglo-Irish exile in the United States: Hugh Kearney, *The British Isles: A History of Four Nations* (Cambridge University Press, 1989). Our own inquiries have been inspired by this Britannic perspective.

English Jews have not often come to the fore in Jewish-*qua*-Jewish histories, except after their return in 1650 and emancipation in the nineteenth century. Even more so than in the case of English historiography, Jewish historical writing has been restricted to Jews and has tended to be parochial in concept. Most chapters on England as well as local histories of communities belong, moreover, to what Salo Baron called "the lachrymose school." This mentality emphasizes relations between Jews and Christians, sometimes disintegrating into a catalogue of grievances and misunderstandings. Its exponents often adopt an openly apologetic stance defending Zionism as one of Jewish history's "obvious" upshots, with all that that interpretation entails. Unintended consequences of historical events are strangely nonexistent in both the English and Jewish practice of history.

Interestingly, however, as Gertrude Himmelfarb ironically discovered, Hebraists in the seventeenth and eighteenth centuries had a different and more positive take on Jewish history. Some were proposing the ancient "Hebrew Commonwealth" as the model for the English government. These suggestions are not unlike the crypto–Jewish behavior we have traced in the present work, from Gildas to Henry of Huntingdon. Surely it was John Toland's English and Irish crypto–Jewish and international mercantile connections that made him even aware of the Italian rabbi and scholar Simone Luzzatto, who published a book in Italian in Venice in 1638 titled in English *Discourse Concerning the Condition of the Jews*. Toland at first declared his intention of translating Luzzatto's book, but in time he went much further in his ideas and wrote a daring book of his own advocating a Mosaic republic in Augustan Britain. At about the same time, Moses Lowman (a Jewish name), who presented himself as a Nonconformist minister, wrote a *Dissertation on the Civil Government of the Hebrews in Which the True Designs and Nature of Their Government Are Explained; The Justice, Wisdom and Goodness of the Mosaical Constitution Are Vindicated*. Without realizing its significance, Himmelfarb also makes animadversion to the inevitable Welshman in the figure of Thomas Morgan, who wrote the "curiously entitled book, *The Moral Philosopher: In a Dialogue Between Philalethes a Christian Deist, and Theophanes a Christian Jew*." We can almost feel her shudder of disapproval at the expression "a Christian Jew."[2]

The early centuries of Christianity were full of Jewish Christians—why can the latter days of Judaism not have room for Christian Jews? Do I cease to be a Jew if I change my religion or decide to be silent about it? Does conversion erase my ancestry and make it inoperative? Without suggesting anything approaching genetic determinism, and without falling into the trap of the biographical fallacy in interpreting the writings of history and literature, we remain satisfied that the questions we have attempted not so much to answer as to raise and address in *When Scotland Was Jewish,* in *Jews and Muslims in British Colonial America* and now in *The Early Jews and Muslims of England and Wales* do in fact matter a great deal. They will never cease to be important, particularly in a world where the nation-state as the essential protagonist of history has succumbed to "history from below." For our interest in history now not only cuts across cultures, embracing categories like ethnicity and gender, "but also moves outward and downward, to the history of the world in one direction and to that of small communities such as the workshop and more often, the village or parish."[3] In this movement, aided and abetted by the power of the Internet and co-production of knowledge by users and consumers, history converges with genealogy. We are glad of this development and endorse it wholeheart-edly, as genealogy serves to make history personal, to infuse it with meaning and to insure that everyone has a share in what society believes important about the past. The significance of Ranke's oft-quoted remark about the immediacy of history is that every past event occurred in a present of its own. It still does and always will. Nothing will "unhappen." The story of Britain's amazing Jewish commercial families and their endurance over thousands of years will always be waiting to be rediscovered and rewritten to suit people's needs and satisfy the tastes of a new age.

Appendix A

Jewish DNA Hot Spots

The modern science of genetics was born in Britain, and the British have not been slow to train it on their own multifaceted national legacy. Several major studies over the past ten years describe the genetic structure of England and Wales and differentiate populations and sub-populations, even down to characterizing fine-scale local patterns. It is our intent in the present appendix to focus on haplogroups E, J and several others from a technical viewpoint and try to determine from the assembled evidence if Jews and other Middle Easterners left any significant traces of deep ancestry or emigration in Britain's DNA record.

In pursuing this investigation, of course, we face several thorny issues. The first is that one can only study the DNA of living persons. Cases of ancient DNA are so rare that we may as well relegate them to the status of interesting curiosities. Their importance in the DNA landscape is like Carlyle's old stone monuments' testimony amid the English countryside: "They stand, but stand in silent and uncommunicative majesty." Second, even in collecting and comparing modern-day samples we must be careful to consider methodology, validity and commensurability of the data in drawing conclusions. One of the nagging problems, as we shall see, is the equivocal definition of who is (or was) Jewish. This is particularly vexing inasmuch as the ethnic origins of Jews are highly mixed from their earliest appearance about 4,000 years ago. Not only are Jews to be approached as a complex diaspora population but the most logical source to sample Jewish DNA today, the state of Israel, is an artificial population composed overwhelmingly of non-native people. Their genetics is a highly sensitive and frequently politicized subject.

Surname studies are increasingly forming part of scientists' tool kits in tackling such subjects.[1] One of the first points we can make in this regard is that Wales and Southwest England have been found to produce quite distinctive surnames. A rough gauge of how specialized and regionalized they are would be to say they are twice as rarefied as those of other parts of England. "Individuals whose surnames are localized to an area are more likely to have ancestry from that area down the male lineage," we read in the project The People of the British Isles (PoBI), "and should be more representative of the region over a long time period." The same project reports that Pembrokeshire (Wales), Cornwall and Devon surnames have a high index for most likelihood quantization (MLQ) compared to what might be expected for their sample sizes. Mentioned are Jones, Davies, Evans, Thomas, Hughes, James and Phillips, all common Welsh surnames we have encountered already in this book. Surnames are judged to have a highly distinctive regional occurrence also in Kent and Sussex, but nowhere approaching the levels of Wales.[2]

PoBI combines Cornwall, Pembrokeshire and Devon to represent southwest England on the grounds that these regions provide the closest surrogate to the Ancient British. It segregates Orkney DNA as a special case owing to the Northern Isles' atypical heritage. More than one-third of Orkney men carry haplotype R1a, considered a Viking signature, and this circumstance is often reflected in surnames.[3] The other regions are Central-North or CN (Oxfordshire and the Forest of Dean, corresponding approximately to medieval Mercia), East or E (Sussex, Kent, Norfolk and Lincolnshire) and North or N (Cumbria, Yorkshire and the North East). PoBI uses samples from these

regions qualified by the criteria of rural grandparental ancestry to lay bare the genetic signatures and signals in the British Isles' five main demographically defined historical populations—Ancient British, Norse, Anglo-Saxon, Roman and Danish/Norman. (Note the absence of anything called "Celtic.") The project published its first results in 2011 based on 3865 carefully chosen samples and aims to provide a UK-control population for future research.

One of the oldest and still most useful surveys of Britain's genetic diversity was the study authored by James F. Wilson and collaborators in 2001. Wilson's team aimed to assess the demographic context of cultural change in British history.[4] The Wilson study explored the relative contributions of male versus female lines (Y chromosome and mitochondrial haplotypes) during major invasions against a background of what was presumed to be the little-changing genetic bedrock of the British Isles. Making its first appearance was the Atlantic Modal Haplotype (AMH), a form of male lineage R1b, which was found to be dominant in Basque and other western European populations, rising to a level of 90 percent in Irish samples. Wilson et al. were the first to correlate Basque and British population histories, but in equating pre–Roman British DNA with "Celtic speaking populations" they opened the door to many popular misinterpretations concerning "Celtic DNA" in the British Isles.[5] For our part, we are more interested in the minor Middle Eastern, African and Mediterranean lineages exposed by their survey.

Following the standard haplogroup division, Wilson et al. genotyped the British Isles mitochondrial DNA specimens available at that time for the following female lineages: J, T, I, W, X, K, U, V, HV1, preHV, N1b, HV*, U*, R*, H and L. In analyzing the patterns of female variation, they found that Britain was similar to other western European countries and that Turkey and Syria provided the clearest opposite paradigms. These two Middle Eastern populations "are distinct with much lower frequencies of the most common European hg (H) and large proportions of hgs not present or extremely rare in the European samples."[6] They concluded that Britain's matrilineal legacy indicated "that one or more of these pre–Anglo-Saxon cultural revolutions had a major effect on the maternal genetic heritage of the British Isles," without speculating whether the contrasting female history of Britain was due to the spread of Neolithic agriculture or some other event, saying only that "at least one of the Neolithic or Iron Age cultural transitions in the British Isles involved some female immigration."[7]

Neither Wilson nor his followers elaborate much on the female population history implied

Opposite: **Jewish DNA hotspots in England and Wales' historic counties (map by Donald Yates).**

Legend for Historic Counties Map

CODE	Historic County	CODE	Historic County	CODE	Historic County	CODE	Historic County
ABN	Aberdeenshire	CUM	Cumberland	KNR	Kinross-shire	RDN	Radnorshire
AGL	Anglesey	DBH	Denbighshire	KCB	Kirkcudbrightshire	RNF	Renfrewshire
ANG	Angus	DRB	Derbyshire	LNK	Lanarkshire	RSS	Ross-shire
ANM	Antrim	DVN	Devon	LCS	Lancashire	RXB	Roxburghshire
ARG	Argyllshire	DRS	Dorset	LCR	Leicestershire	RTL	Rutland
ARH	Armagh	DWN	Down	LNC	Lincolnshire	SKK	Selkirkshire
AYS	Ayrshire	DMF	Dumfriesshire	LDR	Londonderry	SHT	Shetland
BNF	Banffshire	DUN	Dunbartonshire	MRN	Merionethshire	SHP	Shropshire
BED	Bedfordshire	DRH	Durham	MSX	Middlesex	SMS	Somerset
BER	Berkshire	ELT	East Lothian	MLT	Midlothian	STF	Staffordshire
BRW	Berwickshire	ESE	Essex	MNM	Monmouthshire	STL	Stirlingshire
BRN	Brecknockshire	FRM	Fermanagh	MTG	Montgomeryshire	SFF	Suffolk
BUC	Buckinghamshire	FFE	Fife	MOY	Morayshire	SUR	Surrey
BTE	Buteshire	FLT	Flintshire	NRN	Nairnshire	SUS	Sussex
CRN	Caernarfonshire	GLM	Glamorgan	NRF	Norfolk	SRL	Sutherland
CTN	Caithness	GLC	Gloucestershire	NHP	Northamptonshire	TYN	Tyrone
CMB	Cambridgeshire	HMP	Hampshire	NHB	Northumberland	WRW	Warwickshire
CRD	Cardiganshire	HRF	Herefordshire	NOT	Nottinghamshire	WLT	West Lothian
CRM	Carmarthenshire	HTF	Hertfordshire	ORN	Orkney	WML	Westmorland
CHE	Cheshire	HNT	Huntingdonshire	OXD	Oxfordshire	WGT	Wigtownshire
CLM	Clackmannanshire	INS	Inverness-shire	PBS	Peeblesshire	WTS	Wiltshire
CNW	Cornwall	KNT	Kent	PMB	Pembrokeshire	WRC	Worcestershire
CRT	Cromartyshire	KNC	Kincardineshire	PRT	Perthshire	YRK	Yorkshire

in mitochondrial haplogroup frequencies for Britain. As we have touched on above, though, Jewish females of haplogroups T, J, U and K were clearly present early on in numbers unlike those of other Atlantic-facing countries, demanding an explanation beyond simply the demic spread of agriculture from the Middle East.[8] One of the few studies we are aware of that might shed light on Jewish female haplotype distribution in Britain, a 2004 publication, finds high levels of several specific J haplotypes clustered in different regions: J2 defined by the mutation at 16193, a common Jewish type characteristic of Sephardic Jews and notable in Scotland which the study calls British Celtic (106); J1b1, a more eastern European Jewish type with a strong branch denoted by the mutation 16192 in Iceland, Scotland, Cornwall and Wales (which the study also terms British Celtic, 102– 104); and J1a, the "most clear-cut Germanic mtDNA type" within group J, with a mutation at 16231, found in amounts above 2 percent not only in central Europe, Spain, Turkey and the Middle East but also in southeast England (Kent) and Brittany (106–07).[9]

What do Wilson et al. imply about possible Jewish male lineages? The nomenclature for Y chromosome haplogroups can be confusing in the early literature, so we give the following conversion table.[10]

The next data we would like to look at for possible signals of Jewish DNA stem from the classic survey by Capelli and team at University College London published in 2003.[11] This study analyzed 1,772 Y chromosome specimens from 25 predominantly urban locations and compared them with sample sets from Norway, Denmark and Germany to assess the impact of Germanic

	Jobling 2000	Hammer (2001)	Race Archives	Karafet (2001)	Semino (2000)	Defining Mutation	YCC	Popular Label
R1b	1	1L	HG 1	42	Eu18	R-P25*	R1b	Aurignac, Western Atlantic
Q	18	1G	--	41	Eu 22	Q-M3*	Q	Native American, sometimes Ashkenazic
R1a1	3	1D	HG 3	43	Eu16, 18, 19	R-M17*	R1a	Eastern European, Viking
J	9	Med	HG 9	23, 24	Eu 9-10	J-12f2a, J-M172	J, J2, J*	Jewish, Semitic
E3a	8	5	HG 8	15	Eu 2	E-M2	E1b1a	Bantu
E3b	25	4	HG 21	14	Eu4	E-M2	E1b1b	North African, Moorish
I	--	--	HG 2	21	Eu7, Eu 8	I-P37-38, 40	I	Viking, Epi-Gravettan
C	10	V	HG 1, 22	16-19	Eu6	C3b=C-P39	C	Old Eurasian
G2	?	1H	?	22	Eu11	G-P15	G	No.Caucasian
T (K)	23	1E, 1U	HG 12, 26	25	Eu15, Eu 16	SRY9138, P27, Tat	T (K1, K*)	Phoenician
N	12	1I	HG 16	26	Eu13, Eu 14	M178	N*, N1	Uralic, Saami, Finnish

Conversion table for Y chromosome (male) lines (DNA Consultants/Donald Yates).

invasions and patterns of genetic continuity across the British Isles. Castlerea in central Ireland was selected to represent the indigenous populations, as having had no known history of contact with Anglo-Saxon or Viking invaders—a choice that may have been less than felicitous. The twenty-five sampling locations were Shetland, Orkney, Durness and Western Isles in northern Scotland; Stonehaven, Pitlochry and Oban in central Scotland; Morpeth and Penrith in northern England; the Isle of Man; York; Southwell and Uttoxeter in the Midlands; Llandiloes, Llangefni and Haverfordwest in Wales; Castlerea and Rush, near Dublin in Ireland; Chippenham (Wiltshire, medieval Mercia in central England); Faversham (Kent); Midhurst (West Sussex); Dorchester (Dorset, on the English Channel in southern England); Cornwall; and the Channel Islands. Some highlights taken from Capelli's table of haplogroup frequencies are discussed above, in chapter 1, and we will not attempt to critique the study's extrapolations on the relative importance of Viking types versus Anglo-Saxon or "British" DNA, but we should like to draw attention to some pockets of Jewish and Middle Eastern influence that seem to be discernible in Britain's genetic landscape.

Midhurst and Dorchester on the central southern coast of England leap out as an area registering some degree of all the haplogroups reported, that is, they have the highest diversity on this basis. They, along with Irish locations (taken, one recalls, as representing pre–Germanic substrate populations), preserve the unusual Mediterranean haplogroup I2 (formerly called I1b2), a lineage only otherwise noteworthy in the maritime crossroads of the Channel Islands and invasion-sheltered Midlands. Registering levels of 2–3 percent in the British locations where it does survive, I2, according to Capelli, is "found almost exclusively in British populations that have experienced little or no continental genetic input. Intriguingly, earlier studies have shown that it is present in the Iberian Peninsula at low frequencies (0–5.4 percent) and in Sardinia at a significant percentage (35.1 percent)."[12] We suggest that I2, like T and E1b1b, reflects vestiges of England and Wales' Phoenicians, a mercantile and metal-mining people with important colonies in Sardinia and Spain. I2 is also a well characterized, if minor, Jewish lineage. Fellow-traveler T is found in approximately 3 percent of Sephardic and 2 percent of Ashkenazi Jews.[13]

The fine-scale data in a related Y chromosome study by Weale et al. permit us to consider the genetic diversity in two East Midlands locations, Ashbourne (Derby) and Southwell (Nottinghamshire, site of the Southwell Minster mentioned in chapter 1).[14] In the former, relatively high levels are shown for J (3.7 percent) and E1b1b (5.6 percent), and in the latter, we find both J and E1b1b at frequencies of 5.7 percent. Whereas many regions of England register minimal or zero amounts of these Middle Eastern haplogroups, the East Midlands not only have significant levels of them but also multiple haplotypes or varieties (1015–16). Again, we encounter high diversification where, if these were marginal or accidental populations, we would expect the opposite. Setting aside the question of how Danish and other Viking incursions may have affected the population, we suggest that the Midlands in the center of England experienced a remarkable continuity of Mediterranean influences, one featuring Jews and North Africans as well as Romans.

This brings us to the final article we would like to glance at with an eye to detecting possible traces of early Jews and other Middle Easterners in Britain. Steven Bird in "Haplogroup E3b1a2 as a Possible Indicator of Settlement in Roman Britain by Soldiers of Balkan Origin,"[15] is, as the title makes clear, interested in proving a Roman Balkan origin for the haplotype now known as E1b1b1a, the most common type in Europe of the haplogroup E1b1b (formerly denominated E3b). The structure and subclades of this very ancient North African Caucasian lineage have only recently been resolved and overhauled, and the ink is not yet quite dry. But the data used by Bird with the sometimes confused or outdated nomenclature of older reports can still provide valuable clues for our purposes. One must only proceed with caution in making too many distinctions in the tangled branches of the E tree. We must bear in mind that the target haplotype E1b1b1a2 (also called E-V13) represents 85 percent of the parent haplogroup E1b1b (also denoted as the E-M78 clade) and keep simple E before us without splitting hairs.

Bird's study appeared in one of the first publications of the *Journal of Genetic Genealogy*, an online journal of the International Society of Genetic Genealogy (ISOGG), founded in 2005 primarily by DNA project administrators associated with Family Tree DNA, "who share the common vision of the promotion and education of genetic genealogy." Bird's is an ambitious work with a very narrow goal. It uses arguments not only from genetics and statistics but also archaeology, geography, history, anthropology and linguistics, often involving such fine points as the epigraphy of a Spanish soldier's diploma from the British Museum issued in 103 CE and the detailed movements of Thracian *cohors II* and *VII* in the Roman army. Bird's theory about the origins of E1b1b unfortunately became enshrined in popular belief overnight. In the "genetic genealogy community's" view England was soon awash with Thracian legionnaires. We do not wish to appear ungrateful for such a welcome colorful addition to English history but there are problems.

Bird's first mistake occurs in his review of the literature. He misreads Stephen Oppenheimer and represents the author of *The Origins of the British* as having British E "originating from the Balkan peninsula (26)." If we open Oppenheimer's book to the page cited (207) we see a map illustrating "Near Eastern [British English for American English 'Middle Eastern'] Neolithic male migrations via the Mediterranean of E3b [i.e. E1b1b] and J." The vector standing for the migration of these types launches forth from the Peloponnese in Greece at the cropped lower right corner, obviously intending to suggest origins from that general direction, not "the Balkan Peninsula." There is no mention of Balkan DNA in Oppenheimer except as part of the bigger picture. The archeological sites Bird adduces as evidence for E settlements in the Bronze Age are not necessarily associated "directly" or solely or chiefly with "proto–Thracian culture," whatever that term may mean. Nova Zagora in Bulgaria is a Stone Age multi-site. Ezero Culture occupied most of Bulgaria and extended far north into the Danube region of Romania. Yunatsite, Dubene-Sarovka and the other "proto–Thracian culture" examples Bird mentions date to before Thracians or even Greeks. They cannot tell us anything about haplogroup E. If anything, all these sites vindicate Oppenheimer's theory of the demic spread of Middle Eastern (read Anatolian) agriculture, which Bird calls "flawed fundamentally" (27). The center for the diffusion of E in the Balkans is not in Bulgaria or Thrace but northwestern Greece, Albania and Kosovo. But the Balkan Peninsula does not have to be the only place from which Bird can manage to derive E and get it to Britain in time to become part of the historical record. It is also strong throughout Greece, Cyprus, the Greek parts of southern Italy, North Africa and even parts of Spain. In fact, its presence in many of those locations is acknowledged to be "due to a founder effect, i.e. the migration of a small group of settlers carrying mostly this lineage (but also a small amount of other North-East African lineages, notably E-M123 and T."[16]

Despite these failings relating to statement of thesis and validity of arguments, Bird's work is based on useful data which are not likely to be superseded. Three population surveys with frequencies for E in Britain were available to him: the data sets of Capelli, Weale and Sykes. Notwithstanding the nomenclature confusion, only the Sykes data set has true shortcomings, as the Oxford Genetic Atlas Project at the time contained only forty E haplotypes, too small for a valid sample. There are problems comparing them, as Bird realizes, but trends and general conclusions are certainly possible. Before attempting to analyze haplogroup E variation in Britain, though, we must address the matter of time depth.

We have no quarrel with geneticists' and genetic genealogists' methods of gauging coalescence times. Thus, Bird reiterates that the "time to most recent common ancestor" or TMRCA of Cruciani and others led to the "important finding ... that E-V13 [read 85 percent of E] and J-M12 [read J] had essentially identical population coalescence times (27)." E and J are companion types that expanded from their Middle Eastern homelands together in the same fashion and probably reinforced each other in multiple phases of gene flow. But who is to say in any specific case of a haplotype that it arrived in Britain 4,000 years ago (TMRCA) or at any subsequent time, including the time when our grandfathers lived. The TMRCA sets a haplotype's time of origin but not its place of origin, except by inference. We hypothesize geographical origins from a host of other factors, chiefly present-day clusters, genetic distance between types and high concentration of haplotype diversity. Using TMRCA, Bird argues that a specific form of E "could not have arrived in Britain during the Neolithic era (6.5–5.5 kya) if it had not yet expanded from the southern Balkans (27)." We prefer to believe that it entered the British Isles in several stages from the same general source, first in Neolithic times but later with the Phoenicians, Jews, Egyptians, Iberians and related peoples.

Right Pew, Wrong Church

Bird cherry-picks the data to support his Roman Balkan, or what might be called his Diocletian, thesis, but data are data. The data can just as easily be interpreted to bear out the overall storyline we present and, within the same historical context, namely Roman times, to represent the existence of certain hot spots for Jewish and Middle Eastern DNA in England and Wales. We agree somewhat with Bird that the Welsh cluster for E is "underestimated by an arbitrary division by Sykes into two geographic regions ('Wales' and 'Northern England') ... [creating] an impression of a large number of 'Eshu' haplotypes located throughout Northern England, when in fact the northern English cluster is linked to Welsh cluster geographically (29)." Only, we would see in that Northern English cluster the remains of the historical Welsh Old North (chapters 1 and 7). We would not necessarily see in the Wales-to-Nottingham cluster the fading footprints of "the Ordovices, the Deceangi, the Cornovii, the Brigantes and the Coritani tribes (30)," about whom little is known in any event; rather, we would see a belt of pre-existing Mediterranean culture reinforced by Roman occupation and somewhat resistant to Anglo-Saxon and Viking intrusions. Another shrinking pocket of the old British culture is shown in the elevated frequencies for both E and J in Strathclyde and Cumbria, part of the Welsh Old North.

Bird has an informative map of Britain illustrating E1b1b distribution according to the Kriging method (34). In this illustration one can detect all the major pockets of Mediterranean and Jewish DNA. Leaving aside Scotland, and the Midlands pocket already mentioned, our eye is drawn to north Wales (with a clear wall of high incidence surrounding it as though beating back the forces of history on all sides), Dorset, London and East Anglia. It cannot be coincidence that these are the very regions where we have diagnosed the presence of historical Jews and picked up their trail through the chapters of our book.

As a final note, a 2005 paper by Robert Tarín provides phylogenetic analyses of E1b1b haplotypes that cast serious doubt on Bird's assertions and confirm rather our reading of the evidence.[17] Tarín used 290 individual Y chromosome results to characterize "a separate cluster of mostly Iberian haplotypes which seem to represent a North African entry into Iberia distinct from the E3b [E1b1b] in Europe that may have arisen from Neolithic or other migratory events." He wrote that "it is unknown whether this finding reflects relatively recent gene flow from the Islamic rule of Spain or an older influx possibly from the Phoenicians"—the same quandary about timeframe and coalescence we see above. Utilizing the Y Chromosome Haplotype Reference Database (YHRD),[18] Tarín found levels of the Iberian E haplotype as high as 61 percent in one Tunisian population (Zriba, near ancient Carthage), while Andalusian Arabs and Tunisian Berbers both showed frequencies of about 7 percent. We believe this Iberian haplotype is a small but important Jewish lineage that expanded from Tunisia to the Iberian Peninsula with the Berbers who aided Arab armies in conquering Spain. Interestingly, it accompanied Spanish Jews to Mexico and other places in the diaspora following the events of 1492. Its distribution in Britain should reveal an implantation originally under the Phoenicians reinforced by periodic migrations of Sephardic North African and Spanish or French Jews throughout the medieval and early modern periods of British history.

Appendix B

Post-Conquest and Angevin Jews

I. Chronology from Joseph Jacobs (1893), *The Jews of Angevin England*

810	Jews are said to flee from Germany to England and Spain to escape battles between Moors and Christians (Joseph Cohen 1575).
1100s	Jewish rabbis and judges are referred to as "bishops" in English records.
1145/1150	Solomon ben Isaac converts to Islam. Seal found in Scotland. Solomon may have arrived in London from Spain.
1146	R. Simon, an English Jew, is slain in Cologne by Crusaders for refusing baptism. Vives, a Jew from England, buys a house in Cologne.
1158	Other Spanish Jews found in London (Abraham ibn Exra).
1170	There are Christian usurers in England, who may have formerly been Jews.
1180–1182	"Ysaac of Russia" arrives in England from Tchernigoff, Russia.
1186	Ysaac Medicus (Isaac the Doctor) is in London. Moses de Hyspan (Moses the Spaniard) is in London. Josce Mauritij (Joseph the Moroccan) is in London.
1190	Jews of York massacre: The traditional account is a copy of Eleasar of Masada taken directly from Josephus and may not accurately represent what occurred at York.
1198	Jews working with tin mining and shipping in Cornwall and Devon. Place-name "Market Jew."
1199	Leo the Jew is King John's goldsmith.
1203	Rouen and English Jews in close familial contact.
1204–1206	Mention of a Hervery Bagod (Muslim surname) in Northampton.
1279	Mention of the Hagin family in London.

II. Names of Jewesses in England (Adler)

Alemandina	Brunetta	Ermina	Iveta	Milla	Roesia (Rose)
Almonda	Chera	Fleur de Lys	Joie	Mirabel	Sabina
Antera	Ciclaton	Floretta	Joietta	Motta	Salvea
Bacceva	Claricia	Floria	Juliana	Muriel	Sapphira
Bate	Columbina	Floricote	Julietta	Pasturella	Sarabella
Belaset	Damete	Fluria	Jurna	Pigorna	Sigge
Belassez	Denicosa	Francisca	Licoricia	Pimenta	Solal
Belia	Dona	Genta	Malecote	Popelina	Swetecot
Belicote	Duce	Gentil	Margalicia	Pucella	
Belina	Dulce	Gertelote	Margaret	Pulcella	
Bella	Duzelina	Giva	Margot	Preciosa	
Blanche	Dura	Glorietta	Maydin	Prude	
Bona	Engelesia	Godenote	Megge	Reyna	

198

III. Names of Jews Taken from the Royal Exchequer Accounts (date unknown)

(Public Records Office, Exchequer K.R. Accounts, No. 249, 2, Kent and Canterbury.)

De Samson' de Cantuar'
De Jacobo de Cahntuar'
De Samuele f' Jacob
De Isaac juveni de Cant'
De Isaac sene de Cantuar'
De Cresse fil' suo
De Gosce fil' suo
De Deuuelcresse Levi
De Meus fil' Benjamin'
De Simone nepote Jacob
De Jacobo de Cant'
De Aaro' fil' suo
De Jossce Gaudi de Cant'
De Bened' de Rouec'
Kent per manum Will' de Bukingham

De Isaac le gros
De Jacob de Kant'
De Meus gener Jacob
De Sampson
De Simund
De Josce fil' Isaac
De Abraam gener Josce
De Isaac
De Jurnet
De Delecresse le Cresp
De Josce Gaudin
De Solomun gener Isaac
De heredibus Benedict le Cresp
De Simund de Madling'

IV. Names of Jews Who Contributed Aid for the Dowry of Princess Joan (1221)

(Public Records Office, Exchequer 401, No. 4.)

Kantuar'

i

De Viueo filio Isaac
De Pictauin filio Isaac
De Aaron filio Feulecreisse
De Angeuin filio Isaac
De Samsone de Kantuar
De Benedicto Deulecreisse et Bono
De Josceo filio Sampson
De Mosseo filio Sampson
De Antera Vidua
De Isaac filio Meir

De Josceo filio Meir
De Jacobo filio Samuel et Aaron Genero suo
De Josceo fratre Sampsonis
De Aaron filio Joscei
De Melka Vidua
De Duelebenie et Genero suo
De Isaac filio Simonis
De Pictauin' filio Joscei
De Mosseo filio Joscei

ii

De Benedicto Cresselin' et Bonami
De Mosseo Presbytero
De Josceo fratre Bonami
De Isaac filio Meir
De Milka Vidua
De Aaron genero Milka

De Peiteuin et Mosseo fratre suo
De Jacobo filio Samuel'
De Aaron filio Cresselin'
De Josceo filio Aaron
De Angeuin' filio Isaac
De Viueo filio Isaac

V. Names of Jews from the Tallage Recipt Roll (1223)

(Public Records Office, Exchequer 401, No. 6)

Kancia

De Milka
De Benedicto Bonami et Cresselin'
De Aaron filio Josc'
De Aunstervidua
De Josc et copin genero suo
De Aaron filio Cresselin
De Meir filio Josc
De Isaac filio Jurnett
De Pictauin filio Josc
De Viueo filio Isaac

De Angeuin filio Isaac
De Peiteuin filio Isaac
De Sampsone de Kant
De Deuebenie
De Isaac filio Meir
De Josceo filio Sampsonis
De Ursell filio Samuel'
De Jacobo filio Samuel'
De Josceo filio Meir
De Benedicto Cresp et sociis suis

VI. Names of Jews from the Tallage Receipt Roll (1226)

(Public Records Office, Exchequer 401, No 8.)

Cantuaria

De Josceo filio Aaron
De Aaron filio Milka
De Copin' filio Milka

De Meir
De Milka vidua David
(9 more names illegible)

VII. Names of Jews from the Tallage Receipt Roll (1260)

(Public Records Office, Exchequer 401, No. 43)

De Solom de Cantebrig'
De Solom de Stamford
De Bonamy filio Isaac
De Samps' filio Avegaye
De Aaron filio Josc'
De Cress' filio Josc'
De Ben filio Cress
De Aaron filio Ben
De Popeline vidua
De Solom filio Gen
De Josc fil Salom

De Samuel le Evesk'
De Isaac fil Abr'
De Viuo de Wynton'
De Mosseo gener' Biues
De Josceo filio Abr'
De Ben' filio Bone
De Solom' filio Josc'
De Aaron filio Salom
De Leon' gener' Salom
De Manasser Purnas

VIII. Bonds Owing to Jews at the Expulsion

(Public Records Office, Exchequer Accounts, No. 250, 6)

Obligationes et Carte de Nouis Cistin Judeorum anglie que ad manus Regis deuenerunt post abiuracionem eorundem a Regno. Inrotulate coram Magistro W. de March' Thesaurario et Baronibus de Scaccario. Anno Regni Regis Edwardi vicesimo.

(The full text is printed in Trans., iv, 79–89. The dates of the 95 bonds are from September 25, 1280, to March 26, 1290.)

Summary

	Corn	£	s.	d.
Moses le Petit	316 qrs.	93	10	0
Leo son of Master Elias Baggard	270 qrs.	84	16	0
Aaron of Winchester	194 qrs.	56	0	0
Jose son of Ursell	104 qrs.	42	0	0
Aaron son of Cresse of Winchester and Hagin his brother	120 qrs.	40	0	0
Moses son of Salle	124 qrs.	37	13	4
Cok (Isaac) son of Benedict of Winchester	137 qrs.	34	0	0
Bella of Stamford	120 qrs.	32	0	0
Vives of Winchester	86 qrs.	28	3	4
Aaron son of Peitavin	83 qrs.	24	6	8
Hagin son Cresse	62 qrs.	15	0	0
Aaron son of Cresse of Winchester	42 qrs.	11	16	8
Elias son of Hagin	35 qrs.	10	8	4
Aaron son of Benedict of Winchester	18 qrs.	5	14	8
Cok of Winchester and Hagin son of Popelina	20 qrs.	4	0	0
Popelina widow of Abraham Pernas	14 qrs.	4	0	0
Jose Gileberd son of Aaron	10 qrs.	3	6	8
Belaset daughter of Benedict of Winchester	8 qrs.	2	8	0

IX. Names of Jews in Canterbury

(Michael Adler, *Jews of Medieval England*.
London: The Jewish Historical Society of England, 1939.)

1160–1200

Dieulecresse

Samson

Jacob Senex; Samuel his son; Aaron his son; Meir his son-in-law; Simon his nephew

Isaac Senex; Cresse (Cresslin) his son; Jose his son; Solomon his son-in-law

Isaac le Gros

Isaac Juvenis

Benedict Parvus

Benedict Longus

Diulecresse Levi le Cresp

Bonami

Jose Gaudi

Benedict of Rochester

Simon of Malling

Jacob son of Dieulesaut

Joseph son of Dieudonne

Abraham son-in-law of Jose

Meir son of Benjamin

Jurnet

1200–1240

Aaron son of Samson

Jose brother of Samson

Joseph son of Moses

Vives son of Isaac

Joseph Pictavin son of Isaac

Jacob Angevin son of Isaac

Milka widow of David; Aaron her son; Copin (Jacob) her son; Aaron her son-in-law

Moses son of Jacob

Elias son of Benedict

Aaron son of Benedict

Benedict Deulecress

Aaron son of Deulecress (Cresselin)

Jose son of Meir

Jacob son of Samuel; Aaron his son-in-law

Jose son of Samson

Manasser

Isaac son of Simon
Engelesia daughter of Benedict
Moses Presbyter
Chera, wife of Augustine the convert
Zerach, son of Benjamin
Moses of Cambridge
Antera widow of Jacob Molkin
Esther widow of Jacob son of Isaac
Dieubenie son of Isaac

Isaac son of Jacob; Bona his wife
Samuel son of Deudone
Isaac son of Meir
Pictavin son of Jose
Moses son of Jose
Jose son of Benjamin
Ursell son of Samuel
Jose son of Aaron

1240–1270

Aaron son of Benjamin
Aaron son of Jose of Leicester
Aaron son of Salle
Abraham son of Isaac
Abraham son of Leo
Abraham son of Salle
Abraham son of Samuel
Avegaye wife of Salle
Benedict son of Cresse (chirographer); his
    sons Elias, Aaron, Isaac
Benjamin son of Meir (a)
Benjamin son of Meir (b)
Benjamin son of Isaac
Benedict son of Isaac
Bonavie
Bonenfant son of Cresse
Bona widow of Meir son of Zerach
Bona wife of Isaac son of Zerach
Benjamin son of Bona
Deulecresse (Solomon) son of Genta
Hannah wife of Samuel Molkin
Isaac son of Abraham
Isaac son of Benedict of Bedford
Isaac son of Isaac
Moses son of Jose
Moses son of Salle
Moses son of Samson
Moses son of Vives
Popelina wife of Abraham Pernas
Salle son of Jose
Samson son of Abegaye
Samson son of Isaac
Samson son of Jose
Samuel son of Aaron Molkin
Samuel son of Benjamin
Samuel son of Isaac
Isaac son of Salle

Isaac son of Samson
Isaac Bigelin
Isaac son of Zerach
Isaac of Sittingbourne
Jacob son of Jacob
Jacob son of Isaac
Jacob son of Jose
Jacob son of Dieulesaut
Jacob son of Meir (Miles)
Jacob son of Molkin
Jehozadok son of Jehozadok (rabbi)
Jose son of Salle
Jose son of Abraham
Jose son of Samson
Jose brother of Samson
Jose son of Joshua
Jose son of Moses
Leo son of Abraham
Leo son of Solomon
Manasser Purnaz
Meir son of Edra (Zerach?)
Meir son of Isaac
Menahem son of Jose
Moses son of Magister Aaron (Le Petit)
Moses son of Abraham (chirographer)
Moses son of Jacob
Samuel son of Meshullam Halevi
Samuel son of Samson
Samuel of Ospring
Samuel le Evesk
Solomon of Cambridge
Solomon of Stamford (chirographer)
Solomon son of Isaac
Vives of Winchester
Vives (Hayim) son of Yom Tob
Yom Tob son of Isaac
Zerach son of Meir

1270–1290

Samson son of Isaac Presbyter (le Chapeleyn)
Jose Molkin
Samuel le Francois
Joye widow of Vives of Winchester
Moses of Bedford
Aaron son of Jose Grubbe
Elian son of Samson of Northanpton
   (chirographer)
Jornin son of Meir
Slema wife of Jornin
Solomon son of Jornin
David son-in-law of Jornin
Abbe of Dog Street
Moses of Dog Street
Aaron son of Benedict of Winchester
   (chirographer)

Belaset daughter of Benedict of Winchester
Isaac son of Benedict of Winchester
Aaron son of Cresse of Winchester
Hagin son of Cresse of Winchester
Caleman
Samson son of Meir
Cresse son of Samson
Leo son of Master Elias Baggard
Hagin son of Abraham Pernas
Bella of Stamford
Sara la Belle
Sara la Petite
Jose son of Ursell
Jose Gileberd son of Aaron
Aaron son of Peitavin
Isaac Top

X. Names of Jews in Bristowe

(Michael Adler, *Jews of Medieval England.*
London: The Jewish Historical Society of England, 1939.)

De Isaac filio Josse
De Isaac le Veske
Willelmi de Buking'
De Isaac filio Juda
De Abraham Gabbai
De Benlivinger
De Precieuse
De Isaac Furmager
De Abraham filio Vives
De Isaac Episcopo
De Manasser

De Salaman filio Isaac
De Jacobo filio Josce
De Deulecresse Furmager
De Judas Gabbay
De Samuele le Pointur
De Benefey fratre suo
De Viveo le Puintur
De Leone nepote Abraham
De Jacobo Filio Samuelis de Oxonia
De Milone Episcopo

XI. Names of Jews from the Tallage Receipt Roll (1226)

(Public Records Office, Exchequer 401, No. 8., see p. 208.)

BRISTOLL'

De Josceo Furmag'
De Jacobo filio Samuelis
De Isaac filio Bonefei
De Viveo filio Abraham
De Viveo Le Pointur

De Michaele Genero suo
De Benefey Michel
De Isaac Episcopo
De Salomone le Turk
De Milone Episcopo

XII. Names of Jews from the Tallage Receipt Roll (1226)

(Public Records Office, Exchequer 401, No. 8. See p. 208.)

BRISTOLL'

De Jospin Formage
De Viveo Pointur

De Michaele le Vesque
De Milone Episcopo

De Isaac fratre suo
De Moss' fiilio Bonefei
De Abrahyam Gabay

De Levi filio Deuben
De Aunter' filia Jacobi

XIII. Names of Jews in Bristol

(Michael Adler, *Jews of Medieval England.*
London: The Jewish Historical Society of England, 1939.)

1154–1200

Samuel (?)
Moses, son of Rabbi Isaac; his wife Belassez
Rabbi Yom Tob, son of Moses
Isaac, son of Moses
Simon, son of Moses
Benedict; his wife Leah
Moses, son of Benedict
Joseph, son of Benedict
Sturmis (?)
Isaac, son Judah⁻
Benlivinger
Preciosa

Isaac Furmager
Deulacresse Furmager
Abraham, son of Vives
Isaac Episcopus (le Veske)
Manasser
Solomon, son of Isaac
Jacob, son of Jose
Judah Gabbay
Abraham Gabbay
Samuel le Pointur
Amiot

1200–1250

Jacob, son of Samuel of Oxford; his daughter
    Antera
Joseph Furmager; his daughters Beunetta,
    Glorietta and Ciclaton
Bonefey Furmager; his sons Isaac and Moses
Dulce Furmager
Vives le Pointur; his son-in-law Michael
Leo, nephew of Abraham Gabbay
Solomon, son of Abraham
Milo Episcopus (le Veske)
Isaac Episcopus (le Veske)
Isaac of Bath
Isaac, son of Jurner (Jacob)
Cresse, son of Milo le Veske (chirographer)
Jacob of Coutances; Filee; Jacob, his son
    Isaac; their mother, Saphira

Abraham Folet and his sister
Vives, son of Abraham
Bonefey Michael
Solomon le Turk
Michael le Veske
Levi, son of Dieubenie
Aaron (Adrian); his wife Rachel (Richolda)
Lumbard (chirographer)
John; his sister Joan / Converts
Christina
Solomon, son of Aaron (chirographer)
Solomon of Ilchester; his wife Belecote
Filee
Jacob, son of Filee; his wife Bella

1250–1290

Elias of Chippenham
Jose of Caerleon
Isaac, son of Jose of Caerleon (chirographer)
Aaron, son of Jose of Caerleon
Cresse, son of Isaac of Caerleon
Samuel, son of Isaac of Caerleon
Henne, wife of Samuel of Caerleon
David of Caerleon

Jose, son of Isaac; Jose, his son-in-law
Isaac, son of Isaac
Dieulebenie, son of Samuel
Samuel, son of Aaron of Wilton
    (chirographer)
Solomon, son of Samuel of Wilton
Isaac, son of Ursell
Belasez (murdered)

Cressant, son of Pictavin (chirographer)

Hak (Isaac) le Prestre (chirographer)

Aaron of Ireland, son of Benjamin of
Colchester

Saffre, son of Duelecresse

Moses of Kent; his wife Gyna

Aaron (murdered)

Cok (Isaac) of Strygyl

Solomon, son of Isaac of Wilton

Isaac Haripurd of Wilton (Isaac of
Marlborough)

Abraham Honiprud or Hariprud

Leo le Mire; his wife Melka

Covele, son of Reyke; his wife Bate

Leo of Stamford; his wife Reyke

Abraham Levy; his brother Sale

Bonamy of Kaune; his wife Roesia

Manser, son of Solomon of Calais

Mendaunt, son of Isaac

Deulegard, son of Vives

Preciosa

Aaron, son of Aaron

Isaac of Sodbury

Saphira, daughter of Selke

Bonamy, son of Jose

Hak (Isaac), son of Meir

Swetman, son of Meir

Sarah the widow

Solomon, son of Hagin

Sarah, daughter of Benedict

Jacob, son of Jacob

Sampson, son of Isaac of Winchester

Appendix C

London Merchants 1300–1500

Below we have listed a set of merchants working in London whom we propose to have Jewish ancestry, based upon their occupations and/or Judaic name (e.g., goldsmith, importer, pepperer, lender, Adam, Simon, Hamo). The names are distilled from *The Merchant Class of Medieval London*, (Sylvia L. Thrupp, 1948).

Abbott, John
Abyndon, Isabella
Alexander, Ann
Alley, Richard
Armentier, John de
Astrie, Geoffrey
Aubrey, Andrew
Babham, Thomas
Bacon, John
Bally, Isabella
Bamme, Adam
Barentyn, Andrew
Baron, William
Barton, Henry
Bassett, Robert
Bataill, Thomas
Berby, John
Bernes, John de
Betoyne, Richard
Blakden, John
Bolet, Simon
Bonifaunt, Richard
Boseham, Felicia
Bowes, Thomas
Brabazon, Adam
Brembre, Idonia
Brice, Hugh
Brokle, John
Bureford, John de
Bury, Adam de
Bys, Alianora
Calle, Richard
Cantelowe, Adam
Canynges, John
    (Bristol family)

Capel, Dorothea
    (married into
    Zouche family)
Carlille, Adam
Cavendish, Pyek
Cely, Richard
Changeour, Adam
Chichele, Robert
Chigwell, Hamo de
Chircheman, John,
    Emma
Clarell, Thomas
Constantyn, Idonia,
    William
Cornewe, John
Corp, Simon
Cosyn, William
Cote, Henry
Coumbys, Simon
Covele, William
Coventre, Philippa,
    John
Crepyn, Walter
Croke, John
Crowde, Agnes
Davy, Elys
Davynell, Giles
De Carlile, adam
De Chigwell, Hamo
Deumars,
    Bartholomew
Doget, Walter
Dolseley, Simon
Donat, Nicholas
Dytton, Benedict de

Eland, John, esq.
Elys, Thomas
Eyre, Simon
Fauconer, Thomas
Felding, Geoffrey
Franke, John
Fraunceys, Adam
Frowyk, Henry
Gisors, Anketin
Godard, Simon
Goldwell, Thomas
Hakedy, Richard
Hicheman, John
Honilane, Elias de
Hotoft, John, esq.
Kempe, William
Le Blund, John
Lok, John
Love, John
Lovekyn, John
Lyffin, Clement
Lyonhill, John
Lyons, Richard
Malewayn, John
Malpas, Philip
Marowe, Thomas
Muscell, John
Myne, Bartholomew
Nontey, Ralph
Olney, John
Olyver, John
Ostrich, Thomas
    (Ostrich =
    Osterreich/Austria)
Oxenford, Roger

Paris, John
Parke, Jankyn
Payn, John
Peche, John
Perfay, John
Petit, John
Picard, Henry
Prince, Gilbert
Pynchon, Baptist
Pyryman, Thomas
Rich, Richard
Romayn, Roesia,
    Thomas
Romesey, John
Russel, Pentecost
Salman, Stephen
Sampson, William
Selle, John
Servat, William
Sibyle, Walter
Smyth, Simon
Starkey, Elizabeth
Stokes, Raulyn
Stratton, Augustine
Sy, Thomas
Thorney, William
Toky, Richard
Tregoran, John
Trente, William
Trussevbus, John
Twygge, Robert
Urswyck, Thomas
Wood, Thomas
Wyche, Hugh
Yevele, Henry

Chapter Notes

Chapter 1

1. William Flavelle Monypenny, *The Life of Benjamin Disraeli, Earl of Beaconsfield*, vol. I, 1804–1837 (New York: Macmillan, 1910), 1.

2. L. G. Pine, *The Genealogist's Encyclopedia* (New York: Collier, 1969), 153.

3. C. Baurain and C. Bonnet, *Les Phéniciens. Marins de Trois Continents* (Paris: Armand Colin, 1992). C. Shell in M. Ryan, ed., *The Origins of Metallurgy in Atlantic Europe. Proceedings of the Fifth Atlantic Colloquium* (Dublin, 1979), 259–61. Barry Cunliffe, *Facing the Ocean. The Atlantic and Its Peoples* (New York: Oxford University Press, 2004) and id., *The Extraordinary Voyage of Pytheas the Greek* (New York: Penguin, 2002) is one of the "weighty exceptions," inasmuch as he dismisses "the romantic idea, popular in the nineteenth century and still sometimes repeated today, that Cornwall was swarming with Phoenician traders" (72–73). Maria Eugenia Aubet, *The Phoenicians and the West*, 2nd ed. (Cambridge: Cambridge University Press, 2001) does not mention Britain at all.

4. See Ruth Fillery-Travis, "Archeological Copper Bibliography" at http://findsandfeatures.wordpress.com/bibliographies/reading-list-for-archaeological-copper.

5. Glenn E. Markoe, *The Phoenicians* (London: Folio, 2005), 254.

6. "Britannia," *Der Kleine Pauly* 1:196.

7. J.M.P. Calise, *Pictish Sourcebook: Documents of Medieval Legend and Dark Age History* (Westport, CT: Greenwood, 2002) 208.

8. Cunliffe, *Extraordinary Voyage*, 74–75.

9. Robin R. Mundill, *The King's Jews* 2 n. 8, citing B. Susser, *The Jews of Devon and Cornwall from the Middle Ages until the 20th Century*, Ph.D. thesis, University of Exeter, 2.

10. Raphael Patai, *The Children of Noah: Jewish Seafaring in Ancient Times* (Princeton: Princeton University Press, 1998), 31.

11. Cyrus H. Gordon, *Canaanite Mythology*, ed. Samuel Noah Kramer (New York: Doubleday, 1961).

12. For instance, Hanno says, "*Anno byn mytthymballe udradait annech*" (or, *Hanno Muthumballe bachaëdreanech*) and Milphio translates, "*Hannonem se esse ait Carthagine, Carthaginiensis Mytthumbalis filium*" ("He says that he is Hanno from Carthage, a Carthaginian, son of Muthumbal"), *Poenulus* V.ii.994–97.

13. Jory S. Brooks, "The Hebrew-Celtic Connection: Language, Cultural and Religious Ties." *Midwestern Epigraphic Journal* 15 (2001): 88–90.

14. Ibid., 90.

15. In 1675, Charles Edwards, a Welsh Puritan, published a number of Welsh-British Hebraisms in which he attempted to demonstrate that whole phrases in Welsh echoed whole phrases in Hebrew. See "Hebrew Linguistic Traits in Welsh," available at http://britam.org/language.html. Some are very striking. For instance, he claimed that in Welsh *Nesa awyr peneu chwi* means "Lift thou up the light of thy countenance," and in Hebrew this is *Nasa aor panec* (Psalms 4:6).

16. See Nora Chadwick, *The Celts,* with introduction by Barry Cunliffe (London: Folio, 2001), esp. 40.

17. According to Canadian historian Farley Mowat, "Although in ancient times Britain bore the name of Alba, she was by no means alone in doing so. Tens of scores of place names derived from *alb* were scattered all the way from the Hindu Kush of Afghanistan to the Atlantic Ocean." He mentions the Alps, Alban Hills outside Rome, River Elbe, Appenines, Albania, Alborz massif of northeastern Iran, Olbia on the shore of the Black Sea, Elbistan in Turkey and Alba and Albicet in Spain. Mowat also regards the etymology of *albh* as pre–Indo-European and associates its survival in mountainous and other marginal regions with the displacement of the original indigenes of Europe by Indo-European invaders. See *The Farfarers: A New History of North America* (New York: Skyhorse, 2002), 46–47.

18. Bede, *History of the English Church and People*, trans. Leo Shirley-Price, rev. by R. E. Latham (London: Folio, 2010), 8.

19. Chadwick 32.

20. Cunliffe, *Extraordinary Voyage* 98, 107.

21. According to Shlomo Sand, Salo Baron's estimate of eight million Jews in the first century CE was exaggerated, although this number was scaled down from even larger figures given by ancient sources. Four million was the "more reasonable" number suggested by Arthur Ruppin and Adolf von Harnack that was to become standard (*The Invention of the Jewish People* [London: Verso, 2009], 146).

22. Ibid., 154–61.

23. Ibid., 210–49.

24. *When Scotland Was Jewish* 81–85; *Jews and Muslims* 140.

25. The Khazars were unusual not only in perpetuating Turkic names like Bulan ("elk") and Bugha ("bull") but in adopting convert names from Jewish holidays including Hanukkah, Purim, Yomtov and Pesach (Passover).

26. Stephen Oppenheimer, *The Origins of the British.*

A Genetic Detective Story: The Surprising Roots of the English, Irish, Scottish, and Welsh (New York: Carroll & Graf, 2006).

27. Ibid., 3.
28. Ibid., 5.
29. Ibid., Part 1: "The Celtic Myth: Wrong Myth, Real People," 19–95.
30. Ibid., 7, 87.
31. Ibid., 91.
32. Ibid., 193.
33. Bryan Sykes, *Saxons, Vikings, and Celts: The Genetic Roots of Britain and Ireland* (W. W. Norton, 2006), published previously in the UK under the title *Blood of the Isles: Exploring the Genetic Roots of Our Tribal History*. Clan 1 is Oisin (R1b), Clan 2 is Wodan (I), Clan 3 is Sigurd (R1a), Clan 9 is Re (J) and Clan 21 is Eshu (E).
34. See Ibid. 290–91 for distribution tables and maps for British mitochondrial and Y chromosome lineages.
35. Oppenheimer covers the groundwork (91ff.) and lists five key sources on British male lines in note 41 on 463. We've not gone into more detailed a study of it than to examine Capelli's original survey, but readers may also want to investigate James F. Wilson et al., "Genetic Evidence for Different Male and Female Roles during Cultural Transitions in the British Isles," *Proceedings of the National Academy of Sciences of the USA* 98 (2001): 5078–83.
36. A. Nebel, et al., "The Y Chromosome Pool of Jews as Part of the Genetic Landscape of the Middle East," *American Journal of Human Genetics* 69.5 (2001): 1095–1112.
37. C. Capelli et al., "A Y-Chromosome Census of the British Isles," *Current Biology* 13 (2003): 979–984.
38. Sykes 206, 290.
39. "'Extraordinary' Genetic Make-up of North-east Wales Men," BBC News North East Wales, article retrieved January 2012 at http://www.bbc.co.uk/news/uk-wales-north-east-wales-14173910. On Dienekes' Anthropology Blog there is speculation about whether the main sub-clade involved is Balkan or North African E; posts and comments retrieved January 2012 at http://dienekes.blogspot.com/2011/07/eastern-mediterranean-marker-in.html.
40. William F. Skene, *The Four Ancient Books of Wales* (Edinburgh, 1868, republished 2007 by Forgotten Books), 206.
41. Turi E. King et al., "Thomas Jefferson's Y Chromosome Belongs to a Rare European Lineage," *American Journal of Physical Anthropology* 132.4 (2007): 584–89. A later study by Mendez et al. (2011) confirmed that the Jefferson haplotype is Egyptian and belongs to T1a*.
42. L. I. Shlush et al, "The Druze: A Population Genetic Refugium of the Near East," *PLoS ONE* 3.5 (2009): e2105.
43. Sykes 290.
44. Caesar, *The Gallic War*, with an English trans. by H. J. Edwards (Cambridge: Harvard University Press, 1997).
45. Tacitus, *The Agricola and Germania*, trans. R. B. Townshend (London: Methuen, 1894), 12–13.
46. Maev Kennedy, "Ancient Roman Village Discovered in Parkland around Stately Home," *The Guardian*, November 16, 2010, accessed online in 2011 at http://www.guardian.co.uk/science/2010/nov/17/ancient-roman-village-parkland?CMP=twt_fd.
47. On the Devereux's, Percys,' Sidneys' and Seymours' suspected Jewish ancestry, see *Jews and Muslims* 20–21, 51.
48. On Bacon, Ibid., 179–80.
49. Joseph Jacobs, "Personal Names," quoting N. Pulvermacher, "Berliner Vornamen," Berlin, 1902.
50. Lars Menk, *A Dictionary of German-Jewish Surnames* (Bergenfield, NJ: Avotaynu, 2005) 405. A famous bearer of the name in America was *Julius* Rosenberg, convicted and executed with his wife Ethel in 1953 for conspiracy to commit espionage. Another was Julius Schwartz, editor of *Superman* comics, whose parents were Jews from Romania.
51. Cf. W. N. Johns, *Historical Traditions and Facts Relating to Newport and Caerleon* (1880), 54–57, accessed in 2011 at: http://books.google.com/books?id=Y2IZAAAAYAAJ&dq.
52. Prudence Jones and Nigel Pennick, *A History of Pagan Europe* (New York: Barnes & Noble, 1995).
53. Sand 167.
54. Robin R. Mundill, *The King's Jews: Money, Massacre and Exodus in Medieval England* (Continuum, 2010), 2; S. Appelbaum, "Were There Jews in Roman Britain," *TJHSE* 17 (1953): 189.
55. Sand 146.
56. Theodor Mommsen, quoted Ibid. 154.
57. Cicero, quoted Ibid. 145.
58. Ibid. On the Jews of Alexandria and Cyrenaica, see Shimon Appelbaum, *Jews and Greeks in Ancient Cyrene* (Leiden: Brill, 1979).
59. Sand 191.
60. Ibid., 146.
61. Josephus, *Ant. Iud.* XX.viii.11, p. 423.
62. Pliny the Younger, *Letters* 10.96–97.
63. Sand 171.
64. Ibid., 171–72.
65. Ibid., 177.
66. "During the first millennium CE, Jewish believers in Europe knew no Hebrew or Aramaic" (Ibid., 208). It remained for the twentieth century to "revive" Hebrew as a living language.
67. Ibid., 174.
68. Ibid., 182.
69. Peter Hunter Blair, *Roman Britain and Early England 55 BC–AD 871* (New York: W. W. Norton, 1963), 3.
70. Ibid., 34.
71. Cunliffe, *Facing the Ocean* 390, 402.
72. PW s. v. "Papagei."
73. The prominence of the Roman frontier province of Arabia in the second and third centuries is shown by the fact that one of the emperors, Philip the Arab (244–249), was of a family that originated there. It bordered on Palestine. It was rumored that the Emperor Philip belonged to the Jewish faith.
74. Gil Marks, *Encyclopedia of Jewish Food* (New York: Wiley, 2010), 117.
75. There do not appear to be any Christian subjects. Study them all in Jeremy K. Knight, *Caerleon Roman Fortress* (Cadw, 2010), 18.
76. Ibid., 403–04.
77. Ibid., 406–15.
78. Rebecca Fraser, *The Story of Britain: From*

Romans to the Present (New York: Norton, 2003), 23–24.

79. E. G. Shaye and J. D. Cohen, *The Beginnings of Jewishness: Boundaries, Varieties, Uncertainties* (Berkeley: University of California Press, 1999).

80. Paul Johnson, *A History of the Jews* (New York: Harper, 1987), 146.

81. Sand 269.

82. An imperial edict of 428 lists Christian denominations that were not allowed to meet in public places, receive donations or build churches: "Arians, Macedonians, Pneumatomachians, Apollinarians, Novatians, Sabatians, Eunomians, Tetradites, Tessarecaedecadites, Valentinians, Paulians, Papianists, Montanists, Priscillians, Phyrgians, Pepuzites, Marcionists, Boborites, Messalians, Euchites, Enthusiasts, Donatists, Audians, Hydroparastetes, Tascodrogies, Batracites, Hermogenians, Photinians, Paulinists, Marcellians, Ophites, Encratitians, Carpocratitians, Saccophores, and Manicheans, who have sunk to the worst depravity of crimes." The Manicheans were "to be driven out of cities and subject to severe penalty," their possessions confiscated and their adherents "deprived of all aid, whether military or civil, of the law courts, the defenders and judges." Richard Valantasis, ed., *Religions of Late Antiquity in Practice* (Princeton: Princeton University Press, 2000), 271.

83. Ibid., 273.

Chapter 2

1. Colin McEvedy, *Cities of the Classical World*, ed. Douglas Stuart Oles (London: Allen Lane, 2011), 96, 187.

2. Rebecca Fraser, *A People's History of Britain* (London: Chatto & Windus, 2003), 25.

3. Ibid., 27.

4. Peter Hunter Blair, *Roman Britain and Early England, 55 BC—AD 871* (New York: Norton, 1966).

5. Ibid., 174.

6. David Keys, *Catastrophe: An Investigation into the Origins of the Modern World* (New York: Ballantine, 1999), 119–20.

7. Ibid., 122.

8. Norman Davies, *Vanished Kingdoms: The Rise and Fall of States and Nations* (New York: Viking, 2012), 44.

9. *When Scotland Was Jewish* 192–95.

10. Bede, *History of the English Church and People*, trans. Leo Shirley-Price, rev. by R. E. Latham (London: Folio, 2010), 35.

11. John Davies, *A History of Wales* (London: Allen Lane, 1993), 44–45.

12. Ibid., 48.

13. Norman Golb, *The Jews of Medieval Normandy* (Cambridge: Cambridge University Press, 1998), 1.

14. Robert W. Hanning, *The Vision of History in Early Britain* (New York: Columbia University Press, 1966), 44–62.

15. Max Manitius, *Geschichte der lateinischen Literatur des Mittelalters,* vol. I, *Von Justinian bis zur Mitte des Zehnten Jahrhunderts* (Munich: Beck, 1911), 208.

16. Robert Vermaat, *Vortigern Studies*, http://www.vortigernstudies.org.uk/artsou/gildas.htm.

17. Id, *Vortigern Studies*, http://www.vortigernstudies.org.uk/artsou/gildwhere.htm.

18. *Vortigern Studies*, http://www.vortigernstudies.org.uk/artsou/gildas.htm.

19. *Vile quidem stilo*; cf. Manitius I.209.

20. Gildas, chap. IV; cf. Manitius I.209, authors' translation.

21. Manitius I.159.

22. Renee Doehaerd, *The Early Middle Ages in the West: Economy and Society,* trans. W. G. Deakin (Amsterdam: Horth-Holland, 1978), 193.

23. Also called Gurguintius, Gurgust or Gwrgan "Farfdrwch," i.e. Redbeard.

24. Geoffrey of Monmouth, *The History of the Kings of Britain*, trans. with an introduction by Lewis Thorpe, preface by Richard Barber (London: Folio, 2010), 44.

25. Paul Wexler, *The Non-Jewish Origins of the Sephardic Jews* (Binghamton: SUNY Press, 1996), 75–76. It would appear that in the absence of a biblical or related term, Hebrew writers in the early centuries adapted the Gothic term for "black, dark" to describe Jews not only in Visigothic Spain but Vandal North Africa.

26. Sand 200–201.

27. "What, art thou half a Jew?" (*Instructiones adversos gentium deos* XXXVII). Commodianus is often erroneously assigned to the second century and called "the first Christian poet," but his rhythmic and partly rhyming verse points to a much later period.

28. Guilherme Faiguenboim et al., *Dictionary of Sephardic Surnames,* 2nd ed. (Rio de Janeiro: Fraiha, 2003), 143.

29. John and Sheila Rowlands, *The Surnames of Wales* (Baltimore: Genealogical, 2008), 144.

30. O. J. Padel, "Some South-western Sites with Arthurian Associations," in *The Arthur of the Welsh*, ed. Rachel Bromwich, A. O. H. Jarman and Brynley F. Roberts (Cardiff: University of Wales Press, 1991), 229–30.

31. See Nigel Groom, *A Dictionary of Arabic Topography and Placenames* (Beirut: Liban, 1983) 94, 291.

32. Hanning 6–13, 42–43, 55.

33. J. A. Giles, ed., *The Works of Gildas and Nennius* (London: Bohn, 1841), 11.

34. Hugh Williams, ed. and trans., *Gildas, The Ruin of Britain &c.* (1899), 1.

35. The version in Mark says, "The woman was a Greek, a Syrophenician by nation" (7:26).

36. Most scholars view the alternative form "Damnonia" as a nonce word, Gildas bombastically punning on the Latin word for "damnation." This seems an injudicious verdict for such a careful writer.

37. See M. L. W. Laistner, *Thought and Letters in Western Europe, A.D. 500–900* (Ithaca: Cornell University Press, 1966). R.W. Southern, *The Making of the Middle Ages* (New Haven: Yale University Press, 1967). Jean Leclercq, *The Love of Learning and the Desire for God: A Study of Monastic Culture*, trans. Catharine Misrahi (New York: Fordham University Press, 1961). *Ireland and Europe in the Early Middle Ages: Texts and Transmission*, ed. Próinséas Ní Chatháin & Michael Richter (Dublin: Four Courts, 2001).

38. A fact dismissed by Max Manitius as "apparently out of the question" (I.134).

39. "My mind is expressed in Hebrew, in Hebraic" (William F. Skene, *The Four Ancient Books of Wales* [1868; Forgotten Books, 2007], 426).

40. Manitius 1.401–2.

41. Ambros. L 22 sup, a commentary on Donatus (Ibid. I.521).

42. Szmarag, Smaragd, Smararak, etc. are Polish; see Beider 415. The emerald was also called the Bereket ("flashing like lightning, *barak*") or Stone of Levi.

43. Manitius I.466.

44. "Jenes sachlich so unbedeutende, aber sprachlich so rätselhafte Werk." Manitius I.156–57.

45. For a sketch of Wiener, see Stephen Williams, *Fantastic Archaeology* (Philadelphia: University of Pennsylvania Press), 251–52.

46. Leo Wiener, *Contributions Toward a History of Arabico-Gothic Culture* (New York: Neale, 1917–21).

47. The Jewish biblical scholar and editor of BRIT-AM magazine Yair Davidi overlooks *Hisperica Famina* in his review of the literature on the connections between the Hebrew and Welsh languages; HHMI Newsgroup Archives post retrieved January 2012 at http://hebroots.org/hebrootsarchive/0105nn.html. For the record, we do not subscribe to the theory that Welsh came from Hebrew.

48. *Anglo-Saxon Lore and Learning*, selected by Richard Barber (London: Folio, 2008), xv.

49. *The Coming of the Anglo-Saxons*, selected by Richard Barber (London: Folio, 2008), 27.

50. Paula Frederiksen, *Augustine and the Jews: A Christian Defense of Jews and Judaism* (New Haven: Yale University Press, 2010).

51. Ibid., 329.

52. Quoted in Steinberg 59.

53. Frederiksen 375.

54. Eamon Duffy, *Saints and Sinners: A History of the Popes* (London: Folio, 2009), 75–77, 410.

55. *Coming of the Anglo-Saxons* 317.

Chapter 3

1. Peter Hunter Blair, *Roman Britain and Early England, 55 BC–AD 871* (London: Norton, 1963), 219–20.

2. Gwyn Jones, *The Vikings*, introduction by Magnus Magnusson (London: Folio, 1997), 197.

3. Ibid., 205.

4. Ibid., 198.

5. Ibid., 199–200.

6. Rebecca Fraser, *The Story of Britain: From the Romans to the Present : A Narrative History* (New York: Norton, 2003), 54–55.

7. Ibid., 56.

8. Jones 204.

9. Robin R. Mundill, *The King's Jews* (London: Continuum, 2009), 2 n. 7.

10. Jones 208–09.

11. Ibid., 210, 403–08.

12. Fraser 67.

13. Jones 86, 360ff.

14. Brian Sykes, *Saxons, Vikings, and Celts. The Genetic Roots of Britain and Ireland* (New York: Norton, 2006), 192ff. Sykes calls R1b Oisin, R1a Wodan and I Sigurd.

15. M. E. Weale, et al., "Y Chromosome Evidence for Anglo-Saxon Mass Migration," *Molecular Biology and Evolution* 19 (2002): 1008–1021.

16. See also C. Capelli, et al., "A Y-Chromosome Census of the British Isles," *Current Biology* 13 (2003): 979–84. L. Roewer et al., "Online Reference Database of European Y-chromosomal Short Tandem Repeat (STR) Haplotypes," *Forensic Science International* 118 (2001): 106–113. Z. H Rosser et al., "Y-chromosomal Diversity in Europe Is Clinal and Influenced Primarily by Geography, Rather Than by Language," *American Journal of Human Genetics* 67 (2000): 1526–1543. J. F. Wilson, et al., "Genetic Evidence for Different Male and Female Roles during Cultural Transitions in the British Isles," *Proceedings of the National Academy of Science USA* 98 (2001): 5078–83; E. W. Hill et al, "Y-chromosome Variation and Irish Origins," *Nature* 404 (2000): 351–52.

17. Gerhard Endress, *Islam: An Historical Introduction*, 2nd ed., trans. Carole Hillenbrand (New York: Columbia University Press, 2002).

18. Ibid., 84–85.

19. Ibid., 85, 87–91.

20. Ibid., 108.

21. Charles H. Talbot, *Medicine in Mediaeval England* (London: Oldbourne, 1967), 24.

22. Joseph Cohen, *Emek Habacha* (Valley of Tears), cited by Jacobs 177 and quoted by Mundill 2–3 n. 11.

23. Albert Hourani, *A History of the Arab Peoples* (Cambridge: Harvard University Press, 1991), 47.

24. See Renee Doehaerd, trans. W. G. Deakin, *The Early Middle Ages in the West: Economy and Society* (Amsterdam: North-Holland, 1978), 1–8.

25. Elkan Nathan Adler, *Jewish Travellers in the Middle Ages: 19 Firsthand Accounts* (New York: Dover, 1987), 2–3.

26. Frances Wood, *The Silk Road* (London: Folio, 2002), 96.

27. Endress 88.

28. *When Scotland Was Jewish* 235 n. 17.

29. Ibid., 89.

30. Ibid., 88.

31. Perhaps the same as Sephardic surname Botton (DSS 209).

32. See Louis I. Rabinowitz, *Jewish Merchant Adventurers: A Study of the Radanites* (London: Goldston, 1948).

33. Endress 193, citing *Life of St. John the Almoner*.

34. Available at www.cotswold.gov.uk.

35. Johanna Story, "Anglo-Saxon England and the Wider World," http://www.le.ac.uk/users/grj1/asw.html.

36. See http://www.le.ac.uk/users/grj1/asw.html.

37. Cf. Janet Backhouse, *The Lindisfarne Gospels: A Masterpiece of Book Painting* (London: 1995).

38. Fraser 42.

39. *The Coming of the Anglo-Saxons* 25.

40. Asser, *Life of Alfred*, p. 14

41. *Dictionary of Sephardic Surnames* 429, citing Alexandria. As Jobe, the name appears in Donald Yates' genealogy. His earliest known ancestor in America is John Yates, Esq., born in about 1575 in England and living at Elizabeth City, Virginia, according to a list made on February 16, 1623. Mr. Yates, gentleman, as he was referred to, was evidently in the shipping business. His son John married Joan or Johanna Jobe. Also, Elizabeth Jobe married Joel Cooper, January 20, 1788 in Washington County, Virginia (Watauga).

42. Alessandro Barbero, *Charlemagne: Father of a Continent* (Berkeley: University of California Press, 2004), 115.

43. Tomaž Mastnak, *Crusading Peace: Christendom, the Muslim World, and Western Political Order* (Berkeley: University of California Press, 2002), 99–100.

44. Arthur J. Zuckerman, *A Jewish Princedom in Feudal France 768–900* (New York: Columbia University Press, 1972). One should also consult Solomon Katz, *The Jews in the Visigothic and Frankish Kingdoms of Spain and Gaul* (Cambridge: Mediaeval Academy of America, 1970).

45. *When Scotland Was Jewish* 81–87. *Jews and Muslims*, Chapter 8: "Huguenot South Carolina."

46. Ibid., 74–101.

47. Ibid., 32.

48. Esther Benbassa, *The Jews of France: A History from Antiquity to the Present*, trans. M. B. DeBevoise (Princeton: Princeton University Press, 2001), 12.

49. Ibid., 24–28.

50. Jacques Le Goff, *Medieval Civilization 400–1500*, trans. Julia Barrow (London: Folio, 2011), 36.

51. Doehaerd 51. "In the ninth century, too," notes the same author, "Jews were involved in farming in several cities of the Midi of France."

52. Henry Charles Lea, *The Inquisition of the Middle Ages*, abridgment by Margaret Nicholson (New York: Macmillan, 1961), 27.

53. Ibid., 34.

54. Benbassa 11–13.

55. Jacobs (1901–1906).

56. The Davidson surname is recorded on the following pages in *When Scotland Was Jewish* 62, 83, 97–102, 106, 114–119, 123–38, 155, 165, 169, 171–77, 186, 187, 239.

57. *Librum istum monachus scripsit EADUUIUS cognomento BASAN*. D. N. Dumville, *English Caroline Script and Monastic History: Studies in Benedictinism, A.D. 950–1030* (Rochester: Boydell, 1992), 120, 128. Dumville and others take the word *cognomentum* in the sense of "nickname," but its first and usual meaning in dictionaries is "surname."

58. DSS 192.

59. Basan (or its variants Basson, Baison and Basin) is particularly common in Dorset, where we find, for instance, the given names Davidina, Mariam, Mansell, Jesse, Beatrice, Ixa and Lilian in the local records, suggesting Judaism survives to the present day in the very place where we find some of the earliest traces of it.

60. Quoted in Theodore L. Steinberg, *Jews and Judaism in the Middle Ages* (Westport, CT: Praeger, 2008), 3.

61. Quoted in H. S. Q. Henriques, *Jewish Marriages and the English Law* (Clark: Lawbook Exchange, 2006), 52.

62. Steinberg 118.

Chapter 4

1. Steinberg 119.

2. Oxford Jewish Heritage: http://www.oxford jewishheritage.co.uk.

3. Steinberg writes, "The history of the Jews in England is depressingly similar, as is the history of Jews in other countries" (118).

4. David C. Douglas, *William the Conqueror. The Norman Impact upon England* (Berkeley: University of California Press, 1964), 379–82.

5. Wikipedia article "Herleva," retrieved January 2012 at http://en.wikipedia.org/wiki/Herleva.

6. Edward A. Freeman, *The History of the Norman Conquest of England*, vol. II (London: Macmillan, 1868), 286–88.

7. Elisabeth M. C. van Houts, "The Origins of Herleva, Mother of William the Conqueror," *English Historical Review* 101.399 (1986): 399–404.

8. Ibid., 402, n. 1.

9. David Couch, *The Normans* (London: Continuum) 58.

10. Ibid., 24–25.

11. Henry Barber, *British Family Names: Their Origin and Meaning, with Lists of Scandinavian, Frisian, Anglo-Saxon and Norman Names* (London: Stock, 1903), 218.

12. K. S. B. Keats-Rohan, "Poppa of Bayeux and Her Family, *The American Genealogist* 72 (1997): 187–204.

13. See post by David Greene on Gen-Medieval-L, retrieved January 2012 at archiver.rootsweb.ancestry.com/th/read/GEN-MEDIEVAL/1999-12/094475 7135.

14. Amuletic names were used to protect children and ensure they lived long lives. Shmuel Gorr, *Jewish Personal Names*, notes regarding Alter ("old man"), "If a male child died soon after birth or very young, the next born male child was sometimes given the name *Alter* alone, or in combination with another name. The parents, in giving the name, expressed their prayer that the newborn child should live to be an *old* man. See also *Alte*. The family name *Alter* is a derivative (3). In fact, this may be the case with Danish Poppo, the name given to a second son, as it seems to mean "father."

15. Itta: Gorr 89f.

16. Sand 210.

17. Marie Antoinette traced her ancestry back to the twelfth-century figure Bertha von Putelendorf (Jehaes 1998). Although most royal genealogies stop with Bertha, we have found that one authority gives her great-great-grandmother as Judith of Schweinfurt, born before 1050 (Stamp, "Ahnenliste"). Furthermore, Judith's mother was a descendant of Frederuna of France, consort of Charles the Simple, and Frederuna herself was a daughter of Count Theodoricus, an illegitimate younger son of Charlemagne by Adel. Thus Marie Antoinette's female heritage goes back to the wife or concubine of Theodoricus (French Thiérry), who according to Einhard's *Life of Charlemagne* was imprisoned in a monastery by his half-brother the emperor Louis the Pious ("Achternamenlist").

18. The name of Teresa Panther-Yates's grandmother, Etalka Good (the "good name"), of a Melungeon family from Tennessee. Etalka named one of her daughters Elzina (Arabic for "beautiful").

19. See Zuckerman 29–35. On European heraldy, which flourished beginning with the Crusades, see L. G. Pine 177–220.

20. Alessandro Barbero, *Charlemagne, Father of a Continent* (London: Folio, 2006), 16, 20.

21. See I. Levi, "Le Roi Juif de Narbonne et le Philomene," *REJ* 48 (1904): 197–207; id., *REJ* 49

(1904): 147–50; and the sources and studies in chapter 5 below. Zuckerman examines these sources at length; but his thesis—that Narbonne's Jewish princes are identical with certain Provençal counts, understood as being Christians and with entirely different names in the Latin sources—is a superficial reading. See *A Jewish Princedom in Feudal France 768–900.* (New York: Columbia University Press, 1972).

22. Norman Golb, *The Jews in Medieval Normandy: A Social and Intellectual History* (Cambridge: Cambridge University Press, 1998), 18.

23. This is an important theme in one of the age's satiric masterpieces, the animal epic *Ysengrimus,* which makes fun of wolves or rapacious clergy in sheep's clothing and has scenes allegorizing the skinning of the bear Bruno as well as the wolf Ysengrimus. See A. van Geersom, "Bruno, de Auteur van de Ysengrimus," *Verslagen en Mededelingen van de Koninklijke Vlaamse Academie voor Taal- en Letterkunde* (1962), 5–73.

24. M. A. Deville, *Observations sur l'époche de la naissance de Guillaume-le-Conquérant,* in *Memoire de la societé des antiquaries de Normandie,* vol. I (1840), 183–4.

25. Douglas, *William the Conqueror* 45, 381.

26. Henri Gross, *Gallia Judaica: Dictionnaire géographique de la France d'après les sources rabbiniques,* transl. Moïse Bloch (Paris: Cerf, 1897), 36.

27. Ibid., 476–83.

28. Golb 87–89.

29. Gross 222.

30. Heinrich Walter and Eva I. Guggenheim, *Jewish Family Names and Their Origins. An Etymological Dictionary* (New York: KTAV, 1992), 322–26. It is probably the origin of Harlow ("Mount of the Levite").

31. Gross 323–24.

32. William Hunt, "Brompton, John," *DNB* 6 (1885–1900); retrieved January 2012 at http://en.wikisource.org/wiki/Brompton,_John_DNB00. "Brompton's" Latin history, which goes to the death of Richard I, was adapted into French in the compilation known as *Les chroniques et excellents faits des ducs de Normandie* (1535) and included in Sir Roger Twysden's *Historiae Anglicanae Scriptores Decem* published in 1652. "Brompton" has been criticized as "the means of importing many fables into our history," but the miscellany also has much value.

33. *Biographia Britannica, or the Lives of the Most Eminent Persons in Great-Britain and Ireland,* ed. William Oldys, vol. 1 (London, 1747), 182.

34. Golb 3, 547.

35. Ibid., 3–18.

36. Ibid., 15–16.

37. Ibid.

38. Fraser 98–99.

39. Clayton Roberts, David Roberts, Douglas R. Bisson, *A History of England: Prehistory to 1714* (Upper Saddle River, NJ: Prentice Hall, 2002), 78.

40. Golb 113.

41. L. G. Pine, *They Came with the Conqueror: A Study of the Modern Descendants of the Normans* (New York: Putnam, [1954]), 43. Leslie Gilbert Pine was born in 1907 in Bristol, Gloucestershire, and died in 1987. From 1935 to 1940 he served as an assistant editor at Burke's Peerage and until 1960 as Burke's executive director, editing *Burke's Peerage* (1949–1959), *Burke's*

Landed Gentry of Great Britain (1952), *Burke's Landed Gentry of Ireland* (1958) and *Burke's Distinguished Families of America* (1939, 1947).

Chapter 5

1. Elizabeth M. Hallam, *Domesday Book through Nine Centuries* (London: Thames and Hudson, 1986), 36.

2. G. H. Martin in *Domesday Book. A Complete Translation,* ed. Ann Williams and G. H. Martin (London: Penguin, 2002), vii.

3. The Domesday Book Online, accessed January 2012 at http://www.domesdaybook.co.uk/compiling.html.

4. *Domesday Book* vii.

5. The Domesday Book Online, accessed January 2012 at http://www.domesdaybook.co.uk/compiling.html.

6. Ibid.

7. K. S. B. Keats-Rohan, *Domesday People: A Prosopography of Persons Occuring in English Documents 1066–1166.* I: *Domesday Book* (Woodbridge: Boydell, 1996), 75.

8. Hallam 48.

9. Anthony J. Camp, *My Ancestors Came with the Conqueror: Those Who Did and Some of Those Who Probably Did Not* (Baltimore: Genealogical Publishing, 1990), 53. In sorting out the various versions of the famous Battle Abbey Roll, Camp finds only a handful of English families with an ancestor who was definitely at the Battle of Hastings. The eight sources include the Falaise Roll of the companions of the Conqueror (1931), and all mix fact and fiction. Of interest to us is his long list of those who pretended to have a connection to William and his known family and retainers.

10. Ibid., 89.

11. S. A. Rahman, *A Dictionary of Muslim Names* (New Delhi: Goodword, 2011), 17.

12. Ibid., 18–19. Camp 29.

13. See Bagho (Faiguenboim 189) and compare Arabic Bakoda, recorded from early times in Toledo (Faiguenboim et al., 53). Those of an opposite orientation derive the surname from Old Germanic Bago, meaning "bag." The surname Bigod/Bigot may be related. Others, e.g., Reaney and Wilson, derive it from Frenchmen observing Normans' always saying "By God." This explanation of the name seems patently ridiculous. Normans would not have sworn in English but French. They would have said something like "Mon Dieu."

14. Camp 57.

15. Farman: Rahman 24.

16. Cf. Gollanz, "Hollander": Menk 314–15.

17. Golda, "golden personality": Gorr 65–66.

18. Mortagne, Mortain: Camp 67.

19. Domesday 356.

20. Salam: Rahman 75.

21. Algar was the son of Earl Leofric of Mercia and Lady Godiva, famous for her naked bareback protest ride on a horse in Coventry. He was made earl of East Anglia and regranted many, but not all, of his holdings.

22. The lord of Penfou (Penfound Manor), one of Cornwall's oldest inhabited sites, reconfirmed from Count Robert.

23. DSS "Boa," 207, noted in Lisbon before 1492.

24. According to Joan M. Gaskin writing on the Bowhay surname page in the website "Guild of One-Name Studies," accessed January 2012 at http://www.one-name.org/profiles/bowhay.html, "From the 1500s BOWHAYs and variants are found in parish registers in Devon (Blackawton, Braunton, Crediton, Georgeham, Stoke Gabriel, Totnes) and Cornwall (St. Dominick, Stoke Climsland)."

25. The Trelawny ("homestead of the Levites") family multiply intermarried with the Hawkins; see *Jews and Muslims in British Colonial America,* ch. 1.

26. Gamelin was a Cornish nobleman and Odo FitzGamelin his son. Both were regranted holdings. See J. J. Alexander and W. R. Hooper, *The History of Great Torrington in the County of Devon* (1948), 8, 215.

27. Asgar the Cramped was reconfirmed in holding two royal salthouses at Ermington (Hermentona) and Blackawton (Aveton). Later, his widow carried on the business.

28. Edeva the Fair, possibly King Harold's mistress, ended up with holdings scattered through several counties. Some of them were reapportioned to Norman lords.

29. Lew, Lewe, and Leuya, coming, we believe, from Levi, were place-names for several manor houses and two rivers. Lew Trenchard Manor near Okehampton, Devon was the ancient seat of the Rev. Sabine Baring-Gould, who in the nineteenth century "plundered various Tudor houses to decorate his own."

30. Originating in Hebrew Haim, rendered Aimon and the like in Old Occitan and used as a name for the Nesim, this mutates into English Emory, Emery, etc.

31. Beatrix was regranted Bradford Mill on the Little Dart River and Blackberry Castle, an Iron Age hill fort. Her brother William Cheever (Hebrew surname) was confirmed in numerous holdings.

32. Tovi held Militona (Jewish name + ton, "town").

33. Camp 41.

34. Keats-Rohan 469.

35. Menk 651. On Cooper, see *WSWJ* 31 and *Jews and Muslims* 13, 36, 43, 50, 90, 100, 103, 120, 125–26, 129, 137–38, 147–48, 161–62, 167, 171, 185–86. Famous Cheever descendants are the Boston merchant William Cheever (1752–1786), who kept a diary about the Siege of Boston, and John William Cheever (1912—1982), American novelist and short story writer. Reaney and Wilson (92) derive Cheever (*Cheure*) from the word for "nanny goat" and seem to confound it with the surname *le Chiuer,* explaining that the name denoted agility—a good example of a folk etymology accepted uncritically.

36. Totenais: Camp 82.

37. John Bryan Williams, "Judhael of Totnes: The Life and Times of a Post-Conquest Baron," *Anglo-Norman Studies,* 16 (1993): 271–289.

38. Briouze: Camp 36.

39. Ibid., 31.

40. Chaward: Camp 40.

41. Geoffrey de Mombray, bishop of Coustances, is verified by William of Poitiers as present at the Battle of Hastings. He was in charge of prayers for the Norman army's success. Camp 66–67.

42. Ibid., 53.

43. Ibid., 58.

44. Ibid., 66.

45. Ibid., 74.

46. Cf. *When Scotland Was Jewish,* App. B., "Naming and Jewish Priest-Kings," 218–19.

47. Talah "stretch": Nigel Groom, *A Dictionary of Arabic Topography and Placenames* (Beirut: Liban, 1983) 284. Perhaps zealous local antiquarians will confirm how many of the Arabic etymologies listed in this and the next chapter correspond to the topography in question.

48. Ibid., 173.

49. Araj, Urjah, Arja: Ibid., 43.

50. Ajza: Ibid., 36.

51. Ibid., 82.

52. Ulawah: Ibid., 298.

53. Tawiy: Ibid., 288.

54. Hamah: Ibid., 102–3.

55. Dimnah: Ibid., 77.

56. Ibid., 103–04.

57. Ibid., 153.

58. Vital: Camp 87.

59. Groom 54.

60. Ibid.

61. Ibid., 139.

62. Gha'ir: Ibid., 91.

63. Ibid., 63.

64. Kharayim "steppes": Ibid., 142.

65. Haja: Ibid., 100.

66. Menk 220.

67. According to Keats-Rohan (131–32), "The first Aubrey de Vere was a Domesday tenant of the powerful Breton tenant-in-chief Count Alan Rufus, and was among a handful of Alan's Bretons who were also tenant-in-chief of their own fees. Aubrey's family probably came from Vair in Ancenis, in the Nantais ... he is usually assumed to have originated at Ver (Manche, arr. Coutances)." She mentions that a Walter de Ver, "a Breton (Britonis), in Suffolk," was a justiciar or sheriff in Henry I's reign and was buried in Abingdon, which he and his wife Beatrice founded.

68. Asla: Groom 48.

69. Dimnah: Ibid., 77.

70. Wathan (?) "boundary stone": Ibid., 307.

71. Perhaps from Kanf "quarter, tract": Ibid., 136.

72. Manaj: Ibid., 172.

73. Ibid., 28.

74. Azhar: Ibid., 16.

75. Hamo dapifer: Camp 54.

76. Tayn "field": Groom 288.

77. Markaz "chief town": Ibid., 179.

78. Marmas (?) "graves": Ibid., 239.

79. Buhrah "town": Ibid., 68.

80. Ismail (Hebrew) is the biblical Ishmael (Ibid., 38). Named for Ismā il ibn Ja far, Ismailism is the second largest branch of Shia Islam after the Twelvers or followers of the Twelve Imams. Ismailite Muslims were strong in Egypt, Syria, North Africa and Spain.

81. Groom, 41.

Chapter 6

1. Rahman 9.
2. Mutali "exalted": Ibid., 58.
3. Haram "sacred precinct": Groom 104.
4. Rahman 22.

5. Jalha, Jilha'ah "town": Groom 130.

6. This sketch of Hereford Jewry is taken mainly from the work of Joe Hillaby, a foremost expert on Medieval Jewry. The story was published as a series of articles in the *Woolhope Club Transactions* (vol. XLV 1985/87, 1982/84 and XLVI 1988–90). Other material comes from *The Jews of Britain* by Pamela Fletcher-Jones. All of these volumes are available in the library in Hereford. More information can be obtained in *The Anguish of the Jews* by E. H. Flannery and the BBC Radio 4 series *Jewish Journey*.

7. Souche: Camp 79.

8. Rahman 57.

9. Ibid., 242.

10. Groom 87.

11. Camp 86.

12. Ibid., 80.

13. Ibid., 52.

14. Ibid., 60.

15. Ibid., 41.

16. Mahir "skillful": Rahman 46.

17. Camp 29.

18. Ibid., 65.

19. Ibid., 88.

20. Alan Comes, Alan Rufus (fl. 1050–93), second of at least seven legitimate sons of Count Eudo, regent of Brittany, and Agnes alias Orguen his Angevin wife: Keats-Rohan 127–29. Camp 75.

Chapter 7

1. Eamon Duffy, *Saints and Sinners: A History of the Popes* (London: Folio Society, 2009), 151.

2. Adriaan H. Bredero, *Bernard of Clairvaux: Between Cult and History* (Grand Rapids, MI: Eerdmans, 2001), 130 n. 93. See also Mary Stroll, *The Jewish Pope* (Leiden: Brill, 1987).

3. Manitius I 242.

4. Toreigny: Camp 82.

5. Manitius III 481–85.

6. Clive Beeke, "Ramsey Abbey," http://www.ramseyabbey.co.uk.

7. J.C. Almond, "Ramsey Abbey," 1911 Encyclopedia Britannica article at http://www.1911encyclopedia.org/Ramsey%2C_England. "According to a 12th-century chronicle of one of the monks, the name Ramsey is derived from the words "ram," referring to the tradition of a solitary ram having taken up its abode here, and "ey" meaning an island. Ramsey, however, was not completely insulated, like some of the monasteries of the Fen district." "Ram's Island" strikes us as feeble, however. The element Ram- is a frequent component of Arabic, Egyptian and Jewish place-names meaning little more than "land."

8. Lucy Freeman Sandler, "Christian Hebraism and the Ramsey Abbey Psalter," *Journal of the Warburg and Courtauld Institutes* 35 (1972): 123–34.

9. At least one other English Hebrew scholar of Christian origin is the *Magister Andreas, natione Anglus* mentioned by Roger Bacon. Master Andrew the Englishman is identified by S. A. Hirsch with an Augustinian monk who lived about 1150 (S. A. Hirsch, "Early English Hebraists: Roger Bacon and His Predecessors," *Jewish Quarterly Review* 12 [1900]: 34–88 at 44).

Hirsch also examines the possibilities that Bede and Alcuin (born 735) knew Hebrew but rejects them. Alcuin claimed that the library of his native York contained Hebrew books. Another interesting tidbit dismissed by Hirsch is the claim of several English Hebraists based on William of Malmesbury that King Ethelstan had the Bible translated into Anglo-Saxon in the late tenth century "from the pure Hebrew."

10. Cf. also *When Scotland Was Jewish*, App. C: "Early Jewish Names in France and England," 220–28.

11. Michael Adler, *Jews of Medieval England* (London: Jewish Historical Society of England, 1936), 302–303, for the years 1280–1286.

12. Eli Barnavi, *A Historical Atlas of the Jewish People* (New York: Schocken, 1992), 114.

13. Nigel Saul, *The Oxford Illustrated History of Medieval England* (Oxford: Oxford University Press, 2001), 5.

14. Ibid., 45.

15. Ibid., 159.

16. See Robert Bartlett, *England under the Norman and Angevin Kings, 1075–1225* (Oxford: Oxford University Press, 2000).

17. Roberts, Roberts and Bisson 100–101.

18. Bartlett 177.

19. Ibid., 220.

20. Ibid., 226.

21. Ibid., 343.

22. Adler lists them, and so does Camp 33.

23. Golb 174.

24. Ibid., 117.

25. Ibid., 119.

26. Fraser 153.

27. *Jews and Muslims* 173–74.

28. Bartlett 236.

29. Ockham appears in Domesday as *Bocheham*, in Surrey. It was held by Almaer [Arabic name] before William placed it under Richard Fitz Gilbert, the first of the earls of Clare. Almaer also held nearby Ockley. See http://en.wikipedia.org/wiki/Ockham,_Surrey—cite_note-1. It used to be thought that the philosopher was born in Ockham, Yorkshire; see Rega Wood, *Ockham on the Virtues* (Lafayette: Purdue University Press, 1997), 3, 6–7 n.1.

30. Manitius III 784.

31. Umar "prosperous": Rahman 86.

32. Adler 80.

33. Bartlett 425.

34. Shira Lander, "Martyrdom in Jewish Traditions," available online at http://www.bc.edu/dam/files/research_sites/cjl/texts/cjrelations/resources/articles/Lander_martyrdom/index.html.

35. Susan Einbinder, *Beautiful Death: Jewish Poetry and Martyrdom in Medieval France* (Princeton: Princeton University Press, 2002).

36. Lander's summary of Einbinder.

37. Ibid.

Chapter 8

1. *The Surnames of Wales* 8.

2. In Latin, Giraldus Cambrensis. His works include *Descriptio Walliae, Itinerarium Kambriae,* and *Descriptio Kambriae.* He also compiled a *Topographia Bri-*

tannica, Mappa Kambriae, Topographia Hibernica and *Life of St. David.* Manitius III 622–37.

3. Henry of Huntingdon, *The History of the English*, ed. Thomas Arnold (London: Longman, 1879), ix–xiii.

4. J.M.P. Calise, *Pictish Sourcebook* (Westport: Greenwood, 2002), 198.

5. Kai, Kauius, Keu, Cai, Cei fab Cynr: *Arthur of the Welsh* 108–12, 277.

6. There was an important provincial governor of Mauritania named Publius Aelius Aelianus. Eilian became a Sephardic surname.

7. Ashraf: Rahman 14.

8. Lleu, Llaw. The plural means "army." See also Gorr 3 for the Jewish forms.

9. Calise 192.

10. Calise 180. Rahman 12.

11. "Gracious": Gorr 68.

12. Calise 252.

13. Calise 192.

14. Rahman 9.

15. Ibid., 83.

16. Ibid., 64.

17. Skene 188.

18. Sims-Williams 54.

19. Fa'iyah, "an extensive, elevated place": Groom 81.

20. Michael Brett and Elizabeth Fentress, *The Berbers* (Oxford: Blackwell, 1996), 35.

21. Herodotus, *The Histories* (London: Folio, 2006), 273.

22. See Patrick Sims-Williams, "The Early Welsh Arthurian Poems," in Bromwich, Jarman and Roberts 33–61.

23. Brynley F. Robert, "Culhwch ac Olwen, the Triads, Saints' Lives, in Ibid., 91–92.

24. J. E. Caerwyn Williams, "Brittany and the Arthurian Legend," in Ibid., 250 (citing Nora Chadwick).

25. John Davies, *A History of Wales* (London: Allen Lane, 1993). Note that even his surname, *Davies*, denotes a Jewish ancestry. Davies is one of the most common surnames in Wales, together with Jones (originally pronounced Jon-as), and Williams, after William I, the Conqueror.

26. Cadwaladr (7th century) was confused by some historians with Caedwalla, king of Wessex. Calise 192–93.

27. Nell Irvin Painter, *The History of White People* (New York: W. W. Norton, 2010), 396.

28. Keys 110.

29. Ibid., 111.

30. Ibid., 112.

31. Ibid., 113.

32. Ibid., 115.

33. Skene 338–39.

34. Ibid., 340.

35. The last not to be confused with Norman Deakin. John and Sheila Rowlands, *The Surnames of Wales* (Baltimore: Genealogical Publishing, 1996), 49, 88–89.

36. Ibid., 167.

37. Itidal "clemency": Rahman 38. Anwar "rays of light, lustre; pl. of Nur 'light'": Ibid., 12–13.

38. Catholic Encyclopedia, "Consanguinity (in Canon Law)," available at http://www.newadvent.org/cathen/04264a.htm.

39. Jacob and its many forms was generally avoided as a name by Muslims because it was so Jewish, although the biblical patriarch was also part of Islam's heritage.

40. Davies 111.

41. Bleddyn ap Cynfyn, d. 1075, was prince of the kingdoms of Gwynedd and Powys in north Wales. His name possibly comes from Blaidd-ddyn = wolf-person. It may have been modeled on the Anglo-Saxon name Werestan/Gwerstan. At any rate, it is pronounced "Blethin." The unrelated surname Blevin/Blevins has been conflated with Bleddyn, but Blevins is *not* Welsh. Both authors of the present work have Blevins ancestry and have heard all their lives that "the Blevins came from Formby, Wales, and that the name means something like wolf-cub." Formby, however, is not in Wales, but Lancashire, where there are many Blevins to be discovered in eighteenth- and nineteenth-century English census records, while not one instance of a Blevins can be found in any Welsh record from any time. The mischief can be traced to the American editions of Charles Wareing Bardsley's *A Dictionary of English and Welsh Surnames*, which began appearing after 1900 (pp. 110–11 in the widely reprinted editions from Genealogical Publishing). Reaney and Wilson make the same mistake. The true meaning of Blevins, common in the north of England, is unknown. Given the Jewish affiliation of certain lines, we would propose *(a)b* + *Levin* "son of Levin." Supporting this derivation, Blevins Y chromsomal DNA is E1b1b, a classic Sephardic type.

42. John and Sheila Rowlands 9.

43. Calise 179–80.

44. Sims-Williams, in Bromwich, Jarman and Robert 37.

45. Holinshed says, "Onelie it is certaine (as Hector Boetius affirmeth) that Arthur liued in the daies of Iustinianus the emperor, about which time the Gotthes, Vandals, Burgonions, & Frenchmen did inuade sundrie parts of the Romane empire, pitifullie wasting and spoiling the same, where such writers as haue set foorth those warres, make no mention of Arthur at all" (Raphael Holinshed, *Chronicles* [London: Folio, 2012], 64).

46. Sims-Williams 38.

47. Ibid., 58.

48. See Toby D. Griffen, "Arthur's Name," Celtic Studies Association of North America, April 8, 1993, Athens, Georgia, available at http://www.fanad.net/csana94.pdf.

49. Calise 268.

50. Groom 141.

51. Sims-Williams 54. Calise 259.

52. See, for instance, *Ibn Khallikan's Biographical Dictionary*, trans. B. Mac Guckin de Slane IV (Paris: Oriental Translation Fund of Great Britain and Ireland, 1871). The prefix *ar* also appears in toponyms, e.g., ar–Ramla, ar–Rusafa and ar–Roha (=Edessa). It would be a worthwhile exercise to determine how many English and Welsh place-names have derivations still denoted by their beginning in Ar-; we would start with perhaps Arun (an alternative name for the Isle of Man) and Arundel in the south of England.

53. Skene 403.

Chapter 9

1. *Anglia Judaica* (Oxford 1738) 245.
2. Eli Barnavi, *A Historical Atlas of the Jewish People* (New York: Schocken, 1992), 120–21.
3. Saul 160.
4. David M. Gitlitz, *Secrecy and Deceit: The Religion of the Crypto-Jews* (Albuquerque: University of New Mexico Press, 2002), 6.
5. "Court Jews," article in the 1906 *Jewish Encyclopedia*, available at http://www.jewishencyclopedia.com/articles/4709-court-jews. Selma Stern, *The Court Jew: A Contribution to the History of Absolutism in Central Europe,* trans. Ralph Weiman (Philadelphia: Transaction, 1950).
6. See David Cesarini, *Port Jews: Jewish Communities in Cosmopolitan Maritime Trading Centres, 1550–1950* (London: Frank Cass, 2004).
7. Faiguenboim et al. 361; Stern 44.
8. Ephraim Russell, "The Societies of the Bardi and the Peruzzi and Their Dealings with Edward III, 1327–4," Centre for Metropolitan History, *Finance and Trade under Edward III*, ed. George Unwin (originally published 1918) 93–135, "The London Lay Subsidy of 1332," available at "http://www.british-history.ac.uk/report.aspx?compie=33008 (date accessed: 20 March 2009).
9. Peruzzi 474 to 476.
10. Peruzzi 250–65.
11. Malachi Beit-Arié, *The Only Dated Hebrew Manuscript Written in England (1189 CE) [?] and the Problem of the Pre-Expulsion Anglo-Hebrew Manuscripts,* book review by Menahem Schmelzer in *Jewish Quarterly Review* 77 (1986) 88–90.

Chapter 10

1. Rowlands 157.
2. Elizabeth or Elisabeth is the Greek form of the Hebrew name Elisheva, meaning "God's promise," "oath of God," "awesome one" or "I am God's daughter." Elizabeth/Elisabeth begat the names of Lisa, Liza, Lilly, Lizzie, Liz, Beth, Betty, Ella, Elisa, Elise and Eliza, and Elsa, Bitsy, Betsy, Isabel (French and Scottish), Isobel and Isabella are variants. After the greatly venerated Catholic St. Elizabeth of Hungary became popular in the thirteenth century, the name was avoided by Jews. Like Christopher, however, it became a good *crypto*-Jewish name. Elizabeth I was described by her contemporaries as the Deborah of Israel. A 22-foot-long illustrated scroll made in 1559 identified the descent she claimed from great leaders of the distant past, King David among them. There was a star of David emblazoned on the façade of Hatfield House Old Palace, her childhood home and favorite residence.
3. Gorr 37.
4. Zuckermann 120–21.
5. maximiliangenealogy.co.uk/burke/AncestryoftheRoyalHouseofTudor.htm
6. *Domesday People* I 428. The territory was probably Maelor Suesneg, the "English-speaking Maelor," an area of Wales along the northeastern border corresponding approximately to the later parishes of Bersham, Erbistock, Marchwiel, Ruabon and Wrexham in the his-

toric county of Denbighshire; see Max Lieberman, *The Medieval March of Wales* (Cambridge University Press: 2010), 122.
7. Called the "Helen of Wales" because of her beauty. Nest is said to be a Welsh version of Agnes (Greek).
8. Skene 57.
9. Notably, Caxton was a successful London merchant who ventured to Flanders, where he learned the art of printing (from Jews).
10. Fraser 233–34.
11. Shor is Hebrew for "bull," related to the name Joseph (Deut. 33:17): Gorr 671. For Shore in the English colonies in America, see *Jews and Muslims* 54.
12. Roth (1942) 133.
13. Census of Devon and Cornwall and open shaft mining (1450–1550).
14. Roughly "Khan of the English."
15. Nabil I. Matir, *Turks, Moors and Englishmen in the Age of Discovery* (New York: Columbia University Press, 1999) 25.
16. "Caboto" means sailor in Italian. Caboto is believed to have been of Sephardic Jewish decent, just like Christobal Colon (Columbus); *Jews and Muslims* 80.
17. Francesco Guidi-Bruscoli, "John Cabot and His Italian Financiers," *Historical Research* (April 2012): DOI: 10.1111/j.1468–2281.2012.00597.x.
18. Adler (1935).
19. Malden (1900), xiv.
20. See Englishhistory.net/Tudor/citizens/Cromwell.
21. Roth (1942) 136.

Chapter 11

1. Winston Churchill, *A History of the English-Speaking Peoples* (New York, 1956) I, 290.
2. See Hirschman and Yates, *When Scotland Was Jewish* (Jefferson, NC: McFarland, 2007), 205–14.
3. William Prynne, qtd. from Avrom Saltman, *The Jewish Question in 1655: Studies in Prynne's Demurrer* (Jerusalem, 1995), 43, and Gertrude Himmelfarb, *The People of the Book: Philosemitism in England, from Cromwell to Churchill* (New York: Encounter, 2011), 23.
4. On the Wakefields and their immediate circle and successors, see Magne Saebo, *Hebrew Bible/Old Testament: The History of Its Interpretation from the Renaissance to the Englightenment* (Vandenhoeck & Ruprecht, 2008), 521–24. The Englishman Robert Shirwood followed Robert Wakefield as a Hebrew teacher at Louvain in 1520. Both Wakefield and Sherwood have deep associations with the mythic outlaw Robin Hood ("Rueben Hud, the Jew"), identified by many as Earl of Huntingdon. The Wakefields of Newarke in Nottinghamshire intermarried with the Drakes.
5. Walter Elias "Walt" Disney, who was Irish and German, traced his descent to Robert d'Isigny, a Norman. The village of Norton Disney is south of the city of Lincoln, in the county of Lincolnshire. Isigny is in Normandy, near Bayeux.
6. See "Domus Conversorum," *Jewish Encyclopedia*, online at: http://www.jewishencyclopedia.com/articles/5271-domus-conversorum.
7. G. Lloyd Jones, *The Discovery of Hebrew in Tudor England: A Third Language* (Manchester: Manchester University Press, 1983), 272.

8. The Carys were a crypto–Jewish family originally from Devon.

9. Ibid., 240, where it is noted that Paschali (Jewish convert name) dedicated to Elizabeth in 1592 his translation, published in Geneva, of the Psalms from Hebrew into Italian verse.

10. Jason P. Rosenblatt, *Renaissance England's Chief Rabbi, John Selden* (Oxford University Press, 2008).

11. See Raphael Mostel, "Jews in the Court," *Jewish Daily Forward*, October 6, 2006, available at http://forward.com/articles/4829/jews-in-the-court.

12. Jonathan Karp and Adam Sutcliffe, *Philosemitism in History* (Cambridge University Press, 2011), esp. 80–81.

13. Philip Almond, "Thomas Brightman and the Origins of Philo-semitism: An Elizabethan Theologian and the Restoration of the Jews to Israel," *Reformation and Renaissance Review: Journal of the Society for Reformation Studies* 9.1 (2007): 3–25.

14. One is encouraged to read between the lines and peer behind the portraits in the carefully cosmeticized family history by John Martin Robinson, *The Dukes of Norfolk. A Quincentennial History* (Oxford: Oxford University Press, 1982). The Dukes of Norfolk are considered by many the foremost aristocratic house in England, being for centuries Earls Marshall and heads of the College of Arms. "Formerly," writes British genealogist L. G. Pine, "there was current an extraordinary story that Howard was really Hereward written short in mediaeval English, and that the Howards derived their ancestry from the celebrated Hereward the Wake. Curious how great is the posthumous fame of this hero, of whom England in his lifetime was not worthy. So many noble families claim him as their own ... I understand that [the Baronness Herries, who married the fifteenth duke] stood guard over the Hereward legend, as the dragon in *Beowulf* shielded the fairy gold, and none durst touch it while she lived. However, a Norman male line descent the Dukes of Norfolk have not got, and most probably they descend from a Saxon origin, though not from Hereward. Through the marriage of Sir Robert Howard with the Lady Margaret, elder daughter of Thomas de Mowbray, Duke of Norfolk, they have their royal descent and consequent Norman blood, in the female line from Edward I. Hence, too, their honours and estates, and the right to quarter the royal arms" (*They Came with the Conqueror: A Study of the Modern Descendants of the Normans,* New York: Putnam, n.d., 58).

15. See Jacobs, "Personal Names"; Menk 294.

16. "He [i.e., Henry VIII] also got the Jews to give their opinions of the laws in Leviticus, that they were moral and obligatory—that when a brother died without issue, his brother might marry his wwidow within Judea, for preserving their families and succession; although that might not be done out of Judea." *Foxe's Book of Martyrs* (London: Knight, 1856), 308.

17. John Edwards, "A Spanish Inquisition? The Repression of Protestantism under Mary Tudor," *Reformation and Renaissance Review* 4 (2000): 62–74.

18. Ibid., 72.

19. Probably from Bocar (DSS 207).

20. From Segni, a locality in Lazio; see DSS 388.

21. For these and other cases, see Fines 324.

22. See John Fines, "'Judaising' in the Period of the English Reformation—the Case of Richard Bruern," *Transactions of the Jewish Historical Society of England* 21 (1962–1967): 323–26.

23. Brightman qtd. in Almond 13.

24. See David Katz, *Philosemitism and the Readmission of the Jews to England, 1603–1655*.

25. Daniel Rawlinson of Graythwaite was a vintner, a friend of Pepys and a staunch royalist. His son Thomas Rawlinson became Lord Mayor of London in 1705, and his grandson Richard Rawlinson became a great benefactor to the Bodleian Library. He died in 1679.

26. Samuel Pepys, *The Diary of Samuel Pepys, 1663* (Echo Library, 2006), 191–92.

27. Claire Tomalin, *Samuel Pepys: The Unequalled Self* (New York: Vintage, 2003), 42.

28. B. Netanyahu, *The Marranos of Spain from the Late 14th to the Early 16th Century, According to Contemporary Hebrew Sources*, Third ed., updated and expanded (Ithaca: Cornell University Press, 1999).

29. Lloyd P. Gartner, "A Quarter Century of Anglo-Jewish Historiography," *Jewish Social Studies* 48/2 (1986): 105–26.

30. Himmelfarb notes (158) that even though "philo–Semitic" appeared as early as 1934 in the works of Cecil Roth, it quickly fell out of favor in the ordained histories of Judaism. "In his essay, 'England in Jewish History' (1949), he speaks of the 'strong philosemitic movement in the country' even before the readmission of the Jews."

31. Endress 10.

32. Ibid., 12.

Chapter 12

1. John Richetti, *The Life of Daniel Defoe* (Malden: Blackwell, 2005), vii–viii.

2. Variants, some dubious, appear to be Fow, Fowe, Fohe, Fohee, Faeoe, Foy, Fay, Foye, Fooe and Fou. Reaney and Wilson have no entry for either Foe or Defoe. Excellent information on Foe's origins and writings can be found in the article on him in the *Dictionary of National Biography* written by its first editor, Sir Leslie Stephen, vol. 5 (London: Oxford University Press, 1921), 730–43.

3. Richetti 18.

4. The name of Defoe's mother is so spelled in the only records mentioning her, though biographers usually take this as a parish clerk's error and "normalize" it to Alice. Ailsey is a Jewish name.

5. Maximillian E. Novak, *Daniel Defoe, Master of Fictions. His Life and Ideas* (Oxford: Oxford University Press, 2001), 20–21.

6. See, for instance, Sheldon Rogers, *Notes & Queries* 56.2 (2009): 226–28.

7. Roza was very popular among Sephardic women; see Gorr 80–81.

8. Novak 14.

9. Ibid., 17–18.

10. *Jews and Muslims* 10–15.

11. Novak 19.

12. Alice E. Miller, *Cecil County, Maryland, A Study in Local History* (Elkton: C&L, 1949), 150–53.

13. Mary E. Ireland, "The Defoe Family in America," *Scribners Monthly* 12 (1876): 61–64.

14. DSS 260, with branches in Rome, Bari, Busseto,

Borgotaro, Colorno, Genoa, Venice, Asti, Milan, Napoli, Pisa, Varesa, Ivrea, Trieste, Florence, Turin, Parma, Alexandria, Lucca, Leghorn, Reggio Emilia, Casale Monferrato, Modena, Paris, Bordeaux, Marseille, Amsterdam, Tunisia, Buenos Aires, Sao Paulo and New York. Foix was the capital of a province of the same name, now the *département* of Ariége just south of Toulouse, the seat of Machir the Exilarch and center of southern French Jewry. "In the Middle Ages, one finds a number of Jews in the county of Foix and particularly at Pamiers, where they were treated with high regard by the local rulers and officials of the Church" (Gross, *Gallia Judaica* 438–439). Queen Katherine's aunt, Eleanor of Aragon, married Gaston IV de Foix (she had other Jewish ancestry as well). Following the expulsion of Jews from France, the count of Foix pleaded to be allowed to keep the Jews, a scenario that occurred as far back as the twelfth century. In Hebrew the name was pronounced *Po-eesh* and in the Provençal language "Foish"; in other words the final consonant was sounded, distinguishing it from the word *foi*. Our favorite whipping boy Reaney and Wilson notes several occurrences in England (including John Foys, 1359, Devon) but derives all from Old French *foi* "faith," despite the fact that *foi* has no *s* (DES 176). The last count of Foix, also king of Navarre, Francis Phoebus, had a Jewish name which may point to the true origin of the place-name Foix, instead of the apocryphal St. Faith.

15. Novak 19.
16. *The Earlier Life and the Chief Earlier Works of Daniel Defoe*, ed. Henry Morley (London: Routledge, 1886), 17.
17. Richetti 22.
18. Paula R. Backschneider, *Daniel Defoe: His Life* (Baltimore: Johns Hopkins University Press, 1989), 13.
19. Richetti 3.
20. Ibid. 20.
21. Daniel Defoe, *The Life and Strange Surprizing Adventures of Robinson Crusoe of York, Mariner: Who lived Eight and Twenty Years, all alone in an uninhabited Island on the Coast of AMERICA, near the Mouth of the Great River of OROONOQUE; Having been cast on Shore by Shipwreck, wherein all the Men perished but himself. WITH An Account how he was at last as strangely deliver'd by PYRATES. Written by Himself*, with an Intro. by J. M. Coetzee (Oxford: Oxford University Press, 1999), v.
22. Daniel Defoe, *Serious Reflections during the Life and Surprising Adventures of Robinson Crusoe: With His Vision of the Angelick World* (London: Taylor, 1720) A3–A4, 4.
23. William Minto, *Daniel Defoe* (London: 1879), 169.
24. DSS 220. The famous tenor Enrico Caruso (1873–1921) was born in Naples but had a genealogy that can be traced back to Gaspare Caruso (Spanish first name and surname), born in Palermo, Sicily, in about 1545, who married Filippa Amato (Spanish first name and another Sephardic surname).
25. Malcolm H. Stern, *Americans of Jewish Descent: A Compendium of Genealogy* (Cincinnati: Hebrew Union College Press, 1960), 98, 69.
26. George MacKenzie, ed., *Colonial Families of the United States* I (Baltimore: Genealogical Publishing, 1995) under Wills.

27. Family Tree of the Jewish People at jewishgen.org.
28. Mordechai Arbell, *The Jewish Nation of the Caribbean* (Jerusalem: Gefen, 2002), 14–17.
29. Arbell 18, citing Malcolm Stern, "Follow Up on the Jews of Recife," a manuscript Arbell consulted in New York.
30. *Jews and Muslims* 159–60.
31. Coetzee ix.
32. Joel Reed, "Nationalism and Geoculture in Defoe's History of Writing," *Modern Language Quarterly* 56.1 (1995): 31–53.

Epilogue

1. See John Burrow, *A History of Histories. Epics, Chronicles, Romances and Inquiries from Herodotus and Thucydides to the Twentieth Century* (New York: Knopf, 2008), esp. ch. 19, "Antiquarianism, Legal History and the Discovery of Feudalism," 283–301.
2. See Gertrude Himmelfarb, *The People of the Book: Philosemitism in England, from Cromwell to Churchill* (New York: Encounter, 2011), 44–47.
3. John Burrow, *A History of Histories*, 476–77.

Appendix A

1. T. E. King et al., "Genetic Signatures of Coancestry within Surnames," *Current Biology* 16 (2006): 384–88. T. E. King et al., "Founders, Drift and Infidelity: The Relationship between Y Chromosome Diversity and Patrilineal Surnames," *Molecular Biology and Evolution* 26 (2009): 1093–1102.
2. Bruce Winney et al., "People of the British Isles: Preliminary Analysis of Genotypes and Surnames in a UK-control Population," *European Journal of Human Genetics* (2011): 3–5.
3. Ibid. 4.
4. James F. Wilson et al., "Genetic Evidence for Different Male and Female Roles during Cultural Transitions in the British Isles," *PNAS* 98.9 (2001): 5078–5083.
5. See chapter 1 above.
6. Wilson et al., 5082.
7. Ibid., 5083.
8. See chapter 1.
9. Peter Forster et al., "MtDNA Markers for Celtic and Germanic Language Areas in the British Isles," in M. Jones, ed., *Traces of Ancestry: Studies in Honour of Colin Renfrew* (Cambridge: McDonald Institute for Archeological Research, 2004), 99–111.
10. "Conversion Table for Y Chromosome Haplogroups," retrieved January 2012 at http://dnacon sultants.com/images/conversion.pdf. The first phylogenetic chart to unify nomenclature was published in 2002 by the Y Chromosome Consortium (YCC) at the University of Arizona. The International Society of Genetic Genealogy maintains a phylogenetic tree with important links to haplogroup information at http://www.isogg.org/tree.
11. C. Capelli et al., "A Y Chromosome Census of the British Isles," *Current Biology* 13 (2003): 979–84.
12. Ibid., 983.
13. Fernando L. Mendez et al., "Increased Resolu-

tion of Y Chromosome Haplogroup T Defines Relationships among Populations of the Near East, Europe, and Africa," *Human Biology* 83.1 (2011): 39–53. T achieves a high level in Roman Jews (6%) and Moroccan Jews (7%).

14. Michael E. Weale et al., "Y Chromosome Evidence for Anglo-Saxon Mass Migration," *Molecular Biology and Evolution* 19.7 (2002): 1008–1021.

15. Steven C. Bird, "Haplogroup E3b1a2 as a Possible Indicator of Settlement in Roman Britain by Soldiers of Balkan Origin," *Journal of Genetic Genealogy* 3.2 (2007): 26–46.

16. "Haplogroup E1b1b," retrieved January 2012 at http://www.eupedia.com/europe/Haplogroup_E1b1b_ Y-DNA.shtml.

17. Robert L. Tarín, "An Iberian Sub-Cluster Is Revealed in a Phylogenetic Tree Analysis of the Y-chromosome E3b [E1b1b] Haplogroup," published online November 2005 and retrieved January 2012 at http://garyfelix.tripod.com/E3bsubcluster.pdf.

18. S. Willuweit and L. Roewer, on behalf of the International Forensic Y Chromosome User Group, Y chromosome haplotype reference database (YHRD): "Update." *Forensic Science International: Genetics* (2007) 2. Release 37 consists of 97,575 haplotypes within 739 populations. Available online at http://www.yhrd.org.

References

Adler, Elkan Nathan. *Jewish Travellers in the Middle Ages: 19 Firsthand Accounts*. New York: Dover, 1987.

Adler, Michael. *Jews of Mediaeval England*. London: Jewish Historical Society of England, 1936.

Alexander, J. J., and W. R. Hooper. *The History of Great Torrington in the County of Devon*. Sutton: Advance Studio, 1948.

Almond, J.C. "Ramsey Abbey." 1911. Encyclopaedia Britannica article at: http://www.1911encyclopedia.org/Ramsey%2C_England.

Almond, Philip. "Thomas Brightman and the Origins of Philo-Semitism: An Elizabethan Theologian and the Restoration of the Jews to Israel," *Reformation and Renaissance Review: Journal of the Society for Reformation Studies* 9.1 (2007): 3–25.

Appelbaum, Shimon. *Jews and Greeks in Ancient Cyrene*. Leiden: Brill, 1979.

_____. "Were There Jews in Roman Britain." *Transactions of the Jewish Historical Society of England* 17 (1953).

Arbell, Mordechai. *The Jewish Nation of the Caribbean*. Jerusalem: Gefen, 2002.

Backhouse, Janet. *The Lindisfarne Gospels, a Masterpiece of Book Painting*. London: British Library, 1995.

Backschneider, Paula R. *Daniel Defoe: His Life*. Baltimore: Johns Hopkins University Press, 1989.

Barber, Henry. *British Family Names: Their Origin and Meaning, with Lists of Scandinavian, Frisian, Anglo-Saxon and Norman Names*. London: Stock, 1903.

Barber, Richard. *Anglo-Saxon Lore and Learning*. London: Folio, 2008.

_____. *The Coming of the Anglo-Saxons*. London: Folio, 2008.

Barbero, Alessandro. *Charlemagne: Father of a Continent*. Berkeley: University of California Press, 2004.

Barnavi, Eli. *A Historical Atlas of the Jewish People*. New York: Schocken, 1992.

Baron, Salo W. *Economic History of the Jews*. New York: Schocken, 1976.

Bartlett, Robert. *England under the Norman and Angevin Kings, 1075–1225*. Oxford: Oxford University Press, 2000.

Baurain, C., and C. Bonnet. *Les Phéniciens. Marins de Trois Continents*. Paris: Armand Colin, 1992.

Bede. *History of the English Church and People*, trans. Leo Shirley-Price, rev. by R. E. Latham. London: Folio, 2010.

Beeke, Clive. "Ramsey Abbey." N.d. http://www.ramseyabbey.co.uk.

Beit-Arié, Malachi. Rev. of *The Only Dated Hebrew Manuscript Written in England (1189 CE) [?] and the Problem of the Pre-Expulsion Anglo-Hebrew Manuscripts*, by Menahem Schmelzer. *Jewish Quarterly Review* 77 (1986): 88–90.

Benbassa, Esther. *The Jews of France. A History from Antiquity to the Present*, trans. M. B. DeBevoise. Princeton: Princeton University Press, 2001.

Benbassa, Esther, and Aron Rodrigue. *Sephardi Jewry*. Berkeley: University of California Press, 2000.

Biale, David, ed. *Cultures of the Jews: A New History*. New York: Schocken, 2002.

Bird, Steven C. "Haplogroup E3b1a2 as a Possible Indicator of Settlement in Roman Britain by Soldiers of Balkan Origin." *Journal of Genetic Genealogy* 3.2 (2007): 26–46.

Blair, Peter Hunter. *Roman Britain and Early England 55 BC–AD 871*. New York: W. W. Norton, 1963.

Bodian, Miriam. *Hebrews of the Portuguese Nation: Conversos and Community in Early Modern Amsterdam*. Bloomington: Indiana University Press, 1997.

Bredero, Adriaan H. *Bernard of Clairvaux: Between Cult and History*. Grand Rapids, MI: Eerdmans, 2001.

Brett, Michael, and Elizabeth Fentress. *The Berbers*. Oxford: Blackwell, 1996.

Bromwich, Rachel, A.O.H. Jarman and Brynley F. Roberts, eds. *The Arthur of the Welsh. The Arthurian Legend in Medieval Welsh Literature*. Cardiff: University of Wales Press, 1991.

Brooks, Jory S. "The Hebrew-Celtic Connection: Language, Cultural and Religious Ties." *Midwestern Epigraphic Journal* 15 (2001): 88–90.

Burrow, John. *A History of Histories*. New York: Knopf, 2008.

Caesar. *The Gallic War*, with an English trans. by H. J. Edwards. Cambridge: Harvard University Press, 1997.

Calise, J.M.P. *Pictish Sourcebook: Documents of Medieval Legend and Dark Age History*. Westport, CT: Greenwood, 2002.

Camp, Anthony J. *My Ancestors Came with the Conqueror: Those Who Did and Some of Those Who Probably Did Not*. Baltimore: Genealogical Publishing, 1990.

Capelli, C., et al. "A Y Chromosome Census of the British Isles." *Current Biology* 13 (2003): 979–984.

Cesarini, David. *Port Jews: Jewish Communities in Cosmopolitan Maritime Trading Centres, 1550–1950*. London: Frank Cass, 2004.

Chadwick, Nora. *The Celts*, with intro. by Barry Cunliffe. London: Folio, 2001.

Chatháin, Próinséas Ní, and Michael Richter, eds. *Ireland and Europe in the Early Middle Ages: Texts and Transmission*. Dublin: Four Courts, 2001.

Christensen, Penelope. *Parishes & Registration Districts in England & Wales*. Toronto: Heritage Productions, 2001.

Churchill, Winston. *A History of the English-Speaking Peoples*. New York: Macmillan, 1956.

"Cooper Miniature Sells, Warts and All" (2007). *Telegraph* (London) news report from June 7, 2007, available at http://www.telegraph.co.uk/news/uknews/1553848/Cromwell-miniature-sells-warts-and-all.html.

Couch, David. *The Normans: The History of a Dynasty*. London: Hambledon Continuum, 2007.

"Court Jews." Article in the 1906 *Jewish Encyclopedia*, available at http://www.jewishencyclopedia.com/articles/4709-court-jews.

Cunliffe, Barry. *The Extraordinary Voyage of Pytheas the Greek*. New York: Penguin, 2002.

_____. *Facing the Ocean: The Atlantic and Its Peoples*. New York: Oxford University Press, 2004.

Davies, John. *A History of Wales*. London: Allen Lane, 1993.

Davies, Norman. *Vanished Kingdoms: The Rise and Fall of States and Nations*. New York: Viking, 2011.

Defoe, Daniel. *The Life and Strange Surprizing Adventures of Robinson Crusoe of York, Mariner: Who lived Eight and Twenty Years, all alone in an uninhabited Island on the Coast of AMERICA, near the Mouth of the Great River of OROONOQUE; Having been cast on Shore by Shipwreck, wherein all the Men perished but himself. WITH An Account how he was at last as strangely deliver'd by PYRATES. Written by Himself*, with an Intro. by J. M. Coetzee. Oxford: Oxford University Press, 1999.

_____. *Serious Reflections during the Life and Surprising Adventures of Robinson Crusoe: With His Vision of the Angelick World*. London: Taylor, 1720.

DES *see* Reaney and Wilson

Deville, M. A. *Observations sur l'époque de la naissance de Guillaume-le-Conquérant*. In: *Memoire de la societé des antiquaries de Normandie* XI. 1840.

Dienekes' Anthropology Blog. Available at http://dienekes.blogspot.com.

Doehaerd, Renee. *The Early Middle Ages in the West: Economy and Society*, trans. W. G. Deakin. Amsterdam: North-Holland, 1978.

"The Domesday Book Online." Website at http://www.domesdaybook.co.uk/compiling.html.

"Domus Conversorum." Article in *Jewish Encyclopedia*, available online at: http://www.jewishencyclopedia.com/articles/5271-domus-conversorum.

Douglas, David C. *William the Conqueror: The Norman Impact upon England*. Berkeley: University of California Press, 1964.

DSS *see* Faiguenboim et al.

Duffy, Eamon. *Saints and Sinners: A History of the Popes*. London: Folio, 2009.

Dumville, D. N. *English Caroline Script and Monastic History: Studies in Benedictinism, A.D. 950–1030*. Rochester: Boydell, 1992.

Edwards, John. "A Spanish Inquisition? The Repression of Protestantism under Mary Tudor." *Reformation and Renaissance Review* 4 (2000): 62–74.

Einbinder, Susan. *Beautiful Death: Jewish Poetry and Martyrdom in Medieval France*. Princeton: Princeton University Press, 2002.

Endress, Gerhard. *Islam: An Historical Introduction*, 2nd ed., trans. Carole Hillenbrand. New York: Columbia University Press, 2002.

"'Extraordinary' Genetic Make-up of North-east Wales Men." BBC News North East Wales article retrieved January 2012 at http://www.bbc.co.uk/news/uk-wales-north-east-wales-14173910.

Faiguenboim, Guilherme et al. *Dictionary of Sephardic Surnames*, 2nd ed. Rio de Janeiro: Fraiha, 2003.

Fillery-Travis, Ruth. "Archeological Copper Bibliography." N.d. http://findsandfeatures.wordpress.com/bibliographies/reading-list-for-archaeological-copper.

Fines, John. "'Judaising' in the Period of the English Reformation—the Case of Richard Bruern," *Transactions of the Jewish Historical Society of England*. 21 (1968): 323–36.

Forster, Peter, et al. "MtDNA Markers for Celtic and Germanic Language Areas in the British Isles." In M. Jones, ed., *Traces of Ancestry: Studies in Honour of Colin Renfrew*, pp. 99–111. Cambridge: McDonald Institute for Archeological Research, 2004.

Foxe, John. *Foxe's Book of Martyrs*. London: Knight, 1856.

Fraser, Rebecca. *The Story of Britain: From Romans to the Present*. New York: Norton, 2003.

Frederiksen, Paula. *Augustine and the Jews: A Christian Defense of Jews and Judaism*. New Haven: Yale University Press, 2010.

Freeman, Edward A. *The History of the Norman Conquest of England*. II. London: Macmillan, 1868.

Gartner, Lloyd P. "A Quarter Century of Anglo-Jewish Historiography." *Jewish Social Studies* 48.2 (1986): 105–26.

Geersom, A. van. "Bruno, de Auteur van de Ysengrimus." *Verslagen en Mededelingen van de Koninklijke Vlaamse Academie voor Taal- en Letterkunde* (1962): 5–73.

Geoffrey of Monmouth. *The History of the Kings of Britain*, trans. with intro. by Lewis Thorpe, preface by Richard Barber. London: Folio, 2010.

Gerber, Jane S. *The Jews of Spain*. New York: Free, 1992.

Gibbon, Edward. *The History of the Decline and Fall of the Roman Empire*, ed. J.B. Bury with intro. by W.E.H. Lecky. New York: de Fau, 1906. Online at http://oll.libertyfund.org.

Gidlow, Christopher. *Revealing King Arthur*. Stroud: History, 2010.

Giles, J. A., ed. *The Works of Gildas and Nennius*. London: Bohn, 1841.

Gitlitz, David M. *Secrecy and Deceit: The Religion of the Crypto-Jews*. Albuquerque: University of New Mexico Press, 2002.

Golb, Norman. *The Jews in Medieval Normandy: A Social and Intellectual History*. Cambridge: Cambridge University Press, 1998.

Gordon, Cyrus H. *Canaanite Mythology*, ed. Samuel Noah Kramer. New York: Doubleday, 1961.

Gorr, Shmuel. *Jewish Personal Names: Their Origin, Derivation and Diminutive Forms,* ed. Chaim Freedman. Teaneck, NJ: Avotaynu, 1992.

Griffen, Toby D. "Arthur's Name." Celtic Studies Association of North America, April 8, 1993, Athens, Georgia, available at http://www.fanad.net/csana94.pdf.

Groom, Nigel. *A Dictionary of Arabic Topography and Placenames*. Beirut: Liban, 1983.

Gross, Henri. *Gallia Judaica. Dictionnaire géographique de la France d'après les sources rabbiniques*, transl. Moïse Bloch. Paris: Cerf, 1897.

Guidi-Bruscoli, Francesco. "John Cabot and His Italian Financiers." *Historical Research*. DOI: 10.1111/j.1468–2281.2012.00597.x. 2012.

Guild of One-Name Studies. Website accessed January 2012 at http://www.one-name.org/profiles/bowhay.html.

Hallam, Elizabeth M. *Domesday Book through Nine Centuries*. London: Thames and Hudson, 1986.

Hanning, Robert W. *The Vision of History in Early Britain*. New York: Columbia University Press, 1966.

Henriques, H.S.Q. *Jewish Marriages and the English Law*. Clark: Lawbook Exchange, 2006.

Henry of Huntingdon. *The History of the English*, ed. Thomas Arnold. London: Longman, 1879.

Herber, Mark. *Ancestral Trails. The Complete Guide to British Genealogy and Family History,* 2nd ed. Baltimore: Genealogical Publishing, 2005.

Herodotus. *The Histories*. London: Folio, 2006.

Hill, E. W., et al. "Y-chromosome Variation and Irish Origins." *Nature* 404 (2000): 351–52.

Himmelfarb, Gertrude. *The People of the Book: Philosemitism in England, from Cromwell to Churchill*. New York: Encounter Books, 2011.

Hirsch, S. A. "Early English Hebraists: Roger Bacon and His Predecessors." *Jewish Quarterly Review* 12 (1900): 34–88.

Hirschman, Elizabeth C., and Donald N. Yates. *Jews and Muslims in British Colonial America. A Genealogical History*. Jefferson, NC: McFarland, 2012.

_____. *When Scotland Was Jewish: DNA Evidence, Archeology, Analysis of Migrations, and Public and Family Records Show Twelfth Century Semitic Roots*. Jefferson: McFarland, 2007.

Holinshed, Raphael. *Chronicles*. London: Folio, 2012.

Hourani, Albert. *A History of the Arab Peoples*. Cambridge: Harvard University Press, 1991.

Hunt, William. "Brompton, John." 1889. Article in *Dictionary of National Biography* 6, retrieved January 2012 at http://en.wikisource.org/wiki/Brompton,_John_DNB00.

Hyamson, Albert Montefiore. *A History of the Jews in England*. London: Chatto, 1908.

Ibn Khallikan's Biographical Dictionary. trans. B. Mac Guckin de Slane, IV. Paris: Oriental Translation Fund of Great Britain and Ireland, 1871.

Ireland, Mary E. "The Defoe Family in America," *Scribners Monthly* 12 (1876): 61–64.

Jacobs, Joseph. "Personal Names." In *The Jewish Encyclopedia. A Descriptive Record of the History, Religion, Literature, and Customs of the Jewish People from the Earliest Times to the Present Day*, pub. by Isidore Singer and ed. by Cyrus Adler. Orig. published in London. Reprint by KTAV Publishing House, 1980. Available online at http://www.JewishEnclopedia.com.

Johns, W. N. *Historical Traditions and Facts Relating to Newport and Caerleon*. 1880. Accessed in 2011 at http://books.google.com/books?id=Y2IZAAAAYAAJ&dq.

Johnson, Paul. *A History of the Jews*. New York: Harper, 1987.

Jones, G. Lloyd . *The Discovery of Hebrew in Tudor England: A Third Language*. Manchester: Manchester University Press, 1983.

Jones, Gwyn. *The Vikings*, intro. by Magnus Magnusson. London: Folio, 1997.

Jones, Prudence, and Nigel Pennick. *A History of Pagan Europe*. New York: Barnes & Noble, 1995.

Josephus. *Complete Works*, trans. William Whiston, foreword by William Sanford LaSor. Grand Rapids, MI: Kregel, 1976.

Karp, Jonathan, and Adam Sutcliffe (2011). *Philosemitism in History*. Cambridge: Cambridge University Press.

Katz, David. *Philosemitism and the Readmission of the Jews to England, 1603–1655.* Oxford: Clarendon, 1982.

Katz, Solomon. *The Jews in the Visigothic and Frankish Kingdoms of Spain and Gaul.* Cambridge, MA: Mediaeval Academy of America, 1970.

Keats-Rohan, K. S. B. *Domesday People. A Prosopography of Persons Occuring in English Documents 1066–1166.* I: *Domesday Book.* Woodbridge: Boydell, 1996.

_____. "Poppa of Bayeux and Her Family." *The American Genealogist* 72 (1997): 187–204.

Kennedy, Maev. "Ancient Roman Village Discovered in Parkland around Stately Home." *The Guardian,* November 16, 2010, accessed online in 2011 at http://www.guardian.co.uk/science/2010/nov/17/ancient-roman-village-parkland?CMP=twt_fd.

Keys, David. *Catastrophe: An Investigation into the Origins of the Modern World.* New York: Ballantine, 1999.

King, T. E., et al. "Founders, Drift and Infidelity: The Relationship between Y Chromosome Diversity and Patrilineal Surnames," *Molecular Biology and Evolution* 26 (2009): 1093–1102.

_____. "Genetic Signatures of Coancestry within Surnames." *Current Biology* 16 (2006): 384–88.

_____. "Thomas Jefferson's Y Chromosome Belongs to a Rare European Lineage." *American Journal of Physical Anthropology* 132.4 (2007): 584–89.

Knight, Jeremy K. *Caerleon Roman Fortress.* Cardiff: Cadw, 1988.

Laistner, M. L. W. (1966). *Thought and Letters in Western Europe, A.D. 500–900.* Ithaca, NY: Cornell University Press.

Lander, Shira. "Martyrdom in Jewish Traditions," N.d. http://www.bc.edu/dam/files/research_sites/cjl/texts/cjrelations/resources/articles/Lander_martyrdom/index.html.

Lea, Henry Charles. *The Inquisition of the Middle Ages,* abridg. Margaret Nicholson. New York: Macmillan, 1961.

Leclercq, Jean. *The Love of Learning and the Desire for God: A Study of Monastic Culture,* trans. Catharine Misrahi. New York: Fordham University Press, 1961.

Le Goff, Jacques. *Medieval Civilization 400–1500,* trans. Julia Barrow. London: Folio, 2011.

Levi, I. "Le Roi Juif de Narbonne et le Philomene," *Revue des études juives* 48 (1904): 197–207, 49 (1904): 147–50.

Lieberman, Max. *The Medieval March of Wales.* Cambridge University Press, 2010.

MacKenzie, George, ed. *Colonial Families of the United States.* I. Baltimore: Genealogical Publishing, 1995.

Manitius, Max. *Geschichte der lateinischen Literatur des Mittelalters,* I, *Von Justinian bis zur Mitte des Zehnten Jahrhunderts.* Munich: Beck, 1911.

Marks, Gil. *Encyclopedia of Jewish Food.* New York: Wiley, 2010.

Matir, Nabil I. *Turks, Moors and Englishmen in the Age of Discovery.* New York: Columbia University Press, 1999.

McEvedy, Colin. *Cities of the Classical World,* ed. Douglas Stuart Oles. London: Allen Lane, 2011.

Mendez, Fernando L., et al. "Increased Resolution of Y Chromosome Haplogroup T Defines Relationships among Populations of the Near East, Europe, and Africa." *Human Biology* 83.1 (2011): 39–53.

Menk, Lars. *A Dictionary of German-Jewish Surnames.* Bergenfield, NJ: Avotaynu, 2005.

Markoe, Glenn E. *The Phoenicians.* London: Folio, 2005.

Mastnak, Tomaž. *Crusading Peace: Christendom, the Muslim World, and Western Political Order.* Berkeley: University of California Press, 2002.

Miller, Alice E. *Cecil County, Maryland, A Study in Local History.* Elkton: C&L, 1949.

Minto, William. *Daniel Defoe.* London, 1879.

Monypenny, William Flavelle. *The Life of Benjamin Disraeli, Earl of Beaconsfield.* I, *1804–1837.* New York: Macmillan, 1910.

Morley, Henry. *The Earlier Life and the Chief Earlier Works of Daniel Defoe.* London: Routledge, 1886.

Morris, John, ed. and trans. *Nennius: British History and the Welsh Annals.* London: Phillimore, 1980.

Mostel, Raphael. "Jews in the Court." *Jewish Daily Forward,* October 6, 2006, available at http://forward.com/articles/4829/jews-in-the-court.

Mowat, Farley. *The Farfarers. A New History of North America.* New York: Skyhorse, 2002.

Mundill, Robin R. (2010). *The King's Jews: Money, Massacre and Exodus in Medieval England.* New York: Continuum, 2010.

Nebel, A., et al. "The Y Chromosome Pool of Jews as Part of the Genetic Landscape of the Middle East." *American Journal of Human Genetics* 69.5 (2001): 1095–1112.

Netanyahu, B. *The Marranos of Spain from the Late 14th to the Early 16th Century, According to Contemporary Hebrew Sources,* 3rd ed., updated and expanded. Ithaca, NY: Cornell University Press, 1999.

Novak, Maximillian E. *Daniel Defoe, Master of Fictions: His Life and Ideas.* Oxford: Oxford University Press, 2001.

Oldys, William, ed. *Biographia Britannica, or the Lives of the Most Eminent Persons in Great-Britain and Ireland.* 1. London: 1747.

Oppenheimer, Stephen. *The Origins of the British. A Genetic Detective Story: The Surprising Roots of the English, Irish, Scottish, and Welsh.* New York: Carroll & Graf, 2006.

Oxford Jewish Heritage. http://www.oxfordjewishheritage.co.uk.

Padel, O. J. "Some South-western Sites with Arthurian

Associations." In *The Arthur of the Welsh*, ed. Rachel Bromwich, A. O. H. Jarman and Brynley F. Roberts. Cardiff: University of Wales Press, 1991.

Painter, Nell Irvin. *The History of White People*. New York: W. W. Norton, 2010.

Patai, Raphael. *The Children of Noah: Jewish Seafaring in Ancient Times*. Princeton: Princeton University Press, 1998.

Pepys, Samuel. *The Diary of Samuel Pepys, 1663*. Teddington: Echo Library, 2006.

Pine, L.B. *The Genealogist's Encyclopedia*. New York: Collier, 1969.

_____. *They Came with the Conqueror: A Study of the Modern Descendants of the Normans*. New York: Putnam, 1954.

Rabinowitz, Louis I. *Jewish Merchant Adventurers, a Study of the Radanites*. London: Goldston, 1948.

Rahman, S. A. *A Dictionary of Muslim Names*. New Delhi: Goodword, 2011.

Reaney, P. H., and R. M. Wilson. *A Dictionary of English Surnames*. Oxford: Oxford University Press, 1997.

Reddish, Elisabeth "The Fourteenth-Century Tree of Jesse in the Nave of York Minster." N.d. http://www.york.ac.uk/teaching/history/pjpg/jesse.pdf.

Reed, Joel. "Nationalism and Geoculture in Defoe's History of Writing." *Modern Language Quarterly* 56.1 (1995): 31–53.

Richetti, John. *The Life of Daniel Defoe*. Malden, UK: Blackwell, 2005.

Roberts, Clayton, David Roberts, Douglas R. Bisson. *A History of England: Prehistory to 1714*. Upper Saddle River, NJ: Prentice Hall, 2002.

Robinson, John Martin. *The Dukes of Norfolk: A Quincentennial History*. Oxford: Oxford University Press, 1982.

Roewer, L., et al. "Online Reference Database of European Y-chromosomal Short Tandem Repeat (STR) Haplotypes." *Forensic Science International* 118 (2001): 106–113.

Rogers, Sheldon. "Daniel Defoe's Birth Date." *Notes & Queries* 56.2 (2009): 226–28.

Rosenblatt, Jason P. *Renaissance England's Chief Rabbi, John Selden*. Oxford: Oxford University Press, 2008.

Rosser, Z. H., et al. "Y-chromosomal Diversity in Europe Is Clinal and Influenced Primarily by Geography, Rather Than by Language." *American Journal of Human Genetics* 67 (2000): 1526–1543.

Roth, Cecil. *The Life of Menasseh Ben-Israel: Rabbi, Printer and Diplomat*. New York: Arno, 1961.

_____. "Les Marranes à Rouen." *Revue des études juives* 10 (1929): 113–55.

_____. *The Spanish Inquisition*. New York: Norton, 1937.

Rowlands, John, and Sheila Rowlands. *The Surnames of Wales*. Baltimore: Genealogical Publishing, 2008.

Russell, Ephraim. "The Societies of the Bardi and the Peruzzi and Their Dealings with Edward III 1327–4." Centre for Metropolitan History, *Finance and Trade under Edward III*, ed. George Unwin (originally published 1918), pp. 93–135. "The London Lay Subsidy of 1332." Accessed March 20, 2009 at "http://www.british-history.ac.uk/report.aspx?compie=33008.

Ryan, M., ed. *The Origins of Metallurgy in Atlantic Europe: Proceedings of the Fifth Atlantic Colloquium*. Dublin: Rech, 1979.

Saebo, Magne. *Hebrew Bible/Old Testament: The History of Its Interpretation from the Renaissance to the Enlightenment*. Goettingen: Vandenhoeck & Ruprecht, 2008.

Saltman, Avrom. *The Jewish Question in 1655: Studies in Prynne's Demurrer*. Jerusalem: Bar Ilan University Press, 1995.

Sand, Shlomo. *The Invention of the Jewish People*. London: Verso, 2009.

Sandler, Lucy Freeman. "Christian Hebraism and the Ramsey Abbey Psalter." *Journal of the Warburg and Courtauld Institutes* 35 (1972): 123–34.

Saul, Nigel. *The Oxford Illustrated History of Medieval England*. Oxford: Oxford University Press, 2001.

Shaye, E. G., and J. D. Cohen. *The Beginnings of Jewishness: Boundaries, Varieties, Uncertainties*. Berkeley: University of California Press, 1999.

Shlush, L. I., et al. "The Druze: A Population Genetic Refugium of the Near East." *PLoS ONE* 3.5 (2009): e2105.

Skelton, R. A. *Saxton's Survey of England and Wales with a Facsimile of Saxton's Wall-Map of 1583*. Amsterdam: Nico Israel, 1974.

Skene, William F. *The Four Ancient Books of Wales*. Edinburgh: Forgotten, 1868, 2007.

Southern, R.W. *The Making of the Middle Ages*. New Haven: Yale University Press, 1967.

Steinberg, Theodore L. *Jews and Judaism in the Middle Ages*. Westport, CT: Praeger, 2008.

Stephen, Leslie. Article in *Dictionary of National Biography* 5:730–43. London: Oxford University Press, 1921.

Stern, Malcolm H. *Americans of Jewish Descent: A Compendium of Genealogy*, 1st ed. Cincinnati: Hebrew Union College Press, 1960.

Stern, Selma. *The Court Jew: A Contribution to the History of Absolutism in Central Europe*, trans. Ralph Weiman. Philadelphia: Transaction, 1950.

Story, Johanna "Anglo-Saxon England and the Wider World." N.d. http://www.le.ac.uk/users/grj1/asw.html.

Stroll, Mary. *The Jewish Pope*. Leiden: Brill, 1987.

Susser, Bernard. "The Jews of Devon and Cornwall from the Middle Ages until the 10th Century." Ph.D. thesis, University of Exeter, 1977.

_____. *Jews of South West England: The Rise and De-*

cline of Their Mediaeval and Modern Communities. Exeter: University of Exeter Press, 1993.

Sykes, Bryan. *Saxons, Vikings, and Celts: The Genetic Roots of Britain and Ireland.* New York: W. W. Norton, 2006.

Tacitus. *The Agricola and Germania,* trans. R. B. Townshend. London: Methuen, 1894.

Talbot, Charles H. *Medicine in Mediaeval England.* London: Oldbourne, 1967.

Tarín, Robert L. "An Iberian Sub-Cluster Is Revealed in a Phylogenetic Tree Analysis of the Y-chromosome E3b [E1b1b] Haplogroup." Article published online November 2005 and retrieved January 2012 at http://garyfelix.tripod.com/E3bsubcluster.pdf.

Thomas, Charles. *Tintagel: Arthur and Archaeology.* London: Batsford, 1993.

Thrupp, Sylvia L. *The Merchant Class of Medieval London: 1300–1500.* Chicago: University of Chicago Press, 1948.

Tomalin, Claire. *Samuel Pepys: The Unequalled Self.* New York: Vintage, 2003.

Valantasis, Richard, ed. *Religions of Late Antiquity in Practice.* Princeton: Princeton University Press, 2000.

Van Houts, Elisabeth M. C. "The Origins of Herleva, Mother of William the Conqueror." *English Historical Review* 101 (1986): 399–404.

Vermaat, Robert. "Gildas (Early Sixth Century AD)." N.d. http://www.vortigernstudies.org.uk/artsou/gildas.htm.

_____. "Where Did Gildas Write?" N.d. http://www.vortigernstudies.org.uk/artsou/gildwhere.htm.

Wall, Moses. *Menasseh ben Israel, The Hope of Israel. The English Translation by Moses Wall, 1652,* ed. with intro and notes by Henry Méchoulan and Gérard Nahon. Oxford: Oxford University Press, 1987.

Walter, Heinrich, and Eva I. Guggenheim. *Jewish Family Names and Their Origins: An Etymological Dictionary.* New York: KTAV, 1992.

Watt, Ian. *The Rise of the Novel: Studies in Defoe, Richardson and Fielding.* Berkeley: University of California Press, 2001.

Weale, Michael E., et al. "Y Chromosome Evidence for Anglo-Saxon Mass Migration." *Molecular Biology and Evolution* 19.7 (2002): 1008–1021.

Wexler, Paul. *The Non-Jewish Origins of the Sephardic Jews.* Binghamton: SUNY Press, 1996.

Whiznitzer, Arnold. *Jews in Colonial Brazil.* New York: Columbia University Press, 1960.

Wiener, Leo. *Contributions Toward a History of Arabico-Gothic Culture.* New York: Neale, 1917–21.

Williams, Ann, and G. H. Martin, eds. *Domesday Book. A Complete Translation.* London: Penguin, 2002.

Williams, Hugh, ed. and trans. *Gildas, The Ruin of Britain &c.* London: Nutt, 1899.

Williams, John Bryan. "Judhael of Totnes: The Life and Times of a Post-Conquest Baron." *Anglo-Norman Studies* 16 (1993): 271–289.

Willuweit S., and L. Roewer, on behalf of the International Forensic Y Chromosome User Group. "Y Chromosome Haplotype Reference Database (YHRD): Update." *Forensic Science International: Genetics* 1.2 (2007): 83–87. Database available at http://www.yhrd.org.

Wilson, James F., et al. "Genetic Evidence for Different Male and Female Roles during Cultural Transitions in the British Isles." *Proceedings of the National Academy of Sciences* 98.9 (2001): 5078–5083.

Winney, Bruce, et al. "People of the British Isles: Preliminary Analysis of Genotypes and Surnames in a UK-Control Population." *European Journal of Human Genetics* 20 (2012): 203–10.

Winterbottom, Michael, ed. *Gildas.* London: Phillimore, 1978.

Wood, Frances. *The Silk Road.* London: Folio, 2002.

Wood, Rega. *Ockham on the Virtues.* Lafayette: Purdue University Press, 1997.

Ziegler, Konrat, and Walther Sontheimer, ed. *Der Kleine Pauly,* 5 vols. Munich: Deutscher Taschenbuch Verlag, 1979.

Zuckerman, Arthur J. *A Jewish Princedom in Feudal France 768–900.* New York: Columbia University Press, 1972.

Index

Entries in ***bold italics*** indicate pages with illustrations.